Lecture Notes in Computer Science 7592

Commenced Publication in 1973
Founding and Former Series Editors:
Gerhard Goos, Juris Hartmanis, and Jan van Leeuwen

Flavio De Paoli   Ernesto Pimentel
Gianluigi Zavattaro (Eds.)

Service-Oriented and Cloud Computing

First European Conference, ESOCC 2012
Bertinoro, Italy, September 19-21, 2012
Proceedings

 Springer

Volume Editors

Flavio De Paoli
University of Milano-Bicocca, Italy
E-mail: depaoli@disco.unimib.it

Ernesto Pimentel
University of Málaga, Spain
E-mail: ernesto@lcc.uma.es

Gianluigi Zavattaro
University of Bologna, Italy
E-mail: zavattar@cs.unibo.it

ISSN 0302-9743   e-ISSN 1611-3349
ISBN 978-3-642-33426-9   e-ISBN 978-3-642-33427-6
DOI 10.1007/978-3-642-33427-6
Springer Heidelberg Dordrecht London New York

Library of Congress Control Number: 2012947011

CR Subject Classification (1998): H.3.4-5, D.2.11, D.2.m, K.6.5, K.6.3,
H.2.8, C.2.4, J.1

LNCS Sublibrary: SL 2 – Programming and Software Engineering

Typesetting: Camera-ready by author, data conversion by Scientific Publishing Services, Chennai, India

Printed on acid-free paper

Springer is part of Springer Science+Business Media (www.springer.com)

Preface

The first European Conference on Service-Oriented and Cloud Computing (ESOCC) was held in Bertinoro (Italy) on September 19–21, 2012. This was the first meeting in a new conference series born on the past experience of the Steering Committee with the organization of the ECOWS (European Conference on Web Services) conference series. The start of this new series was based on the desire to renew and broaden the original scope of ECOWS and to provide a forum where researchers and practitioners could discuss the latest advances on the topics of service-oriented and cloud computing, and foster future collaborations in Europe and beyond.

The program of the main conference was structured in two days (September 20th and 21st, 2011), with the presentation of selected research papers and of three invited keynote talks by John Domingue (KMI, UK), on "Linked Services for the Web of Data"; Bryan Stephenson (HP Labs, UK), on "Service Management in the Cloud", and Paolo Traverso (FBK-ICT, Italy), on "Territory-Wide People-Centric Services". A total of 57 submissions of research papers were received and, after a rigorous peer review process that provided at least 3 reviews per paper, only 12 papers were accepted, yielding an acceptance rate of 21%. In addition, 3 short papers and 3 posters were accepted. This allowed us to select a high-quality program with papers giving important insights on Web services and cloud computing, which were clustered in four sessions on composition, security, modeling, and adaptation.

The conference also hosted an industrial track, which featured seven presentations – four accepted after a peer review process led by the industrial track chairs, and three invited talks. The industrial program was enriched by a workshop on "Servitisation in ICT Industry". ESOCC 2012 also hosted a PhD symposium on September 19th, 2012, as well as a tutorial on "Smart Work Roadmap Workshop for Business & IT: Cloud Powered".

Three satellite workshops were also hosted:

FLACOS 6th International Workshop on Formal Languages and Analysis of Contract-Oriented Software

WAS4FI 2nd International Workshop on Adaptive Services for the Future Internet

Mashups 6th International Workshop on Web APIs and Service Mashups

The success of ESOCC 2012 was the result of the work of many people, whom we would like to warmly thank for their efforts and dedication: the Local Organization Committee, the Industrial Track Chairs Thomas Gschwind and Sergio Gusmeroli, the Workshop Chairs Ivan Lanese and Cesare Pautasso, the

PhD Symposium Chair Wolf Zimmermann, the Steering Committee, the Program Committee, the Industry Track Program Committee, as well as the additional reviewers. We also express our gratitude to the Dipartimento di Scienze dell'Informazione, University of Bologna, for sponsoring the conference. Last but not least, we would like to thank all of the authors of the accepted papers for their great presentations.

We do hope that the contributions reported in this volume will be valuable and inspiring for your work, and perhaps also encourage you to participate in future ESOCC events.

July 2012

Flavio De Paoli
Ernesto Pimentel
Gianluigi Zavattaro

Organization

Program Committee

Marco Aiello	University of Groningen
Farhad Arbab	CWI and Leiden University
Luciano Baresi	DEI - Politecnico di Milano
Sami Bhiri	DERI, National University of Ireland
Mario Bravetti	University of Bologna
Antonio Brogi	University of Pisa
Christoph Bussler	Xtime, Inc.
Manuel Carró	IMDEA Software
Siobhan Clarke	Trinity College Dublin
Flavio De Paoli	University of Milano-Bicocca
Jürgen Dunkel	FH Hannover - University for Applied Sciences and Arts
Schahram Dustdar	TU Wien
Rik Eshuis	Eindhoven University of Technology
David Eyers	University of Otago
Chris Giblin	IBM Zurich Research Lab
Claude Godart	LORIA
Paul Grefen	Eindhoven University of Technology
Thomas Gschwind	IBM Research
Reiko Heckel	University of Leicester
Martin Henkel	Stockholm University
Dionisis Kehagias	Centre for Research and Technology Hellas
Ernö Kovacs	NEC Europe Ltd.
Akhil Kumar	Pennsylvania State University
Birgitta König-Ries	Friedrich Schiller University of Jena
Peep Küngas	University of Tartu
Frederic Lang	INRIA Rhône-Alpes / VASY
Frank Leymann	Institute of Architecture of Application Systems
Welf Löwe	Linnaeus University
Ingo Melzer	DaimlerChrysler AG
Roy Oberhauser	Aalen University
Claus Pahl	Dublin City University
George Papadopoulos	University of Cyprus
Ernesto Pimentel	University of Malaga
Christophe Ponsard	CETIC
Manfred Reichert	University of Ulm

Wolfgang Reisig	Humboldt-Universität zu Berlin
Ulf Schreier	Furtwangen University
Rainer Unland	University of Duisburg-Essen, ICB
Marten J. Van Sinderen	University of Twente
Erik Wilde	UC Berkeley
Umit Yalcinalp	Adobe Systems
Olaf Zimmermann	ABB Corporate Research
Wolf Zimmermann	Universität Halle

Additional Reviewers

Achilleos, Achilleas
Addanki, Ramesh
Comuzzi, Marco
Cubo, Javier
De Landtsheer, Renaud
Gierds, Christian
Herranz, Ángel
Ivanovic, Dragan
Kapitsaki, Georgia
Khosravi, Ramtin
Kloos, Reinhold
Kokash, Natalia
Leitner, Philipp
Martín, José Antonio

Müller, Richard
Nguyen, Tuan Anh
Pagani, Giuliano Andrea
Panayiotou, Christoforos
Pautasso, Cesare
Prüfer, Robert
Rubio Bonilla, Daniel
Santini, Francesco
Sürmeli, Jan
Truong, Hong-Linh
Van Gorp, Pieter
Vanderfeesten, Irene
Vizzari, Giuseppe
Warriach, Ehsan

Table of Contents

Adaptation

Short Papers

Posters

Industrial Track

Papers

Presentations

Automatic Code Generation
for the Orchestration of Web Services with Reo

Sung-Shik T.Q. Jongmans[1], Francesco Santini[1], Mahdi Sargolzaei[2],
Farhad Arbab[1], and Hamideh Afsarmanesh[2]

[1] Centrum Wiskunde & Informatica, Amsterdam, Netherlands
{S.S.T.Q.Jongmans,F.Santini,Farhad.Arbab}@cwi.nl
[2] Universiteit van Amsterdam, Amsterdam, Netherlands
{H.Afsarmanesh,M.Sargolzaei}@uva.nl

Abstract. We present a compositional construction of Web Services,
using Reo and Constraint Automata as the main "glue" ingredients. Reo
is a graphical and exogenous coordination language based on channels.
We propose a framework that, taking as input the behavioral description
of services (as Constraint Automata), their WSDL interfaces, and the description of their interaction in Reo, generates all the necessary Java code
to orchestrate the services in practice. For each Web Service, we automatically generate a proxy that manages the communication between
this service and the Reo circuit. Although we focus on Web Services,
we can compose different kinds of service-oriented and component technologies at the same time (e.g., CORBA, RPC, WCF), by generating
different proxies and connecting them to the same coordinator.

1 Introduction and Motivations

A *Web Service* (WS) can be very generally described as a software system de-
signed to support interoperable machine-to-machine interaction over a network.
The standards at the basis of WSs are the *Web Services Description Language*
(WSDL) [18], which describes the interface in a machine-processable format, and
Simple Object Access Protocol (SOAP) [17], which is used to format the exchanged
messages, typically conveyed using HTTP with an XML serialization.

Web Services are strongly loosely-coupled by definition, and therefore, two
fundamental combination paradigms have emerged in the literature, permitting
complex combinations of WSs: *orchestration* and *choreography* [16]. Nowadays,
there exist many workflow-description-based languages, defined to orchestrate or
to choreograph WSs, including BPEL4WS [15] and WS-CDL [20] (see Sec. 2). However, such proposals remain at the description level, without providing any kind
of formal reasoning mechanisms or tool support based on the proposed notation
for checking the compatibility of WSs [11]. Despite all the efforts, composition
of WSs is still a critical problem.

In this paper, we orchestrate WSs using the graphical language Reo [1]. Several
(rather theoretical) studies on service orchestration using Reo already exist,
including [11,12,13]. We build atop ideas presented in those papers, approaching

F. De Paoli, E. Pimentel, and G. Zavattaro (Eds.): ESOCC 2012, LNCS 7592, pp. 1–16, 2012.

them from a more practical perspective: we present a tool that enables employing Reo for orchestrating *real* WSs, deployed and running on different servers.

The Reo language has a strong formal basis and promotes loose coupling, distribution, mobility, exogenous coordination, and dynamic reconfigurability. *Constraint Automata* (CA) [2] provide compositional formal semantics for Reo. The formal basis of Reo guarantees possibilities for both model checking and verification [10], as well as well-defined execution semantics of a Web Service composition [11]. Exogenous coordination of components in Reo by channels makes it suitable for modeling orchestration. In this modeling, WSs play the role of components and the orchestrator is the Reo circuit that coordinates them. In other words, Reo as a modeling language for service composition can provide service connectivity, composition correctness, automatic composition, and composition scalability, which are vital and valuable for modeling WSs.

In the rest of the paper, we present how to generate all the necessary Java code in an automated way, starting from the description of the orchestration (given as a Reo circuit), the description of the WSs interfaces (given as WSDL files), and the description of the WSs behavior (given as automata). For each WS, we generate a proxy application that acts as an intermediary relaying messages between its WS and the Reo orchestrator, i.e., between the "WS world" and the "Reo world." All the output code necessary to manage the orchestration in practice is generated automatically, in a manner completely transparent to both client and WSs developers, whose programmers do not have to be concerned with this middleware at all. Although we focus on WSs in this paper, the same framework can be used to compose different kinds of service-oriented and component technologies at the same time (e.g., CORBA, RPC, WCF), by generating different proxies and connecting them to the same Reo circuit. Therefore, we make Reo a complete language for the verification and (with this work) implementation of WS orchestration.

The paper is organized as follows: in Sec. 2 we describe the related work and further motivate this paper with respect to the literature. In Sec. 3, we summarize the necessary background notions about Reo. Section 4 forms the core of the paper, since it details the architecture of our Reo-based orchestration platform and how we implemented it. In Sec. 5 we present two case studies of WS combination that can be automatically generated with our tool, and in Sec. 6 we draw the final conclusions and describe our future work.

2   Related Work

In literature we can find two main coordination paradigms to combine Web Services (WS): either through *orchestration* or *choreography* [16] languages. In orchestration, the involved WSs are under the control of a single endpoint central process. This process coordinates the execution of different operations on the WSs participating in the process. An invoked WS neither knows nor needs to know that it is involved in a composition process and that it is playing a role in a business process definition. Choreography, in contrast, does not depend on a central orchestrator. Each WS that participates in the choreography has to know exactly when to become active and with whom to interoperate: they must be conscious of the business process, operations to execute, messages to exchange, as well as the timing of message exchanges. However, in real-world scenarios, corporate entities are sometimes unwilling to delegate control of their business processes to their integration partners. Therefore, in this paper we focus on the orchestration paradigm, although Reo can be used to describe choreographies [11] as well.

Many languages have emerged and been proposed in academia and industry for composition and execution of Web Services, according to the choreography or orchestration principles: some examples are BPEL4WS [15], WS-CDL [20], BPML and WSCI [19], and BPMN [6] and BPEL4CHOR [6]. The *Business Process Execution Language for Web Services* (BPEL4WS) is an orchestration language with an XML-based syntax, supporting specification of processes that involve operations provided by one or several WSs. Furthermore, BPEL4WS draws upon concepts developed in the area of workflow management. When compared to languages supported by existing workflow systems and to related standards (for example, WSCI), it relatively appears to be more expressive. BPEL4CHOR is a choreography-oriented version of WS-BPEL instead. The *W3C Web Service Choreography Description Languages* (WS-CDL) is a W3C candidate recommendation in the area of service composition. Like WSCI, the intent of WS-CDL is to define a language for describing multiparty interaction scenarios (or choreographies), not necessarily for the purpose of executing them using a central scheduler but rather with the purpose of monitoring them and being able to detect deviations with respect to a given specification. The *Business Process Modeling Notation* (BPMN) offers a rich set of graphical notations for control flow constructs and includes the notion of interacting processes where sequence flow (within an organization) and message flow (between organizations) are distinguished [6]. Several formal proposals have been made for representing WSs using, for example, Labeled Transition System, Process Algebra, Petri nets, and Reo itself [7,3,21,11].

Considering the existing implementations, we can find service-oriented workflow research tools, as *BliteC* [4] and *JOLIE* [14], and commercial offers, as *IBM WebSphere, BEA WebLogic Integrator, Microsoft Web Services Support*, and *WF*. These systems provide a design tool and an execution engine for business processes in workflow specification languages. For example part of the *BizTalk* suite (another Microsoft product) is the *BizTalk Orchestration Engine*, which implements XLANG (a precursor of BPEL4WS). *Windows Workflow Foundation* (*WF*) is a Microsoft technology that provides an API, an in-process workflow engine, and a rehostable designer to implement long-running processes as workflows within .NET applications. *BliteC* [4] is a software tool that translates service orchestrations written in *Blite*, into readily executable WS-BPEL programs. *JOLIE* [14] is a Java-based interpreter and engine for orchestration programs, with a mathematical underlying model.

Comparing our solution with the related work presented in this section, none of the XML-based languages in the proposed standards, e.g., BPEL4WS [15] or WS-CDL [20], comes with tools for a direct formal verification and model checking

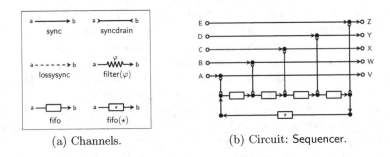

(a) Channels.   (b) Circuit: Sequencer.

Fig. 1. Graphical syntax of common channels and a circuit

Name	Behavior
sync	Atomically fetches an item on its source end a and dispatches it on its sink end b.
syncdrain	Atomically fetches (and loses) items on both of its source ends a and b.
lossysync	Atomically fetches an item on its source end a and, non-deterministically, either dispatches it on its sink end b or loses it.
filter(φ)	Atomically fetches an item on its source end a and dispatches it on its sink end b if this item satisfies the filter constraint φ; loses the item otherwise.
fifo	Atomically fetches an item on its source end a and stores it in its buffer.
fifo($\star$)	Atomically dispatches the item $\star$ on its sink end b and clears its buffer.

Fig. 2. Channel behavior

of programs or specifications in that language; therefore, verification of specifications in these languages requires a translation to a higher level of abstraction, in contrast to other formal techniques, such as Process Algebra [3] and Petri nets [21]. Moreover, with Reo a user is able to compose two orchestrators such that global synchronicity emerges from the synchronous behavior of the individual orchestrators [1]. This can be useful when different coordination protocols, designed for different services, need to be merged together in order to integrate all of them in the same single protocol. This advantage is granted by the formal definition of the *join* operator on two circuits [1]. Furthermore, the Reo language yields more declarative to directly specify an interaction, while with Process Algebra one has to define a sequence of actions to achieve the same interaction.

3   Reo

As its main feature, Reo facilitates compositional construction of *circuits*: communication mediums that coordinate interacting parties (in this paper, Web Services), each built from a number of simple *channels*. Every channel in Reo has exactly two *ends*, and each such end has exactly one of two types: a channel end either accepts data items—a *source end*—or it offers data items—a *sink end*.[1] Figure 1a shows six different channels at the disposal of Reo users; Figure 2 describes their behavior. Interestingly, Reo does not fix which particular channels one may use to construct circuits with. Instead, Reo supports an *open-ended set of channels*, each of which exhibits a unique behavior. This feature enables users of Reo to define their own channels, tailored to their specific needs.

We call the act of "gluing" channel ends together to build circuits *composition*. One can think of composite circuits as digraphs with nodes and edges (channels) and compare their behavior to plumbing systems. In such systems, "fluids" flow through "pipes and tubes" past "fittings and valves." Similarly, in Reo circuits, "data items" flow through "channels" (along edges) past "nodes." Usually, the interacting parties themselves supply the data items that flow through the circuits they communicate through. To this end, every circuit defines an interface. Such an interface consists of the *boundary nodes* of a circuit: parties write and take data items only to and from boundary nodes.

Figure 1b shows a circuit, named Sequencer, that one can construct from the channels in Fig. 1a. This circuit imposes an order on when parties can write and take data items to and from its boundary nodes (shown as open circles): first A and V, second B and W, ... , fifth E and Z, subsequently A and V again, etc. In general, one derives the behavior of a circuit from the behavior of the channels and nodes that it consists of—circuits exhibit *compositionality*. We skip the details here, however, for brevity and because they do not matter for the rest of this paper—see [1] for details.

Importantly, there exist various *semantic models* to formally describe the behavior of circuits. These semantic models,[2] among other applications, enable one to reason about the correctness of service orchestrations. For example, Kokash et al. employ the mCRL2 toolkit to verify the correctness of Reo translations of business process models [10]. In this paper, however, we use formal models of circuits for two other purposes. First, we employ *Constraint Automata* (CA) [2] to automatically compile Reo circuits—i.e., orchestrators—to Java code. Second, we formalize the behavior of WSs in terms of CA (see Sec. 4).

Constraint Automata resemble classical finite state machines in the sense that they consist of finite sets of states and transitions. States represent the internal configurations of a circuit, while transitions describe its atomic coordination steps. Formally, we represent a transition as a tuple of four elements: a source state, a *synchronization constraint*, a *data constraint*, and a target state. A synchronization constraint specifies which nodes synchronize—i.e., through which nodes a data item flows—in some coordination step; a data constraint specifies which particular data items flow in such a step. Figure 3 shows the CA of the channels and circuits in Fig. 1.

---

[1] However, channels do not necessarily have *both* a source end *and* a sink end: they can also have two source ends or two sink ends.

[2] See [9] for a recent survey on the various semantic formalisms for Reo.

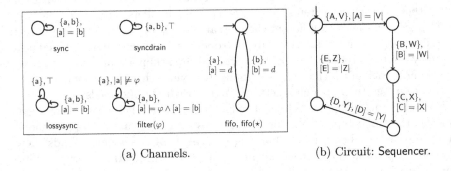

(a) Channels.   (b) Circuit: Sequencer.

Fig. 3. Constraint Automata of common channels and a circuit

4   Orchestrating Web Services with Reo

Conceptually, orchestrating Web Services (WS) using Reo proceeds in three steps: (i) design an orchestrator circuit, (ii) deploy and run this circuit, and (iii) connect some WSs to it. The *Extensible Coordination Tools* (ECT),[3] a collection of Eclipse plug-ins constituting the default IDE for Reo, perfectly supports step (i): it allows users of Reo to design circuits using a drag-and-drop interface. But unfortunately, steps (ii) and (iii) involve less straightforward activities. How can we go from a circuit diagram to executable code? And how can we connect WSs oblivious to Reo to this executable circuit? In this section, we present two tools that address these questions. We call these tools the *Reo Compiler* and the *Proxy Generator*:

- The Reo Compiler compiles circuit diagrams to Java, addressing step (ii).
- The Proxy Generator generates *proxies* for WSs. Postponing the details until Sec. 4.2, a proxy serves as an intermediary between a circuit and a WS. Essentially, it relays data items from a circuit to a WS and vice versa, bridging the gap between them, addressing step (iii).

Figure 4 shows the architecture of our two tools and the intended workflow for using them. We elaborate on this figure in the next three subsections.

4.1   Reo Compiler: From Circuit Diagrams to Java

The Reo Compiler works as follows. Suppose a user of Reo has drawn a circuit diagram using the ECT and wishes to compile it to Java. Internally, the ECT stores this diagram as an XML document, which subsequently serves as input to the Reo Compiler; the box labeled "Reo Circuit" in Fig. 4 represents such an XML document. On input of an XML document `conn.xml` describing some circuit C, the Reo Compiler first parses this file; the component labeled "Reo Parser" represents the component involved. Subsequently, the Reo Compiler computes

---

[3] `http://reo.project.cwi.nl`

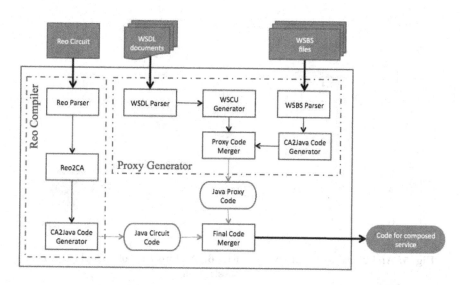

Fig. 4. Architecture of our code generation framework

the Constraint Automaton (CA) that models the behavior of C. For this purpose, it uses functionality that the ECT already ships with; the box labeled "Reo2CA" in Fig. 4 represents the component involved. This computation has a complexity exponential in the number of buffers—fifo channels—in C. Finally, based on the CA just computed, the Reo Compiler generates a Java class; the boxes labeled "CA2Java" and "Java Circuit Code" in Fig. 4, respectively, represent the component involved and the generated class. This computation has a complexity linear in the size of the CA. The generated class extends the `Thread` class, overriding the default `run()` method. In particular, `run()` now executes a state machine that simulates the CA computed previously, as follows.

Suppose a Java class `Conn` generated as described above for some circuit C. At runtime, an instance `conn` of `Conn` awaits requests for writing or taking data items at particular nodes. We call the concurrent data structures that register such requests *synchronization points*: for each node that a circuit allows interaction on—its boundary nodes—we have a synchronization point in the implementation. To make a transition, `conn` first checks the synchronization points of the nodes involved in that transition, i.e., the synchronization constraint in the corresponding transition of the CA of C. This check has a complexity linear in the size—the number of nodes—of the synchronization constraint. If appropriate requests exist, `conn` invokes a simple solver to check if the data items involved in those requests satisfy certain conditions, i.e., the data constraint in the corresponding transition of the CA of C. If they do, the transition fires: the requests resolve and data items flow according to the conditions checked before.

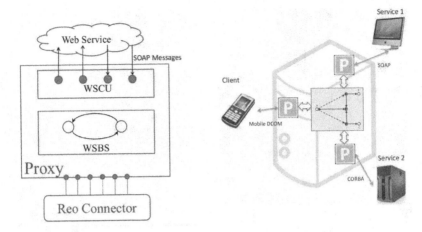

Fig. 5. Architecture of a proxy   **Fig. 6.** Architecture of a deployed orchestration

Importantly, interacting parties can communicate with compiled circuits at runtime only through synchronization points. As detailed in Section 4.2, this causes issues if we want to connect WSs to a circuit compiled as described.

4.2   Proxy Generator: Connecting Web Services to Circuits

First, we discuss in more detail why we need proxies and how they work. Thereafter, we describe the process of generating them.

Background on Proxies: Suppose a WS deployed remotely—from the viewpoint of the machine on which the orchestrator runs—that we wish to include in a service composition orchestrated by a circuit. Ideally, we would simply send this WS the synchronization points of the boundary nodes it should connect to. Subsequently, this WS would perform I/O operations directly on the synchronization points it received. Unfortunately, however, this approach does not work: no WS supports direct communication through circuits—to adopt this as a prerequisite for service orchestration with Reo would constitute an unacceptable limitation. Instead, we take a different approach for including WSs in service compositions orchestrated with Reo (including existing ones): *service proxying.*

In service proxying, one creates a proxy for each WS in a service composition. These proxies then serve as intermediaries between a circuit and the orchestrated WSs.[4] To a WS, however, its proxy looks just like any other client. To explain service proxying in more detail, Fig. 5 shows the architecture of a proxy P, together with a circuit C and a WS S. Essentially, P consists of two *sides*:

---

[4] Note that the concept of service proxies works also for other orchestration languages.

a *circuit side* and a *service side*. On the circuit side, P has access to a number of synchronization points. Thus, this side allows P to write and take data items directly to and from C. On the service side, P has access to the network infrastructure that connects P with S. Thus, this side allows P to directly send and receive messages to and from S. Essentially, P has two tasks:

– Take data items from C on its circuit side; encode these data items into messages that it can send to S on its service side; send these messages.
– Receive messages from S on its service side; encode these messages into data items that it can write to C on its circuit side; write these data items.

Circuit Side. The circuit side of a proxy contains synchronization points connected to a Java implementation of a Constraint Automaton (CA). This CA implementation resembles the implementation discussed in Sec. 4.1. The box labeled "Simulation Automaton" in Fig. 5 represents this executable CA, which *simulates* the behavior of the WS involved. In particular, it simulates the *external view* [11] of this WS: every state represents an externally observable internal configuration of the WS, while every transition represents the exchange of one or more messages.[5] More precisely, the synchronization points that the simulation automaton inside a proxy has access to represent the *names* of the messages exchanged by a WS; the data items passing through these synchronization points constitute the actual payloads. (Recall from Section 4.1 that a CA implementation has a synchronization point for each boundary node appearing in one of its transitions.) For instance, one may have a synchronization point for a message named `addIntegersRequest` and a (serialized) data item "x=1;y=2" (the actual payload of `addIntegersRequest`).

Proxies require simulation automata for the following reason. First, we observe that *stateful* WSs—WSs with more than one internal configuration—may permit the exchange of different messages in different such configurations. The correct functioning of proxies depends crucially on this information: proxies must know which messages their WSs can exchange in each state to decide which synchronization points to allow interaction on. To illustrate this, suppose a WS that at some point permits only the receipt of a `multIntegersRequest` message. In that case, it makes no sense for its proxy to take data items from the synchronization point for the `addIntegersRequest` message: the proxy may try to relay data items taken from this synchronization point, but it will certainly fail. After all, the WS does not permit `addIntegersRequest` messages in its current state! Proxies must know the present configuration of their WSs to avoid such faulty behavior. However, WSs encapsulate their states and generally, they do not provide means to share them with clients. By simulating their respective WS behavior, proxies compensate for this: every time a proxy exchanges a message with its WS, its simulation automaton makes a corresponding transition. In this way,

---

[5] We model stateless WSs with singleton automata.

a proxy can always derive which message exchanges its WS permits, namely from its simulation automaton.[6]

Service Side. The service side of a proxy contains components that facilitate network communication, e.g., using SOAP: a standardized protocol for exchanging structured information in computer networks [17]. To implement this, we use Apache Axis2 [8], because it is a very flexible and easily extensible framework. Moreover, it supports many standards, including WSDL [18] and SOAP [17].

In short, Axis2 provides us the technology for exchanging messages with WSs over a network. Consequently, we had to implement only a connection between Axis2 and the simulation automata in our proxies. The box labeled "WSCU" in Fig. 5 represents the component of the proxy that does this, called *Web Service Communication Unit* (WSCU). Roughly, a WSCU works as follows.

- A WSCU monitors the simulation automaton. If this automaton makes a transition, it registers the data items and the synchronization points involved. Subsequently, it packs these data items—payloads—and synchronization points—message names—into an appropriate message format (using Axis2), e.g., SOAP. Finally, it sends these messages over the network to the actual WS (again using Axis2).
- Concurrently, a WSCU receives messages sent by the actual WS (using Axis2). Subsequently, it unpacks these messages (e.g., removes headers) and writes their payload as data items on the appropriate synchronization points. Importantly, a WSCU forces the simulation automaton to make a corresponding transition. Otherwise, this automaton and the actual WS can diverge.

In our current implementation, proxies of WSs run on the same machine as the circuit orchestrating them. This has a practical reason: typically, we cannot deploy applications on the remote machines on which the WSs run.

Generating Proxies. Previously, we outlined why we need proxies and how they work. Next, we describe how the Proxy Generator generates them. To generate a proxy for a single WS, the Proxy Generator requires two inputs: a WSDL document and a WS *behavior specification* (WSBS). The WSDL document specifies the syntax and technical details of the interface of the WS; the WSBS formally describes its (externally observable) behavior.[7]

To explain in more detail how the Proxy Generator works, suppose a WSDL document `service.wsdl` and a WSBS file `service.wsbs`. (Suppose they describe the same WS.) The Proxy Generator proceeds in three steps.

---

[6] Currently, we assume that a WS and a simulating automaton *start* and *stay* in sync. Communication errors, for instance, can take the two out of sync, but a proxy can detect such situations and recover or reset itself to reestablish its sync with its respective actual service.

[7] We assume that WS providers publish sufficient information about the externally visible behavior of their WSs to construct a faithful WSBS in some formalism. Note that not only our approach requires such a behavioral description: generally, if WS providers want to enable others to compose the services they provide, this comprises essential information (especially in the case of stateful WSs).

- First, the Proxy Generator parses `service.wsdl` using Axis2 technology; the box labeled "WSDL Parser" in Fig. 4 represents the component involved. (Note that both the Proxy Generator and the generated proxy use Axis2, albeit in different ways.) Subsequently, the Proxy Generator generates a Web Service Communication Unit (WSCU) based on the previous parsing; the box labeled "WSCU Generator" represents the component involved.
- Second, the Proxy Generator parses `service.wsbs`; the box labeled "WSBS Parser" in Fig. 4 represents the component involved. More precisely, this component parses the content of `service.wsbs` to a Constraint Automaton (CA). Subsequently, similar to the Reo Compiler (see Section 4.1), the Proxy Generator generates Java code for the CA resulting from parsing `service.wsbs`. In fact, the boxes labeled "CA2Java Code Generator" in the Reo Compiler and Proxy Generator refer to the same component. Instances of the resulting Java class serve as simulation automata at runtime, as described above.

  The current version of the Proxy Generator handles WSBS files describing CA. We aim to experiment with other languages for specifying WS behavior: in principle, our approach supports any modeling language for which we can devise a mapping to CA. For instance, we can use the tool presented in [5] to automatically translate UML Sequence Diagrams to Reo circuits. Combined with the Reo2CA component in Fig. 4, this yields CA that can serve as WSBSs. We outline this further in Sec. 5.
- Finally, the Proxy Generator combines the generated WSCU and the generated simulation automaton class by adding glue code between them. More concretely, this step yields a Java class `Proxy`. The box named "Java Proxy Code" in Fig. 5 represents this class. Instances of `Proxy` run as proxies, encapsulating the constituent WSCU and simulation automaton.

4.3   Gluing Together Orchestrators and Proxies

We discuss how to combine generated proxies of WSs with a compiled circuit that orchestrates them—we describe the box named "Final Code Merger" in Fig. 4. We start with some notation. Suppose an XML document `conn.xml` specifying a circuit C. Moreover, suppose a set of $\langle$WSDL, WSBS $\rangle$-pairs $\widehat{S}$ representing the set of WSs S that C orchestrates. Let `Conn` denote the Java class the Reo Compiler yields on input of `conn.xml` (i.e., the box named "Java Circuit Code"); let `Proxy` denote the class the Proxy Generator yields on input of some $\langle$`service.wsdl`, `service.wsbs`$\rangle \in \widehat{S}$ (i.e., the box named "Java Proxy Code").

The box named "Final Code Merger" in Fig. 4 represents the component that glues together `Conn` and the `Proxy` of every $\widehat{s} \in \widehat{S}$. This gluing yields a collection of Java classes that, once deployed, orchestrate the WSs in the set S as desired. The "Final Code Merger" produces a gluing Java class that comprises the following activities.

1. Create a synchronization point for each boundary node of C.
2. Create an instance `conn` of the class `Conn` generated by the Reo Compiler on input of `conn.xml`. Moreover, pass the synchronization points created in the

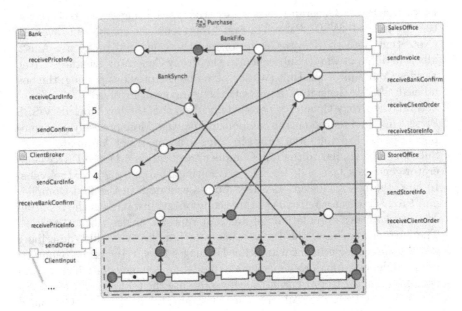

Fig. 7. The sequential coordination of four WSS represented as a Reo circuit: the numbers represent the ordering of the exchanged messages

previous step to `conn`. These synchronization points constitute the interface through which proxies communicate with `conn` (see Sec 4.1).

3. Create an instance `proxy` of the class `Proxy` generated by the Proxy Compiler on input of $\widehat{s} = \langle$`service.wsdl`, `service.wsbs`$\rangle$ for each $\widehat{s} \in \widehat{S}$. Importantly, pass to this instance the *appropriate* synchronization points created in step (1). The sharing of synchronization points between `conn` and `proxy` establishes the link between the orchestrator and a WS.

5   Case Studies

In this section, we first present a simple yet nontrivial example of orchestration to familiarize the reader, and then, we extend the Reo circuit of this first example to show a more complex interaction protocol among (almost) the same services of the first example, to show the expressiveness of Reo at full.

In Fig. 7 we can see the complete representation of the circuit for the orchestration of four WSS. The image has been created with the ECT. With the aid of the Reo Compiler (see Sec. 4.1) we generated the *Purchase* circuit describing the interaction among the four WSS named *ClientBroker*, *StoreOffice*, *SalesOffice*, and *Bank*. This scenario implements the classical purchase-online example. The *ClientBroker* service takes care of interfacing the real client to the other services, which deal with: the information about the store (i.e., the *StoreOffice* service), the procedure to prepare the invoice (i.e., the *SalesOffice* service), and the

ClientBroker: The *ClientBroker* interfaces the real client with the other WSs:
1. It issues the order information, for example, the product ID of the object (e.g., #3, corresponding to a pair of sport shoes), and a string of characters with a complementary description (e.g., "color blue"). Both the *SalesOffice* and the *StoreOffice* require this information.
2. It waits for the price confirmation of the order (which comes from the *SalesOffice*).
3. It issues the credit card information of the client, which the *Bank* needs to proceed with the payment for the order.
4. It receives the confirmation or the refusal of the payment (which comes from the *Bank*).

StoreOffice: The *StoreOffice* checks the availability of the order request:
1. It receives the order (e.g., "ID and String"), which comes from the *ClientBroker*.
2. It issues a confirmation that the object is in the store or not (a Boolean and a String with additional comments), which the *SalesOffice* needs for further processing.

SalesOffice: The *SalesOffice* computes the final price (a Real) and sends the corresponding invoice information:
1. It receives the order information, which comes from *ClientBroker*.
2. It receives the confirmation that the product is in the store (issued by *StoreOffice*), with possible further shipping info and price.
3. It computes the final price and issues it together with the account number of the company (an Integer), which both the *ClientBroker* and the *Bank* need to proceed with the transaction.
4. It accepts the confirmation of the payment (or the rejection), which comes from the *Bank*.

Bank: The *Bank* manages the payment, issued by the *ClientBroker*, according to the price information issued by the *SalesOffice*:
1. It synchronously (thanks to the *BankFifo* fifo and the **BankSynch** syncdrain channels in Fig. 7) receives the card info (from the *Client*) and the price of the transaction (from the *SalesOffice*).
2. It issues back the confirmation (or the refusal) of the payment, which goes to both the *Client* and the *SalesOffice*.

Fig. 8. Description of the services in Fig. 7

effective payment management (i.e., the *Bank* service). The complete high-level behavior of these services is described in Fig. 8.

The dashed rectangle in Fig. 7 highlights a **Sequencer** of the messages (see Sec. 3), i.e., a Reo subcircuit that enforces the correct ordering of the messages exchanged among the WSs. Therefore, the interaction of the WSs is sequential: the sequence consists of five steps, whose ordering is shown in Fig. 7 with ordinal numbers beside the sink ports of the components.[8]

We programmed and deployed the WSs on a server machine, and afterwards we automatically generated their proxies with the help of the Proxy Generator (see Sec. 4.2). We described the four WSs as UML *Sequence Diagrams* as represented in Fig. 9, where labels correspond to the types of exchanged SOAP messages. From this description, we can generate the corresponding CA as described in Sec. 4.2.

In Fig. 10, we show essentially the same purchase interaction as in Fig. 7, albeit with a more complex behavior. The scenario in Fig. 10 is closely derived from [15] and the related circuit is named *ComplexPurchase*. As in the first

---

[8] The presence of the **Sequencer** in Fig. 9 may appear redundant as the WSs themselves already impose an ordering on their interactions. However, the sequencing of the messages *is* also part of the protocol among the WSs and should, therefore, be part of the protocol specification—regardless of what the WSs involved do.

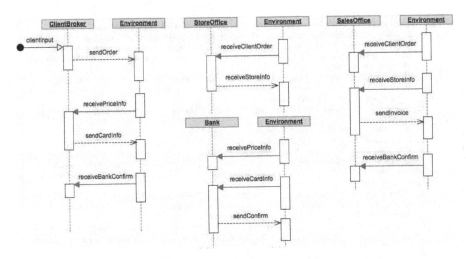

Fig. 9. The UML Sequence Diagrams for the four services in Fig. 7

case study, we represent a *ClientBroker*, a *Bank*, a *SalesOffice*, and a *StoreOffice* service. Additionally, in this second case study, we include a *ShippingOffice*, which accomplishes the task of controlling shipping details, e.g., a shipping fee.

The transaction is initiated by the *ClientBroker*, which on receiving the purchase order message from the customer, initiates parallel flows to handle shipping (*ShippingOffice*), invoicing (*SalesOffice*), and scheduling (*StoreOffice*), concurrently. While some of the activities in the transaction may proceed concurrently, there are control and data dependencies among the services, thus coordination is needed to execute the transaction. For example, to complete the price calculation by the *SalesOffice* service, the shipping price is required. Once the parallel flow is finished, the invoice is delivered to both the *Bank* and the *ClientBroker*. Then, on behalf of the customer, the *ClientBroker* sends the credit card information (which can be accepted or not by the filter channels, see Sec. 3) to the *Bank*, which sends the outcome of the financial transaction back to the *ClientBroker*.

The dashed rectangle in Fig. 7 highlights a Sequencer subcircuit. The high number of fifo channels is due to the fact that the activities of *ShippingOffice*, *StoreOffice*, and *SalesOffice* run in parallel: the fifo channels are used to buffer the messages in case one of these service is not yet ready to accept them.

Note that in this example, we adopt filter channels to check if the format of the message is coherent with the given specifications, e.g., if the expiry date of a credit card is after the current date or not. This shows that Reo circuits can perform such "active" controls. They are not only passive routers of data. One more data-aware action is performed during the final delivery of the invoice and the credit card information to the *Bank*. This is carried out by a *join node*, denoted by $\oplus$ in Fig. 10, which represents a component that accepts data items from all connected sink ends and creates a tuple out of them: all the information is merged into one message only, representing the complete request to the *Bank*.

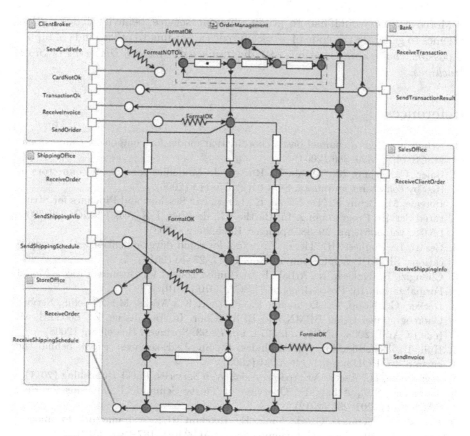

Fig. 10. The example in Fig. 7 with a more complex interaction

6   Conclusion

In this paper, we have shown how to automatically generate an orchestration framework for WSs. The orchestration is defined by using the Reo language, and the generated Java code is used to compose the behavior of the services in a way transparent to the client and all the services. The input of our generation tool consists of the externally observable behavior of each service, the WSDL description file of each service, and the specification of the orchestration as a Reo circuit. From all this information, it is then possible to automate the Java code generation process from a Reo circuit and a proxy (see Sec. 4.2) for each service. This proxy component is in charge of managing the communication between the technology behind the service and the Reo environment.

This research can proceed in the future along different lines. Our first intention is to be able to generate different communication units for the proxy (not only the WSCU, see Sec. 4.2), in order to include other technologies in the orchestration of components and services, e.g., CORBA, RPC, WCF. We intend to have a multi-technology platform to integrate several kinds of third-parties.

Moreover, we would like to study different service behavioral description schemes to generate the code of service proxies according to other kinds of input. A possible choice can be various UML diagrams, e.g., *Activity Diagrams* or *State Machines*.

References

1. Arbab, F.: Reo: a channel-based coordination model for component composition. MSCS 14(3), 329–366 (2004)
2. Baier, C., Sirjani, M., Arbab, F., Rutten, J.: Modeling component connectors in Reo by constraint automata. SCP 61(2), 75–113 (2006)
3. Boreale, M., Bruni, R., De Nicola, R., Loreti, M.: Sessions and Pipelines for Structured Service Programming. In: Barthe, G., de Boer, F.S. (eds.) FMOODS 2008. LNCS, vol. 5051, pp. 19–38. Springer, Heidelberg (2008)
4. Cesari, L., Pugliese, R., Tiezzi, F.: A tool for rapid development of ws-bpel applications. SIGAPP Appl. Comput. Rev. 11(1), 27–40 (2010)
5. Changizi, B., Kokash, N., Arbab, F.: A Unified Toolset for Business Process Model Formalization. In: Proceedings of FESCA 2010 (2010)
6. Decker, G., Kopp, O., Leymann, F., Pfitzner, K., Weske, M.: Modeling Service Choreographies Using BPMN and BPEL4Chor. In: Bellahsène, Z., Léonard, M. (eds.) CAiSE 2008. LNCS, vol. 5074, pp. 79–93. Springer, Heidelberg (2008)
7. Hull, R., Benedikt, M., Christophides, V., Su, J.: E-services: a look behind the curtain. In: PODS, pp. 1–14. ACM (2003)
8. Jayasinghe, D., Azeez, A.: Apache Axis2 Web Services. Packt Publishing (2011)
9. Jongmans, S.S., Arbab, F.: Overview of Thirty Semantic Formalisms for Reo. SACS 22(1), 201–251 (2012)
10. Kokash, N., Krause, C., de Vink, E.: Reo+mCRL2: A framework for model-checking dataflow in service compositions. FAC 24(2), 187–216 (2012)
11. Meng, S., Arbab, F.: Web Services Choreography and Orchestration in Reo and Constraint Automata. In: Proceedings of SAC 2007, pp. 346–353 (2007)
12. Meng, S., Arbab, F.: QoS-Driven Service Selection and Composition Using Quantitative Constraint Automata. FI 95(1), 103–128 (2009)
13. Meng, S., Arbab, F.: A Model for Web Service Coordination in Long-Running Transactions. In: Proceedings of SOSE 2010, pp. 121–128 (2010)
14. Montesi, F., Guidi, C., Lucchi, R., Zavattaro, G.: JOLIE: a Java Orchestration Language Interpreter Engine. ENTCS 181, 19–33 (2007)
15. Web services business process execution language (2007),
    http://docs.oasis-open.org/wsbpel/2.0/
16. Peltz, C.: Web Services Orchestration and Choreography. IEEE Computer 36(10), 46–52 (2003)
17. Simple Object Access Protocol (2000), http://www.w3.org/2000/xp/Group/
18. Web Service Description Language (2001), http://www.w3.org/TR/wsdl
19. Web Service Choreography Interface (2002), http://www.w3.org/TR/wsci/
20. Web Services Choreography Description Language (2005), http://www.w3.org/TR/ws-cdl-10/
21. Zhang, J., Chung, J.-Y., Chang, C., Kim, S.: WS-Net: A Petri-net Based Specification Model for Web Services. In: Proceedings of ICWS 2004, pp. 420–427 (2004)

Reactive Service Selection in Dynamic Service Environments

Lina Barakat, Simon Miles, and Michael Luck

Department of Informatics, King's College London, London, UK
{lina.barakat,simon.miles,michael.luck}@kcl.ac.uk

Abstract. Due to the highly dynamic nature of services (web services can enter or leave the system at any time, or change their characteristics), adaptation to change during service composition is necessary to meet user needs. Yet current approaches to change handling detect quality violations and service unavailability only after their occurrence (after executing the corresponding service), resulting in undesired situations at execution time from which recovery (usually through costly replanning) might not always be possible. In response, this paper presents a novel reactive selection algorithm, which adapts to changes in the environment efficiently while performing the selection, ensuring that the selected composite service is executable, satisfactory and optimal prior to execution. The algorithm's effectiveness is demonstrated via experimental results.

Keywords: service composition, adaptive service selection, quality of service.

1 Introduction

Service Oriented Architecture (SOA) is becoming widely adopted for enterprise development, allowing seamless and dynamic integration of loosely-coupled components (services), thus enabling more flexible distributed systems that better accommodate the complex and changing user requirements. Web services offer a promising paradigm for implementing SOA, by providing a set of platform-independent standards, such as WSDL, UDDI, SOAP, and BPEL, to describe, locate, invoke, and compose services over the web. A composite application is usually specified as a graph-based workflow, comprising a set of abstract tasks. The allocation of web services to these tasks is performed at run time, based on functional suitability, and the user's QoS criteria specified in service level agreements (SLAs). Such quality-based service selection is not trivial in open environments due to the huge number of available services providing similar functionalities with different qualities (e.g. in grid settings, each of thousands of nodes may act as a service for performing a particular processing job, but with widely varying speeds, robustness, storage capacity etc.), and the constantly changing service environment, where services can enter or leave the system at any time, or change their qualities.

Most current web service composition approaches assume a static environment during selection, and handle changes by monitoring the behaviour of selected services during execution, so that whenever service unavailability or contract violations are observed, re-selection is performed for the non-executed part of the workflow. In other words, even if service changes occur during selection, they are only detected after faulty

F. De Paoli, E. Pimentel, and G. Zavattaro (Eds.): ESOCC 2012, LNCS 7592, pp. 17–31, 2012.

or quality-violating services are executed [11], resulting in undesired effects at execution time, such as reduced performance due to replanning and, in some cases, inability to find a satisfactory solution given the already executed services. In response, this paper presents a novel reactive selection algorithm, capable of adapting efficiently to changes during *selection*, with a minimal number of modifications, thus ensuring, when execution starts, that the selected composite service is executable, satisfactory, and optimal according to the current environment state.

This paper is organised as follows. A summary of the basic selection model (originally introduced in [12]) is provided in Section 2. Sections 3 and 4 present a motivating example and our novel reactive selection algorithm, respectively. Experimental results are provided in Section 5. Section 6 discusses related work and conclusions.

2   Basic Model

2.1   Planning Knowledge Model

The planning knowledge for achieving a goal task $t \in T$ (T is the set of all tasks), is a set of abstract plans, $abspln(t)$, each representing an alternative way of decomposing task t into smaller sub-tasks. The sub-tasks of each abstract plan are partially ordered, and are annotated with semantic descriptions specifying their functional requirements, e.g., in terms of OWL-S or WSDL-S. Assuming all abstract plans have a sequential structure (other structures can be transformed to the sequential structure using existing techniques [8]), the planning knowledge for task t can be represented as a directed graph, called *plan paths graph*, where the paths between the start and end nodes correspond to task t's alternative decompositions (abstract plans). An example of such a graph for task *plan holiday* is shown in Figure 1, where two possible abstract plans are available (note that sub-task B is achieved by a service providing both hotel and sightseeing bookings as a package).

Given the set of all available services S, the candidate services for a task $t \in T$ are those services $cnd(t) \subset S$ providing task t's required functionality. These functionally equivalent services are differentiated according to their quality of service (QoS) values (the non-functional properties), which can be defined as a function $sv(s, a)$ that assigns to service s its value for the quality attribute a. QoS attributes usually have either an increasing direction (quality increases as attribute value increases, e.g. reliability), or a decreasing direction (quality decreases as attribute value increases, e.g. price). For simplicity, henceforth we assume that all quality attributes are decreasing.

The abstract plans of task $t \in T$ can be *instantiated* to a set of *actual plans*, $actpln(t)$, each representing an alternative composite service for achieving task t. More specifically, $actpln(t) = \bigcup_{p \in abspln(t)} (ins(p))$, where $ins(p)$ maps p to its possible *instances* (the set of composite services replacing the task nodes in p with a particular combination of their candidate services). The value of a particular quality attribute a for an actual plan (composite service) p_s, $cv(p_s, a)$, is some aggregation function **aggr** of the corresponding quality values for the component services, where the type of **aggr** depends on the attribute. For example, the possible aggregation functions for *execution time*, *reliability*, and *throughput* are the summation, multiplication and min functions, respectively.

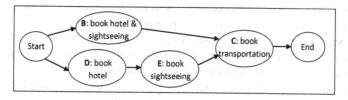

Fig. 1. Plan paths graph for task *plan holiday*

2.2 Service Selection Problem

A user request can be defined in terms of three elements: the goal task to be accomplished $rt \in T$; the quality constraints function $rc(a)$, which specifies, for each quality attribute a, an upper bound on its allowed value (note that $rc(a) = undefined$ in case of no restrictions on a value by the user); and the quality weights function $rw(a) \in [0,1]$, which associates each quality attribute a with a weighting factor reflecting its relative importance to the user, s.t. $\sum_a rw(a) = 1$.

The utility of an atomic service $s \in cnd(t)$ with respect to the user's request is a function $su(t, s) \in [0, 1]$ s.t. $su(t, s) = \sum_a (rw(a) * \frac{tmx(t,a)-sv(s,a)}{tmx(t,a)-tmn(t,a)})$, where $tmx(t, a)$ returns the max (and $tmn(t, a)$ the min) value offered for quality attribute a by task t's candidate services. Similarly, the utility of a composite service $p_s \in actpln(rt)$ is a function $cu(p_s) \in [0, 1]$ s.t. $cu(p_s) = \sum_a (rw(a) * \frac{rmx(a)-cv(p_s,a)}{rmx(a)-rmn(a)})$, where $rmx(a)$ returns the max (and $rmn(a)$ the min) value offered for quality attribute a by the requested task's actual plans (these max/min values can be estimated by aggregating for each abstract plan the tmx/tmn values of its tasks, and then calculating the max/min of these aggregated values).

Based on this, service selection problem involves finding the best actual plan (composite service) to achieve the goal rt, that satisfies the user quality constraints rc, while maximising the overall utility cu with respect to the user-defined quality weights.

2.3 Static Service Selection

We model the service selection problem as a multi-constrained optimal path selection problem in a requested task's plan paths graph (V_{PK}, E_{PK}), and we utilise the optimal paths concept of the multi-constrained Bellman-Ford algorithm [1] to solve this problem. Moreover, to improve selection efficiency, candidate services per node (task) are reduced such that only request-based non-dominated candidates for the current request, denoted $rcnd(v)$, are kept for each node v in the plan paths graph. Service $s_j \in cnd(v)$ request-based dominates (r-dm) service $s_i \in cnd(v)$ **iff** s_j is better for all *constrained quality attributes* AR, and the *utility* value, i.e.

$$(\forall a \in AR, \ sv(s_i, a) \geq sv(s_j, a)) \land (su(t, s_i) \leq su(t, s_j)) \land$$
$$([\exists a \in AR, \ sv(s_i, a) > sv(s_j, a)] \lor [su(t, s_i) < su(t, s_j)])$$

Dominated services are not candidates for the optimal solution, so their elimination will not affect the ability to find the optimal satisfactory composite service (when it exists).

To illustrate, consider two composite services to achieve a task: $p_s = s_1...s_i...s_n$ and $p'_s = s_1...s'_i...s_n$, where s'_i r-dm s_i, and suppose the user is interested in minimising price while satisfying a particular constraint on execution time. Given that p_s satisfies the imposed execution time constraint, p'_s will also meet the same constraint (since its execution time is shorter), but with better utility (lower price).

Besides uninteresting services, unsatisfactory abstract plans (denoted UNS) whose available instances are all guaranteed to violate the quality constraints, are also pruned from the planning search space prior to service selection. An abstract plan p is unsatisfactory, i.e. $p \in UNS$, if $\exists a \in AR, \textbf{\textit{aggr}}_{t \in nds(p)}(tmn(t,a)) > rc(a)$, where function **aggr** depends on attribute a. To achieve such pruning, each node v in the plan paths graph is associated with the set of its valid predecessors $vldprd(v)$, which can be defined as follows: given a path $p_v + v$ from the start node to v, path p_v is considered a valid predecessor of node v if there exists at least one path p_i from v to the destination node, such that $p_v + p_i$ is a satisfactory abstract plan, i.e. $p_v + p_i \notin UNS$.

Based on the above sets $rcnd(v)$ and $vldprd(v)$ for each node, our service selection algorithm is as follows. Each node v in the plan paths graph stores the optimal instances, denoted as $oi(v, p_v)$, for each path $p_v + v$ discoved so far from the start node to v such that $p_v \in vldprd(v)$. In order to maximise utility, the concept of optimal paths in the original Bellman-Ford algorithm is updated so that an instance of path p is considered optimal if no other possible instance of the same path has both better values for all the constrained attributes and better utility. Moreover, to reduce the number of optimal instances, only those satisfying the quality constraints are maintained in each node. After traversing all graph nodes in topological order, the solution is the optimal composite service that has the best utility at the destination node. More details on this static service selection can be found in [12].

3   Motivating Example for Reactive Selection

Consider an example in which the user has issued a request to *plan holiday*, and is interested in minimising price while satisfying the following constraint on execution time ($ex \leq 100$). The request-based non-dominated candidate services and the valid predecessors of the sub-tasks in Figure 1 are shown in Figure 2. Notice that plan BC is unsatisfactory since $tmn(B, \text{ex}) + tmn(C, \text{ex}) = 105 > 100$.

Now, suppose the selection algorithm visits the nodes in the following topological order: $start, B, D, E,$ and C. Visiting the start node $start$ involves processing its outgoing edge $(start, D)$, which results in storing the request-based non-dominated services of node D as its optimal instances (see Figure 3). Node B does not have any valid predecessor, and thus is ignored. Next, node D is visited, and edge (D, E) is processed by combining the optimal instances at node D with node E's request-based non-dominated candidate services, resulting in four possible instances of the path DE (Figure 3, where symbol **d** indicates the instance is dominated by another instance). Being dominated by the instance $s_{D2}s_{E1}$, instance $s_{D1}s_{E2}$ is not considered optimal, and thus is not recorded at node E. Similarly, after traversing node E, four optimal instances of the path DEC are maintained in node C.

Node	B	C	D	E
$rcnd$ (ex, pr)	$s_{B1}(90,30)$	$s_{C1}(30,30)$ $s_{C2}(15,50)$	$s_{D1}(40,10)$ $s_{D2}(20,30)$	$s_{E1}(20,5)$ $s_{E2}(15,35)$
$vldprd$	$\emptyset$	SDE	S	SD

Fig. 2. Sets $rcnd$ and $vldprd$ for nodes in Figure 1 (S = start node)

Node	B	D	E	C
$vldprd$	$\emptyset$	S	SD	SDE
oi	$\emptyset$	$s_{D1}(40,10)$ $s_{D2}(20,30)$	$s_{D1}s_{E1}(60,15)$ $s_{D1}s_{E2}(55,45)$(**d**) $s_{D2}s_{E1}(40,35)$ $s_{D2}s_{E2}(35,65)$	$s_{D1}s_{E1}s_{C1}(90,45)$ $s_{D1}s_{E1}s_{C2}(75,65)$(**d**) $s_{D2}s_{E1}s_{C1}(70,65)$ $s_{D2}s_{E1}s_{C2}(55,85)$ $s_{D2}s_{E2}s_{C1}(65,95)$(**d**) $s_{D2}s_{E2}s_{C2}(50,115)$

Fig. 3. Optimal instances estimation for nodes

Change 1: Suppose that after processing node E, the world changes and service s_{E1} becomes unavailable. Neglecting this change leads to the selection of the composite service $s_{D1}s_{E1}s_{C1}$ with the highest utility (lowest price) to perform the requested task, which is invalid (not executable). Moreover, simply removing the optimal instances that include service s_{E1} from node C results in considering service $s_{D2}s_{E2}s_{C2}$ the solution service. This is not optimal for price as the composite service $s_{D1}s_{E2}s_{C1}(85,75)$ is optimal in this case. Since the instance $s_{D1}s_{E2}$ is not recorded in node E (dominated by $s_{D2}s_{E1}$), acquiring the cheapest satisfactory composite service ($s_{D1}s_{E2}s_{C1}$) requires updating the optimal instances of nodes E and C. Consequently, to tackle this change, nodes D and E need to be reprocessed. Figure 4 shows the result of revisiting nodes D and E. As can be seen, only three optimal instances are stored in node C , of which, instance $s_{D1}s_{E2}s_{C1}$ has the minimum price.

Node	E	C
$vldprd$	SD	SDE
oi	$s_{D1}s_{E2}(55,45)$ $s_{D2}s_{E2}(35,65)$	$s_{D1}s_{E2}s_{C1}(85,75)$ $s_{D1}s_{E2}s_{C2}(70,95)$ (**d**) $s_{D2}s_{E2}s_{C1}(65,95)$ $s_{D2}s_{E2}s_{C2}(50,115)$

Fig. 4. Optimal instances reestimation in response to change 1

Change 2: Suppose that after revisiting nodes D and E, the world changes again and a new service $s_{B2}(60,35)$ joins the candidate services of task B, thus changing node B's minimum quality value for execution time from 90 to 60. As a result, plan BC becomes satisfactory, and its instance $s_{B2}s_{C1}(90,65)$ is now a better solution (regarding price) than $s_{D1}s_{E2}s_{C1}(85,75)$. Therefore, in order to take advantage of the path BC, which was considered unsatisfactory before the addition of s_{B2}, the valid predecessors of nodes B and C should be modified as follows: $vldprd(B) = vldprd(B) \cup \{S\}$, and $vldprd(C) = vldprd(C) \cup \{SB\}$. The selection algorithm execution should then roll-back to the start node $start$ so that the optimal instances at nodes B and C can be updated. Notice that, being already processed, edges $(start, D)$, (D, E), and (E, C) need not be reprocessed when revisiting nodes $start$, D, and E. Figure 5 shows the optimal instances of nodes B and C after processing edges $(start, B)$ and (B, C) (symbol **ns** indicates the instance is not satisfactory).

Node	B	C	
$vldprd$	S	SB	SDE
oi	$s_{B1}(90, 30)$	$s_{B1}s_{C1}(120, 60)$**(ns)**	$s_{D1}s_{E2}s_{C1}(85, 75)$
	$s_{B2}(60, 35)$	$s_{B1}s_{C2}(105, 80)$**(ns)**	$s_{D2}s_{E2}s_{C1}(65, 95)$
		$s_{B2}s_{C1}(90, 65)$	$s_{D2}s_{E2}s_{C2}(50, 115)$
		$s_{B2}s_{C2}(75, 85)$	

Fig. 5. Optimal instances reestimation in response to change 2

4   Reactive Service Selection

The service selection algorithm presented in Section 2.3 assumes the space of available services for performing the different tasks remains static during service selection. However, this is not always true in open environments in which services can enter or leave at any time, or change their quality values. Such service changes during selection in dynamic enough environments can affect the request-based non-dominated services considered and, as a result, can alter the optimal instances recorded at nodes, as well as the satisfactory abstract plans. In response, this section presents a *reactive* selection algorithm, allowing selection of the best combination of web services in highly dynamic environments, where potential future changes cannot be predicted in advance.

As has been seen in the example of Section 3, in order for the selection algorithm to be reactive (capable of handling changes that occur in the environment), some nodes already visited might require reprocessing so that the changes are reflected. To maintain the algorithm's efficiency, we need to ensure that only the optimal instances affected by the change are modified when revisiting nodes. To achieve this, the valid predecessors p_v of each node v are associated with either a *processed* (pr) or an *unprocessed* (up) status, where $sts(v, p_v) = $ pr indicates that the optimal instances of path $p_v + v$ are already recorded at node v, so there is no need to recompute them when reprocessing the edge $(en(p_v), v)$, and $sts(v, p_v) = $ up indicates that the optimal instances of path $p_v + v$ require (re)calculation.

In addition to introducing the status function, responding to changes in the environment involves adding the following four steps to the selection algorithm: updating the request-based non-dominated services of the node where the change occurred, updating the status of nodes in the plan paths graph so that the affected optimal instances are modified, updating the valid predecessors of nodes to reflect the change (if any) in the satisfactory plans, and identifying the node to which the algorithm should roll back. The last step depends on the set of nodes, NTR, to be revisited as a result of the change,

---

Algorithm 1. R-WS-Selection-Algorithm

1: generate plan paths graph $g_{PK} = (V_{PK}, E_{PK})$
2: assign to each node $v \in V_{PK} \setminus \{v_{start}\}$ its valid predecessors $vldprd(v)$: $\forall p_v \in vldprd(v), sts(v, p_v) =$ up
3: sort the nodes in V_{PK} topologically
4: store the empty instance at v_{start} and empty service at v_{dest}
5: nextInd $\leftarrow 0$
6: **while** nextInd $< |V_{PK}| - 1$ **do**
7:     $v \leftarrow$ the node at position $nextInd$ according to the topological order
8:     currInd=nextInd
9:     nextInd=nextInd+1
10:    **if** $v = v_{start}$ **or** $vldprd(v) \neq \emptyset$ **then**
11:        $E = \{(v, u) \in E_{PK}\}$
12:        **while** (**not** $empty(E)$) **and** (nextInd $>$ currInd) **do**
13:            $(v, u) \leftarrow$ an element from E
14:            $E \leftarrow E \setminus \{(v, u)\}$
15:            r-process-edge(v,u,currInd,nextInd)
16: $ins_{solution}$ is the instance at v_{dest} with the highest cu

---

specified in the second and third steps, and including the nodes that require reprocessing in order for the change to be considered (the node from which to start reprocessing is first in the topological order, among the nodes in NTR). This reactive selection algorithm is provided in Algorithm 1, with the above four steps being summarised in Procedure 4. The first three steps are explained next, using the following notation and functions: α_o and α_n represent α before and after the occurrence of a change, $nds(p)$ returns the nodes of path p, $en(p)$ returns the last node in path p, $ion(p, v)$ returns the index of node v in path p, $es(ins)$ returns the last service in instance ins, and $sai(ins, i)$ returns the service that appears at index i in instance ins.

4.1 The Effect on Request-Based Non-dominated Services

A change to the available services for a task $v \in V_{PK}$ while processing a particular request, can affect the task's set of request-based non-dominated services, causing the addition of new services (AD) while removing existing ones (RM), i.e. $rcnd_n(v) = (rcnd_o(v) \setminus RM) \cup AD$. The sets AD and RM depend on the kind of change that has occurred (service addition, service deletion, or changes to service qualities), and thus is specified for each case separately.

Addition of a Service. Where a new service s_n joins the candidate services of task v, i.e. $cnd_n(v) = cnd_o(v) \cup \{s_n\}$, two cases are distinguished. If $\exists s \in rcnd_o(v)$ s.t. s r-dm s_n, no change is made to the set $rcnd_o(v)$, i.e. $AD = RM = \emptyset$. Otherwise, service s_n is added to the set $rcnd_o(v)$, i.e. $AD = \{s_n\}$, removing from this set all the services request-based dominated by s_n, i.e. $RM = \{s \in rcnd_o(v) \mid s_n$ r-dm $s\}$.

Deletion of a Service. Where an existing candidate service s_o of task v becomes unavailable, i.e. $cnd_n(v) = cnd_o(v) \setminus \{s_o\}$, the following two cases are distinguished.

Procedure 2. r-process-edge(v,u,currInd,nextInd)

1: $P \leftarrow \{p_u \in vldprd(u) \mid en(p_u) = v\}$
2: **while** (**not** $empty(P)$) **and** (nextInd > currInd) **do**
3:      $p_u \leftarrow$ an element from P
4:      $p_v \leftarrow p_u - v$
5:      $P \leftarrow P \setminus \{p_u\}$
6:      **if** $sts(u, p_u) =$ up **then**
7:          **for** each $s \in rcnd(u)$ **do**
8:              **for** each optimal instance $ins_v \in oi(v, p_v)$ **do**
9:                  **if** $\forall a \in AR, cv(ins_v + s, a) \leq rc(a)$ **then**
10:                     check-instance-optimality($ins_v + s$,u,p_u)
11:         $sts(u, p_u) \leftarrow$ pr
12:     **else**
13:         do-nothing
14:     observe the world
15:     **if** change occurred **then**
16:         process-changes(nextInd)

Procedure 3. check-instance-optimality(ins,u,p_u)

1: flag $\leftarrow 1$
2: **for** each optimal instance $ins_u \in oi(u, p_u)$ **do**
3:      **if** ins_u r-dm ins **then**
4:          flag $\leftarrow 0$
5:          **break**
6:      **else if** ins r-dm ins_u **then**
7:          remove ins_u from the instances at $oi(u, p_u)$
8: **if** flag=1 **then**
9:      add ins to the instances $oi(u, p_u)$

If service s_o is not a member of the set $rcnd_o(v)$, its deletion does not affect this set, i.e. $AD = RM = \emptyset$. Otherwise, s_o is removed from $rcnd_o(v)$, i.e. $RM = \{s_o\}$, adding to it all task v's candidate services not previously included in this set which, as a result of eliminating s_o, become non-dominated according to the current request, i.e. $AD = \{s \in sd(s_o) \mid \forall s_i \in (rcnd_o(v) \setminus \{s_o\}) \cup sd(s_o), \neg(s_i$ r-dm $s)\}$, where $sd(s_o) = \{s_i \in cnd_n(v) \mid s_o$ r-dm $s_i\}$ is the set of candidate services request-based dominated by service s_o.

Changes in the Quality Values of a Service. Where a candidate service s_o of task v changes its quality values, i.e. $cnd_n(v) = (cnd_o(v) \setminus \{s_o\}) \cup \{s_{ch}\}$, with s_{ch} denoting this service after the change, the following two cases are distinguished. *Case1:* $s_o \notin rcnd_o(v)$. Here, if service s_o r-dm s_{ch}, no change to the set $rcnd_o(v)$ is required, i.e. $AD = RM = \emptyset$. Otherwise, this case is treated similarly to the addition of a new service $s_n = s_{ch}$. *Case2:* $s_o \in rcnd_o(v)$. Here, we have the following three sub-cases. *Case2.1:* s_{ch} r-dm s_o. In this case, service s_o is replaced with service s_{ch}, removing from $rcnd_o(v)$ all the services that are request-based dominated by s_{ch}, i.e. $AD = \{s_{ch}\}, RM = \{s_o\} \cup \{s \in rcnd_o(v) \setminus \{s_o\}, s_{ch}$ r-dm $s\}$. *Case2.2:*

Procedure 4. process-changes(nextInd)

1: $v \leftarrow$ the node where the change occurred
2: $NTR \leftarrow \emptyset$ (the nodes to be reprocessed)
3: $rcnd(v) = (rcnd(v) \setminus RM) \cup AD$
4: update $sts(u, p_u)$ of each $p_u \in vldprd(u \in V_{PK} \setminus \{v_{start}\})$
5: **if** $\exists a \in AR, tmn_n(v, a) \neq tmn_o(v, a)$ **then**
6:    update $vldprd(u)$ of each $u \in V_{PK} \setminus \{v_{start}\}$
7: nextInd $\leftarrow$ the smallest index among the nodes in NTR

---

s_o r-dm s_{ch}. In this case, the sets AD and RM are similar to those in the deletion case, i.e. $AD = \{s \in sd(s_o) \mid \forall s_i \in (rcnd_o(v) \setminus \{s_o\}) \cup sd(s_o), \neg(s_i \text{ r-dm } s)\}$, $RM = \{s_o\}$ (notice that $s_{ch} \in sd(s_o)$ in this case). *Case2.3:* s_{ch} and s_o are incomparable according to the current request. In this case, if $\exists s \in rcnd_o(v) \setminus \{s_o\}$ s.t. s r-dm s_{ch}, then the sets AD and RM are defined as in *Case2.2*. Otherwise, the services to be added are service s_{ch} along with all task v's candidate services not previously included in $rcnd_o(v)$ which, as a result of replacing s_o with s_{ch}, become non-dominated according to the current request, i.e. $AD = \{s_{ch}\} \cup \{s \in sd(s_o) \mid \forall s_i \in (rcnd_o(v) \setminus \{s_o\}) \cup \{s_{ch}\} \cup sd(s_o), \neg(s_i \text{ r-dm } s)\}$. The services to be removed are service s_o plus all the services in $rcnd_o(v) \setminus \{s_o\}$ that are request-based dominated by s_{ch}, i.e. $RM = \{s_o\} \cup \{s \in rcnd_o(v) \setminus \{s_o\}, s_{ch} \text{ r-dm } s\}$.

4.2 The Effect on Status Function

Altering the request-based non-dominated services of task $v_{ch} \in V_{PK}$ can lead to corresponding changes in the optimal instances of each path containing node v_{ch} in the plan paths graph. For instance, in Section 3, removing service s_{E1} from the request-based non-dominated services of task E requires modifying the optimal instances of paths DE and DEC. One way to take account of these changes is by *recalculating* the optimal instances of all affected paths. More specifically, each *processed* valid predecessor $p_v \in vldprd(v_{ch})$, as well as the *processed* valid predecessors $p_u \in vldprd(u \in V_{PK})$ including node v_{ch} (i.e. $v_{ch} \in nds(p_u)$) are assigned an *unprocessed* status. Since recomputing the optimal instances of a path $p_u + u$ requires revisiting node $en(p_u)$, the last node of each *processed* valid predecessor of node v_{ch} should be added to NTR. Finally, the status of all *unprocessed* valid predecessors, and those not including node v_{ch} (whose optimal instances are not affected by the change), remains the same.

   Although this way of reacting to changes is effective, it causes unnecessary full recalculation of the affected paths' optimal instances. More efficient change handling can be achieved by ensuring that only the necessary updates are made to these instances, instead of recomputing them from scratch. For example, when a new service joins the request-based non-dominated services of task $v \in V_{PK}$, new instances (that include the additional service) become available for each path containing node v. Taking account of these additional instances requires checking their optimality against the existing optimal instances of the affected paths, without recalculating the latter from scratch. Similarly, when a request-based non-dominated service of task $v \in V_{PK}$ is deleted, updating the optimal instances of an affected path involves removing all instances including the deleted service, in addition to checking the optimality of all this path's instances that are dominated by at least one eliminated instance.

To accomplish this, the status function semantics is updated as follows: $sts(u, p_u) =$ up indicates that the optimal instances of path $p_u + u$ are not computed yet, while $sts(u, p_u) =$ pr indicates that these instances are already recorded at node u, but might require some modifications specified in terms of three sets: an *additional services* function $as(u, p_u) \subset cnd(u)$ specifying what services of node u need to be joined with path p_u's optimal instances when updating the optimal instances of path $p_u + u$; an *additional instances* function $ai(u, p_u, i \in \mathbb{Z}^+) \subset S$ specifying what optimal instances of path p_u need to be joined with node u's services when updating the optimal instances of path $p_u + u$ (i.e. $s \in ai(u, p_u, i)$ indicates that, of the additional optimal instances ins of path p_u to be combined with node u's services, are those including service s at position i); and a *domination check* function $dc(u, p_u) \subset ins(p_u + u)$ specifying what optimal instances of path $p_u + u$ become unavailable, thus, when updating the optimal instances of path $p_u + u$, all its instances previously dominated by at least one instance in $dc(u, p_u)$ should be checked for optimality. Note that $as(u, p_u) = ai(u, p_u, i \in \mathbb{Z}^+) = dc(u, p_u) = \emptyset$, when no modifications to the optimal instances of path $p_u + u$ are required, or when $sts(u, p_u) =$ up. Given this new semantics of the status function, the steps in Figure 6 should replace line 13 of Procedure 2.

The sets as, ai, and dc, associated with each valid predecessor, are modified each time a change occurs in the environment. This modification depends on the change type, and thus is defined for each case separately.

Addition of a Service. Where a new service s_n joins the candidate services of node $v \in V_{PK}$ s.t. $s_n \in AD$, the sets as, ai, and dc of each valid predecessor $p_u \in vldprd(u \in V_{PK})$ are updated according to the following three cases. *Case1:* p_u is not processed yet, i.e. $sts(u, p_u) =$ up, or is not affected by this addition, i.e. $(u \neq v) \wedge (v \notin nds(p_u))$. In this case, no change is made to the sets as, ai, and dc associated with p_u. *Case2:* p_u is a *processed* valid predecessor of node v, i.e. $(sts(u, p_u) =$ pr$) \wedge (u = v)$. In this case, only set $as(u, p_u)$ is modified, by adding to it the new service s_n while removing all the services belonging to RM, i.e. $as_n(u, p_u) = (as_o(u, p_u) \setminus RM) \cup AD$. In addition, all existing optimal instances ending with a service in RM are eliminated, i.e. $oin(u, p_u) = oi_o(u, p_u) \setminus \{ins \in oi_o(u, p_u) \mid es(ins) \in RM \setminus as_o(u, p_u)\}$. Finally, to allow the update of the optimal instances, node $en(p_u)$ is added to the set of nodes to be revisited, i.e. $NTR = NTR \cup \{en(p_u)\}$. *Case3:* p_u is a *processed* valid predecessor including node v at position i, i.e. $(sts(u, p_u) =$ pr$) \wedge (v \in nds(p_u)) \wedge (ion(p_u, v) = i)$. In this case, only set $ai(u, p_u, i)$ is modified, by adding to it the new service s_n while removing all the services that are members of RM, i.e. $ai_n(u, p_u, i) = (ai_o(u, p_u, i) \setminus RM) \cup AD$. Like the previous case, all the optimal instances including a service from RM at position i are eliminated, i.e. $oi_n(u, p_u) = oi_o(u, p_u) \setminus \{ins \in oi_o(u, p_u) \mid sai(ins, i) \in RM \setminus ai_o(u, p_u, i)\}$.

Deletion of a Service. Where a request-based non-dominated service s_o of node $v \in V_{PK}$ becomes unavailable, the sets as, ai, and dc of each valid predecessor $p_u \in vldprd(u \in V_{PK})$ are updated according to the following five cases. *Case1:* p_u is not processed yet, i.e. $sts(u, p_u) =$ up, or is not affected by this deletion, i.e. $(u \neq v) \wedge (v \notin$

if $dc(u, p_u) \neq \emptyset$ **then**
    for each $s \in rcnd(u) \setminus as(u, p_u)$ **do**
        for each $ins_v \in oi(v, p_v)$ s.t. $\forall i \in \mathbb{Z}^+, sai(ins_v, i) \notin ai(u, p_u, i)$ **do**
            if $\exists ins \in dc(u, p_u), ins$ r-dm $ins_v + s$ **then**
                check-instance-optimality($ins_v + s$,u,p_u)
if $\exists i \in \mathbb{Z}^+, ai(u, p_u, i) \neq \emptyset$ **then**
    for each $ins_v \in oi(v, p_v)$ s.t. $\exists i \in \mathbb{Z}^+, sai(ins_v, i) \in ai(u, p_u, i)$ **do**
        for each $s \in rcnd(u) \setminus as(u, p_u)$ **do**
            if $\forall a \in AR, cv(ins_v + s, a) \leq rc(a)$ **then**
                check-instance-optimality($ins_v + s$,u,p_u)
if $as(u, p_u) \neq \emptyset$ **then**
    for each $s \in as(u, p_u)$ **do**
        for each $ins_v \in oi(v, p_v)$ **do**
            if $\forall a \in AR, cv(ins_v + s, a) \leq rc(a)$ **then**
                check-instance-optimality($ins_v + s$,u,p_u)
$as(u, p_u) \leftarrow \emptyset; ai(u, p_u, i \in \mathbb{Z}^+) \leftarrow \emptyset; dc(u, p_u) \leftarrow \emptyset$

Fig. 6. Modification to Line 13 of Procedure 2 with new status semantics

$nds(p_u)$). In this case, no change is made to the sets as, ai, and dc associated with p_u.
Case2: p_u is a *processed* valid predecessor of node v, i.e. $(sts(u, p_u) = \text{pr}) \wedge (u = v)$,
and the eliminated service $s_o \in as_o(u, p_u)$. In this case, only set $as(u, p_u)$ is modified, by adding to it all the services in AD while eliminating the deleted service s_o, i.e.
$as_n(u, p_u) = (as_o(u, p_u) \setminus RM) \cup AD$. Here, there is no need to add node $en(p_u)$
to the set NTR, since the valid predecessor p_u had not been reprocessed before the
occurrence of the current change $(as_o(u, p_u) \neq \emptyset)$. *Case3:* p_u is a *processed* valid predecessor of node v and service $s_o \notin as_o(u, p_u)$. In this case, all the existing optimal
instances ending with s_o, $IE = \{ins \in oi_o(u, p_u) \mid es(ins) \in RM\}$, are eliminated
from $oi(u, p_u)$, i.e. $oi_n(u, p_u) = oi_o(u, p_u) \setminus IE$, and added to the set $dc(u, p_u)$, i.e.
$dc_n(u, p_u) = dc_o(u, p_u) \cup IE$. Additionally, the end node of p_u is regarded as a node to
be revisited, i.e. $NTR = NTR \cup \{en(p_u)\}$. *Case4:* p_u is a *processed* valid predecessor
including node v at position i, i.e. $(sts(u, p_u) = \text{pr}) \wedge (v \in nds(p_u)) \wedge (ion(p_u, v) = i)$,
and the eliminated service $s_o \in ai_o(u, p_u, i)$. In this case, only set $ai(u, p_u, i)$ is modified, by adding to it all the services in AD, while eliminating the deleted service s_o, i.e.
$ai_n(u, p_u, i) = (ai_o(u, p_u, i) \setminus RM) \cup AD$. *Case5:* p_u is a *processed* valid predecessor
including node v at position i and service $s_o \notin ai_o(u, p_u, i)$. In this case, all the existing optimal instances containing service s_o at position i, $IAI = \{ins \in oi_o(u, p_u) \mid$
$sai(ins, i) \in RM\}$, are eliminated from $oi(u, p_u)$, i.e. $oi_n(u, p_u) = oi_o(u, p_u) \setminus IAI$,
and added to the set $dc(u, p_u)$, i.e. $dc_n(u, p_u) = dc_o(u, p_u) \cup IAI$.

Changes in the Quality Values of a Service. Changes in the quality values of a
request-based non-dominated service s_o of node $v \in V_{PK}$, with s_{ch} denoting this service after the change, can be defined in terms of the deletion and addition of a service,
as follows. If service s_o r-dm s_{ch}, or service $s_{ch} \notin AD$, this case is modelled as the
deletion of service s_o with $AD_{del} = AD$, $RM_{del} = RM$. Therefore, the same updates
to the sets as, ai, and dc in the deletion case are applied here. Otherwise, this case
is treated similarly to the deletion of a request-based non dominated service s_o with

$AD_{del} = AD \setminus \{s_{ch}\}$, $RM_{del} = \{s_o\}$, followed by a subsequent addition of service s_{ch} with $AD_{add} = \{s_{ch}\}$, $RM_{add} = RM \setminus \{s_o\}$.

4.3   The Effect on Valid Predecessors

A modification in the request-based non-dominated services of a task $v \in V_{PK}$, can affect the best quality values offered by this task's services for the constrained attributes and, as a result, might alter the set of unsatisfactory plans UNS. Hence, the valid predecessors of each node $u \in V_{PK}$ should be recalculated correspondingly. Moreover, the status of each newly added valid predecessors $p_u \in vldprd_n(u) \setminus vldprd_o(u)$ ($\forall u \in V_{PK}$) is set to *unprocessed*, i.e. $sts(u, p_u) = $ up, and its end node is added to the nodes to be revisited, i.e. $NTR = NTR \cup \{en(p_u)\}$.

5   Experiments and Results

In this section, we present an experimental evaluation of our reactive selection algorithm, focusing on performance, in terms of execution time, and gain in utility achieved by reacting to changes during selection. Here, the candidate services of each task are generated randomly (each service is assumed to have 5 quality attributes). Request quality constraints and quality weights are also set to random values. For simplicity, all quality attributes are assumed to be additional (**aggr** is the sum function).

To evaluate performance, four selection algorithms are compared in terms of time: static selection (*s-alg*), which ignores changes during selection; reactive selection with the first status semantics (*r-fs-alg*); reactive selection with the second status semantics (*r-ss-alg*), which utilises sets as, ai and dc; and replanning from scratch (*rpl-alg*), which restarts static selection whenever a change occurs. The time of each is averaged over 20 different random requests, and 20 different graph instances, each containing 16 alternative abstract plans, with up to 16 tasks per plan (see Figure 8).

Figures 7(a), 7(b), and 7(c) show the running time of the algorithms (regarding the candidates number per task) where a single change occurs during selection, with each figure corresponding to a different change type (addition, deletion, or changes in the qualities of a request-based non-dominated service for a randomly selected node). The results indicate that both *r-fs-alg* and *r-ss-alg* significantly outperform *rpl-alg* which requires almost twice the time required by *r-ss-alg* to produce the same optimal solution. Moreover, as expected, *r-ss-alg* performs better than *r-fs-alg*, especially as the number of candidates grows, and is only slightly less efficient than the static algorithm *s-alg*. The same observations are made in Figure 7(d), where execution time corresponds to three changes per selection (addition, deletion, and changes in qualities).

To further compare the performance of *r-fs-alg* and *r-ss-alg* in relation to the number of changes during selection, the number of candidates per task was fixed at 1000, while the number of changes varied between 1 and 5 (change types and locations were selected randomly). As shown in Figure 7(e), the efficiency of both algorithms decreases with the increasing environment dynamism, since more rollbacks are required as change increases. We can also observe that *r-ss-alg* performs better than *r-fs-alg* in all cases.

To evaluate utility gain, *s-alg* and *r-ss-alg* are compared in terms of solution *optimality*, estimated as $\frac{cu_{act}}{cu_{opt}}$, where cu_{act} and cu_{opt} denote the algorithm's actual utility

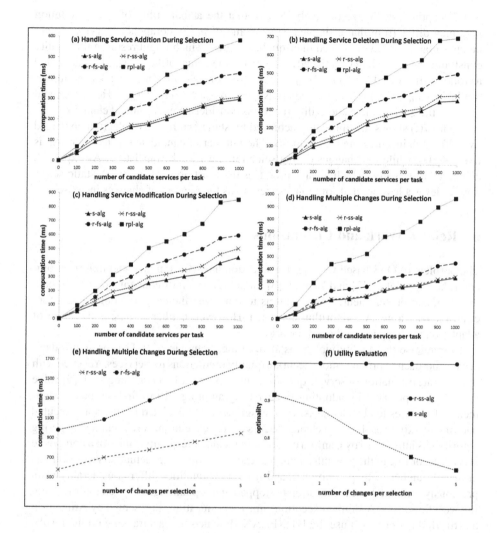

Fig. 7. Evaluating the reactive selection algorithm

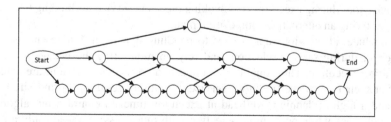

Fig. 8. Plan paths graph used for evaluation

and the optimal utility, respectively. Notice that the actual utility of *s-alg*'s solution p_{salg} may differ from that estimated, since some of p_{salg}'s component services might be unavailable, or have changed their quality values (which might result in the quality constraints being no longer satisfied). Therefore, the actual utility of *s-alg* is calculated as follows. If $\exists a \in AR$ s.t. $cv_{ch}(p_{salg}, a) > rc(a)$, or $\exists s \in nds(p_{salg})$ s.t. s is no longer available, $cu_{act}(p_{salg})$ is set to 0. Otherwise, $cu_{act}(p_{salg}) = cu_{ch}(p_{salg})$. Here, cv_{ch} and cu_{ch} are the quality value and utility functions considering environment changes.

Figure 7(f) shows the optimality achieved by static and reactive selection, averaged over 20 graph instances and 20 requests. The number of candidate services per task is fixed at 500, while the changes during selection are varied from 1 to 5. As expected, compared to *r-ss-alg* (which always produces the most optimal solution), static selection retrieves a less optimal solution, especially as the number of changes increases.

6   Related Work and Conclusions

The problem of QoS-based web service selection has gained much attention from others. Like us, Yu et al. [2] and Li et al. [3] model it as a multi-constrained optimal path problem, and present heuristic algorithms to improve efficiency. In contrast, Canfora et al. [4] take a genetic algorithm approach. However, neither addresses the issue of adaptation to changes in a dynamic world.

To minimise the quality violations at run time, Ivanovic et al. [13] present a data-driven approach to produce more accurate quality predictions for services. Yet even with the accurate estimation of service qualities, changes can still occur. Zeng et al. [5] solve the selection problem by adopting Integer Programming (IP) to find the best assignments of services to abstract tasks, with assignments recalculated for the non-executed part of a workflow each time a change occurs during execution. A replanning triggering algorithm is introduced by Canfora et al. [7], to recalculate quality values of a composite service according to the new information at execution time (e.g. actual service qualities, or actual number of loop iterations), and if the new qualities differ considerably from previously estimated ones, execution is stopped and replanning is triggered for remaining workflow tasks. A similar execution-time reoptimisation is presented by Ardagna et al. [6]. Berbner et al. [9] use the H1_RELAX_IP heuristic, backtracking on the results of a relaxed integer program, to perform recomposition in a timely manner, when the actual qualities of an executed service deviate from those expected. Finally, three error-recovery strategies are suggested by Baresi et al. [10] to handle service unavailability or faulty behaviour during execution: re-invoking the same service, re-binding to another service, or trying an alternative composition plan.

To conclude, all previous approaches to handling dynamism ignore changes that might occur during service selection, and rely on monitoring the behaviour of services during execution. Thus, quality violations and erroneous behaviour are detected only after their occurrence (i.e. after service execution), resulting in undesired situations and a high replanning overhead at execution time. In contrast, our algorithm reacts to changes while performing selection with much less overhead (only a small number of modifications are required, as opposed to existing approaches where reselection is performed from scratch), and without delaying detection of these changes to execution (when recovery may not be possible). This selection-time reactive algorithm can act as a basis for efficient execution-time adaptivity.

The paper presented a novel reactive selection algorithm handling service changes during selection. Based on request-based dominance, it identifies whether the changes occurred could have an impact on the optimal solution, and makes corresponding modifications to the search graph. The results show that the algorithm can find the best solution in highly dynamic environments with only a small overhead. Our recent work considers service quality dependencies during selection [14], while future work involves a theoretical complexity analysis and case study evaluation on real-world datasets.

References

1. Yuan, X., Liu, X.: Heuristic algorithms for multi-constrained quality of service routing. IEEE/ACM Trans. Netw. 10, 244–256 (2002)
2. Yu, T., Zhang, Y., Lin, K.: Efficient algorithms for Web services selection with end-to-end QoS constraints. ACM Trans. Web. 1 (2007)
3. Li, L., Wei, J., Huang, T.: High Performance Approach for Multi-QoS Constrained Web Services Selection. In: Krämer, B.J., Lin, K.-J., Narasimhan, P. (eds.) ICSOC 2007. LNCS, vol. 4749, pp. 283–294. Springer, Heidelberg (2007)
4. Canfora, G., Penta, M.D., Esposito, R., Villani, M.L.: An approach for QoS-aware service composition based on genetic algorithms. In: 2005 Genetic and Evolutionary Computation Conference, pp. 1069–1075 (2005)
5. Zeng, L., Benatallah, B., Ngu, A.H.H., Dumas, M., Kalagnanam, J., Chang, H.: QoS-aware Middleware for Web Services Composition. IEEE Trans. Softw. Eng. 30, 311–327 (2004)
6. Ardagna, D., Pernici, B.: Adaptive Service Composition in Flexible Processes. IEEE Trans. Softw. Eng. 33, 369–384 (2007)
7. Canfora, G., Penta, M.D., Esposito, R., Villani, M.L.: QoS-Aware Replanning of Composite Web Services. In: 2005 IEEE International Conference on Web Services, pp. 121–129 (2005)
8. Cardoso, J., Miller, J., Sheth, A., Arnold, J.: Quality of service for workflows and web service processes. Web Semant. 1, 281–308 (2004)
9. Berbner, R., Spahn, M., Repp, N., Heckmann, O., Steinmetz, R.: Dynamic Replanning of Web Service Workflows. In: 2007 IEEE International Conference on Digital Ecosystems and Technologies, pp. 211–216 (2007)
10. Baresi, L., Ghezzi, C., Guinea, S.: Towards Self-Healing Service Compositions. In: PriSE 2004, First Conference on the Principles of Software Engineering (2004)
11. Nitto, E.D., Ghezzi, C., Metzger, A., Papazoglou, M., Pohl, K.: A journey to highly dynamic, self-adaptive service-based applications. Autom. Softw. Eng. 15, 313–341 (2008)
12. Barakat, L., Miles, S., Poernomo, I., Luck, M.: Efficient Multi-granularity Service Composition. In: 2011 IEEE International Conference on Web Services, pp. 227–234 (2011)
13. Ivanovic, D., Carro, M., Hermenegildo, M.: Towards Data-Aware QoS-driven Adaptation for Service Orchestrations. In: 2010 IEEE International Conference on Web Services, pp. 107–114 (2010)
14. Barakat, L., Miles, S., Luck, M.: Efficient Correlation-aware Service Selection. In: 2012 IEEE International Conference on Web Services (to appear)

GEMBus Based Services Composition Platform for Cloud PaaS

Yuri Demchenko[1], Canh Ngo[1], Pedro Martínez-Julia[2], Elena Torroglosa[2], Mary Grammatikou[3], Jordi Jofre[4], Steluta Gheorghiu[4], Joan A. Garcia-Espin[4], Antonio D. Perez-Morales[5], and Cees de Laat[1]

[1] University of Amsterdam, Amsterdam, Netherlands
{y.demchenko,c.t.ngo,delaat}@uva.nl
[2] Dept. Information and Communication Engineering, University of Murcia, Murcia, Spain
{pedromj,emtg}@um.es
[3] University of Athens, Athens, Greece
mary@netmode.ntua.gr
[4] Distributed Applications and Networks Area, i2CAT Foundation, Barcelona, Spain
{jordi.jofre,steluta.gheorghiu,joan.antoni.garcia}@i2cat.net
[5] RedIRIS, Madrid, Spain
antonio.perez@rediris.es

Abstract. Cloud Platform as a Service (PaaS) provides an environment for creating and deploying applications using one of popular development platforms. This paper presents a practical solution for building a service composition platform based on the GEMBus (GEANT Multi-domain Bus) that extends the industry accepted Enterprise Service Bus (ESB) platform with automated services composition functionality and core services to support federated network access to distributed applications and resources, primarily targeted for GEANT research and academic community. The ESB is widely used as a platform for SOA and Web Services based integrated enterprise solutions. However in existing practices ESB design is still based on manual development, configuration and integration. GEMBus with its extended functionality and orientation on distributed resources integration can be considered as a logical choice for creating cloud PaaS services composition and provisioning platform. The paper describes Composable Services Architecture that creates a basis for automated services composition and lifecycle management and explains how this can be implemented with GEMBus. The paper describes the combined GEMBus/ESB testbed and provides an example of the simple services composition.

Keywords: Cloud Platform as a Service, Services Composition, Composable Services Architecture, GEMBus (GEANT Multi-domain Bus), Enterprise Service Bus (ESB).

1   Introduction

Cloud computing [1, 2] defines three basic service models: Infrastructure as a Service (IaaS), Platform as a Service (PaaS), and Software as a Service (SaaS). Cloud PaaS

F. De Paoli, E. Pimentel, and G. Zavattaro (Eds.): ESOCC 2012, LNCS 7592, pp. 32–47, 2012.

provides an environment for creating and deploying applications using one of popular development platforms such as current available on the market Windows Azure, Google App Engine, VMware Foundry, SaleForce.com's Force.com, Flexiant's Flexiscale, or specialised proprietary enterprise platforms.

Customers use PaaS services to deploy applications on controlled, uniform execution environments available through the network. IaaS gives a way to bind hardware, operating systems, storage and network capacity over the Internet. The cloud based service delivery model allows the customer to acquire virtualized servers and associated services. We will first discuss how a distributed service-oriented infrastructure can ease the deployment of service instances in the cloud, and how it can facilitate the usage of Cloud infrastructural services as well.

The paper introduces the GEMBus, GEANT Multi-domain Bus, being developed in the GEANT3 project JRA3 Task 3 Composable Network Services [3, 4]. GEMBus uses SOA paradigm to provide a framework to define, discover, access and combine services in the federated GÉANT multi-domain environment. It intends to span over different layers, from the infrastructure up to application elements. The GEMBus architecture is based on a general framework for composable services, founded on the industry adopted Enterprise Service Bus (ESB) [5] and extended to support dynamically reconfigurable virtualised services. GEMBus facilitates the deployment of services, supports the composition of services (spanning different management domains) and enables the automation of a particular task of business process.

The paper refers to the Composable Services Architecture (CSA) proposed by the authors that provides a basis for flexible integration of component services [4, 6]. The CSA provides a framework for the design and operation of composite services, provisioned on-demand. Since it is based on the virtualisation of component services, which in its own turn is based on the logical abstraction of the (physical) component services and their dynamic composition, it does naturally fit in the cloud distributed virtualization philosophy.

GEMBus is an interoperability and integration platform that extends the functionality of traditional enterprise-wide service-oriented architectures to a distributed multi-domain environment - therefore enabling them to be located within the cloud. It acts as enabler for new services that can be deployed in the cloud using a well-defined API, as well as integrating enterprise services and cloud based services. In this way, GEMBus intends to provide a middleware platform to support the integration of cloud-based applications, services and systems.

The paper is organised as follows. Section 2 provides general motivation for combining SOA and cloud technologies to build the advanced community oriented cloud PaaS platform. Section 3 describes Composable Services Architecture, on which the GEMBus is based, and the services lifecycle management model. Section 4 describes the general architecture of GEMBus and section 5 extends on the GEMBus component services. Section 6 provides information about GEMBus implementation status and GEMBus/ESB testbed. And finally, section 7 discusses future development of the GEMBus as a prospective cloud PaaS platform.

2   Clouds and SOA for Services Composition

There are two main directions in which mutual influence in the evolution of cloud infrastructures and Service-Oriented Architecture (SOA) [7] can translate into benefits for the maturity and usability of both technologies. First of all, service deployment and operation can greatly benefit from a supporting cloud infrastructure able to transparently provide elastically and on-demand computational and storage resources. On the other hand, cloud infrastructure services are essentially service-oriented and therefore suitable to take advantage from supporting services, such as messaging, security, accounting, composition and therefore simplifying their integration into business processes. In any of the above directions, multi-domain issues have to be considered from the beginning: service deployment in any cloud infrastructure beyond enterprise limits, as well as access to cloud interfaces out of those limits require mechanisms spanning several management domains. Other, more complicated use cases like collaborating services supported by different infrastructures, or access to different cloud providers imply much more complicated settings although they are clear application environments in the short term, if not already required.

PaaS service provisioning model [1] suggests that besides actual platform for deploying services, the PaaS platform provides also a number of automated services management functions such as remote automatic deployment, configuration of underlying platform/infrastructure services, elastic/dynamic computing and storage capacities resources allocation (by PaaS platform provider), usage statistics/accounting, and platform security such as firewalling, intrusion detection, etc.

Definition of PaaS brings benefits of creating the community oriented platform, in particular for adopted for GEANT Research and Education community in Europe. It can provide a basic set of infrastructure services and usage templates, in particular, allowing integration with campus networks. On the other hand, moving to PaaS service model will require devoted operational support facilities and staff.

3   Composable Services Architecture (CSA)

Composable Services Architecture (CSA) provides a framework for cloud based services design, composition, deployment and operation [6, 8]. CSA allows for flexible services integration of existing component services. The CSA infrastructure provides functionalities related to Control and Management planes, allowing the integration of existing distributed applications and provisioning systems, thus simplifying their deployment across network and cloud infrastructures.

CSA provides also a basis for provisioning distributed composite services on-demand by defining composable services lifecycle that starts from the service request and ends with the service decommissioning. CSA is based on the virtualisation of component services that in its own turn is based on the logical abstraction of the component services and their dynamic composition. Composition mechanisms are provided as CSA infrastructure services.

3.1   CSA Functional Components

Fig. 1 shows the major functional components of the proposed CSA and their interaction. The central part of the architecture is the CSA Middleware (CSA-MW), which supports message exchange through a normalized container that provides seamless access to a set of general infrastructure services supporting reliable and secure delivery and operation of composite services:

- A Service Lifecycle Metadata service (MD SLC) that stores service management metadata and code.
- A Registry service that holds information about service instances.
- Security services that ensure the proper operation of the infrastructure.
- Logging mechanisms able to provide operational information for monitoring and accounting purposes.

It must be noted that both logging and security services can be also provided as component services that can be composed with other services in a regular way.

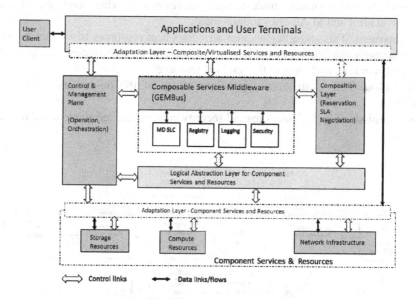

Fig. 1. Composable Service Architecture and main functional components

The Logical Abstraction Layer (LAL) defined by CSA eases service relocation across highly distributed infrastructures that can span different management domains, enabling service developers to simply fit them to satisfy the requirements to make them able to be seamlessly deployed in the cloud, as shown in "Component Services & Resources" in the diagram above. Composite services offer compatible interfaces through the Service Composition layer, which in a simple case can be provided by standard workflow management systems adapted through the Logical Abstraction Layer.

3.2   Service Provisioning Workflow and Service Lifecycle Management

While this architecture provides a good basis for creating and composing services, making them suitable to support and make advantage of the dynamical re-configurability associated with cloud infrastructures also requires them to rely on a well-defined Services Lifecycle Management (SLM) model. Most of existing services development and lifecycle management frameworks and definitions are oriented towards rather traditional human-driven services development and composition [9, 10]. Dynamically provisioned and re-configured services will require re-thinking of existing models and proposing new security mechanisms at each stage of the provisioning process.

The proposed service lifecycle includes the following main stages, depicted in the diagram (Fig. 2) below:

- **Service Request.** It relies on service metadata and supports SLA negotiation, described in terms of QoS and security requirements.
- **Composition/Reservation.** It provides support for complex reservation process in potentially multi-domain, multi-provider environment. This stage may require access control and SLA/policy enforcement.
- **Deployment.** This stage begins after all component resources have been reserved and includes distribution of the common composed service context (including the security context) and binding the reserved resources.
- **Operation.** This is the main operational stage of the on-demand provisioned services.
- **Decommissioning.** It ensures that all security contexts are terminated, and data are cleaned.

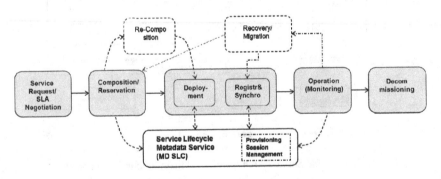

Fig. 2. Services Lifecycle Management Diagram

To take advantage of a distributed infrastructure, two additional stages can be initiated from the Operation stage based on the running service state, such as its availability or SLA requirements from its user composite services:

- Re-composition or re-planning, allowing incremental infrastructure changes.
- Recovery/Migration, can be initiated both by the user and the provider. It may also require re-composition/modification

It is important to mention that the implementation of the proposed provisioning workflow requires a number of special services to support consistent provisioned (on-demand) service life cycle management such as Service Lifecycle Metadata Service, Service Repository and Service Monitor, that should be implemented as a part of the CSA middleware.

Defining different lifecycle stages allows using different level of service presentation and description at different stages, and addressing different aspects and characteristics of the provisioned services. However, to ensure integrity of the service lifecycle management, consistent service context management mechanisms should be defined and used during the whole service lifecycle, including the corresponding security mechanisms to protect integrity of the services context. The problem here is that such mechanisms are generically stateful, what imposes problems for a SOA environment, which is defined as generically stateless. The MD SLC functional component shown in Figure 2 is intended to services lifecycle metadata.

4   GEMBus

The GEMBus framework, being developed within the GEANT project, aims to build a multi-domain service bus for the GEANT community to provide a common platform for integration of the existing and new GEANT services. With the GEMBus as a development and integration platform, new services and applications can be created by using existing services as building blocks. The foundation of the GEMBus framework includes the necessary functionality to create composite (composed) services and effectively use the widely accepted Service Oriented Architecture (SOA) to building autonomic and manageable services using the provided mechanisms for composition, adaptation, and integration of services [11, 12]. The GEMBus uses the federation approach and mechanisms for services integration and operation that is natively applicable for such multi-domain environment as GEANT community. Federation preserves management independence for each party as long as they obey the (minimum) set of common policies and technological mechanisms that define their interoperation. Metadata constitute the backbone of such federations, as they describe the components provided by each party and their characteristics in what relates to the federated interfaces.

To facilitate the GEMBus based services integration and interoperability with other cloud platforms, the core functionalities provided by GEMBus are accessible and managed via the OCCI (Open Cloud Computing Interface) [13].

The main goal of GEMBus framework is to define, discover, access, and combine network services of different layers (infrastructure, platform, service). Thus, the framework will expose to the application elements both the infrastructure-level and service-level elements. It provides the basis for a federated, multi-domain service bus designed to integrate any services within the GEANT community, and provide flexible negotiation of service provision capabilities interactively on mutual basis, avoiding centralized service deployment and management.

Fig. 3 shows the intended use of GEMBus in a cloud infrastructure. A common service registry and a service repository provide the metadata backbone for the federated SOA, together with the deployable service code. Service instances are deployed within the supporting infrastructure from the repository, allowing for re-composition, modification and migration. Description and metadata information of the deployed instant services are updated in the common registry and populated among all participating entities (services and applications). The GEMBus core supports the CSA LAL through a common messaging infrastructure plus supporting infrastructure services for security, accounting and composition.

The GEMBus core is constituted by those elements that provide the functionality required to maintain the federation infrastructure, allowing the participant SOA frameworks to interoperate in accordance with the principles previously described. The GEMBus core comprises two types of elements, combined to provide the functional elements described below according to the functionalities of the service frameworks connected to GEMBus:

- The core components that form the federation fabric, enforcing its requirements in regard to service definition and location, routing of requests/responses and security. These elements are implemented by specific software elements and by extending and profiling the service frameworks to be connected.
- A set of core services that provide direct support to any service to be deployed in GEMBus, such as the STS or the Workflow Server described below. These core services are invoked by the core elements as part of their functions. They can be called from the code implementing any service deployed in GEMBus. Furthermore, as any other service taking part in the infrastructure, they are suitable to be deployed anywhere, and integrated within composite services.

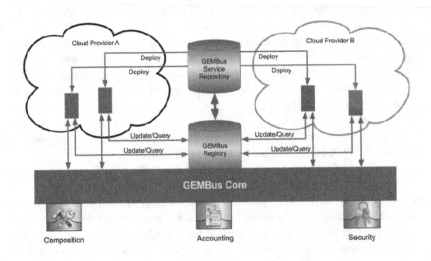

Fig. 3. GEMBus as platform for cloud services integration

GEMBus includes a set of core services that jointly constitute the GEMBus composable service platform and can be used to support user defined services:

- Federated Service Registry: stores and provides information about GEMBus services.
- Service Repository: stores service bundles, thus allowing their deployment via GEMBus.
- Composition Service: enables services composition and supported by the orchestration engine.
- Security Token Service: issues, verifies and translates security tokens to allow the authentication of requesters in a federated, multi-domain environment.
- Accounting Service: provides configurable and aggregated access to the GEMBus login service to support monitoring, auditing, diagnostics, and troubleshooting.
- Messaging service that provides underlying infrastructure for composable services interaction, integration and QoS management.

5   GEMBus Component Services

5.1   Composition Service

Being based on SOA principles, the ecosystem around GEMBus comprises a group of loosely coupled, reusable, composable and distributed services, mainly coming from the GÉANT community. Therefore, there is a need for a feasible and reliable way to compose those services to build up more complex and smarter services. This functionality is provided by the composition engine, a core service that enables GEMBus to aggregate multiple general services, as well as other composed services, into new services and applications. In summary, GEMBus allows to use existing services as building blocks of other (bigger) services with additional functionality that extends the aggregated functionality provided by the individual services.

To achieve this objective, the GEMBus framework follows existing procedures and standard SOA mechanisms, and extends them to support multi-domain operations, in particular using Business Process Execution Language (BPEL) [14] and available ESB-based workflow execution engines to enable services orchestration. They are connected with a specific description and control tool (first prototype implemented as an Eclipse plug-in) based on Business Process Modeling Notation (BPMN) [15], which is a graphical representation for Business Processes Modeling. BPMN is aimed to fill the gap between the different stakeholders that take place from the analysis of a business process to the implementation and management. It also provides a mapping to the underlying constructs of execution languages (BPEL).

The most important feature of the composition aspect offered by GEMBus is the possibility to compose any kind of services that implement standard Web Services API. For instance, the infrastructure services available in cloud IaaS may be composed with other computing services by using the OCCI standard. GEMBus allows directly consuming the services that support OCCI by connecting them to other services through the composition engine.

In addition to the orchestration service, a workflow management system will be provided by integrating the Taverna [16] environment, a cross-platform set of tools enabling users to compose not only web services, but also local Java services (Beanshell scripts), local Java APIs, R scripts and import data from Excel or in CVS format. The GEMBus composition service allows integration of other workflow engine. Thus it is dynamically extended to meet the requirements of the specific applications and services that rely on GEMBus.

5.2   Security Token Service

The GEMBus architecture bases its operation on the Security Token Services (STS) defined in WS-Security [17] and WS-Trust [18] as a security mechanism to convey security information between services that can also be easily extended to the federated security required by the GEMBus composable services. The STS makes it possible to issue and validate security tokens such as SAML [19], JWT [20], and X.509 certificates [21]. It also supports services (identity) federation and federated identity delegation.

In the GEMBus STS, different elements support token issues and validation, as shown in Fig. 4. The Ticket Translation Service (TTS) is responsible for generating valid tokens in the system according to the received credentials, renewing and converting security tokens. Token validation is performed by the Authorisation Service (AS), which can also retrieve additional attributes or policy rules from other sources to perform the validation.

The TTS mostly relies on external identity providers that must verify the identity of the requester based on valid identification material. To support a large amount of services, the application of different authentication methods must be ensured. This must include the support of currently standardized authentication methods as well as methods incorporated in future. In this respect, there will be a direct usage of the eduGAIN identity federation service [22], or TERENA Certificate Service (TCS) [23] and other accredited identity federation service.

The AS is responsible for checking the validity of the presented tokens. In this case, the requester is usually a service that has received a token along with a request message and needs to check the validity of the token before providing a response. Checks carried out on the token can be related to issue date, expiration date or signature(s). If the token is valid, the AS provides an affirmative answer to the service. This process can also be associated with more complex authorisation processes that involves additional attributes request and authorisation policy check.

The interaction between services in GEMBus is based on message exchanges. Whether deployed inside GEMBus or running as an external service, the STS can be used in a service composition to transparently provide its capabilities.

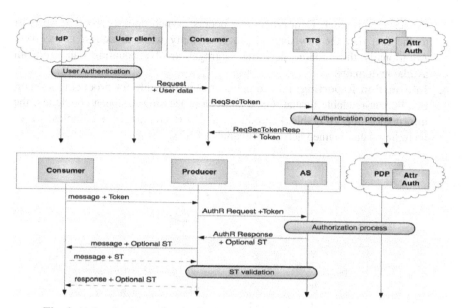

Fig. 4. Authentication and authorization processes in GEMBus security services

5.3 GEMBus Accounting Service

The GEMBus multi-domain nature requires specific mechanisms for producing and processing meaningful accounting information. The Accounting Service is deployed at every participating ESB; the collected data are stored locally, within each service instance.

The Accounting Module consists of the following main building blocks (see Fig. 5):

1. **Data Collection:** this block is in charge of collecting basic, "raw" data about the services. Data collection is done at the ESB level. This is an asynchronous operation, as it is triggered each time a service is being called. In particular, the services integrated in GEMBus use the message-oriented middleware infrastructure to communicate. The function of this block is to capture every message exchanged between services, as those messages are precisely the source of information to evaluate GEMBus services behavior and performance.

2. **Data Storage:** this component stores the raw data. This operation occurs in conjunction with data collection; in other words, the collection operation is always followed by the operation of storing the collected raw data locally. Consequently, this is an asynchronous operation as well.

3. **Data Processing:** this block computes the metrics of interest related to each service. In order to fulfill this operation, the Accounting Service must be aware of the metrics it should compute for each of the services registered with the system. Which metrics are appropriate for a particular service or how to define them is out-of-scope of our work. Instead, we assume the metrics are either part of a basic set provided by the Accounting Service itself, or they are specified by

the service provider. Data processing occurs asynchronously; by that we refer to the fact that the raw data is processed only when a request is received. Additionally this module performs aggregation of accounting data from all available domains.

4. **Information Reporting:** this component is responsible for producing a report in a human-readable format. Once the data processing has been concluded, the information reporting block produces a report containing a complete view, including data obtained across all available ESBs.

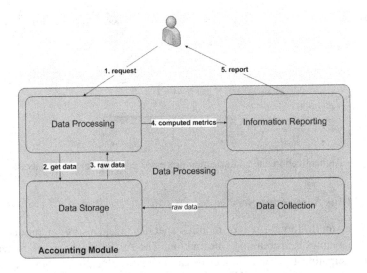

Fig. 5. Accounting service architecture

In order to support the multi-domain nature of GEMBus, the Accounting Service must allow inter-domain data aggregation. To this end, each Accounting instance informs the Registry on the services about which it has collected raw data. Next, when a request about a specific service is received at one of the Accounting Services, it will query the Registry for the list of other Accounting instances with data on that service. Once the Registry returns the list, the Accounting will contact the other instances to obtain the data of interest, which will further be aggregated with the local data and the resulting report will be presented to the issuer of the request.

Let us give a short example to explain the workflow in the Accounting Service, also illustrated in Fig. 5. We consider a situation when a system user or system administrator from domain A/ESB A would like to get information on a certain service, denoted by Service X. In the following, we use the term "local" to refer to the Accounting System receiving the request, and the term "remote" to refer to other instances that have collected data about the service under consideration.

The user/administrator issues a request to the local Accounting Service (Step 1 from Fig. 6). Next, the Accounting Service from domain A obtains from the Registry the list of remote instances (i.e. the Accounting Service from domains B and C) with information on Service X (Steps 2 and 3), and contacts each of them (Steps 4 and 5).

At the same time, the Data Processing component from the Accounting Service in domain A retrieves from the Data Storage the raw data collected locally , and it computes the metrics of interest. Once the reports from the remote Accounting instances arrive, all data are aggregated and passed to the local Information Reporting component. This block will further produce a final report, to be delivered to the system user or system administrator who issued the request in the first place (step 6).

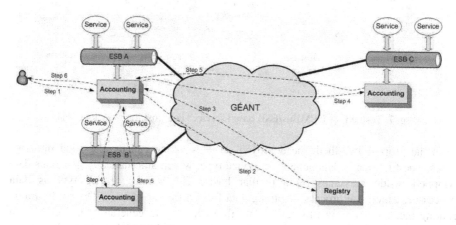

Fig. 6. Workflow in the Accounting Service

6   Testbed for ESB Based PaaS Platform

The proposed solutions and GEMBus/ESB based platform for services composition have been implemented as a cloud PaaS tested at University of Amsterdam. The testbed provides a facility for testing technologies and developing them as an open cloud PaaS platform.

Fig. 7 shows the testbed structure and implementation details. The lower layer infrastructure uses OpenNebula Virtual Machines (VM) management environment [24]. Each VM runs a Fuse ESB [25] instance that may host one or more services that can be provided and deployed as OSGi bundles [26].

Services interconnections is realised based on such ESB functional components as Message Broker (based on Apache ActiveMQ [27]) and Message Router (based on Apache Camel). Component services can be deployed in ESB environment using VM's with preinstalled and pre-configured ESB instances. Final services interconnection topology can be created by pre-configuring ESB instances or dynamically changing their configuration after deployment and during run-time, what is supported by ESB functionality.

Communication between GEMBus domains is done either over underlying transport network infrastructure or using dedicated network infrastructure provisioned as Network as a Service (NaaS). In the latter case NaaS can controlled via dedicated GEMBus service. Current testbed implementation uses only underlying transport network infrastructure.

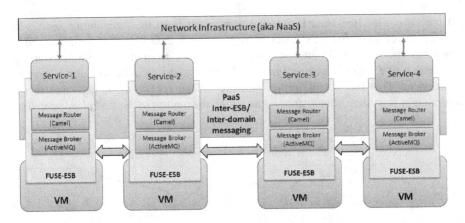

Fig. 7. Testbed for GEMBus/ESB based services composition as a cloud PaaS

In the proposed testbed, the deployed services which can be classified into two types. The first one is data generator service type, which automatically generates data wrapped inside messages on a regular basis. The second service type is data processor, which can process incoming data from different sources. The configurable routing mechanism allows to define data flows from data generator services to data processor services. All services are deployed in separated VMs that can be distributed between different hosting computers and physical locations. They can be dynamically connected into single logical topology by network of brokers as shown in Fig. 8. Theoretically, the testbed could allow to deploy as many services as possible, not only in existing VMs, but also by extending network of brokers when provisioning new VMs.

Fig. 8 provides graphical illustration of the services topology realization using Message Router and network of Brokers. The listing provides example of Message Broker configuration in bean.xml for a simple demonstrator shown in Fig. 9.

Current testbed configures that service data generators produce data messages every second. The service data processor receives data messages from different sources and processes them to produce new data and send them to the visualization output. Problems relating to message transport such as delay and message ordering can be illustrated by the visualization result. For example, with the service data generators to produce sin signal and square signal, and the service processor realising an addition function engine, the output is a combination of sin and square signals. The demonstrator helped to reveal the importance of services synchronisation and controlling message sequencing in a distributed environment due to possible communication delays and even changed sequence of messages arrival.

The ongoing testbed development addresses discovered services synchronisation and load balancing issues which are particular important for industry oriented applications. Some known approaches deal with these problems are using message processing mechanisms available in ActiveMQ Message Broker and Camel Normalised Message Router, but their dynamic deployment and configuration in multi-domain environment remain a subject of the future research.

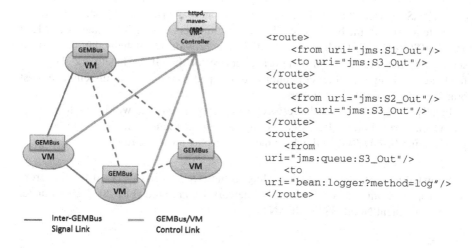

```
<route>
    <from uri="jms:S1_Out"/>
    <to uri="jms:S3_Out"/>
</route>
<route>
    <from uri="jms:S2_Out"/>
    <to uri="jms:S3_Out"/>
</route>
<route>
    <from
uri="jms:queue:S3_Out"/>
    <to
uri="bean:logger?method=log"/>
</route>
```

Fig. 8. Message Router and network of Brokers and example of bean.xml configuration

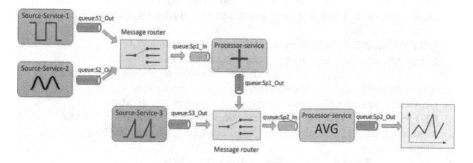

Fig. 9. GEMBus/ESB services composition Demonstrator.

7 Conclusion and Future Development

In this paper we described the architecture and initial implementation of the GEMBus framework as a generic SOA service bus implementing the proposed in the GEANT project Composable Services Architecture (CSA). Besides serving as a middleware platform for CSA, the GEMBus offers composition and orchestration services for automated services creation, deployment, and execution. The paper also describes how the GEMBus can be used as a cloud PaaS platform.

It is important to mention that GEMBus is being developed as a part of the GÉANT project, so it inherits a wide base of already developed services and the user community of all European National Research and Education Networks (NREN) which is currently positioned as a federated community of independent networks and service operators. GEMBus provides all the necessary functionality to integrate services from different domains and resolve the inter-domain issues. The future work will include the deployment of a GEANT wide GEMBus testbed to be provided as a cloud PaaS service that will allows creating new services and applications and integrate them with the basic GEANT infrastructure services such as AutoBAHN [24] and PerfSONAR [25] which correspondingly provide the bandwidth on-demand service and the multi-domain monitoring service for the GÉANT network. This will facilitate exchange of the community developed services and disseminate best practices among GEANT members.

Finally, it is planned that the research results presented here will be contributed to the Open Grid Forum Research Group on Infrastructure Services On-Demand provisioning (ISOD-RG) [30], where the authors play an active role.

Acknowledgement. The research leading to these results has received funding from the European Community's Seventh Framework Programme (FP7 2007-2013) under Grant Agreement No. 238875 (GÉANT).

References

[1] NIST SP 800-145, A NIST definition of cloud computing, `http://csrc.nist.gov/publications/drafts/800-145/Draft-SP-800-145_cloud-definition.pdf`

[2] NIST SP 500-292, Cloud Computing Reference Architecture, v1.0, `http://collaborate.nist.gov/twiki-cloud-computing/pub/CloudComputing/ReferenceArchitectureTaxonomy/NIST_SP_500-292_-_090611.pdf`

[3] GEANT Project, `http://www.geant.net/pages/home.aspx`

[4] GN3 Project JRA3 Task 3 Composable services, `http://www.geant.net/Research/Multidomain_User_Application_Research/Pages/GEMBus.aspx`

[5] Chappell, D.: Enterprise Service Bus. O'Reilly (June 2004)

[6] Grammatikou, M., Marinos, C., Demchenko, Y., Lopez, D.R., Dombek, K., Jofre, J.: GEMBus as a Service Oriented Platform for Cloud-Based Composable Services. In: Proc. 3rd IEEE Conf. on Cloud Computing Technologies and Science (CloudCom 2011), Athens, Greece, November 29-December 1 (2011) ISBN: 978-0-7695-4622-3

[7] OASIS Reference Architecture Foundation for Service Oriented Architecture 1.0, Committee Draft 2 (October 14, 2009), `http://docs.oasis-open.org/soa-rm/soa-ra/v1.0/soa-ra-cd-02.pdf`

[8] Generic Architecture for Cloud Infrastructure as a Service (IaaS) Provisioning Model, Release 1. SNE Techn. Report SNE-UVA-2011-03 (April 15, 2011), `http://staff.science.uva.nl/~demch/worksinprogress/sne2011-techreport-2011-03-clouds-iaas-architecture-release1.pdf`

[9] Demchenko, Y., van der Ham, J., Ghijsen, M., Cristea, M., Yakovenko, V., de Laat, C.: On-Demand Provisioning of Cloud and Grid based Infrastructure Services for Collaborative Projects and Groups. In: The 2011 International Conference on Collaboration Technologies and Systems (CTS 2011), Philadelphia, Pennsylvania, USA, May 23-27 (2011)

[10] TMF Service Delivery Framework, `http://www.tmforum.org/servicedeliveryframework/4664/home.html`

[11] Martinez-Julia, P., Lopez, D.R., Gomez-Skarmeta, A.F.: The gembus framework and its autonomic computing services. In: Proceedings of the International Symposium on Applications and the Internet Workshops, pp. 285–288. IEEE Computer Society, Washington, DC (2010)

[12] Martinez-Julia, P., Marin Cerezuela, A., Gomez-Skarmeta, A.F.: A service oriented architecture for basic autonomic network management. In: Proceedings of the IEEE Symposium on Computers and Communications, pp. 805–807. IEEE Computer Society, Washington, DC (2010)

[13] GFD.183: Open Cloud Computing Interface – Core. Open Grid Forum, http://ogf.org/documents/GFD.183.pdf

[14] OASIS Web Services Business Process Execution Language (WSBPEL), http://www.oasis-open.org/committees/wsbpel/

[15] Business Process Modelling Notation (BPMN), http://www.bpmn.org/

[16] Taverna, http://www.taverna.org.uk/

[17] WS-Security, http://www.oasis-open.org/committees/ tc_home.php?wg_abbrev=wss

[18] WS-Trust, http://docs.oasis-open.org/ws-sx/ws-trust/v1.3/ ws-trust.html

[19] Cantor, S., et al.: Assertions and Protocols for the OASIS Security Assertion Markup Language (SAML) V2.0 (SAML Core). OASIS Standard (2005)

[20] Jones, M., et al.: JSON Web Token (JWT) Network Working Group, Internet Engineering Task Force (IETF) (December 2011), http://tools.ietf.org/ html/draft-jones-json-web-token

[21] Lawrence, K., Kaler, C.: Web Services Security: X.509 Certificate Token Profile 1.1. Web Services Security (WSS) (November 2006)

[22] eduGain – Federated access in GEANT services network, http://www.geant.net/ service/edugain/pages/home.aspx

[23] TERENA Certificate Service, http://www.terena.org/activities/tcs/

[24] OpenNebula, http://opennebula.org/

[25] FUSE ESB Platform, http://fusesource.com/products/ enterprise-servicemix/

[26] OSGi Service Platform Release 4, Version 4.2, http://www.osgi.org/Download/ Release4V42

[27] Apache ActiveMQ Performance, http://activemq.apache.org/performance.html

[28] AutoBAHN Bandwidth on-demand provisioning tool, http://www.geant.net/ service/autobahn/pages/home.aspx

[29] PerfSONAR Multidomain monitoring service for GEANT service area, http://www.geant.net/service/perfsonar/pages/home.aspx

[30] Open Grid Forum Research Group on Infrastructure Services On-Demand provisioning (ISOD-RG), http://www.ogf.org/gf/event_schedule/ index.php?event_id=17

Interface-Based Service Composition with Aggregation

Mila Dalla Preda[1], Maurizio Gabbrielli[1], Claudio Guidi[2],
Jacopo Mauro[1], and Fabrizio Montesi[3]

[1] Lab. Focus, Department of Computer Science/INRIA, University of Bologna, Italy
{dallapre,gabbri,jmauro}@unibo.it
[2] italianaSoftware srl, Imola, Italy
cguidi@italianasoftware.com
[3] IT University of Copenhagen, Denmark
fabr@itu.dk

Abstract. Service-oriented architectures (SOAs) usually comprehend in-the-middle entities such as proxies or service mediators that compose services abstracting from the order in which they exchange messages. Although widely used, these entities are usually implemented by means of ad-hoc solutions.

In this paper we generalise this composition mechanism by identifying the primitive notion of *aggregation*. We formally define the semantics of aggregation in terms of a process calculus. We also provide a reference implementation for this primitive by extending the Jolie language, thus allowing for the experimentation with real SOA scenarios.

1 Introduction

Service-Oriented Computing (SOC) is a programming paradigm for distributed systems based upon the composition of services, autonomous computational entities which can be dynamically discovered and invoked in order to form complex and loosely coupled systems. Service-oriented systems are called Service-Oriented Architectures (SOAs).

Composition is the key aspect of SOC, and it is usually obtained through programming methodologies that impose specific orders of interactions between services. Examples are orchestration and choreography, where the order of interactions is respectively specified from the point of view of a single service or from that of the whole network. We call this kind of composition *flow-based*, referring to its explicit programming of the interaction flows. However, mechanisms based on constraining a specific order of interactions are not the only possible approaches to composition [13]. In practice, it is often the case that distributed networks are supported by entities such as proxies and service buses, which can act as transparent intermediaries between services. These entities are especially useful for handling the topology of an SOA, linking different networks together, or for enacting some functionality that does not depend on the order of interactions between the bridged services (e.g., logging). We call this kind of composition *flow-transparent*.

Flow-based and flow-transparent compositions are represented by a multitude of tools and specifications. For example, in Web Services, orchestration is usually achieved by using WS-BPEL; choreography is addressed in terms of WS-CDL, YAWL, or BPMN.

F. De Paoli, E. Pimentel, and G. Zavattaro (Eds.): ESOCC 2012, LNCS 7592, pp. 48–63, 2012.

On the other hand, many commercial platforms for SOC implement flow-transparent composition through an Enterprise Service Bus (ESB) [6], a middleware that provides an abstraction layer to integrate different services in a single SOA. The consumer services communicate with the ESB which translates incoming messages by using a suitable protocol (e.g. REST , JNI, SOAP, etc.) and then routes their translated version to the correct service. Flow-transparent composition comprehends also all the proxy services used for specific tasks in network architectures, such as caching proxies, reverse proxies, and load balancers. Even though flow-transparent composition is widely used, there is no work, to the best of our knowledge, that studies its basic characteristics at the foundational level of a programming model. In this paper we provide such a study, presenting an interpretation in terms of a process calculus. We identify a basic mechanism called *aggregation* for programming flow-transparent composition. Aggregation defines a proxy entity, called *aggregator*, which composes *aggregated* services in a flow-transparent way. Aggregators can change the topology of an SOA by exposing the *interfaces* (collections of operations and their types) of some aggregated services. They can also implement custom functionalities through the specification of code that, by construction, abstracts from the order in which communications are performed. These enhanced aggregators, called *smart aggregators*, can for instance check the content of a message for authorization credentials and then decide whether it must be forwarded or rejected, or it can store some logging information.

We use our model to formalise some properties that we expect in flow-transparent composition. For example, we show that for some aggregators flow-transparent composition does not interfere with the behaviour of flow-based composition, i.e. the order of communications is always preserved. Moreover, we show that aggregators are transparent to operations and interfaces allowing the design of a system that could be easily maintained and adapted to small but also even structural changes.

We show how our study can be used in practice by presenting a reference implementation that extends Jolie [18], a full-fledged service-oriented programming language for building SOAs which is based on the formal process calculus SOCK [8]. We introduce smart aggregation in Jolie building on its support to interface-based composition and structured data types [9,16]. Our formal model is based on SOCK, ensuring that the properties that we present are preserved in the implementation. It is worth noting that even though Jolie was originally conceived for orchestrating services, its extension to include flow-transparent composition is rather smooth since it exploits primitive Jolie notions such as sessions and input/output operations. The rest of this article is structured as follows: in Section 2 we present some basic notions. In Section 3 we describe the primitive for aggregation in terms of some simple examples while in section 4 we provide its formalization in SOCK. Section 5 presents the implementation in the Jolie language while Section 6 concludes, discussing some related work and indicating directions for future research.

2 Network Model

In this section we describe the basic notions that we need to define the deployment of a network of services and, therefore, to define aggregation. A network consists of some service definitions deployed at some locations and the structure of the connections between them. Our notion of *connection* depends on those of *interfaces* and *communication points*, which we define in the following.

We consider the following disjoint sets: the set *Var* of variables ranged over by x, y; the set *Val* of values ranged over by v; the set *Loc* of locations ranged over by l; the set $\mathcal{O}$ of operation names ranged over by o. Finally, we use the bold notation $\mathbf{k}$ to denote a vector $\langle k_0, k_1, \ldots, k_n \rangle$.

In SOC, an *interface* describes the operations exposed by a service. Here we use a simple definition inspired by the WSDL standard [3].

Definition 1 (Interface). *An interface I is a set of* one-way *(OW) and* request-response *(RR) operations with different names.*

An OW operation describes an invocation that does not wait for a response; it is denoted by $o(\mathbf{x})$, where o is the name of the operation and $\mathbf{x}$ are its arguments. An RR operation, denoted by $o(\mathbf{x})(\mathbf{y})$, describes an invocation that waits for a response, so together with the name o of the operation and its arguments $\mathbf{x}$ here we have also the arguments $\mathbf{y}$ that are received back by the invoker. We assume that an interface I cannot contain two operations with the same name. We write $o \in I$ to indicate that an interface I contains an operation whose name is o, omitting the arguments.

Service aggregation is based on the creation of a service (the *aggregator*) with an interface that incorporates other interfaces of existing services. Therefore we introduce a specific operation for manipulating interfaces. In particular, we introduce *argument extension*, which is captured by the (overloaded) function *extend* that takes an (OW or RR) operation, a list of arguments names and returns a new operation:

$$extend(o(\mathbf{x}), \mathbf{x}') = o(\mathbf{xx}') \qquad extend(o(\mathbf{x})(\mathbf{y}), \mathbf{x}') = o(\mathbf{xx}')(\mathbf{y})$$

The *extend* function can be defined over interfaces in the natural way:

$$extend(I, \mathbf{x}') = \{ extend(o(\mathbf{x}), \mathbf{x}') \mid o(\mathbf{x}) \in I \} \cup \{ extend(o(\mathbf{x})(\mathbf{y}), \mathbf{x}') \mid o(\mathbf{x})(\mathbf{y}) \in I \}$$

The deployment of a service $\mathcal{S}$ is defined in terms of its *communication points*.

Definition 2 (Communication point). *A communication point is a pair (I, l), where I is an interface and l is a location.*

We distinguish between *input* and *output communication points*. An input communication point (I, l) defines the operations (those contained in the interface I) that a service exposes at the location l. These are the functionalities that other services can invoke. An output communication point (I, l), on the other hand, specifies the operations (those in I) that a service will invoke on location l. These are the functionalities that the service requires from a given location. Given a service $\mathcal{S}$ we denote with $In(\mathcal{S})$ its input communication points and with $Out(\mathcal{S})$ its output communication points.

In order to define the deployment of a network we need to define how its services are connected. Intuitively a connection between a service $\mathcal{S}$ and a service $\mathcal{S}'$ allows the first to invoke the operations of the second: connections are directed. We call a connection between different services *external connection*.

Definition 3 (External connection). *Given services S and S', an external connection is a pair of communication points (out, in) such that $in = (I, l) \in In(S)$, $out = (I', l) \in Out(S')$ and $I \subseteq I'$.*

Next we enrich the communication capability of a service by introducing the notion of *internal connection*, which consists of a link between an input and an output communication point in the same service. This notion allows the programming of bridge services that can forward messages received on an input communication point to an output communication point (thus another service).

Definition 4 (Internal connection). *Given a service S an internal connection is a pair (in, out) where $in = (I, l) \in In(S)$, $out = (I', l') \in Out(S)$ and there exists a list $\mathbf{k}$ of names of arguments such that $I = extend(I', \mathbf{k})$.*

Observe that the interface of $in \in In(S)$ can be an extension of the interface of $out \in Out(S)$ because we want to be able to modify the interfaces of aggregated services.

We say that a service is *directly linked* to another when there exists an external connection from the first to the second. More loosely, a service is *linked* to another, and can therefore invoke it, if there exists a (directed) path consisting of external and internal connections from the first to the second.

3   Some Motivating Examples

In order to highlight the key concepts and advantages of our primitives for service aggregation we consider, as an example, the case of a printer service exposing its functionalities to an intranet. The intranet is trusted, so no authentication is required for the invokers that want to use the printer. When we extend the use of the printer service functionalities to an untrusted network, say the Internet, we require that the invokers send an authentication token together with the other data required for using the printer. We can easily model this scenario by using a *smart aggregator* service that forwards calls from the Internet to the printer service, which acts as an aggregated service. This aggregator, for each message received from the Internet, checks the authentication token and, if it is correct, it forwards the rest of the message to the printer service. Conversely, the messages coming from the intranet do not need any authentication, hence they are directly sent to the printer. Note that we do not modify the printer service: the aggregator is an external service, and the printer service is not aware of its existence.

Graphically a scenario where two printers exposing the same interface are aggregated is depicted in the following way:

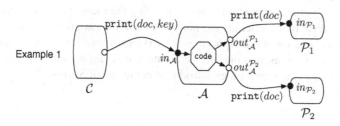

Now a scenario that constraints the printer at location loc1 to accept requests only from internet users knowing the key "0000" while the printer at location loc2 can be used only by users providing the key "1111" can be implemented allowing the aggregator service to execute the following code at every operation invocation.

```
if key == "0000" then
    forward loc1
else if key == "1111" then
    forward loc2
```

It is worth noting that aggregating services could also enhance the behavior of the services since the aggregator could also provide new functionalities on its own. For example, the aggregator service $\mathcal{A}$ in the printing setting could provide a new operation get_key($user\_id$)(key) that, given an identifier of the client, returns the key that could be used to exploit the printing facilities. In this scenario the client should first try to get the key from the service $\mathcal{A}$ through the invocation of the operation get_key and then, by using the obtained key, it could proceed by invoking the print operation.

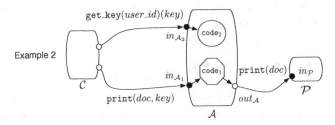

The new functionalities added by the aggregating services can be extremely useful in practice. In the previous case, for instance, the operation get_key could be exploited for dynamically balancing the workload of the two printers.

4   The Formal Model

SOCK [8] is a process calculus for Service-Oriented Computing, featuring request-response invocations as a native primitive. It provides the theoretical basis for the implementation of the Jolie language [18]. In this section we extend SOCK with aggregation. We will omit some details that do not influence our presentation. Full definitions can be found in [7].

First we introduce the notion of courier session, which specifies the code that has to be executed by the aggregator before forwarding the message to the final recipient. Next we introduce in the calculus the notion of communication points, which provide an explicit specification of the deployment of services. This allows us to model internal and external connections, and therefore communication among services which are not directly linked (see the terminology introduced at the end of Section 2).

Table 1. Process Syntax

$P ::= \mathbf{0}$	null process	$P; P$	sequence
$\bar{\epsilon}$	output	$P \mid P$	parallel
$\Sigma_i \epsilon_i; P_i$	external choice	$Wait(c, \mathbf{y})$	wait after solicit
$x := e$	assignment	$Exec(c, o, \mathbf{y}, P)$	exec after request
if e then P else Q	if then else		

output $\bar{\epsilon} ::= o(\mathbf{x})@out$	notification	input $\epsilon ::= o(\mathbf{x})$	reception
$o(\mathbf{x})(\mathbf{y})@out$	solicit	$o(\mathbf{x})(\mathbf{y})\{P\}$	request

4.1 Session

A service in SOCK is a process that can instantiate multiple inner processes equipped with a local state, called sessions. Sessions can send/receive messages and perform computations. Session *behaviours* $P, Q, \ldots$ define the actions to be performed by sessions. A selection of their syntax is reported in Table 1. We denote with $\mathbb{P}$ the set of possible session behaviours. $\mathbf{0}$ is the null process; $\bar{\epsilon}$ is an output, while ϵ is an input; $\Sigma_i \epsilon_i; P_i$ is a standard input-guarded choice; $x := e$ assigns the evaluation of expression e to variable x. We leave the syntax for expressions undefined, assuming that they are first-order expressions including variables and values in *Val*. if e then P else Q is an if-then-else choice; $P; P$ and $P \mid P$ represent, respectively, sequential and parallel composition. $Exec(c, o, \mathbf{y}, P)$ and $Wait(c, \mathbf{y})$ are runtime terms that are only used in the semantics. $Exec(c, o, \mathbf{y}, P)$ represents a server-side running request-response: P is the process computing the answer, o the name of the operation, $\mathbf{y}$ the vector of variables to be used for the answer, and c the private channel to use to send back the answer. Symmetrically, $Wait(c, \mathbf{y})$ is the process waiting for the response on client-side: c is the channel used for receiving the answer and $\mathbf{y}$ the vector of variables to be used for storing the answer. An input ϵ can either be a one-way (OW) $o(\mathbf{x})$ or a request-response (RR) $o(\mathbf{x})(\mathbf{y})\{P\}$, where o is the name of the operation, $\mathbf{x}$ is the vector of variables where to store the received information, and P is the process that has to be executed before sending the information contained in $\mathbf{y}$. An output $\bar{\epsilon}$ can either be the invocation of an OW operation $o(\mathbf{x})@out$ (called notification) or of an RR operation $o(\mathbf{x})(\mathbf{y})@out$ (called solicit-response), where o is the operation name, $\mathbf{x}$ is the vector of variables containing the information to send, $\mathbf{y}$ the vector of variables to store the response, and *out* specifies the output communication to invoke. An output $o(\mathbf{x})@out$ (or $o(\mathbf{x})(\mathbf{y})@out$) is well formed if o is contained in the interface of the used output communication point, namely $out = (I, l)$ implies $o \in I$.

Let $\sigma : Var \to Val$ be a memory map that associates values to variables and let $\mathfrak{M}$ denote the set of possible memory maps.

Definition 5 (Service session). *A service session T is a pair (P, σ). We denote with* $\mathbf{P} = \mathbb{P} \times \mathfrak{M}$ *the set of possible service sessions.*

The semantics of a (service) session is specified by a labelled transition system (lts): $(\mathbf{P}, Labels_{\mathbf{P}}, \to_{\mathbf{P}})$. $Labels_{\mathbf{P}}$ is ranged over by α which is defined as follows:

$$
\begin{aligned}
\alpha ::= \ &\tau &\text{Silent Action} &\qquad \uparrow o(\mathbf{v}) \mapsto \nu \mathrm{c}@(I,l) &\text{Solicit} \\
&o(\mathbf{v})@(I,l) &\text{Notification} &\qquad \downarrow \mathrm{c} \mapsto o(\mathbf{v}) &\text{SResponse} \\
&o(\mathbf{v}) &\text{Reception} &\qquad \uparrow \mathrm{c} \mapsto o(\mathbf{v}) &\text{Request} \\
& & &\qquad \downarrow o(\mathbf{v})@\mathrm{c} &\text{RResponse}
\end{aligned}
$$

Table 2. Session semantics

$$\text{RECEPTION:} \quad (o(\mathbf{x}),\sigma) \xrightarrow{o(\mathbf{v})}_{\mathbf{P}} (\mathbf{0}, \sigma[\mathbf{v}/\mathbf{x}])$$

$$\text{NOTIFICATION:} \quad (o(\mathbf{x})@out,\sigma) \xrightarrow{o(\sigma(\mathbf{x}))@out}_{\mathbf{P}} (\mathbf{0},\sigma)$$

$$\text{SOLICIT:} \quad (o(\mathbf{x})(\mathbf{y})@out,\sigma) \xrightarrow{\uparrow o(\sigma(\mathbf{x})) \mapsto \nu \mathrm{c}@out}_{\mathbf{P}} (\mathit{Wait}(\mathrm{c},\mathbf{y}),\sigma)$$

$$\text{SRESP:} \quad (\mathit{Wait}(\mathrm{c},\mathbf{y}),\sigma) \xrightarrow{\downarrow \mathrm{c} \mapsto o(\mathbf{v})}_{\mathbf{P}} (\mathbf{0},\sigma[\mathbf{v}/\mathbf{y}])$$

$$\text{REQUEST:} \quad (o(\mathbf{x})(\mathbf{y})\{P\},\sigma) \xrightarrow{\uparrow \mathrm{c} \mapsto o(\mathbf{v})}_{\mathbf{P}} (\mathit{Exec}(\mathrm{c},o,\mathbf{y},P),\sigma[\mathbf{v}/\mathbf{x}])$$

$$\text{REXE:} \quad \frac{(P,\sigma) \xrightarrow{\alpha}_{\mathbf{P}} (P',\sigma')}{(\mathit{Exec}(\mathrm{c},o,\mathbf{y},P),\sigma) \xrightarrow{\alpha}_{\mathbf{P}} (\mathit{Exec}(\mathrm{c},o,\mathbf{y},P'),\sigma')}$$

$$\text{RRESP:} \quad (\mathit{Exec}(\mathrm{c},o,\mathbf{y},\mathbf{0}),\sigma) \xrightarrow{\downarrow o(\sigma(\mathbf{y}))@\mathrm{c}}_{\mathbf{P}} (\mathbf{0},\sigma)$$

$$\text{CHOICE:} \quad \frac{(\epsilon_i,\sigma) \xrightarrow{\alpha}_{\mathbf{P}} (Q_i,\sigma')}{(\Sigma_i \epsilon_i; P_i,\sigma) \xrightarrow{\alpha}_{\mathbf{P}} (Q_i; P_i,\sigma')} \qquad \text{ASSIGNMENT:} \quad \frac{[\![e]\!]\sigma = v}{(x := e,\sigma) \xrightarrow{\tau}_{\mathbf{P}} (\mathbf{0},\sigma[v/x])}$$

τ is an internal action. $o(\mathbf{v})@(I,l)$ and $o(\mathbf{v})$ model respectively the delivery and the reception of an OW operation. Label $\uparrow o(\mathbf{v}) \mapsto \nu \mathrm{c}@(I,l)$ models the invocation of an RR operation to the output communication point (I,l), where $\nu \mathrm{c}$ denotes the new private channel c created for receiving the response later, while label $\uparrow \mathrm{c} \mapsto o(\mathbf{v})$ models the reception of an RR operation on the private channel c. RR invocations are closed by labels $\downarrow \mathrm{c} \mapsto o(\mathbf{v})$ and $\downarrow o(\mathbf{v})@\mathrm{c}$, which denote respectively the reception and the delivery of the response. The transition relation $\to_{\mathbf{P}}$ is the least relation that satisfies the rules in Table 2 (we report only a selection) and that is closed up to structural equivalence $\equiv$ (namely the least congruence relation satisfying the axioms $P|Q \equiv Q|P$; $P|(Q|R) \equiv (P|Q)|R$; $P|\mathbf{0} \equiv P$; $\mathbf{0}; P \equiv P$). We briefly describe the rules in Table 2. Rules RECEPTION and NOTIFICATION model the reception and deliver of the one-way operation $o(\mathbf{x})$. Rule SOLICIT says that when a service sends a RR operation $o(\mathbf{x})(\mathbf{y})$ it establishes a fresh channel c on which it then waits for the answer. Once the answer is received the results are stored in variables $\mathbf{y}$ as described by rule SRESP. Rule REQUEST models the reception of a request for the RR operation $o(\mathbf{x})(\mathbf{y})\{P\}$ on channel c: the received values are stored in variables $\mathbf{x}$ and then process P is executed. The execution of process P is modeled by rule REXE. Once process P terminates the values contained in variables $\mathbf{y}$ are sent back to the invoking service on channel c, as modeled by rule RRESP. In ASSIGNMENT, $[\![e]\!]\sigma$ denotes the evaluation of expression e on σ. The rule CHOICE is standard.

4.2 Services

We define now the semantics of a service, building on that of a service session. A service is responsible for the creation and management of its sessions that, like threads in processes, are the entities actually implementing the functionalities required by the invokers. We introduce aggregation at the service level with the primitive $\text{agg}(List)$. This primitive specifies the internal connections of the aggregator service and the courier process. A courier $\mathfrak{C}$ has the syntax:

$$\mathfrak{C} ::= o(\mathbf{xz}) \rightsquigarrow \hat{P} \mid o(\mathbf{xz})(\mathbf{y}) \rightsquigarrow \hat{P}$$

where $o(\mathbf{xz})$ and $o(\mathbf{xz})(\mathbf{y})$ are the input operations that should be forwarded and $\hat{P}$ is the process to be executed. The courier process $\hat{P}$ differs from a standard session process P in the fact that it cannot receive inputs, meaning that the term $\Sigma_i \epsilon_i; P_i$ can not appear in $\hat{P}$, and in the fact that it can contain the new term $\text{forward}(out)$ that forwards the message that has activated the courier session to the output communication point out. We denote by $\mathbb{C}$ the set of possible couriers ranged over by $\mathfrak{C}$, and by Δ the parallel composition of couriers, that is: $\Delta = \mathfrak{C} \mid \mathfrak{C}|\Delta$. We assume that two couriers in a Δ never start with a same operation o. We write $\mathfrak{C} \in \Delta$ for saying that $\mathfrak{C}$ is in Δ. The idea is that when an input $o(\mathbf{xz})$ (resp. $o(\mathbf{xz})(\mathbf{y})$) arrives to the service the corresponding courier $o(\mathbf{xz}) \rightsquigarrow \hat{P}$ (resp. $o(\mathbf{xz})(\mathbf{y}) \rightsquigarrow \hat{P}$) is considered and a new session that we call *courier session* is created. The process of this courier session is obtained by replacing every occurrence of the term $\text{forward}(out)$ in $\hat{P}$ by the term $o(\mathbf{x})@out$ (resp. $o(\mathbf{x})(\mathbf{y})@out$). We denote this substitution by $\hat{P}[o(\mathbf{x})]$ when the input message is an OW operation, and by $\hat{P}[o(\mathbf{x})(\mathbf{y})]$ when the input is an RR operation. Thus, when a service receives an input $o(\mathbf{v})$ that matches the courier $o(\mathbf{xz}) \rightsquigarrow \hat{P}$ the service creates a courier session $(\hat{P}[o(\mathbf{x})], \sigma_\perp[\mathbf{v}/\mathbf{xz}])$ where $\sigma_\perp$ denotes a fresh memory map. If instead the input $o(\mathbf{v})(\mathbf{y})$ that matches the courier $o(\mathbf{xz})(\mathbf{y}) \rightsquigarrow \hat{P}$ is received, the service creates a courier session $(Exec(\mathbf{c}, o, \mathbf{y}, \hat{P}[o(\mathbf{x})(\mathbf{y})]), \sigma_\perp[\mathbf{v}/\mathbf{xz}])$ where $\mathbf{c}$ is the channel to be used to send the reply.

Observe that the input operation that activates a courier session and the output operation performed by the forward term are related by the extension function, indeed $o(\mathbf{xz}) = extend(o(\mathbf{x}), \mathbf{z})$ and $o(\mathbf{xz})(\mathbf{y}) = extend(o(\mathbf{x})(\mathbf{y}), \mathbf{z})$. This models the fact that the newly created session executes the process $\hat{P}$ that consumes part of the input (namely $\mathbf{z}$) and then forwards the remaining information [1].

Note also that the term courier session just indicates a session that is created from a courier process $\hat{P}$, once such a session has been created there is no difference with a standard session.

In this paper we abstract from how a service can route an incoming message to the right internal running session, since it is an orthogonal aspect to our presentation. The interested reader may consult [17]. Here we simply assume that messages are delivered to the right session. The sessions in execution at a given instant of time are specified by the execution environment $\mathcal{E}$. We will denote by ε the empty execution environment and by $T_1|\ldots|T_n$ the environment having $T_1, \ldots, T_n$ $(n \geq 1)$ as session. Operator $|$ is commutative. We can now define the primitive for aggregation presented in Section 3. The syntax is $\text{agg}(\mathbb{I})$ where $\mathbb{I}$ is a list of tuples of the form $\langle in, \{out_1, \ldots, out_n\}, \Delta \rangle$ and:

---

[1] In the actual implementation the output communication point in a forward primitive can be omitted if it can be unambiguosly determined by looking at the deployment information of the service.

Table 3. Service semantics

START:
$$\frac{(P, \sigma_\perp) \xrightarrow{\alpha}_P (P', \sigma)}{\langle In, Out \rangle\, P \oplus \mathsf{agg}(\mathbb{I})[\![\mathcal{E}]\!] \xrightarrow{\alpha}_S \langle In, Out \rangle\, P \oplus \mathsf{agg}(\mathbb{I})[\![\mathcal{E}|(P', \sigma')]\!]}$$

COUR$_1$:
$$\frac{\alpha = o(\mathbf{v}) \quad |\mathbf{v}| = |\mathbf{xz}| \quad \langle(extend(I, \mathbf{z}), l), \{out_1, \ldots, out_n\}, \Delta\rangle \in \mathbb{I} \quad o \in I \quad o(\mathbf{xz}) \rightsquigarrow \hat{P} \in \Delta}{\langle In, Out \rangle\, P \oplus \mathsf{agg}(\mathbb{I})[\![\mathcal{E}]\!] \xrightarrow{\alpha}_S \langle In, Out \rangle\, P \oplus \mathsf{agg}(\mathbb{I})[\![\mathcal{E}|(\hat{P}[o(\mathbf{x})], \sigma_\perp[\mathbf{v}/\mathbf{xz}])]\!]}$$

COUR$_2$:
$$\frac{\alpha = \uparrow c \mapsto o(\mathbf{v}) \quad |\mathbf{v}| = |\mathbf{xz}| \quad \langle(extend(I, \mathbf{z}), l), \{out_1, \ldots, out_n\}, \Delta\rangle \in \mathbb{I} \quad o \in I \quad o(\mathbf{xz})(\mathbf{y}) \rightsquigarrow \hat{P} \in \Delta}{\langle In, Out \rangle\, P \oplus \mathsf{agg}(\mathbb{I})[\![\mathcal{E}]\!] \xrightarrow{\alpha}_S \langle In, Out \rangle\, P \oplus \mathsf{agg}(\mathbb{I})[\![\mathcal{E}|(Exec(c, o, \mathbf{y}, \hat{P}[o(\mathbf{x})(\mathbf{y})]), \sigma_\perp[\mathbf{v}/\mathbf{xz}])]\!]}$$

EXE:
$$\frac{(Q, \sigma) \xrightarrow{\alpha}_P (Q', \sigma')}{\langle In, Out \rangle\, P \oplus \mathsf{agg}(\mathbb{I})[\![\mathcal{E}|(Q, \sigma)]\!] \xrightarrow{\alpha}_S \langle In, Out \rangle\, P \oplus \mathsf{agg}(\mathbb{I})[\![\mathcal{E}|(Q', \sigma')]\!]}$$

- $in = (extend(I, \mathbf{x}), l)$ is an input communication point, where $\mathbf{x}$ denotes the array of additional arguments that the incoming messages of interface I should provide;
- $\{out_1, \ldots, out_n\} = \{(I, l_1), \ldots, (I, l_n)\}$ is a nonempty set of output communication points, sharing the same interface;
- Δ denotes the courier behaviour related to the operations of I, such that for every forward(out) contained in the courier processes in Δ we have that $out \in \{out_1, \ldots, out_n\}$.

We can finally formally define a service. We use $\mathcal{S}$ to denote a service and $\mathbf{S}$ to denote the set of all possible services.

Definition 6 (Service). *A service $\mathcal{S}$ is defined as:*

$$\mathcal{S} ::= \langle In, Out \rangle\, P \oplus \mathsf{agg}(\mathbb{I})[\![\mathcal{E}]\!]$$

where In and Out are the set of input and output communication points of the service; P specifies the behaviour of the service sessions; $\mathsf{agg}(\mathbb{I})$ specifies the aggregating behaviour of the service; $\mathcal{E}$ is the environment of the executing sessions.

Observe that the internal connections of a service engine is specified by $\mathbb{I}$. For every element $\langle in, \{out_1, \ldots, out_n\}, \Delta\rangle$ in the list $\mathbb{I}$ we have a corresponding set of internal connections $\{(in, out_i)\,|\,1 \leq i \leq n\}$. Thus, as expected, we have an internal connection every time that we perform aggregation in a service.

A service is *well-formed* if for every input communication point $in = (I, l)$ in In we have that for every operation $o \in I$ exactly one of the following holds:

- P can receive in input the operation o;
- o is aggregated, namely there exists at least one tuple $\langle in, \{out_1, \ldots, out_n\}, \Delta\rangle \in \mathbb{I}$ such that $in = (I, l) \in In$, $\{out_1, \ldots, out_n\} \subseteq Out$, and $o \in I$.

This means that every operation declared by an input communication point of a service engine is either implemented by the service itself or aggregated.

From the above definition we can observe that a service consists of two main components: P and $\mathsf{agg}(\mathbb{I})$. The first one specifies the behaviour of its internally implemented sessions, while the second one specifies which interfaces the service aggregates and how the service manipulates the incoming messages before forwarding them to the aggregated communication points. Observe that a simple form of aggregation where

Table 4. Network semantics

$$
\text{NOT/REC:} \quad \frac{S_1 \xrightarrow{o(\mathbf{v})@(I,l)}_{\mathbf{S}} S_1' \quad S_2 \xrightarrow{o(\mathbf{v})}_{\mathbf{S}} S_2 \quad (I,l)\in Out(S_1) \quad (I,l)\in In(S_2) \quad o\in I}{S_1|S_2 \xrightarrow{\mu(o(\mathbf{v}))}_{\mathbf{N}} S_1'|S_2'}
$$

$$
\text{SOL/REQ:} \quad \frac{S_1 \xrightarrow{\uparrow o(\mathbf{v})\mapsto \nu c@(I,l)}_{\mathbf{S}} S_1' \quad S_2 \xrightarrow{\uparrow c\mapsto o(\mathbf{v})}_{\mathbf{S}} S_2' \quad (I,l)\in Out(S_1) \quad (I,l)\in In(S_2) \quad o\in I}{S_1|S_2 \xrightarrow{\mu(\uparrow o(\mathbf{v}))}_{\mathbf{N}} S_1'|S_2'}
$$

$$
\text{RES:} \quad \frac{S_1 \xrightarrow{\downarrow c\mapsto o(\mathbf{v})}_{\mathbf{S}} S_1' \quad S_2 \xrightarrow{\downarrow o(\mathbf{v})@c}_{\mathbf{S}} S_2'}{S_1|S_2 \xrightarrow{\mu(\downarrow o(\mathbf{v}))}_{\mathbf{N}} S_1'|S_2'} \qquad \text{S-EXE:} \quad \frac{S \xrightarrow{\tau} S'}{S|N \xrightarrow{\tau}_{\mathbf{N}} S'|N}
$$

messages are only forwarded, as in Example 2 of Section 3, can be seen as a special case of the more general notion of smart aggregation where messages are elaborated by the courier process. In fact, in the first case the courier is only composed by the forward primitive ($\hat{P} = \texttt{forward}(out)$). Hence, without loss of generality, we can assume that a courier is defined for every aggregated operation.

The semantics of the service engine is specified by an LTS ($\mathbf{S}$, $Labels_{\mathbf{P}}$, $\rightarrow_{\mathbf{S}}$) where $\rightarrow_{\mathbf{S}} \subseteq \mathbf{S} \times Labels_{\mathbf{P}} \times \mathbf{S}$ is the least relation that satisfies the rules in Table 3, where $\sigma_\perp$ denotes a fresh memory map, and its main features are the following. Rules START, COUR$_1$, and COUR$_2$ model the creation of sessions and courier sessions. Rule START is standard: when an operation implemented by the service is invoked a new session is created that will handle the request. Rules COUR$_1$ and COUR$_2$ are structurally similar: they create a session to handle the arrival of an aggregated operation. These sessions run a courier code where all the forward primitives are replaced by an output primitive. The last rule, EXE, models the execution of an existing session.

4.3 Network

Definition 7 (Network). *A network* N *is a parallel composition of service engines:* N ::= $\mathcal{S}$ | N|$\mathcal{S}$.

As argued above, the different services in a network can communicate when they are connected through their input and output communication points. Table. 4 reports the transition rules for a network of services. The first three rules model the communication between services in a network, while the rule S-EXE models the internal evolution of a service in a network, namely the execution of service actions that do not involve input/output operations. Rule NOT/REC models the one-way communication between two services, while request-response communications are modeled through the two rules SOL/REQ and RES which represents, respectively, the delivery and reception of an RR operation and the delivery and reception of the answer to an RR operation. The communication rules describe both direct communication between directly connected services, and aggregated communication between services connected by a sequence of external and internal connections.

4.4 Properties

We are now going to show the adequacy of our model by formalizing some proprieties that the flow-transparent mechanism of aggregation preserves, namely flow-based neutrality, operation transparency, and interface transparency. In the following $\langle \beta_1, \ldots, \beta_n \rangle$ $(\langle \beta_1, \ldots, \rangle)$ denotes a finite (infinite) trace. The set $[\![N]\!]$ of maximal finite and infinite traces of a network N are defined as follows:

$$[\![N_1]\!] = \{\langle \beta_1, \ldots, \beta_n \rangle | \exists N_2, \ldots, N_{n+1} \; \forall i \; N_i \xrightarrow{\beta_i}_N N_{i+1} \wedge \text{ for any } \beta \; N_{n+1} \xrightarrow{\beta}_N \} \cup$$

$$\{\langle \beta_1, \beta_2, \ldots \rangle | \forall i > 1 \; \exists N_i \; N_{i-1} \xrightarrow{\beta_{i-1}}_N N_i \}$$

The flow-based neutrality propriety states that the behaviour of a system of services does not change when the messages are rerouted through an aggregator. This is guaranteed by the fact that a simple aggregator, i.e. an aggregator that only forwards the messages, does not alter the flow between the invoker and the callee as stated by the following.

Proposition 1 (Flow-based neutrality). *If S_1 is a service having output communication point (I, l), S_2 is a service having input communication point (I, l), A aggregates the interface I of S_2, and S_1' is the service obtained from S_1 by replacing all the locations l with the locations of the A aggregator, then $\langle \beta_1, \beta_2, \ldots \rangle \in [\![S_1|S_2]\!]$ iff $\langle \beta_1', \beta_2', \ldots \rangle \in [\![S_1'|A|S_2]\!]$ where $\beta_i' = \beta_i, \beta_i$ if β_i is a label involving an operation in I, $\beta_i' = \beta_i$ otherwise. Analogously for the finite traces.*

The property of operation transparency states that the forwarding of the messages to aggregated services does not depend on the names of the aggregated functionalities. This property is guaranteed by the `forward(out)` construct. In fact, by definition, this construct does not depend on the name of the single operations in the aggregated interface, but it redirects all the operations in the interface to the corresponding output communication point.

Interface transparency means that it is possible to reuse aggregators definitions whenever the interfaces of the aggregated services are modified. Since addition or deletion of operations to an interface can be seen as merge or partition of interfaces, the interface transparency property is guaranteed by the fact that it is possible to merge two or more aggregators providing different functionalities into one aggregator without modifying the courier code. In the following, we denote with $A_{I,S}$ the aggregator that aggregates the interface I of the service S.

Proposition 2 (Interface transparency). *Assume that I_1, I_2 are interfaces, C, S are services and S has input communication point $(I_1 \cup I_2, l)$. Then $[\![S|C|A_{I_1,S}|A_{I_2,S}]\!] = [\![S|C|A_{I_1 \cup I_2,S}]\!]$.*

We argue that these three properties are the basic ones that a language allowing flow-transparent composition should observe. Indeed the programmer thanks to the flow-based neutrality could reuse existing orchestrators, and thanks to operation and interface transparency can forget about low level, repetitive and usually error prone details. The combination of these three proprieties allows the development of a modular system that can be easily and quickly modified to accommodate the need of a fast changing environment.

5   Implementation in Jolie

In this section we substantiate our approach by showing the use of the new aggregation primitives that have been included in the Jolie language. Here we will just outline the use of this new primitives for the implementation of the examples introduced in Section 3, for a detail description please see [7] instead.

In order to define the aggregator of Example 1 we need to extend the interface of the printer by adding a new argument. The operation that allows us to extend every OW operation of an interface with an additional argument of type *KeyType* can be defined by using the (new) keyword `interface extender` as follows:

```
interface extender AuthIntExtender { OneWay: *(KeyType) }
```

Exploiting this new construct we can now define the new input communication point of the aggregator in the following way

```
inputPort AggregatorPort {
  Location: "socket://localhost:8000"
  Protocol: soap
  Aggregates: { Printer1Port, Printer2Port } with AuthIntExtender
}
```

Here the keyword `Aggregates` that we introduce allows us to specify which services are aggregated. This is obtained by declaring that the output ports *Printer1Port* and *Printer2Port* (defining the output communication points to invoke the printer services) are aggregated in the input port *AggregatorPort* that defines the input communication point of the aggregator service. The input port specifies that messages are accepted on the port 8000 using the socket mechanism and the SOAP protocol.

The primitive `Aggregates` is used here to aggregate the two printers by using the extended interface obtained through the *AuthIntExtender* operator.

To complete the definition of the aggregator we just need to specify the courier session code. If $I_\mathcal{P}$ is the interface of the printers this can be done using the new keyword `courier` as follows:

```
courier AggregatorPort {
  [ interface I𝓟( request ) ] {
    if ( request.key == "0000" ) {
      forward Printer1Port( request )
    } else if ( request.key == "1111" ) {
      forward Printer2Port( request ) } } }
```

The reading of the previous code should be immediate.

Finally, we use Example 2 to show how functionalities can be added to an aggregator service. Here the goal is to have an aggregator that, besides forwarding the messages to the printer, is also able to provide the user with the key needed for accessing the printer service. Such a key can be obtained by invoking the $get\_key(user\_id)(key)$ operation, which is included in the new interface defined as follows

```
interface AggregatorInterface
  { RequestResponse: get_key(string)(string) }
```

Suppose that the behaviour of the aggregator service that we want to model is the following: whenever it receives the get_key(*user_id*)(*key*) operation it returns the key "0000" unless the name of the user is *John*, in which case it returns the key "1010". This can be implemented as follows:

```
main {
  get_key( username )( key ) {
    if ( username == "John" ) { key = "1010" }
    else { key = "0000" } } }
```

Now, in order to completely define the aggregator of Example 2, we just need to modify the input port of the aggregator in the following way.

```
inputPort AggregatorPort {
  Location: "socket://localhost:8000"
  Protocol: sodep
  Interfaces: AggregatorInterface
  Aggregates: Printer1Port with AuthIntExtender
}
```

Notice that now the input port has a new field *Interfaces* that specifies the additional operation that the aggregator provides on its own, in addition to those that are aggregated by using the construct *Aggregates*.

The Jolie code encoding the examples of Section 3 can be retrieved at [1].

6   Related Work and Conclusions

In this work we studied the foundational aspects of flow-transparent composition of services in the context of SOA. We identified a basic mechanism, called aggregation, that allows programmers to join service functionalities in a loosely coupled, interface based, and behavioural transparent way. We formally defined aggregation in terms of a process calculus and we provided a reference implementation in terms of an extension of the Jolie language. Despite the simplicity of the examples that we provided, it should be clear that aggregation can be used to build, in a rather easy way, large applications along the Enterprise Integration Patterns guidelines.

To the best of our knowledge, this work is the first attempt to bring primitives for the aggregation of services at the same level of the language that is used to define the behavior of a service. Indeed, existing approaches provide tools that define aggregation by mixing different existing solutions. Our work goes in the opposite direction: we englobe into a unique language, with a precise semantics, all the features needed to define services and their aggregation. This facilitates the development of correct software, since the aggregating primitive enforces syntactic and semantic checks which allows to easily prove relevant properties, as previously shown. This advantage is particularly relevant when considering practical, commercial tools for services integration and composition: in this context often the Enterprise Application Integration (EAI) framework [21] is used, which is usually composed by a collection of technologies and services. On the market one can find several EAI mature technologies developed by leading IT companies such as IBM, Oracle and Microsoft. Usually these are implemented by enhancing standard middleware products, often using an Enterprise Service Bus (ESB) [6]. Differently from our approach, all these tools need to operate on top of several existing languages and primitives: for instance, it is not usually possible [25] to implement Enterprise Integration Patterns (EIPs) [10] relying solely on BPEL constructs. This complicates the life of programmers and facilitates the introduction of errors.

Our aggregation mechanism could resemble inheritance in object-oriented languages. However, while inheritance allows the reuse of the *code* of methods, in aggregation what is reused is the executing service itself, since the computation for an aggregated operation invocation is delegated to the aggregated service. We see this as a natural difference, given the fact that aggregation operates in a distributed setting and, as such, locality plays an important role.

A similar notion of aggregation is the interoperation hub [12]. This approach however differs from ours because it assumes that workflows and business process specification are given following a data-centric paradigm.

WSDL [3] is a description language for Web Services that features communication ports. WSDL 2.0 features interface inheritance, allowing an interface to be extended with other operations. This recalls our mechanism of extending an interface using the aggregation primitive. However, in WSDL one can not extend the data type of an operation when using interface inheritance, but only add new operations. The literature reports several attempts of using work-flow techniques [5,20], AIP planning [24,4], theorem provers [19,23] to compose service in an automatic way. Usually these approaches are computationally difficult (often these problems are NP-hard), they make a lot of strong assumptions (like the presence of a common ontology to describe the service functionalities) and they do not scale up to larger systems. In our work we focus on a simpler form of composition with less ambitious goals. Our aggregation mechanism is strongly based on interfaces. There exist other models that exploit types for describing service composition, such as those based on session types [11]. These models, however, are mainly *behavioural* since they focus on aspects such as the order of message exchanges used in the composed services. The aggregation mechanism, instead, focuses on the structure of a service-oriented network and set of operations offered by the composed services. Aggregation and typed behavioral composition play two different, complementary, roles and as future work we plan to add behavioral types to our framework. We also plan to introduce a type system for communication points and connections in order to check the absence of "dangling" output communication points. Moreover we believe that flow-transparent composition facilitates the design of a SOA, since some architectural design decisions may be taken rather early, demanding to the implementation of the (code in the) courier sessions some details.

Sometimes the ESB has been called also a architectural style that provides fundamental functionalities for integrating complex architectures via an event-driven and standards-based messaging engine.

As another line of future work we are investigating the introduction of dynamic aggregation of services. We would like to extend the current form of static aggregation in order to support dynamic changes of the network topology, thus allowing dynamic creation and deletion of communication points and connections. This could be important for the development of adaptable systems. In this context Jolie could represent an advantage for supporting session stickyness, i.e. the support to track session references in aggregators such as load balancers, since Jolie statically defines the structure of session references (correlation sets) along with service interfaces [17]. Finally our aggregate primitive could be included also in other service-oriented languages based on Web Services, such as WS-BPEL [2], or in other models that are used to formalise service-oriented programming such as those in [15,14,22].

References

1. JOLIE Examples Files: `http://www.jolie-lang.org/files/esop2012_aggregation/example.zip`
2. Web Services Business Process Execution Language Version 2.0: `http://docs.oasis-open.org/wsbpel/2.0/wsbpel-v2.0.html`
3. Web Services Description Language (WSDL) Version 2.0: `http://www.w3.org/TR/wsdl20/`
4. Bertoli, P., Pistore, M., Traverso, P.: Automated composition of Web services via planning in asynchronous domains. Artif. Intell. 174(3-4), 316–361 (2010)
5. Casati, F., Ilnicki, S., Jin, L., Krishnamoorthy, V., Shan, M.-C.: Adaptive and Dynamic Service Composition in eFlow. In: Wangler, B., Bergman, L.D. (eds.) CAiSE 2000. LNCS, vol. 1789, pp. 13–31. Springer, Heidelberg (2000)
6. Chappell, D.A.: Enterprise Service Bus - Theory in practice. O'Reilly (2004)
7. Dalla Preda, M., Gabbrielli, M., Guidi, C., Mauro, J., Montesi, F.: A language for (smart) service aggregation: Theory and practice of interface-based service composition. Technical Report UBLCS-2011-11, University of Bologna (2011), `http://www.informatica.unibo.it/ricerca/ublcs/2011/UBLCS-2011-11`
8. Guidi, C., Lucchi, R., Gorrieri, R., Busi, N., Zavattaro, G.: SOCK: A Calculus for Service Oriented Computing. In: Dan, A., Lamersdorf, W. (eds.) ICSOC 2006. LNCS, vol. 4294, pp. 327–338. Springer, Heidelberg (2006)
9. Guidi, C., Montesi, F.: Reasoning about a service-oriented programming paradigm. In: YR-SOC, pp. 67–81 (2009)
10. Hohpe, G., Woolf, B.: Enterprise Integration Patterns: Designing, Building, and Deploying Messaging Solutions. Addison-Wesley Longman Publishing Co., Inc., Boston (2003)
11. Honda, K., Yoshida, N., Carbone, M.: Multiparty asynchronous session types. In: POPL, pp. 273–284 (2008)
12. Hull, R., Narendra, N.C., Nigam, A.: Facilitating Workflow Interoperation Using Artifact-Centric Hubs. In: Baresi, L., Chi, C.-H., Suzuki, J. (eds.) ICSOC-ServiceWave 2009. LNCS, vol. 5900, pp. 1–18. Springer, Heidelberg (2009)
13. Khalaf, R., Leymann, F.: On Web Services Aggregation. In: Benatallah, B., Shan, M.-C. (eds.) TES 2003. LNCS, vol. 2819, pp. 1–13. Springer, Heidelberg (2003)
14. Laneve, C., Zavattaro, G.: webπ at work. In: De Nicola, R., Sangiorgi, D. (eds.) TGC 2005. LNCS, vol. 3705, pp. 182–194. Springer, Heidelberg (2005)
15. Lapadula, A., Pugliese, R., Tiezzi, F.: A Formal Account of WS-BPEL. In: Lea, D., Zavattaro, G. (eds.) COORDINATION 2008. LNCS, vol. 5052, pp. 199–215. Springer, Heidelberg (2008)
16. Montesi, F.: Jolie: a service-oriented programming language. Master's thesis, University of Bologna, Department of Computer Science (2010)

17. Montesi, F., Carbone, M.: Programming Services with Correlation Sets. In: Kappel, G., Maamar, Z., Motahari-Nezhad, H.R. (eds.) ICSOC 2011. LNCS, vol. 7084, pp. 125–141. Springer, Heidelberg (2011)

18. Montesi, F., Guidi, C., Zavattaro, G.: Composing Services with JOLIE. In: ECOWS, pp. 13–22 (2007)

19. Rao, J., Küngas, P., Matskin, M.: Logic-based Web Services Composition: From Service Description to Process Model. In: ICWS, pp. 446–453 (2004)

20. Schuster, H., Georgakopoulos, D., Cichocki, A., Baker, D.: Modeling and Composing Service-Based and Reference Process-Based Multi-enterprise Processes. In: Wangler, B., Bergman, L.D. (eds.) CAiSE 2000. LNCS, vol. 1789, pp. 247–263. Springer, Heidelberg (2000)

21. Sherif, M.H.: Handbook of Enterprise Integration. Auerbach Publishers, Incorporated (2009)

22. Vieira, H.T., Caires, L., Seco, J.C.: The Conversation Calculus: A Model of Service-Oriented Computation. In: Drossopoulou, S. (ed.) ESOP 2008. LNCS, vol. 4960, pp. 269–283. Springer, Heidelberg (2008)

23. Waldinger, R.: Web Agents Cooperating Deductively. In: Rash, J.L., Rouff, C.A., Truszkowski, W., Gordon, D.F., Hinchey, M.G. (eds.) FAABS 2000. LNCS (LNAI), vol. 1871, pp. 250–262. Springer, Heidelberg (2001)

24. Wu, D., Sirin, E., Hendler, J.A., Nau, D.S., Parsia, B.: Automatic Web Services Composition Using SHOP2. In: WWW, Posters (2003)

25. Yuan, X.: Prototype for executable EAI patterns. Master's thesis, University of Stuttgart (2008)

A Framework for Modelling Security Architectures in Services Ecosystems

Matthew Collinson, David Pym, and Barry Taylor

University of Aberdeen
Scotland, U.K.
{matthew.collinson,d.j.pym,barry.taylor}@abdn.ac.uk

Abstract. We develop a compositional framework for modelling security and business architectures based on rigorous underlying mathematical systems modelling technology. We explain the basic architectural model, which strictly separates declarative specification from operational implementation, and show architectures can interact by composition, substitution, and stacking. We illustrate these constructions using a running example based on airport security and an example based on (cloud-based) outsourcing, indicating how our approach can illustrate how security controls can fail or be circumvented in these cases. We explain our motivations from mathematical modelling and security economics, and conclude by indicating how to aim to develop a decision-support technology.

Keywords: Services Security and Privacy Systems Modelling, Architectural Models for Cloud Computing, Economics Models and Services, Composition of Services, Service Modelling, Service-oriented Analysis and Design.

1 Introduction

The development of utility computing platforms, such as cloud, and the business ecosystems that they can support, has emphasized clearly the need for systematic approaches to designing and reasoning about security architectures, their associated policies and investment requirements, and their relationship with the core operational concerns of the business model. Moreover, as such systems become integral parts of hybrid cyber-physical systems, the need to identify unifying conceptual structures becomes pressing.

But security and business architectures (they should, of course, be considered together) cannot be understood in isolation from the underlying systems architecture. We propose a conceptual framework (building directly on some earlier basic ideas [1]) for describing security and business architectures that integrates directly with an underlying account of the components of the supporting (distributed) system [2] and an associated account of mathematical systems modelling [3–6]. Building on these foundations, we can hope for a framework that is capable of addressing such challenging issues as how to identify vulnerabilities, and potential attacks, that may arise from the interaction of otherwise appropriately secure architectures. To this end, it is essential that our account of security and business architectures be compositional.

Our approach to a conceptual architecture for security and associated business processes is inspired by several key influences. First, a rigorous yet applicable and robust theory of mathematical systems modelling (supported by a simulation tool [4, 7])

F. De Paoli, E. Pimentel, and G. Zavattaro (Eds.): ESOCC 2012, LNCS 7592, pp. 64–79, 2012.

that will support the requisite compositionality. Second, an increasingly well-developed economics-based account of decision-making about trade-offs in security [8, 9]. Third, a desire to deliver ontologically valuable, executable tools to support decision-makers. Our presentation in this paper is intended to be informal but careful.

In § 2, we summarize our underlying approach to system modelling, aspects of which are needed for our subsequent discussion. In § 3, we explain the basic model of security architecture hierarchies that sits on top of this modelling approach. We use an example that, whilst chosen to be familiar to most readers, illustrates that our approach, though motivated by information architectures, is more broadly applicable. In § 4, we discuss the various ways in which hierarchies can interact in order to combine to form more complex architectures — and so allows us to see how complex situations are composed of simpler ones, so allowing the sources of some security issues to be examined. In § 5, we extend our running example to encompass aspects of outsourcing to the cloud. We conclude, in § 6, with a short discussion of our ongoing work in integrating our structural and economics-based approaches into decision-support tools.

2   Systems Modelling and Systems Economics

2.1   The Core System Concepts

Our underlying approach to mathematical systems modelling builds on a body of theoretical work [3–6, 10], an implemented tool, Core Gnosis, [4, 7, 3], and a body of practical modelling experience (see [3] for references). The approach builds on identifying four key concepts, which can be seen as building on a body of basic work in the theory of distributed systems as summarized, for example, rather elegantly in [2]. The key notions are those of *location, resource, process*, and *environment*, as described below. We mention briefly our mathematical treatment of these concepts, as captured in Core Gnosis and reported extensively elsewhere [3, 4, 7] , but defer any detailed use of these concepts to another occasion.

Location. Locations are the logical and/or physical places in the system architecture at which resources are located. They are connected by links. Mathematically, our treatment of location begins with some observations about some natural and basic properties of locations [3, 5]: a collection of atomic locations — the basic places — which generate a structure of locations; a notion of (directed) connection between locations — describing the topology of the system; a notion of sublocation (which respects connections); a notion of substitution (of a location for a sublocation) that respects connections — substitution provides a basis for abstraction and refinement in our system models. Leading examples are provided by various constructions on (directed) graphs.

Resource. The logical and/or physical entities that enable and are manipulated by the processes that describe the system's operations/services. Mathematically, our notion of resource — which encompasses natural examples such as space, memory, and money — is based on (ordered, partial, commutative) monoids (e.g., the non-negative integers with addition, zero, and less-than-or-equals), which capture basic conceptual notions of resource composition and comparison: each type of resource is based on a basic set of resource elements; resource elements can be combined (and the combination has a unit); resource elements can be compared.

Process. Processes describe the system's operations; the services it provides. Mathematically, we consider a process algebra that is similar to Milner's SCCS [11], but which incorporates notions of location and resource [3–5].

Environment. Such an architecture, as described in terms of location, resource, and process, works well conceptually, but it is isolated — that is, it is not connected to the environment within which it exists. For example, developed below, the processes that describe an airport's security operations apply to passengers (and their luggage) who arrive at the terminal building from the outside world. Clearly, for our present purposes at least, we are not interested in modelling the outside world in any detail. Nevertheless, we must have some way of modelling passenger arrivals at the boundary of our system of interest. In our system modelling point of view, in common with established practice in discrete event simulation, the approach taken is to employ stochastic models of event occurrences (cf. below, the arrival of passengers or other agents).

The incidence of events upon the system of interest is represented by an appropriate choice of probability distribution. Once the model has been connected to its environment in this way, it can be executed, explored, and validated using discrete-event and Monte Carlo-style simulation methods. Core Gnosis, which implements the approach to mathematical systems modelling described above, allows the exploration of a model's properties by Monte Carlo-style experiments.

2.2 A Running Example

We will illustrate our approach to modelling security and other operational architectures using a running example based on airport security. To set this up, we first explain, informally, the underlying system model corresponding to this example, in terms of its locations, resources, processes, and environment. The basic set-up is illustrated in Fig. 1 (cf. [1, 12]), which describes the locations — from the public area outside of the architecture, via airside, to the aircraft — in an airport that are significant for the security architecture, the purpose of which is to ensure the suitability of passengers to be admitted onto aircraft. A passenger (perhaps with luggage) must navigate from groundside to airside, passing through a sequence of checks. These checks are *processes* that are applied to, or act upon, various *resources*, at particular *locations*.

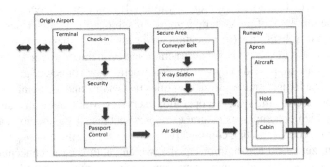

Fig. 1. Running Example: Airport Security Locations Directed Graph (Simplified)

The environment turns this static view into a dynamic one by introducing actors into the system. For example, the arrival of passengers at the airport's terminal building might be captured by a negative exponential distribution, negexp(λ), where the rate parameter λ gives the mean time between passenger arrivals. Similarly, we might capture the arrival of passengers carrying prohibited items with a different negexp parameter.

3   The Basic Architecture Model

Following [1], there are two key layers in our representation of a security architecture, the *Framework Layer* and *Instantiation Layer*. Both are organized through a common hierarchy of rôles, each rôle sub-divided into dependencies, priorities, and preferences.

The hierarchy contains all the relevant rôles that make up the organization being modelled. Rôles are ordered by their ability to influence the security architecture of the system. In other words, they are classified by the toolbox that is available to them for modifying *Security Objects* (that characterize security tasks, defined below). The system accepts multiple and partial orderings. For example, the top level of the model might represent the strategic decision-makers of the organization, such as an airport's security managers or their regulators, while the bottom level might represent an individual employee or user of the organization, such as an airport's check-in staff or a passenger navigating airport security. The rôles, representing positions in the hierarchy that individuals can adopt, do not represent any entity themselves. They are instead populated by *actors*, which are another component in the system and are described below.

Each hierarchy level contains three sections representing the dependencies, priorities and preferences of that level. For our purposes we define the terms as follows:

- *Dependencies* (strong requirement): Externally enforced requirements that actors populating the rôle must meet all of in order to function within the model. Actors occupying this rôle have no choice in whether or not (and possibly even how) to meet these requirements regardless of how resource inefficient they are. Dependencies will often be informed by the environment within which the hierarchy exists;
- *Priorities* (weak requirement): Externally supplied tasks, as many as possible of which should be met by actors in the associated rôle. Actors have some choice in which priorities to meet and how they are approached. In a limited resource environment, actors can select the most resource efficient priorities and methods first. Priorities will often be informed by the rôle that the level represents;
- *Preferences*: Actor-generated tasks that an actor has decided are worth doing from its own perspective — can be derived from an actor's rôles in other hierarchies.

Dependencies, priorities, and preferences (DPP) and the hierarchy of rôles structure are found in both the Framework Layer and the Instantiation Layer.

The use of dependencies, priorities, and preferences is inspired, as described in [1], by utility theory and its use to study resource allocation and investment in information security, as described in [8, 9]. Dependencies and priorities are driven by the utility of the policy-makers that are responsible for the hierarchies (e.g., governments, regulators, system owners/managers). Preferences, representing much weaker choices, are driven by the users of systems (e.g., managers, employees, customers). A systematic integration of these utility-theoretic perspectives is beyond the scope of this short paper.

The form and construction of the security architecture is illustrated in Fig. 2. The key components of this diagram are the following:

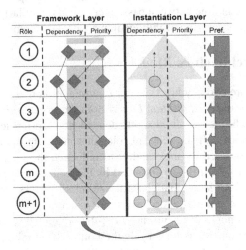

Fig. 2. Security Architecture: Basic Hierarchy

- *The hierarchy of rôles* (far left). Rôles capture the relevant security or business management structure of the organization being modelled. They are ordered by their ability to influence the security architecture of the system;
- *The Framework Layer* (centre left). The Framework Layer is constructed top-down. Dependencies and priorities at a given level in the hierarchy induce dependencies and priorities at lower levels;
- *Security Objects* (trees within Framework Layer, with the requirements at parent nodes being devolved to requirements at child nodes). Security Objects represent the security tasks which, if completed, will satisfy the dependencies and priorities with which they are associated;
- *The Instantiation Layer* (centre right). The Instantiation Layer is constructed bottom-up, starting where the Framework Layer finishes (see below). The Instantiation Layer is a populated image of the Framework Layer;
- *Security Components* (nodes of trees within Instantiation Layer). Security Components perform the operational checks required in order to deliver Security Objects. They do so by returning boolean values up the tree, towards the root, from parent nodes to child nodes, thereby implementing the dependencies and requirements in the corresponding nodes (i.e., those at the same rôle level) of the Framework Layer. They enter the architecture when the Framework is instantiated;
- *Actors* (far right). Actors occupy rôles. They insert preferences into the hierarchy of rôles at the Instantiation Layer.

3.1 The Framework Layer

The Framework Layer represents the underlying architecture. It is declarative, describing requirements, but informs the construction of the corresponding operational Instantiation Layer, providing implementation. A Framework Layer consists in a hierarchy of rôles (cf. RBAC models of access control), with dependencies and priorities assigned to them. Preferences appear in the Instantiation Layer, below, not the Framework Layer. The dependencies and priorities each have a *Security Object* (SO) associated with them. SOs are a unique component of the Framework Layer and represent the security requirements which, if delivered, will satisfy the dependencies and priorities with which they are associated. A typical SO will exist at multiple levels and multiple sections (dependency, priority) in the Framework Layer. It will commonly be the case that an SO created at a higher level will transition through and connect (or create) priorities and dependencies lower in the framework.

For example, in the setting of the running example of airport security that we have begun to introduce, examples of Security Objects include the examining of checked luggage, the checking of hand luggage and passengers — to identify and so remove any prohibited contents — and the tracking of the relationship between passengers and checked luggage. These examples are developed below.

More mathematically, there are many choices of formalization of SO. Our working choice for the purposes of this paper is, roughly speaking, the following:

- SOs are characterized by (directed) and/or forests[1] [2] (Fig. 2, trees in the Framework Layer) associated with dependencies and priorities;
- Internal nodes of the trees are labelled with boolean variables, each associated with a dependency or priority; truth conditions are inherited upwards (towards the root);
- Leaves are nodes for which a boolean instantiation (all components for conjunctions, one component for disjunctions) can be determined at the next level down in the hierarchy of rôles.

Dependencies and priorities are externally generated. In practice, a hierarchy will not encompass all possible contributors to the framework and will be bounded at some sensible level. In our example, we have not represented any rôle higher than the airport security manager. To populate a hierarchy, it is necessary to determine the dependencies and priorities that the top rôle inherits from sources external to the hierarchy. The next step is to assign Security Objects to these dependencies and priorities: see Table 1, where down the table one navigates down the Framework Layer along an SO.

Note, for example, that the SO 'scan luggage and passengers' corresponds to a tree (in Fig. 2) in the Framework Layer. Starting as a node at the Manager's rôle level, it passes to two nodes at the Airport Security Staff level, and acquires a boolean value at the Passenger rôle level (true/false that the passenger and luggage contents are permitted) and will terminate. An SO must always terminate with such a compliance requirement. Table 1 neglects (below the Manager's level) the SOs related to checked luggage.

---

[1] A (directed) forest is a disjoint union of (directed) and/or trees.

[2] A forest is required because a given SO may, in general, derive from more than one dependency or priority.

Table 1. Rôles, Dependencies, and Security Objects

Rôle	Dependencies	Security Objects
Airport Security Manager	Ensure no prohibited materials transit the airport	Scan checked luggage
		Scan hand luggage and passengers
		Track relationship between passengers and checked luggage
Airport Security Staff	Examine all passengers and luggage passing through security checkpoint	Identify contents of hand luggage and verify permitted
		Put passenger through metal detector
Passenger	Comply with SO	

3.2 The Instantiation Layer

Whereas the Framework Layer is declarative, the Instantiation Layer is operational. Two new parts of the architecture are added during instantiation, Security Components (SC) and actors. Actors occupy rôles and insert preferences into the hierarchy of rôles at the Instantiation Layer. Security components combine together to form the operational counterparts of security objects.

The Instantiation Layer is built from the bottom up. SCs lay out the processes and resources needed to perform the boolean checks specified in corresponding SOs. SCs start at the final 'compliance' level of the SO. Once the processes and resources required at this level are in place, we check they are sufficient to complete the SO. If yes, then the SC terminates. If not, then we move up to the rôle above and add additional processes and resources as needed. Again, this process repeats until all SCs are closed. At this point, the Instantiation Layer is complete.

A little more formally, corresponding to the slightly more formal view of SOs sketched above, we can describe how SCs are combined to instantiate SOs as follows:

- SCs are combined according to the and/or forest of the SO that they instantiate;
- Each SC implements a checking process that applies to Actors at the level below;
- SCs return boolean values that instantiate internal nodes of the corresponding SO.

Working through our example again, we work upwards from Passenger until we have sufficient processes and resources in place to return a boolean for the statement 'the passenger and luggage are permitted'. The SCs in this case would be as in Table 2, in which reading up the table one navigates up the Instantiation Layer, along an SC.

In Fig. 2, the SCs correspond to the trees in the Instantiation Layer. Note that whereas the SO terminated in a 'compliance' level the SC terminates at a 'provision' level when it reaches a rôle that can sufficiently provide the resources required to execute the SC without recourse to a higher rôle.

The final component of the Instantiation Layer (and the architecture) are actors. Actors exist independently of any single hierarchy, being entities that can inhabit rôles in multiple hierarchies, this being the key difference between actors and SOs. They can interact with any and all hierarchies present, simultaneously if necessary.

Table 2. SCs

Rôle	Dependencies	Security Components
Airport Manager Security	Ensure no prohibited materials transit the airport	Provide resources (X-ray machine, metal detector, wands)
		Provide data on prohibited materials for X-ray comparison
Airport Staff Security	Examine all passengers and luggage passing through security checkpoint	Monitor X-ray machine and inspect results for prohibited items
		Hand-search suspect luggage
		Hand-scan suspicious passengers
Passenger	Comply with SO	Place luggage on scanner
		Walk through detector

3.3   Context and Related Approaches

The use of actors populating rôles, and of relations between rôles in organizations and in society, has been an important theme in sociology since the mid-twentieth century [13–15]. Indeed, much everyday language now incorporates terminology from that research. The present work is influenced only indirectly — and perhaps unconsciously — through the shared language. Indeed, the focus of the present paper is on setting down in precise, mathematical terms the structure of organizations with a particular focus on their security function. A specific impact of this cultural heritage can be seen in the development in computer security of RBAC, analyzed in the context of the system modelling that underpins this work in [10].

Task Knowledge Structures (TKS) [16] provide a mechanism by which the organization of knowledge the users employ in order to solve problems can be used to support system design, and an alternative approach to task modelling is given in [17].

An alternative approach to systems modelling is provided by System Dynamics [18] explored in the business process modelling context in, for example, [19] and security [20]. System Dynamics is focussed on the dynamics of system models, and does not consider structural properties such as location or the structural properties of resource and process. It also lacks the associated logic of states afforded by our approach [3–6] (and needed, we submit, to consider architecture). Human factors in systems security have been considered by many authors, (e.g., [21–23, 20] are relevant examples for this paper) with social interactions between actors being considered in, for example, [24].

4   Interacting Architectures

The basic architecture model works well for a describing a single, clearly delineated process, such as airport security operations or airport airside business operations. This level of analysis was sufficient for the concerns of [1].

Typically, however, organizations operate many such processes simultaneously, and all of these processes may interact with one another, possibly in unintended ways or with unintended consequences. For the present paper, we restrict our attention to those forms of interaction that are mediated by actors. In the underlying system model, actors will be represented either as resources, when they are passive components of a model or, more typically, as processes, where they manage and navigate through architectures.

We identify three key ways in which hierarchies may interact, namely *composition*, *substitution*, and *stacking*. We conjecture that, given our restriction to actor-mediated interaction, these three forms of interaction are all that is required to describe conveniently and naturally the architectures commonly found in services ecosystems. This conjecture can be formulated precisely in terms of the underlying mathematical systems model, for which there is a rich theory of the expressiveness of concurrent composition operators (e.g., [11, 25, 26]). The details are beyond the scope of this informal paper.

It should be noted here that, although the use of 'actors' is a convenient abstraction here, it remains the case that our intended leading applications are primarily concerned with policy assurance/compliance for organizational hierarchies, with their associated 'human factors'. This intent influences our design decisions directly.

4.1   Composition

Composition, as illustrated in Fig. 3, is perhaps the most basic form of interaction between architectures. A key component of composition is the presence of some actors in both hierarchies — the dotted lines in Fig. 3 indicate that some actors may populate rôles in both hierarchies. In order for this to be possible, we must require that such actors must be able to move themselves and/or resources between the two hierarchies. This in turn requires that locations in the one hierarchy be connected to locations in the other (recall locations can be logical and/or physical). Of course, the two hierarchies in Fig. 3 might have the stronger property of sharing locations L and resources R.

For an example — illustrating the use of our framework to assess security vulnerabilities and possible attacks that may arise from composing architectures — consider again our running example of airport security. Consider the security architecture as sketched so far. Its purpose is to ensure certain integrity properties of people who get airside (no weapons, no liquids that can be used to make bombs, etc.). Now, the airport also exploits the airside location as part of its business process: it seeks to sell stuff to passengers who are waiting to board aircraft, so that bottles of liquids that would be blocked by the security process are available in airside stores.

So, as a result of composing the security architecture and the business architecture, with shared locations, resources, and actors, we have a possible vulnerability and attack. A terrorist clears security with nothing to identify her and nothing that is prohibited. Similarly, an accomplice, who is a staff member in the newsagent's airside store, passes through security without question. However, the newsagent's supply chain is compromised, and there is a shrink-wrapped case of water bottles containing bomb-making fluids, and the location of these bottles in the case is known to the staff-member accomplice (here we assume that the fluids in the bottles for sale airside have not all been individually tested for their chemical composition). The terrorist can then buy the bomb-making liquids from the accomplice, so undermining the security architecture.

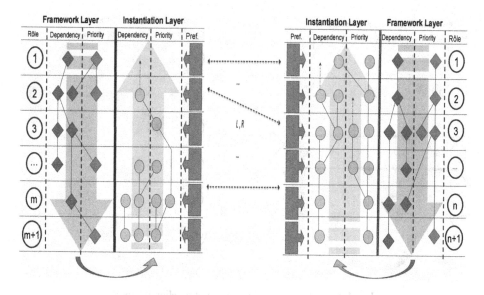

Fig. 3. Security Architecture: Composing Hierarchies

How, then, should we analyse this situation? The problem arises from the sharing of locations and resources by the two architectures, with some actors able to be part of both hierarchies without the integrity properties of actors and the resources to which they have access that are required by one architecture being guaranteed by the other. Moreover, if an actor inhabits rôles in two hierarchies, what are the conflicts between the SOs and SCs associated with those rôles?

Our approach gives a framework within which the factors that contribute to failures and circumventions of security policies and controls can be identified, isolated, and handled. Moreover, when implemented in a simulation tool, the impact of vulnerabilities in a range of threat scenarios can be explored. For example, for a vulnerability such as the 'water bottles' described above, the likelihood of a successful attack can be explored.

4.2 Substitution

The next form of interaction is substitution, illustrated in Fig 4. Here one hierarchy (the child, on the right) is used to refine a rôle in another (the parent, on the left, rôle in bold). We must require that the declarative and operational properties of the rôle that is replaced are respected in the child hierarchy. Note there is no *necessary* requirement here for the parent and child to share resources and locations (cf. stacking, below).

For substitution to be defined, the parent and child hierarchies must fit together properly, as described below. This definition can be given mathematically in terms of the underlying system model; here we aim to give a precise, informal definition of how a child hierarchy is substituted into the parent, replacing a rôle.

- In the Framework Layer, each dependency (resp. priority) that occurs in an SO in the rôle in the parent that is replaced (♯) must have a corresponding dependency

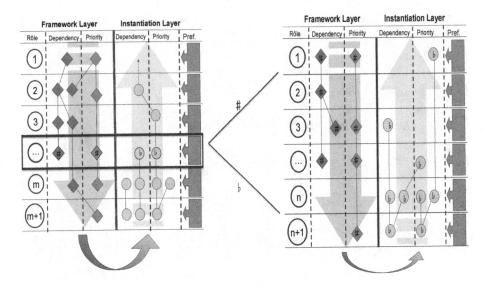

Fig. 4. Security Architecture: Substituting Hierarchies

(respectively priority) at level 1 in an SO in the child that replaces it. Similarly, corresponding to any dependency (resp. priority) in an SO in the parent that is derived from a dependency (resp. priority) in the rôle that is replaced, there must be a dependency (resp. priority) at level $n + 1$ in the child that replaces it. Thus the SO in the child refines the dependencies (resp. priorities) replaced in the parent.

- In the Instantiation Layer, each dependency (resp. priority) that occurs in an SC in the rôle in the parent hierarchy that is replaced (♭) must have a corresponding dependency (respectively priority) at level $n + 1$ in an SC in the child that replaces it. Similarly, any dependency (resp. priority) in an SC the parent that is derived from (going upwards, of course) on any dependency (resp. priority) in the rôle that is replaced must have a corresponding dependency (resp. priority) at level 1 in an SC in the child that replaces it. Thus the SC in the child refines the dependencies (resp. priorities) replaced in the parent.

The child hierarchy must provide all of the declarative and operational capabilities associated with the dependencies and priorities in the rôle that it replaces — formally, this is expressed in terms of processes and resources in the underlying system model, but the details are omitted in this informal description. An example of the use of substitution, together with the associated facility to support the identification of vulnerabilities and associated attacks, is given in § 5.

4.3 Stacking

We can also combine hierarchies vertically — giving a natural approach to modelling multilayered architectures — to form what we call *stacks*, in which one hierarchy sits immediately below another.

The formation of stacks is similar to substitution, in that we can think of them as being formed by substituting (as defined above) a child hierarchy for the bottom rôle in the parent hierarchy. Critically, however, in stacks there may be actors that are common to both the upper and lower hierarchy with, correspondingly, shared locations and resources. Thus stacking combines aspects of both substitution and composition. The left-hand diagram in Fig. 5 illustrates a stack of two hierarchies.

To form this stack of (two) hierarchies, we start with a basic one, as in Fig. 2, with layers 1 to $m+1$. We then substitute a second one, with its own layers labelled 1 to $n+1$, at layer $m + 1$, according to the definition of substitution given above. We then obtain a hierarchy with layers 1 to $m + n + 1$, with layers $m + 1$ to $m + n + 1$ corresponding to the layers 1 to $n + 1$ from the second layer. The right-hand diagram in Fig. 5 depicts the three-layer cloud ecosystem stack, discussed below.

5   Extending the Running Example: Outsourcing to the Cloud

Having established our modelling theory using the familiar example of airport security as an illustrative example, we now consider the example of a cloud-based services ecosystem [27–29]. Three-layered approaches are common in designing and modelling software system architectures (e.g., [30]) and we adopt this approach here. Specifically, we suppose an infrastructure layer, upon which is stacked a service layer, upon which is stacked a social layer.

The infrastructure layer provides the hardware and middleware platforms — that is, the underlying cloud infrastructure — for the ecosystem. The service layer provides the software — both its development and/or maintenance and sales to business users. The social layer is where the end-user customers access services provided by the business users — for example, a bank's personal customers may use security software to support internet banking, with the software being a collection of programs obtained by the bank from a broker in the service layer who aggregates a security service.

The right-hand diagram in Fig. 5, illustrating the cloud ecosystem stack, hides the rôle layers that were replaced when the stack was formed by substitution. For example, the Service Layer replaces a (bottom) rôle in the Social Layer that describes the provision of suitable software.

Table 3 illustrates the dependencies in the Service Layer. Table 4 illustrates how priorities, for example, cross between stacked hierarchies: the SC tree connects the priority of the SaaS Broker to that of the Business User.

To conclude this example, recall the airport security example. Suppose, as part of the security process, some identities must be checked. The security staff may, for example, need to use an email or other messaging service in order to obtain confirmation of an identity. Clearly, establishing the integrity of such messages will be a dependency for the airport's security manager. To this end, the manager might outsource integrity checking to a specialist (SaaS) email scanning provider. In terms of the security architecture, this will be an instance of substitution.

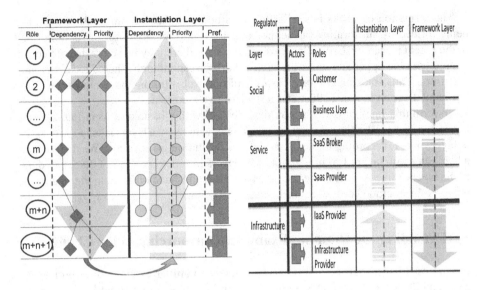

Fig. 5. Security Architecture: Stacking Hierarchies (left) with Cloud Example (right)

Table 3.

Rôle	Dependencies	Security Components
SaaS Broker	Ensure compliance for SaaS requirements	Implement procedure to supply audit outcomes to Regulator
	Ensure availability of SaaS audit data	Implement procedure to obtain audit data from SaaS provider
SaaS Provider	Ensure log data available to SaaS Broker	Implement secure, adequately retrievable archiving

Table 4.

Rôle	Priorities	Security Components
Customer	Obtain a good service	
Business User	Acknowledge contact from customers promptly	Respond to customer by email within 2 working days
SaaS Broker	Contact SaaS Provider with performance feedback sufficiently promptly for feedback to be useful	Email SaaS Provider within 6 months of beginning service contract

The process of sending an email intended for an airport employee is the following: *Original Email → Internet → Airport Firewall → Domain Server → Client PC → Recipient*. A SaaS offering scans email and performs a series of checks to ensure messages are free from malicious software, and their integrity is intact; that is, the apparent originator is the actual sender of a message. Then the process is, essentially: *Original Email* → *Internet* → *SaaS* → *Email Scanned and Tagged* → *Internet* → *Airport Firewall* → *Domain Server* → *Client PC* → *Recipient*. Message tags are added by the SaaS prior to forwarding: *Checked* (message is considered safe); *Spam* (unwelcome or unsolicited source); *Alert* (message has failed a test). The operator has the option of releasing the message. There is clearly a risk that a non-security aware operator will release the message and enable malicious content to attack connected airport IT. There is also a dependency that the SaaS be available.

A larger risk is that the integrity of the data within the email is now trusted to security controls that exist within the SaaS business model: typically, there will be less transparency in the outsourced (i.e., substituted) setting concerning the controls that are applied to determine which actors are used to fill which rôles. In our running example, focus is therefore on differences between airport security controls and those of the SaaS offering. Vetting procedures required for airport staff are in general tougher than those for the staff employed by a SaaS operator. The relevant employee of the SaaS provider will have access to a system able to access airport email traffic, and sign it as secure. In the absence of tougher checks on this particular employee, there is a potential vulnerability that the employee could exploit in order to carry out a targeted attack. If the service has previously performed well, and the user trusts the tags appended to checked messages, then the resulting attack might have a high probability of success. The SaaS provider's ability to hold these contracts is quite tightly bound to their not allowing such breaches, and it is not clear the contractual incentives will necessarily ensure that vetting standards are well-matched to the sensitivities of the tasks determined by the SOs and implemented by the SCs. Our framework provides a way to organize the inclusion of appropriate standards for appropriate tasks in the contractual structure.

Thus, as in § 4.1, we see that our architectural framework provides a framework for identifying, analyzing, and handling the vulnerabilities and associated attack vectors related to with security design choices.

6 Modelling and Tool Support

The next stage of this work has three key aspects. First, we must provide a mathematically precise account of the relationship between the underlying system models (based on locations, resources, and processes [4, 3]) and the architectures described here, including the key relationship between models/architectures and their environments. We have alluded this work here, but defer presentation of the details to another occasion.

Second, we must provide a systematic account of how utility-theoretic approaches to resource allocation and investment decision-making in security are to be integrated with our account of architectures [23, 31, 8, 9].

Third, we must develop tools to support the use of the architectural models described in this paper to assess, systematically, how the interaction between different processes can give rise to security vulnerabilities and attacks. A key aspect of this approach, building on both the first and second steps above, will be to simulate the behaviour of systems and architectures in the presence of different threat intensities; that is, in the terms of § 2, different probabilities of possible attacks that are incident from the environment.

Acknowledgement. We are grateful to Adam Beautement for many helpful discussions related to the topics discussed herein. This paper builds on [1].

References

1. Beautement, A., Pym, D.: Structured systems economics for security management. In: Moore, T. (ed.) Proc. WEIS 2010, Harvard (2010),
   http://weis2010.econinfosec.org/papers/session6/
   weis2010_beautement.pdf
2. Coulouris, G., Dollimore, J., Kindberg, T.: Distributed Systems: Concepts and Design, 3rd edn. Addison Wesley (2000)
3. Collinson, M., Monahan, B., Pym, D.: A Discipline of Mathematical Systems Modelling. College Publications (2012)
4. Collinson, M., Monahan, B., Pym, D.: Semantics for structured systems modelling and simulation. In: Proc. Simutools 2010. ACM Digital Library (2010) ISBN 78-963-9799-87-5
5. Collinson, M., Monahan, B., Pym, D.: A logical and computational theory of located resource. Journal of Logic and Computation 19(b), 1207–1244 (2009)
6. Collinson, M., Pym, D.: Algebra and logic for resource-based systems modelling. Mathematical Structures in Computer Science 19, 959–1027 (2009), doi:10.1017/S0960129509990077
7. Core Gnosis, http://www.hpl.hp.com/research/systems_security/
   gnosis.html
8. Ioannidis, C., Pym, D., Williams, J.: Investments and Trade-offs in the Economics of Information Security. In: Dingledine, R., Golle, P. (eds.) FC 2009. LNCS, vol. 5628, pp. 148–166. Springer, Heidelberg (2009)
9. Ioannidis, C., Pym, D., Williams, J.: Information security trade-offs and optimal patching policies. European Journal of Operational Research 216(2), 434–444 (2012)
10. Collinson, M., Pym, D.: Algebra and logic for access control [and erratum]. Formal Aspects of Computing 22(2, 3-4), 83–104 (2010)
11. Milner, R.: Calculi for synchrony and asynchrony. TCS 25(3), 267–310 (1983)
12. Beautement, A., Pym, D.: The structure and dynamics of systems security economics,
    https://www.abdn.ac.uk/~csc335/actors.pdf
13. Parsons, T.: The Social System. Routledge (1951)
14. Merton, R.: Social Theory and Social Structure. Macmillan (1968)
15. Brown, L., Harding, A.: Social modelling and public policy: application of microsimulation modelling in Australia. Journal of Artificial Societies and Social Simulation 5(4) (2002)
16. Johnson, H., Johnson, P.: Task knowledge structures: Psychological basis and integration into system design. Acta Psychologica 78(1), 3–26 (1991)
17. Souchon, N., Limbourg, Q., Vanderdonckt, J.: Task Modelling in Multiple Contexts of Use. In: Forbrig, P., Limbourg, Q., Urban, B., Vanderdonckt, J. (eds.) DSV-IS 2002. LNCS, vol. 2545, pp. 59–73. Springer, Heidelberg (2002)
18. Sterman, J.D.: Business Dynamics: Systems thinking and modeling for a complex world. McGraw Hill (2000)
19. Pidd, M.: Tools for Thinking: Modelling in Management Science. Wiley (2003)
20. Gonzalez, J., Sawicka, A.: A framework for human factors in information security. In: WSEAS International Conference on Information Security, Rio de Janeiro (2002)
21. Adams, A.L., Sasse, M.A.: Users are not the enemy: Why users compromise security mechanisms and how to take remedial measures. Comm. ACM 42(12), 40–46 (1999)
22. Beautement, A., Sasse, M.: The compliance budget: The economics of user effort in information security. Computer Fraud & Security 10, 8–12 (2009)

23. Beautement, A., Coles, R., Griffin, J., Ioannidis, C., Monahan, B., Pym, D., Sasse, A., Wonham, M.: Modelling the Hum. and Tech. Costs and Bens. of USB Memory Stick Sec. In: Johnson, M.E. (ed.) Managing Inf. Risk and the Econ. of Sec., pp. 141–163. Springer (2008)
24. Kabir, M., Han, J., Colman, A.: Modeling and coordinating social interactions in pervasive environments. In: Proc. 16th IEEE Int. Conf. on Eng. Complex Comp. Sys., pp. 243–252 (2011)
25. de Simone, R.: Higher-level synchronising devices in Meije-SCCS. TCS 37, 245–267 (1985)
26. Hoare, C.A.R.: Communicating Sequential Processes. Prentice-Hall International (1985)
27. Baldwin, A., Pym, D., Shiu, S.: Enterprise information risk management: Dealing with cloud computing. In: Pearson, S., Yee, G. (eds.) Privacy and Security for Cloud Computing: Selected Topics. Communications and Networks. Springer (2012)
28. Wolter, C., Menzel, M., Schaad, A., Miseldine, P., Meinel, C.: Model-driven business process security requirement specification. Journal of Systems Architecture 55(4), 211–223 (2009)
29. Menzel, M., Thomas, I., Meinel, C.: Security requirements specification in service-oriented business process management. In: Proc. ARES 2009, pp. 41–48. IEEE (2009)
30. Blackwell, C.: A multi-layered security architecture for modelling complex systems. In: Proc. 4th Ann. Workshop on Cybersecurity and Information Intelligence Res. ACM (2008)
31. Beres, Y., Pym, D., Shiu, S.: Decision Support for Systems Security Investment. In: Proc. Business-driven IT Management (BDIM 2010). IEEE Xplore (2010)

Much Ado about Security Appeal: Cloud Provider Collaborations and Their Risks

Olga Wenge, Melanie Siebenhaar, Ulrich Lampe, Dieter Schuller, and Ralf Steinmetz

Multimedia Communication Lab (KOM)
Technische Universität Darmstadt, Germany
{Olga·Wenge,Melanie·Siebenhaar,Ulrich·Lampe,Dieter·Schuller,
Ralf·Steinmetz}@KOM.tu-darmstadt.de

Abstract. The lack of capacity, unplanned outages of sub-contractors, a disaster recovery plan, acquisitions, or other financial goals may force cloud providers to enter into collaborations with other cloud providers. However, the cloud provider is not always fully aware of the security level of a potential collaborative cloud provider. This can lead to security breaches and customers' data leakage, ending in court cases and financial penalties. In our paper, we analyze different types of cloud collaborations with respect to their security concerns and discuss possible solutions. We also outline trusted security entities as a feasible approach for managing security governance risks and propose our security broker solution for ad hoc cloud collaborations. Our work provides support in the cloud provider selection process and can be used by cloud providers as a foundation for their initial risk assessment.

Keywords: cloud computing security, cloud collaborations, data privacy, data protection, security broker.

1 Introduction

Nowadays, cloud computing is widely spread in very different industries due to its efficiency, scalability and cost-saving models. The collaboration of clouds opens new perspectives for cloud providers, helping to mitigate technical risks, assure availability and provide customers with a larger range of services. Sometimes, cloud providers *are forced* to enter collaboration immediately, because of an unplanned disaster, as a backup solution, or because of some political and economical decisions.

However, the selection process of a potential collaborative cloud is not trivial. An "ideal" collaborative cloud must fully meet all requirements and criteria, a cloud provider identified for the collaboration. The requirements may include technical aspects, pricing, unique cloud services, mutual benefits, and last but not least – a big bouquet of security requirements.

Security requirements may vary between cloud providers, depending on their business needs, security policies and data classification. In our paper, we define and discuss possible types of cloud collaborations and their security issues, as well as their possible solutions.

F. De Paoli, E. Pimentel, and G. Zavattaro (Eds.): ESOCC 2012, LNCS 7592, pp. 80–90, 2012.

The paper is structured as follows: In Section 2, we discuss different types of multiple clouds and give a holistic definition of cloud collaborations with respect to security metrics. Section 3 provides an overview and evaluation of security risks in cloud collaborations and their possible solutions. In Section 4, we outline information security governance issues in cloud collaborations and discuss trusted security entities (TSEs). We propose here our security broker selection process as a solution for ad hoc collaborations. Finally, Section 5 describes our future work.

2   Security Aware Cloud Collaboration Types

In recent papers about cloud computing many different definitions can be found related to cloud collaborations. Keahey et al. [1] define dynamically provisioned distributed domains over several clouds as *"sky computing"*; Bernstein and Vjj [2] describe *"intercloud"* as *"a network of clouds"* and Wolf et al. [3] as *"Cloud of clouds"*, while Kretzschmar et al. [4] use the *"multi-cloud"* term for their definition; *federation of clouds* is defined by Wolf et al. [3] as "a homogenous environment, where all partners use the same standard". Almutairi et al. [5] propose another view of cloud collaborations with respect to security access control: *federated collaborations* with a metapolicy for the cloud access control, *loosely coupled collaborations* with local security policies for the access control, and *ad hoc collaboration* with the third party provider as a trusted partner for access control verification. The authors in [5] measure tradeoffs between proposed types of collaboration using the following four metrics: *level of interoperation* between cloud providers, their *autonomy*, *level of privacy*, and *verification complexity* of security policies.

In our paper we present a holistic security analysis and explore these three types of cloud collaborations as proposed by Almutairi et al. [5] with respect to *further security risk metrics*, which Cloud Security Alliance (CSA) considers as the critical areas of cloud computing [6]:

— Legal risks
— Proprietary definitions of cloud services and deployment models
— Compliance and audit with regulators
— Insufficient level of security
— Data protection risk
— Data location risk
— Identity and data access risks
— Insufficient monitoring and incident response
— Portability risk
— Insufficient information security governance

We *extend* the definitions of the cloud collaborations, proposed by Almutairi et al. [5], with respect to the classical security domains [7], and define the cloud collaboration types as follows:

Federated collaborations presume a global *metapolicy*, which is conform to all policies of all collaborative partners. Policies can include security policies, data privacy policies, data classification policies, regulators requirements, and local laws.

Compliance of all collaborative partners leads to a strong mutual dependence and trusted interoperation between individual clouds, i.e. all clouds within a federation can interoperate without *"security fear"*.

A *loosely coupled collaboration* allows more autonomy and is managed by local policies between collaborative partners, e.g. service level agreements (SLAs) or other pre-agreed collaboration contracts, which fully meet security requirements of both cloud providers.

An *ad hoc collaboration* does not set any predetermined agreement or rules between individual clouds. The selection of a collaboration partner performs in a dynamic "ad hoc" manner and can be denied if an individual cloud did not persuade with his "security appeal", e.g. sufficient authentication and authorization mechanisms, network encryption, etc. By ad hoc collaboration, cloud providers need some kind of a trustable security interface for the security judgment, e.g. a trusted security entity (TSE).

Fig.1 gives a graphical overview of the cloud collaboration types as described before and tradeoffs between them.

3   Security Concerns and Solutions in Multiple Cloud Environments

In this section, we outline security concerns and issues of the defined types of cloud collaborations with respect to the critical areas, proposed in Section 2.

3.1   Legal Risks

The lack of international standards for data privacy and data transfer is one of the major hurdles for cloud providers. The recent legislations in EU (European Data Protection Directive – Directive 9/46/EC) [8] and Canada (Canada's Personal Information Protection and Electronic Document Act – PIPEDA) [9] restrict transfer of customers' personal data to countries without *"an adequate level of protection"* [10].

While Europe and Canada believe *society* is responsible for protection of private data, the USA considers *individual users* to be responsible for protecting their own data [11]. In some countries data protection laws are still not implemented, as for example in Malaysia [12], or only partly implemented, as in Taiwan [13].

Poor knowledge of laws can lead to privacy breaches; therefore, all cloud providers should be aware of countries' actual laws about data privacy, data protection and other laws, related to their services and collaborative partners.

European Network and Information Agency (ENISA) [14] recommends *a full awareness* of laws and government regulations to be prepared contractually to cooperate with cloud providers from different legal environments. Cloud providers can also implement their own *additional privacy policies* to provide the necessary level of trust [15]. Additional policies must include directives concerning collecting, recording, using, or storing of data and agreed upon with customers, because in some countries, cloud providers cannot transfer data to another provider without customers' explicit permission [11].

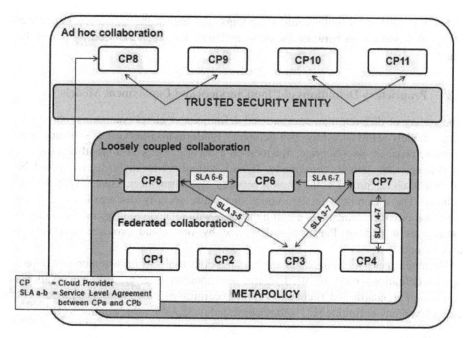

Fig. 1. Cloud collaboration types and tradeoffs between them

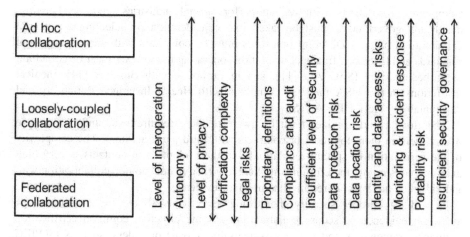

Fig. 2. Evaluation of proposed security metrics in cloud collaborations (the arrow head shows the highest value)

Adoption of international policies, such as Organization for Economic Cooperation and Development (OECD) or Asia-Pacific Economic Cooperation (APEC) guidelines [14] could be a feasible solution as well, especially for ad hoc collaborations [15]. An agreement on global privacy laws could be *a panacea* against international cyber security issues, but this approach is very challenging and complex, because of heterogeneities of local laws and political situations [16].

So, the weaker the collaboration bindings, the higher the risks. We depict our observed dependencies between the cloud collaboration types and security risk in the Fig 2.

3.2   Proprietary Definitions of Cloud Services and Deployment Models

The variety of different non-standardized definitions of cloud computing, cloud service models (Infrastructure-as-a-Service, Platform-as-a-Service, Software-as-a-Service, Database-as-a-Service, Business-as-a-Service, etc.), and cloud deployment models (private, public, community, hybrid, virtual-private hybrid, etc.) could be another issue for proper collaboration between cloud providers, especially in ad hoc manner. The differences on definitions can cause security discrepancy and make the cloud provider vulnerable, e.g. if a database with related security configurations is defined as a part of Platform-as-a-Service by one cloud provider and not by another one.

To avoid these misunderstandings and possible trials with customers, only pre-agreed definitions must be used in the collaboration (e.g. according to National Institute of Standards and Technology (NIST) definitions, cloud reference model [17], cloud taxonomy definition [6]) and documented in SLAs or other contracts [18].

3.3   Compliance and Audit with Regulators

Compliance resolutions with regulators for special industries, such as banking, healthcare, government, must be taken into consideration by selecting a potential collaboration partner. Different industries must be compliant with special industrial standards and laws, e.g. financial institutions operating in the USA must be compliant to Sarbanes-Oxley (Sox) Act [11], and in Europe – with Basel II [14]; medical institutions in the USA must be compliant with Health Insurance Portability and Accountability Act - HIPAA [15].

Therefore, cloud provider must be aware of these requirements and be ready to reflect them in their contracts or contracts with third-party auditors. The complexity of the verification of special regulations and their adoption in contacts is very high and time-consuming, therefore not applicable for a dynamic ad hoc collaboration with individual clouds without required compliance evidence.

In addition, proper security monitoring agreements should be established for sufficient evidence of secure collaborations. Some effective common certification assurance frameworks and risk assessments for (cloud) providers, such as ISO/IEC 27001/27017 [19], COBIT [20], Cloud Security Alliance Control Matrix [21], Bundesamt für Sicherheit in der Informationstechnik (BSI, in Germany) Recommendation for Cloud Providers [22], and Shared Assessment Program [23], can be used as a basis for security control agreements for federative and loosely coupled collaborations, and as a compliance evidence for individual clouds in the ad hoc collaboration.

3.4 Insufficient Level of Security

Before transferring the customers' data to a collaboration partner, the cloud provider must be aware of the security level of a collaborative partner to prevent the compromising of data protection and data privacy laws.

The security assurance of a potential collaborative cloud provider can be provided via a trusted cloud provider certification, risk assessment or information security policy with defined security controls, necessary for a planned type of collaboration [6].

Actual security policies and risk assessments should include all relevant security domains, recommended by security standard institutions such as NIST [24], ISO/IEC 27001/27017 [19], BSI [23] and Information Systems Audit and Control Association (ISACA) [25]:

— Access control
— Encryption and key management
— Security governance
— Network security
— Business continuity management and disaster recovery
— Security monitoring
— Application and infrastructure security
— Physical security
— Virtualization security

The review of policies and assessment results of collaborative partners should be taken to identify their security level and to make a decision on a possible interoperation. The security level of a potential collaborative partner should be at least equal to the cloud provider's level [22].

In the ad hoc collaboration a trusted security entity (e.g., a security broker, a trusted third party) is necessary for a proper decision.

3.5 Data Protection Risk

The data transferring to a collaborative partner should be protected at least at the same level as by the origin cloud provider [22]. Differences between proprietary data protection mechanisms can lead to security gaps and compromising of data.

Agreed data classification and data labeling framework are some of the solutions to identify the needed protection level for data flow. Watson [26] proposes an extended Bell-LaPadula security model for cloud providers, where the permission of data access and data transfer in the multi-level security environment depends on the sensitivity of the data. Role-based access control (RBAC) models for cloud, defined by Berger et al. [27] can be used for automated identification of the data protection level and for assigning a level to a potential collaborative partner for interoperations.

To prevent data leakage and provide data integrity, collaborative cloud providers should use pre-agreed data content patterns, encryption mechanisms and best practice key management solutions, such as trusted platform modules (TPMs), one-time passwords [28], etc.

An implemented data retention policy is also a "nice-to-have" solution for data misuse after service delivery.

3.6 Data Location Risk

A cloud provider must be aware of data location if he transfers the users' data to another cloud provider to be compliant with customers' SLAs and other specific regulations described in Section 3.1 and Section 3.3. Proper defined SLAs with collaborative partners are one of the solutions to prevent non-controlled data movements [29].

3.7 Identity and Data Access Risks

Identity and data access in multiple cloud environments is one of the most serious issues because of its complexity and involvement of several classical security do-mains: encryption, key management, information security, application and infrastructure security. The idea of the *cross-cloud identity and data access* is to provide a dynamic, fast and customer friendly cloud service. The issues of non-proper and non-secure identity and access management are non-standardized identification, authentication and authorization mechanisms between cloud providers.

A *centralized* identity and access administration and governance has to be replaced with a *decentralized* one, because of the overwhelming number of rules to be managed [5]. Secure federated cloud access mechanisms and *good access and authentication practices*, such as Security Assertion Markup Language (SAML), secure single-sign-on [30], as possible solutions should be implemented between cloud providers. Sabahi [31] proposes a control access to all levels, including virtual machines (VMs), and Almutairi et al. [5] bet on a *fine-grained authorization mechanism*, multi-factor authentication and distributed access control architecture. Wolf et al. [3] propose a "message meta model for federated authentication for heterogeneous clouds across different standards", which can be used for ad hoc collaboration as well.

3.8 Insufficient Monitoring and Incident Response

Security monitoring and security incident management are eminent parts of a proper security concept for every cloud provider. An efficiently implemented security monitoring, using a combination of preventive, detective and corrective measurements, can save lots of money, reputation and trouble, if a cloud provider knows what should be monitored. Many researchers are busy with the mapping of traditional security monitoring frameworks to a cloud computing architecture, to define gaps and provide new monitoring metrics. ENISA in "A guide to monitoring of security service levels in cloud contracts" [32] proposes different monitoring parameters for Infrastructure-as-a-Service, Platform-as-a-Service and Software-as-a-Service, including requirements for log management, incidence response, and forensics.

It is strongly recommended to define all *monitoring parameters* and related *vulnerability and incident response processes* in the SLAs with a collaborative partner or with a third-party monitoring provider. Sufficient monitoring evidences can be used to identify fraud, zero-day attacks and support IT forensic science. The costs of security monitoring countermeasures are mostly high: their implementation is time-consuming, they need a lot of storage, and they must be regularly reviewed. Therefore, a business impact analysis (BIA) should be performed to calculate a loss-benefit factor for assets, which need security monitoring.

3.9   Portability, Interoperation and Autonomy

Almost all cloud providers use their own proprietary (and also in addition to open source) security solutions for their services, and do not make them public because of intellectual property rights, hacking issues and other business concerns. The lack of public information ends up with a provider *lock-in* and hampers customer's portability and interoperation.

ENISA [14] and CSA [6] recommend using only standard technologies and solutions for collaboration to avoid a cloud provider lock-in, or to sign a so-called *escrow agreement* in case a cloud provider stops its activity.

As we already mentioned above, federated collaborations assume a high level of *mutual interoperability* and low level of *autonomy*, in comparison to ad hoc collaboration. But, if any security threat occurs in the federation, it can compromise all collaborative partners, as they use one metapolicy.

Viability and capability of a cloud provider is another very important aspect. A potential collaborative partner should provide the existence of *Plan B* – a business continuity and disaster recovery plan, which is especially critical for interoperation with high available and sensitive data [31].

We present our evaluation of described risks in Fig.2; the arrow head shows the highest value.

4   Information Security Governance in Cloud Collaborations

In this section, we discuss a *trusted security entity (TSE)* as a possible solution for information security governance risks and propose our initial TSE approach, which we plan to develop in our future work.

Information security governance in the federated or loosely coupled collaborations is regulated by metapolicy, SLAs or a contracted security provider. The lack of a standardized trusted security entity (TSE) makes the ad hoc collaboration between clouds very difficult. Requests for the necessary security evidence of a potential collaborative partner and responses to it cannot be provided dynamically and without latency. A cloud provider must be *fully aware* of his own security requirements (security policy, SLAs, security standards, etc) to determine security requirements and map them against the TSE output.

To the best of our knowledge there are very different approaches of a TSE for federated or loosely coupled cloud collaborations. Huang et al. [33] propose an *"identity federation broker"*, based on an interaction of transitive federated single sign-on principle. Goyal [34] defines a distributed security method to "end-2-end services security for heterogeneous cloud environments". His method does not require a centralized infrastructure and is based on *the mutual methods of trust and security* used for public key infrastructure (PKI). Ates et al. [35] bet on *"an identity cloud agent"* and propose an *Identity-as-a-Service* approach.

The Shared Assessment Program [23] is an industrial standard self-assessment for cloud providers and third party auditors, and can be used as a standard in the federated collaboration.

CSA [6] recommends the following *five-steps methodology* to identify a potential cloud-ready asset and a potential cloud partner: "1) Identify the asset; 2) Evaluate the asset; 3) Map the asset to the potential cloud deployment model; 4) Evaluate potential cloud service models and providers; and 5) Map out the potential data flow " .

However, the proposed TSE approaches are generally *hardly* applicable to ad hoc cloud collaborations. We suggest the following *six-step TSE selection approach*, our *security broker*, which we consider to be applicable for ad hoc collaborations as well:

Step 1: Security broker performs or gathers security risk assessments of each potential cloud provider, eager to collaborate;

Step 2: Security broker classifies risk assessments results and stores these results in his database;

Step 3: A cloud provider X sends a specified collaboration request, which includes cloud provider's security requirements of the expected security level of a potential collaborative cloud;

Step 4: Security broker analyzes and classifies requirements of a cloud provider X;

Step 5: Security broker maps the classified results with the results of security risk as-assessments in his data base to identify an appropriate collaborative cloud provider;

Step 6: Security broker outputs a list with recommended cloud providers.

Our proposed security broker approach can be used in all types of cloud collaborations, described in Section 2. While storing and classifying of performed security risk assessments of cloud providers, the verification complexity can be avoided, that makes our security broker also applicable for ad hoc collaborations. To provide a proper selection process, our proposed approach needs to be completed with *a proper security assessment classification* and with defined *mapping rules*, which we aim to provide in the future.

5   Conclusion and Future Work

In our paper, we defined different types of cloud collaborations with respect to their security issues and discussed potential solutions. We could see that the different types of cloud collaborations either tend increase or decrease described cloud security risks. Hence, the determination of the risk level indicates whether a specific collaboration type is appropriate or not to conduct the risk assessment.

We have also proposed the application of a *trusted security entity (TSE)* – our *security broker* - for ad hoc collaborations and a corresponding cloud provider selection process.

In the future, we plan to analyze cloud providers' collaboration requirements in more details in order to define a holistic security framework for an "ideal" *cloud security broker,* we outlined in Section 4.

Acknowledgement. This work is supported in part by E-Finance Lab e. V., Frankfurt am Main, Germany (http://www.efinancelab.com).

References

1. Keahey, et al.: Sky Computing. IEEE Internet Computing, 43–51 (September/October 2009)
2. Bernstein, et al.: Intercloud Security Considerations. In: IEEE International Conference on Cloud Computing Technology and Services, pp. 537–544 (2010)
3. Wolf, et al.: A Message Meta Model for Federated Authentication in Service-oriented Architectures. In: IEEE International Conference on Service-Oriented Computing and Applications (SOCA), pp. 1–8 (2009)
4. Kretzschmar, et al.: Security management Spectrum in future Multi-Provider Inter-Cloud Environments – Method to highlight necessary further development. In: 5th International DMTF Academic Alliance Workshop on Systems and Virtualization Management (SVM), pp. 1–8 (2011)
5. Almutairi, A., Sarfraz, M., Basalamah, S., Aref, W., Ghafoor, A.: A Distributed Access control Architecture for Cloud Computing. IEEE Software 29(2), 36–44 (2012)
6. CSA: Security Guidance for Critical Areas of Focus in Cloud Computing, V3.0, https://cloudsecurityalliance.org/research/security-guidance/
7. CISSP Domains, https://www.isc2.org/cissp-domains/default.aspx
8. European Data Protection Directive – Directive 9/46/EC, http://eurex.europa.eu/LexUriServ/LexUriServ.do?uri=OJ:L:1995:281:0031:0050:EN:PDF
9. Canada's Personal Information Protection and Electronic Document Act – PIPEDA, http://www.priv.gc.ca/leg_c/leg_c_p_e.asp
10. Pearson, et al.: Privacy, Security and Trust Issues Arising from Cloud Computing. In: IEEE 2nd International Conference on Cloud Computing Technology and Science (CloudCom), pp. 693–702 (2010)
11. Perkins, et al.: Multinational Data-Privacy Laws: An Introduction for IT Managers. IEEE Transactions on Professional Communication 47(2), 85–94 (2004)
12. Ho, et al.: A Guideline to Enforce Data Protection and Privacy Digital Laws in Malaysia. In: 2nd International Conference on Computer Research and Development, pp. 3–6 (2010)
13. Chen, et al.: Legal Issues on Public Access to Remote Sensing Data in Taiwan. In: Geosciences and Remote Sensing Symposium (2005)
14. ENISA: Security & Resilience in Governmental Clouds (2011), http://www.enisa.europa.eu/activities/risk-management/emerging-and-future-risk/deliverables/security-and-resilience-in-governmental-clouds

15. Wood, K., Anderson, M.: Understanding the complexity surrounding multitenancy in cloud computing. In: IEEE 8th International Conference on e-Business Engineering (ICEBE), pp. 119–124 (2011)

16. Wolf, C.: The Role of Government in Commercial Cybersecurity. In: Telecom World (ITU WT), Technical Symposium at ITU, pp. 13–18 (2011)

17. NIST SP 800-145: The NIST Definition of Cloud Computing, http://csrc.nist.gov/publications/nistpubs/800-145/SP800-145.pdf

18. Bernsmed, K., Jaatun, M.G., Meland, P.H., Undheim, A.: Security SLAs for Federated Cloud Services. In: 6th International Conference on Availability, Reliability and Security (ARES), pp. 202–209 (2011)

19. ISO/IEC 27001: International Standard (2005), http://www.iso.org/iso/catalogue_detail?csnumber=42103

20. COBIT, http://www.isaca.org/Knowledge-Center/COBIT/Pages/Overview.aspx

21. CSA Cloud Control Matrix, https://cloudsecurityalliance.org/research/ccm/

22. BSI-Standard 100-1, Version1.5, https://www.bsi.bund.de/ContentBSI/Publikationen/BSI_Standard/

23. The Shared Assessment Program: Evaluation Cloud Risk for the Enterprise: A Shared Assessment Guide (2010), http://sharedassessments.org/media/pdf-EnterpriseCloud-SA.pdf

24. NIST: Guide for Security-Focused Configuration management of Information Systems (2011), http://csrc.nist.gov/publications/nistpubs/800-128/sp800-128.pdf

25. ISACA: Cloud Computing: Business Benefits With Security, Governance and Assurance Perspectives (2011)

26. Watson, P.: A Multi-level Security Model for Partitioning Workflows over federated Clouds. In: IEEE 3rd International Conference on Cloud Computing Technology and Science (CloudCom), pp. 180–188 (2011)

27. Berger, et al.: Security for the Cloud Infrastructure: Trusted Virtual Data Center Implementation. IBM Journal of Research and Development 53(4), 6:1–6:12 ((2009)

28. Wu, et al.: Alignment of Authentication Information for Trusted Federation. In: EDOC Conference Workshop, pp. 73–80 (2007)

29. Kandukuri, B.R., Paturi, V.R., Rakshit, A.: Cloud Security Issues. In: Services Computing, pp. 517–520 (2009)

30. OASIS-Security-Services, http://www.oasis-open.org/

31. Sabahi, F.: Cloud Computing Security Threats and Responses. In: IEEE 3rd International Conference on Communication Software and Networks, pp. 245–249 (2011)

32. ENISA: Procure Secure: A guide to monitoring of security service levels (2012), http://www.enisa.europa.eu/activities/application-security/test/procure-secure-a-guide-to-monitoring-of-security-service-levels-in-cloud-contracts

33. He, Y.H., Bin, W., Xiao, X.L., Jing, M.X.: Identity Federation Broker for Service Cloud. In: International Conference on Service Sciences (ICSS), pp. 115–120 (2010)

34. Goyal, P.: Application of a Distributed Security Method to End-2-End Services Security in Independent Heterogeneous Cloud Computing Environments. In: IEEE World Congress on Services (SERVICES), pp. 379–384 (2011)

35. Ates, M., Ravet, S., Ahmat, A.M., Fayolle, J.: An Identity-Centric Internet: Identity in the Cloud, Identity as a Service and other delights. In: 6th International Conference on Availability, Reliability and Security (ARES), pp. 555–560 (2011)

Formal Modeling of Resource Management for Cloud Architectures: An Industrial Case Study*

Frank S. de Boer[1], Reiner Hähnle[2], Einar Broch Johnsen[3],
Rudolf Schlatte[3], and Peter Y.H. Wong[4]

[1] CWI, Amsterdam, The Netherlands
f.s.de.Boer@cwi.nl
[2] Technical University of Darmstadt, Germany
haehnle@cs.tu-darmstadt.de
[3] Dept. of Informatics, University of Oslo, Norway
{einarj,rudi}@ifi.uio.no
[4] Fredhopper B.V., Amsterdam, The Netherlands
peter.wong@fredhopper.com

Abstract. We show how aspects of performance, resource consumption, and deployment on the cloud can be formally modeled for an industrial case study of a distributed system, using the abstract behavioral specification language ABS. These non-functional aspects are integrated with an existing formal model of the functional system behavior, supporting a separation of concerns between the functional and non-functional aspects in the integrated model. The ABS model is parameterized with respect to deployment scenarios which capture different application-level management policies for virtualized resources. The model is validated against the existing system's performance characteristics and used to simulate and compare deployment scenarios on the cloud.

1 Introduction

Virtualization is a key technology enabler for cloud computing. Although the added value and compelling business drivers of cloud computing are undeniable [12], this new paradigm also poses considerable new challenges that have to be addressed to render its usage effective for industry. Virtualization makes elastic amounts of resources available to application-level services; for example, the processing capacity allocated to a service may be changed according to demand. Current software development methods, however, do not support the modeling and validation of application-level resource management strategies for virtualized resources in a satisfactory way. This seriously limits the potential for fine-tuning a service to the available virtualized resources. This paper demonstrates how to overcome this limitation by integration of resource management into a formal, yet realistic, model that yields to simulation and analysis.

* Partly funded by the EU project FP7-231620 HATS: Highly Adaptable and Trustworthy Software using Formal Models (http://www.hats-project.eu).

F. De Paoli, E. Pimentel, and G. Zavattaro (Eds.): ESOCC 2012, LNCS 7592, pp. 91–106, 2012.
© Springer-Verlag Berlin Heidelberg 2012

Our long-term goal is the integration of virtualization into the development process of general purpose software services, by leveraging resources and resource management to the modeling of software. Our starting point in addressing this challenge is the recently developed abstract behavioral specification language ABS [19]. ABS is *object-oriented* to stay close to high-level programming languages and to be easily usable as well as accessible to software developers, and it is *executable* to support full code generation and (timed) validation of models.

ABS has been extended with time and with primitives for leveraging resources and their dynamic management to the abstraction level of software models [8,23]. The extension achieves a separation of concerns between the *application model*, which requires resources, and the *deployment scenario*, which reflects the virtualized computing environment and provides elastic resources. For example, an application model may be analyzed with respect to deployments on virtual machines with varying features: the amount of allocated computing or memory resources, the choice of application-level scheduling policies for client requests, or the distribution over different virtual machines with fixed bandwidth constraints. The simulation tools developed for ABS may then be used to compare the performance of a service ranging over different deployment scenarios already at the modeling level.

The main contribution of this paper is a large industrial case study, which demonstrates that it is possible to model aspects of performance, resource consumption, and deployment on the cloud based on this extension of ABS. The non-functional aspects are integrated with a model of the functional system behavior, achieving a separation of concerns between the functional and non-functional aspects. The ABS model is parameterized over deployment scenarios which capture different application-level management policies for virtualized resources. The model is validated against the existing system's performance characteristics and used to simulate and compare deployment scenarios on the cloud. A companion paper [22] details the modeling of the cloud provider and compares our approach to results obtained by simulation tools.

The paper is organized as follows: In Sect. 2 we describe the case study used in this paper; in Sect. 3 we explain how deployment scenarios are modeled in the extended ABS; in Sect. 4 we describe the modeling of the case study in ABS, before we discuss related work in Sect. 5 and conclude in Sect. 6.

2   The Case Study: Background

The Fredhopper Access Server (FAS) is a distributed, concurrent object-oriented system that provides search and merchandising services to e-Commerce companies. Briefly, FAS provides to its clients structured search capabilities within the client's data. Each FAS installation is deployed to a customer according to a deployment architecture; see [34] for a detailed presentation of the individual components of FAS and its deployment model. FAS consists of a set of live environments and a single staging environment. A *live environment* processes queries from client web applications via web services. FAS aims at providing a

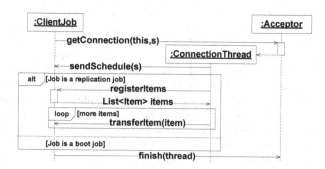

Fig. 1. Interaction between ClientJob, Acceptor, and ConnectionThread

constant query capacity to client-side web applications. A *staging environment* is responsible for receiving data updates in XML format, indexing the XML, and distributing the resulting indices across all live environments according to a *Replication Protocol* which is implemented by the *Replication System*. The Replication System consists of a *SyncServer* at the staging environment and one *SyncClient* for each live environment. The SyncServer determines the schedule and content of replication, while a SyncClient receives data and configuration updates.

The SyncServer communicates to SyncClients by creating *ConnectionThread* objects via its *Acceptor*. ConnectionThreads serve as the interface to the server side of the Replication Protocol. SyncClients schedule and create *ClientJob* objects to handle communications to the client-side of the Replication Protocol. Fig. 1 is a UML sequence diagram that depicts the replication protocol between a ClientJob, a ConnectionThread, and an Acceptor. In this paper we detail a part of the Replication Protocol that is informally described in Fig. 2.

Relevance to Cloud Computing. FAS provides structured search and navigation capabilities within a client's data. For the last decade, FAS installations were deployed as server-based products on client premises with fixed hardware resources. However, on-premise deployment does not scale with increasing demand on throughput and update frequency. This is especially visible when customers experience drastic increase on throughput and data updates at certain time periods. For example, retail customers might expect large throughput during seasonal sales. In these periods, much larger amounts of purchases will be made and stock units would need to be updated very frequently so that customers do not receive incorrect information. Higher throughput requires a larger number of live environments and, in turn, larger number of SyncClients. On-premise deployment cannot cope with on-demand, varying requirements without large up-front investments in hardware which remains unused most of the time.

To cater for these requirements, FAS is deployed as a service (SaaS) over virtualized resources that provide the necessary elasticity. To this end, virtualization makes elastic amounts of resources available to application-level services; for example, the processing capacity allocated to a service can be changed on

1. SyncServer starts the Acceptor, which listens for connections.
2. SyncClient schedules a *Boot* job, and an associated ClientJob object is created and connected to the Acceptor. This corresponds to the message getConnection(**this**,s) in Fig. 1, where s is a schedule.
3. SyncServer creates a ConnectionThread to communicate with this ClientJob.
4. The ClientJob asks the ConnectionThread for *all replication schedules*, denoted by the message sendSchedule(s) in Fig. 1. Replication schedules dictate when and where the SyncServer monitors for changes in the staging environment. These changes are replicated to the live environments through their Sync-Clients. Each schedule specifies a *replication type*; i.e., the number of locations and type of data to be replicated. The schedule also specifies the amount of time until the replication must commence and the deadline of each replication.
5. The ClientJob receives the replication schedules and creates new ClientJob objects representing these schedules. If the old ClientJob object represented a Boot job, it releases the ConnectionThread and terminates.
6. When a *Replication* job is triggered, its associated ClientJob object connects immediately to the Acceptor.
7. SyncServer creates a ConnectionThread to communicate with each ClientJob.
8. A ClientJob asks the ConnectionThread for its replication schedule and recursively creates a new ClientJob object to deal with the next schedule. The ClientJob then receives a sequence of file updates according to its replication type, after which it releases the ConnectionThread and terminates. This is denoted by the message registerItems followed by zero or more transferItem(item) messages in Fig. 1.
9. The ConnectionThread first sends a replication schedule to the ClientJob according to the ClientJob's replication type, then a sequence of file updates according to this replication type, and then it terminates.

Fig. 2. Informal description of the interactions in the Replication Protocol

demand. Fig. 3 shows how an on-demand deployment architecture for the Replication System on virtual environments is implemented using cloud resources. Virtualized resources allow the SyncServer (via the Acceptor) to elastically allocate resources to each replication job based on the *cost* and the *deadline* of the replication to be conducted by the corresponding ClientJob object.

3   ABS Deployment Architecture

ABS is an abstract, executable, object-oriented modeling language with a formal semantics [19], targeting distributed systems. ABS is based on concurrent object groups (COGs), akin to concurrent objects [15,20], Actors [1], and Erlang processes [4]. COGs in ABS support interleaved concurrency based on guarded commands. This allows active and reactive behavior to be easily combined, by means of a cooperative scheduling of processes which stem from method calls. Real-Time ABS extends ABS models with *implicit* time [8]; execution time is not specified directly in terms of durations (as in, e.g., UPPAAL [25]), but rather

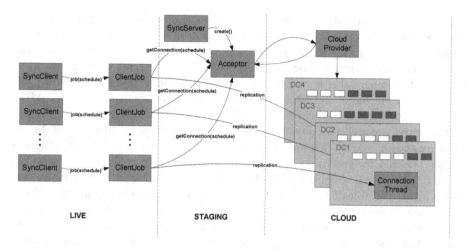

Fig. 3. An on-demand deployment architecture for the Replication System using Cloud resources

observed by measurements of the executing model. With implicit time, no assumptions about execution times are hard-coded into the models. The execution time of a method call depends on how quickly the call is effectuated by the server object. In fact, the execution time of a statement varies with the *capacity* of the chosen deployment architecture and on *synchronization* with (slower) objects.

3.1   Behavioral Modeling in ABS

ABS combines functional and imperative programming styles with a Java-like syntax [19]. COGs execute in parallel and communicate through asynchronous method calls. Data manipulation inside methods is modeled using a simple functional language based on user-defined algebraic data types and functions. Thus, the modeler may abstract from the details of low-level imperative implementations of data structures while maintaining an overall object-oriented design close to the target system. The functional part of ABS consists of algebraic data types such as the empty type Unit, booleans Bool, integers Int; parametric data types such as sets Set<A> and maps Map<A> (for a type parameter A); and functions over values of these data types, with support for pattern matching. In Real-Time ABS, measurements are additionally obtained by comparing values from a global clock, which can be read by an expression **now**() of type Time.

The imperative part of ABS addresses concurrency, communication, and synchronization at the concurrent object level, and defines interfaces, classes, and methods. ABS objects are *active* in the sense that their run method, if defined, gets called upon creation. Communication and synchronization are decoupled in ABS. Communication is based on asynchronous method calls, denoted by assignments f=o!m(e) where f is a future variable, o an object expression, and e are (data value or object) expressions. After calling f=o!m(e), the caller may proceed with its execution *without blocking* on the method reply. Two operations on future variables control synchronization in ABS. First, the statement **await** f? *suspends the active process* unless a return value from the call associated with f has arrived, allowing other processes in the same COG to execute. Second, the return value is retrieved by the expression f.**get**, which *blocks all execution in the object* until the return value is available. Inside a COG, ABS also supports standard synchronous method calls o.m(e).

The active process of an object can be unconditionally suspended by the statement **suspend**, adding this process to the queue, from which an enabled process is then selected for execution. The guards g in **await** g control suspension of the active process and consist of Boolean conditions conjoined with return tests f? on future variables f. Just like functional expressions, guards g are side-effect free. The remaining statements are standard; e.g., sequential composition $s_1; s_2$, assignment x=rhs, and **skip**, **if**, **while**, and **return** constructs. Expressions rhs include the creation of an object group **new cog** C(e), object creation in the group of the creator **new** C(e), method calls, future dereferencing f.**get**, and functional expressions e.

3.2   Deployment Modeling in ABS

The execution capacity of (virtualized) locations can be abstractly captured by *deployment components* (for formal definitions, see [21]). Deployment components share resources between their allocated objects. A deployment component environment with unlimited resources is used for the model's root object and, e.g., clients. Deployment components with different capacities may be dynamically created depending on the control flow of the ABS model or statically created in the main block. Objects are by default allocated to the deployment component of their creator, but they may also be allocated differently.

Deployment components in ABS have the type DC and are instances of the class DeploymentComponent, which takes as parameters a location name and a set of resource bounds. Our focus is on resources reflecting *processing capacity*.

The *resource capacity* of a deployment component is specified by the constructor CPUCapacity(r), where r of type Resource represents the amount of abstract processing resources available between observable (discrete) points in time, after which the resources are renewed. Objects are explicitly allocated to specific deployment components via annotations. They compete for the shared resources to execute methods and may execute until the component runs out of resources or until they are otherwise blocked. The method total("CPU") of a deployment component returns its total amount of allocated CPU resources.

The *cost* of executing statements in ABS is specified by the modeler. A default cost for statements can be set as a compiler option (e.g., defaultcost=10). However, this default cost does not discriminate between different statements. More precise cost expressions are often desirable; for example, if f(x) is a complex expression, then the statement result=f(x) should have a significantly higher cost than **skip**. Fine-grained costs can be introduced via statement annotations;

e.g., [Cost: g(size(x))] result=f(x) where the cost is given by a function g in terms of the *size* of the input values x to the function f.

It is the responsibility of the modeler to specify realistic costs. A behavioral model with default costs may be gradually refined to provide fine-grained resource-sensitive behavior. On the other hand, the modeler may want to capture resource consumption at an *abstract level* without a fully developed model. Cost annotations can be used to abstractly represent the cost of a computation which is not be fully specified; e.g., [Cost: g(size(x))] **skip**.

4   Case Study: The ABS Model

The Replication System, introduced in Sect. 2, is part of the Fredhopper Access Server (FAS). The current Java implementation of FAS has over 150,000 lines of code, of which 6,500 are part of the Replication System. The functional aspects of the Replication System have previously been modeled in detail in ABS [34]. This section describes how the model was extended to capture non-functional and resource aspects of the Replication System. The extended model consists of 40 classes, 17 data types, and 80 user-defined functions (in total 5,000 lines of ABS code, 25% of which capture scheduling information as well as file systems and data bases from third party libraries not included in the Java implementation).

Fig. 4 shows the main data type and interfaces. Data type Schedule records interval, deadline, cost, and file locations to receive updates for each type of replication schedule. The interface ConnectionThread models its objects as active objects (without methods). The interface ClientJob defines the method executeJob() for executing replication schedules, and SyncClient defines the method scheduleJob(Schedule s) for scheduling the given replication schedule s. The getConnection(job, s) method of the Acceptor interface is called from the ClientJob. The acceptor creates ConnectionThread objects on virtual machines acquired from the CloudProvider via the method

```
data Schedule =
  Schedule(String sn, Int il, Int dl, Int ct, List<File> files);
interface ConnectionThread { }
interface ClientJob { Unit executeJob(); }
interface SyncClient { Unit scheduleJob(Schedule s); }
interface Acceptor {
  ConnectionThread getConnection(ClientJob job, Schedule s);
  Unit finish(ConnectionThread thread);
  Unit end();
}
interface CloudProvider {
  DC createMachine(Int capacity);
  Unit acquireMachine(DC vm);
  Unit releaseMachine(DC vm);
  Int getAccumulatedCost();
}
```

Fig. 4. Data types and interfaces of the Replication System

createMachine. The methods acquireMachine and releaseMachine are used to start and stop virtual machines (modeled by deployment components) to let replication schedules be conducted by ConnectThread objects. For presentation purposes, we focus on the interface implementations given in the classes CloudProvider, ConnectionThread, and Acceptor.

The CloudProvider interface (shown in Fig. 4) is implemented by a class of the same name. Virtual machines are modeled by deployment components in ABS, on which the client application can deploy objects. In addition, the cloud provider keeps track of the *accumulated cost* incurred by the client application. This accumulated cost is retrievable by the method getAccumulatedCost() during execution. Accumulated cost is calculated in terms of the sum of the processing capacities of the *active* virtual machines over time; i.e., a call to acquireMachine(vm) starts the accounting for machine vm and a call to releaseMachine(vm) stops the accounting. Inside the cloud provider, an active run() method does the accounting for every time interval. Since we focus on the application-level management of virtualized resources, as implemented by the balancer, and not on a specific strategy for cloud provisioning, we do not detail the cloud provider further.

We model and compare three potential balancing strategies offered by the Acceptor for the application-level management of virtualized resources. An Acceptor gets requests for replication sessions from ClientJob objects. It deploys ConnectionThread objects on cloud instances to conduct replications with the ClientJob objects. The implementations of Acceptor reflect different strategies for interacting with the cloud provider to achieve resource management:

Constant balancing deploys ConnectionThread objects to a single virtual machine sufficient for the expected load, and keeps this machine running;

As-needed balancing calculates the CPU capacity of the virtual machine needed for a specific replication schedule with a given deadline, and deploys ConnectionThread objects to a machine supplying the needed resources disregarding the cost; and

Budget-aware balancing calculates the CPU capacity of the cloud instance for a given budget. Unused funds can be "saved up" to cope with load spikes, but the cost of running the system is still bounded by the overall budget.

The Cloud User Account. Each acceptor encapsulates an Account object that realizes book-keeping for a cloud user account (see Fig. 5). The implementation maintains a data structure in the field is which sorts available machines by CPU processing capacity, the current cost per time unit costPerTimeUnit for the cloud user account, and the time instanceStartUpTime it took the most recent machine to start up. Method getInstance(size) either requests a new virtual machine from the cloud provider or brings online an existing offline machine. The method dropInstance(d) takes a machine offline when it is no longer active.

```
interface Account {
  DC   getInstance(Int size);
  Unit dropInstance(DC d);
  Int  getCostPerTimeUnit();
  Int  getLastInstanceStartUpTime();
}

class AccountImpl implements Account {
  Map<Int, Set<DC>> is = EmptyMap;
  Int costPerTimeUnit = 0; Int instanceStartUpTime = 0;

  DC getInstance(Int size) {
    DC d = null;
    Time t = now();
    costPerTimeUnit = costPerTimeUnit + size;
    if (hasSetFor(is, size)) {
      d = takeOne(lookup(is, size));
      is = removeFrom(is, size, d);
      Fut<Unit> fa = provider!acquireMachine(d); await fa?;
    } else {
      Fut<DC> fdc = provider!createMachine(size);
      await fdc?; d = fdc.get;
    }
    instanceStartTime = timeDifference(t, now());
    return d;
  }
  Unit dropInstance(DC d) {
    Fut<Unit> fr = provider!releaseMachine(d); await fr?;
    Fut<Int> fs = d!total("CPU"); await fs?; Int size = fs.get;
    costPerTimeUnit = costPerTimeUnit - size;
    is = addToSet(is, size, d);
  }
}
```

Fig. 5. The Cloud User Account

Constant balancing over-provisions by processing all replication schedules on a single virtual machine with sufficient capacity, and is captured by the class ConstantAcceptor in Fig. 6. The acceptor initially requests a single machine through its cloud user account and deploys all ConnectionThread objects to this machine after initialization, to process the replication schedules.

As-needed balancing receives a request for a connection from a ClientJob object, calculates the resources needed by the virtual machine to fulfill the replication schedule, and requests a machine of appropriate size through the user account. Implementation details are omitted for brevity.

Budget-aware balancing (class BudgetAcceptor in Fig. 6) is a strategy where the acceptor has a certain *budget per time interval* and may "save resources" for later. The class parameter budgetPerTimeUnit determines this budget and the field availableBudget keeps track of the accumulated (saved) resources. When the acceptor gets a request from a ClientJob it calculates the resources needed to fulfill the replication schedule in wantedResources and the resources it has available on the budget in maxResources. If resources are available on the budget, the acceptor calls getInstance(size) on the user

```
class ConstantAcceptor(SyncServer server,
    Int instanceSize, Account acc) implements Acceptor {
  DC dc = null;
  Unit run() { dc = acc.getInstance(instanceSize); }
  ConnectionThread getConnection(ClientJob job, Schedule schedule) {
    Int cost = scheduleCost(schedule);
    await dc != null; ConnectionThread th = null;
    [DC: dc] th = new cog ConnectionThreadImpl(job,server,cost);
    return th; }
  Unit finish(ConnectionThread t) { }
  Unit end() { acc.dropInstance(dc); }
}

class BudgetAcceptor(SyncServer server, Account acc,
    Int budgetPerTimeUnit) implements Acceptor {
  Int availableBudget = 1; List<Int> budgetHistory = Nil;
  Unit run() {
    while (True) {
      Int cu = acc.getCostPerTimeUnit();
      availableBudget = availableBudget + budgetPerTimeUnit - cu;
      budgetHistory = Cons(availableBudget, budgetHistory);
      await duration(1, 1);} }
  ConnectionThread getConnection(ClientJob job, Schedule schedule) {
    Int cost = scheduleCost(schedule);
    Int dur = durationValue(deadline());
    Int startUp = acc.getLastInstanceStartUpTime();
    Int wantedResources = (cost / dur) + 1 + startUp;
    Int maxResources = (budgetPerTimeUnit - costPerTimeUnit) +
      (max(availableBudget, 0) / dur);
    ConnectionThread th = null;
    if (maxResources > 0) {
      DC dc = acc.getInstance(min(wantedResources, maxResources));
      [DC: dc] th = new cog ConnectionThreadImpl(job,server,cost);}
    return th; }
  Unit finish(ConnectionThread thread) {
    Fut<DC> fdc = thread!release();
    await fdc?; DC instance = fdc.get;
    acc.dropInstance(instance);}
  Unit end() { }
}
```

Fig. 6. The classes ConstantAcceptor and BudgetAcceptor

account to get the best machine according to the budget. The run() method monitors the resource usage and updates the available budget for every time interval. It also maintains a log budgetHistory of the available resources over time.

4.1   Calibration

To obtain a realistic cost model of the Replication System in ABS, we measured the execution time of replication sessions for the different schedules on the Java implementation. We were interested in three types of replication schedules:

Search: A session replicates changes from the search index, i.e., the underlying data structure providing search capability on a customer's product items.

Business rule: A session replicates changes to the business configuration; i.e., the presentation of search results such as the sorting of items and promotions.

Data: A session replicates changes concerning the item and navigation indices, i.e., the core index structures and data model for providing faceted navigation on a customer's product items.

Table 1 shows the average execution time of a single ClientJob for each schedule type for one SyncClient on a reference machine (4 core CPU 2.5GHz, 8GB memory), as well as the cost value subsequently used in the ABS model, which is directly proportional to execution time. Based on these schedule execution times and costs, we extend the functional ABS model of the Replication System with resource and timing information. To determine suitable deadlines for individual schedules and intervals between each ClientJob, we iteratively simulated a Replication System consisting of one SyncClient and a fixed number of replication jobs on a single cloud instance with CPU capacity set to 30 and interval to 11. With these parameters fixed, the lowest deadlines for schedules could be determined for 100% quality of service (QoS). Table 1 also shows the results of this initial simulation.

Table 1. Measurements on the Java implementation of the Replication System and derived simulation parameters

Schedule	Execution Time	Cost	Interval	Deadline
Search	34.0s	14	11	3
Business rules	2.5s	1	11	2
Data	274.9s	110	11	11

We also identified a *hot spot* of the ConnectionThread in the Java implementation of the method transferItem(fileset), which accounts for 99% of the execution time. The hot spot justifies adding a single cost annotation to the ConnectionThread class of the model so that resources are consumed upon invocation of that method. Fig. 7 sketches the implementation of the ConnectionThread interface.

4.2 The Results

Fig. 8 shows simulation results of the different balancing strategies over the number of live environments. We simulated from 1 to 20 environments over 100 time units; 20 environments are typically required to handle large query throughputs over a large number of product items. For each number of environments and scheduling strategy, the graph shows the quality of service (QoS) as a percentage of deadlines that have been met and the total amount of CPU resources made available by the cloud provider during the simulation. The *constant* balancing strategy models machine over-provisioning as mentioned in Sect. 2, with good QoS but the highest cost, independently of the load (QoS degrades once

```
class ConnectionThreadImpl(ClientJob job,
  SyncServer server, Int cost) implements ConnectionThread {
  Maybe<Command> cmd = Nothing;
  Set<Schedule> schedules = EmptySet;

  Unit consumeResource(Int amount) {
    Int c = 0; while (c <= amount) { [Cost: 1] c = c + 1; }}
  Unit run() {
    await cmd != Nothing;
    schedules = this.sendSchedule();
    if (cmd != Just(ListSchedule)) {
      ...
      Int size = size(filesets);
      while (hasNext(filesets)) {
        Pair<Set<Set<File>>,Set<File>> nfs = next(filesets);
        filesets = fst(nfs); Set<File> fileset = snd(nfs);
        this.transferItem(fileset);
        this.consumeResource(cost/size); }
      ... }    }
}
```

Fig. 7. The class `ConnectionThreadImpl`

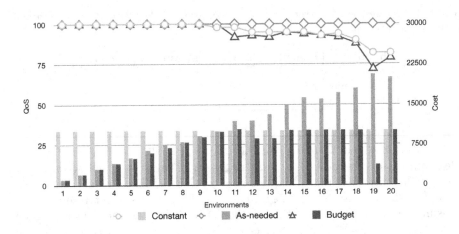

Fig. 8. Simulation results: QoS as percentage of successful sessions (left scale) and accumulated cost (right scale)

more environments are added than provisioned for). As expected, the *as-needed* balancing strategy exhibits 100% QoS, albeit with rising cost. The *budget-aware* balancing strategy exhibits rising cost up to the chosen budget and degrading QoS thereafter.

To compare the simulation results against the running system, we executed the simulation task loads on the Java implementation of the Replication System and measured the execution time. From Fig. 9, it can be seen that there is a direct correlation between simulated cost and measured execution time, except

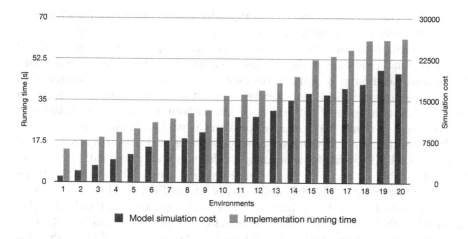

Fig. 9. Comparison of the measured execution time of the implementation (left scale) and the accumulated cost of the simulation for the as-needed policy (right scale)

for a constant factor resulting from system start-up time. Upon reflection, we decided not to model start-up time, since this one-time cost is amortized among all requests made during the server lifetime and hence is a negligible factor in a long-running system such as the FAS Replication System.

5   Related Work

To reduce complexity, general-purpose modeling languages strive for *abstraction* [24]: descriptions primarily focus on the functional behavior and logical composition of software, largely overlooking how the software's deployment influences its behavior. However, by using virtualization technologies an application can *modify resources of its deployment scenario during execution*; e.g., to dynamically create virtual processors. For cyber-physical and embedded systems, it is today accepted that modeling and programming languages need a timed semantics [26]. The Java Real-Time Specification (RTSJ) [11] extends Java with high-resolution time, including absolute time and relative time, and new thread concepts to solve time-critical problems: threads in RTSJ offer more precise scheduling than standard threads, with 28 strictly enforced priority levels. The modeling and analysis of single resources is discussed in, e.g., [2,16,33]. *Resource-aware programming* allows users to monitor the resources consumed by their programs, to manage such resources in the programs, and to transfer (i.e., add or remove) resources dynamically between distributed computations [27].

Resource constraints in the embedded systems domain led to a large body of work on performance analysis using formal models based on, e.g., process algebra [7], Petri Nets [31], and priced [10], timed [3], and probabilistic [6] automata and games (an overview of automata-based approaches is [33]). Related approaches are also applied to web services and business processes with resource constraints [18, 28]. These approaches typically abstract from the data flow and *declare* the cost of transitions in terms of time or in terms of a single resource. The automata-based modeling language MODEST [9] combines functional and non-functional requirements for stochastic systems, using a process algebra with dynamically computed weight expressions in probabilistic choice. Compared to ABS, these approaches do not associate capacities with locations but focus on non-functional aspects of embedded system without resource provisioning and management of dynamically created locations as studied in our paper.

Work on the modeling of object-oriented systems with resource constraints is scarce. The UML profile for scheduling, performance and time (SPT) describes scheduling policies according to the underlying deployment model [17]. Using SPT, the Core Scenario Model (CSM) [30] is informally defined to generate performance models from UML. However, CSM is not executable as it only identifies a subset of the possible system behaviors [30]. Verhoef's extension of VDM++ for embedded real-time systems [32] is based on abstract executable specification and models static deployment of fixed resources targeting the embedded domain, namely CPUs and buses.

Related work on simulation tools for cloud computing is mostly reminiscent of network simulators. Testing techniques and tools for cloud-based software systems are surveyed in [5]. In particular, CloudSim [14] and ICanCloud [29] are simulation tools using virtual machines to simulate cloud environments. CloudSim is a mature tool which has been used for a number of papers, but it is restricted to simulations on a single computer. In contrast, ICanCloud supports distribution on a cluster. EMUSIM [13] is an integrated tool that uses AEF (Automated Emulation Framework) to estimate performance and costs for an application by means of emulations to produce improved input parameters for simulations in CloudSim. Compared to these approaches, our work aims to support the developer of client applications for cloud-based environments at an early phase in the software engineering process and is based on a formal semantics.

In software design, no general, systematic means exists today to model and analyze software in the context of a set of available virtualized resources, nor to analyze resource redistribution in terms of load balancing or reflective operations. None of the cited works directly address the challenges raised by virtualization; in particular, they do not model quantitative resources as data inside the system itself, which is a particular property of virtualized resources.

6   Conclusion and Future Work

In this paper we demonstrated that it is possible to model *low-level* software aspects, including performance, resource consumption, and deployment, in a suitably *abstract* way which is adequate for *cloud computing*. As an immediate benefit this makes it possible to perform comprehensive simulations based on the system *model* that allow to predict and evaluate the consequences of different scheduling, load balancing, or deployment strategies. We demonstrated the feasibility of our approach by modeling part of an industrial e-Commerce product and by comparing the simulated model to the actual code in production.

The modeling in this paper is based on a resource-aware extension of the *abstract behavioral specification* language ABS [8,23]. ABS has a formal semantics and was designed such that the models expressed in it are mechanically *analyzable* with respect to correctness, resource consumption, security, etc. Specifically, it is possible to *automatically* compute symbolic worst-case bounds for resource consumption of ABS programs [2]. We plan to generalize this approach to the extension of ABS used here and apply it to cloud scenarios. This would make it possible to automatically analyze the worst-case resource consumption of programs running in the cloud without actually deploying them.

References

1. Agha, G.A.: ACTORS: A Model of Concurrent Computations in Distributed Systems. MIT Press (1986)
2. Albert, E., Arenas, P., Genaim, S., Gómez-Zamalloa, M., Puebla, G.: COSTABS: a cost and termination analyzer for ABS. In: Proc. Partial Evaluation and Program Manipulation (PEPM 2012), pp. 151–154. ACM (2012)
3. Amnell, T., Fersman, E., Mokrushin, L., Pettersson, P., Yi, W.: TIMES: A Tool for Schedulability Analysis and Code Generation of Real-time Systems. In: Larsen, K.G., Niebert, P. (eds.) FORMATS 2003. LNCS, vol. 2791, pp. 60–72. Springer, Heidelberg (2004)
4. Armstrong, J.: Programming Erlang. Pragmatic Bookshelf (2007)
5. Bai, X., Li, M., Chen, B., Tsai, W.-T., Gao, J.: Cloud testing tools. In: Proc. Service Oriented System Engineering (SOSE 2011), pp. 1–12. IEEE (2011)
6. Baier, C., Haverkort, B.R., Hermanns, H., Katoen, J.-P.: Performance evaluation and model checking join forces. Comm. ACM 53(9), 76–85 (2010)
7. Barbanera, F., Bugliesi, M., Dezani-Ciancaglini, M., Sassone, V.: Space-aware ambients and processes. TCS 373(1-2), 41–69 (2007)
8. Bjørk, J., de Boer, F.S., Johnsen, E.B., Schlatte, R., Tapia Tarifa, S.L.: User-defined schedulers for real-time concurrent objects. Innovations in Systems and Software Engineering (to appear, available online, 2012)
9. Bohnenkamp, H.C., D'Argenio, P.R., Hermanns, H., Katoen, J.-P.: MODEST: A Compositional Modeling Formalism for Hard and Softly Timed Systems. IEEE Trans. Software Eng. 32(10), 812–830 (2006)
10. Bouyer, P., Fahrenberg, U., Larsen, K.G., Markey, N.: Quantitative analysis of real-time systems using priced timed automata. Comm. ACM 54(9), 78–87 (2011)
11. Bruno, E.J., Bollella, G.: Real-Time Java Programming: With Java RTS. Prentice Hall (2009)
12. Buyya, R., Yeo, C.S., Venugopal, S., Broberg, J., Brandic, I.: Cloud computing and emerging IT platforms: Vision, hype, and reality for delivering computing as the 5th utility. Future Generation Computer Systems 25(6), 599–616 (2009)
13. Calheiros, R.N., Netto, M.A., Rose, C.A.F.D., Buyya, R.: EMUSIM: an integrated emulation and simulation environment for modeling, evaluation, and validation of performance of cloud computing applications. Software: Practice and Experience (to appear, available online, 2012)
14. Calheiros, R.N., Ranjan, R., Beloglazov, A., Rose, C.A.F.D., Buyya, R.: CloudSim: a toolkit for modeling and simulation of cloud computing environments and evaluation of resource provisioning algorithms. Software, Practice and Experience 41(1), 23–50 (2011)

15. Caromel, D., Henrio, L.: A Theory of Distributed Objects. Springer (2005)
16. Chander, A., Espinosa, D., Islam, N., Lee, P., Necula, G.C.: Enforcing resource bounds via static verification of dynamic checks. ACM TOPLAS 29(5) (2007)
17. Douglass, B.P.: Real Time UML – Advances in the UML for Real-Time Systems. Addison-Wesley (2004)
18. Foster, H., Emmerich, W., Kramer, J., Magee, J., Rosenblum, D.S., Uchitel, S.: Model checking service compositions under resource constraints. In: Proc. European Software Engineering Conf. and Intl. Symp. on Foundations of Software Engineering (ESEC/FSE 2007), pp. 225–234. ACM (2007)
19. Johnsen, E.B., Hähnle, R., Schäfer, J., Schlatte, R., Steffen, M.: ABS: A Core Language for Abstract Behavioral Specification. In: Aichernig, B.K., de Boer, F.S., Bonsangue, M.M. (eds.) FMCO 2011. LNCS, vol. 6957, pp. 142–164. Springer, Heidelberg (2011)
20. Johnsen, E.B., Owe, O.: An asynchronous communication model for distributed concurrent objects. Software and Systems Modeling 6(1), 35–58 (2007)
21. Johnsen, E.B., Owe, O., Schlatte, R., Tapia Tarifa, S.L.: Dynamic Resource Reallocation between Deployment Components. In: Dong, J.S., Zhu, H. (eds.) ICFEM 2010. LNCS, vol. 6447, pp. 646–661. Springer, Heidelberg (2010)
22. Johnsen, E.B., Schlatte, R., Tapia Tarifa, S.L.: Modeling Resource-Aware Virtualized Applications for the Cloud in Real-Time ABS. In: Proc. Formal Engineering Methods (ICFEM 2012). LNCS. Springer, Heidelberg (to appear, 2012)
23. Johnsen, E.B., Owe, O., Schlatte, R., Tapia Tarifa, S.L.: Validating Timed Models of Deployment Components with Parametric Concurrency. In: Beckert, B., Marché, C. (eds.) FoVeOOS 2010. LNCS, vol. 6528, pp. 46–60. Springer, Heidelberg (2011)
24. Kramer, J.: Is abstraction the key to computing? Comm. ACM 50(4), 36–42 (2007)
25. Larsen, K.G., Pettersson, P., Yi, W.: UPPAAL in a nutshell. Intl. Journal on Software Tools for Technology Transfer 1(1-2), 134–152 (1997)
26. Lee, E.A.: Computing needs time. Comm. ACM 52(5), 70–79 (2009)
27. Moreau, L., Queinnec, C.: Resource aware programming. ACM TOPLAS 27(3), 441–476 (2005)
28. Netjes, M., van der Aalst, W.M., Reijers, H.A.: Analysis of resource-constrained processes with Colored Petri Nets. In: Proc. Practical Use of Coloured Petri Nets and CPN Tools (CPN 2005), DAIMI 576. University of Aarhus (2005)
29. Nuñez, A., Vázquez-Poletti, J., Caminero, A., Castañé, G., Carretero, J., Llorente, I.: iCanCloud: A flexible and scalable cloud infrastructure simulator. Journal of Grid Computing 10, 185–209 (2012), doi:10.1007/s10723-012-9208-5
30. Petriu, D.B., Woodside, C.M.: An intermediate metamodel with scenarios and resources for generating performance models from UML designs. Software and System Modeling 6(2), 163–184 (2007)
31. Sgroi, M., Lavagno, L., Watanabe, Y., Sangiovanni-Vincentelli, A.: Synthesis of embedded software using free-choice Petri nets. In: Proc. Design Automation Conference (DAC 1999), pp. 805–810. ACM (1999)
32. Verhoef, M., Larsen, P.G., Hooman, J.: Modeling and Validating Distributed Embedded Real-Time Systems with VDM++. In: Misra, J., Nipkow, T., Sekerinski, E. (eds.) FM 2006. LNCS, vol. 4085, pp. 147–162. Springer, Heidelberg (2006)
33. Vulgarakis, A., Seceleanu, C.C.: Embedded systems resources: Views on modeling and analysis. In: Proc. Computer Software and Applications Conference (COMPSAC 2008), pp. 1321–1328. IEEE (2008)
34. Wong, P.Y.H., Diakov, N., Schaefer, I.: Modelling Adaptable Distributed Object Oriented Systems Using the HATS Approach: A Fredhopper Case Study. In: Beckert, B., Damiani, F., Gurov, D. (eds.) FoVeOOS 2011. LNCS, vol. 7421, pp. 49–66. Springer, Heidelberg (2012)

A Model-Driven Approach for Virtual Machine Image Provisioning in Cloud Computing

Tam Le Nhan[1], Gerson Sunyé[1,3], and Jean-Marc Jézéquel[1,2]

[1] INRIA Rennes - Bretagne Atlantique, France
[2] University of Rennes 1
[3] University of Nantes
{tam.le_nhan,gerson.sunye,jean-marc.jezequel}@inria.fr

Abstract. The Cloud Computing Infastructure-as-a-Service (IaaS) layer provides a service for on demand virtual machine images deployment. This service provides a flexible platform for cloud users to develop, deploy, and test their applications. However, one major issue of application deployment is to ensure the compatibility of software components installed in a virtual machine image. This paper describes a model-driven approach to manage, create configurations, and deploy images for virtual machine image provisioning in Cloud Computing. This approach considers virtual image as product lines and uses feature models to represent their configurations. It uses model-based techniques to handle automatic deployment and reconfiguration, making the management of virtual images more flexible and easier than traditional approaches.

Keywords: Model-driven deployment, cloud computing, virtual image provisioning, feature models.

1 Introduction

Cloud Computing [2, 13] has been a hot topic in both of research and industry community recently. It can be described as a new kind of computing in which dynamically scalable and virtualized resources are provided as services over the Internet. Cloud users can access cloud system and use the service through different devices and interfaces. They only have to pay what they use according to Service Level Agreement contracts established between Cloud providers and Cloud users [5]. One of the main features of Cloud computing is the virtualization in which all cloud resources become transparent to the user. They do not need any longer to control and maintain the underlying cloud infrastructure. The virtualization in Cloud Computing combines a number of virtual machine images (VMIs) on the top of physical machines. Each virtual image hosts a complete software stack: it includes operating system, middleware, database, and development applications. The deployment of a VMI typically involves booting the image, as well as installation and configuration of software packages. In the traditional approach, the creation of a VMI to fit user's requirements and deploying it in the Cloud environment are typically carried out by the technical

F. De Paoli, E. Pimentel, and G. Zavattaro (Eds.): ESOCC 2012, LNCS 7592, pp. 107–121, 2012.

division of the Cloud service providers. They provide a platform as a service to the user according to SLA contracts signed between the service provider and the user. Usually, it is a pre-packaged platform with installed and configured software components. The standard VMI contains many software packages, which rarely get used and thus the image is typically larger than what would be necessary. This can lead to several difficulties, such as wastage of storage space, memory, operating costs, and waste of network bandwidth when cloning an image and deploying it on the cloud nodes [1].

In the traditional approach, when a cloud user requests a new development platform, the service provider administrators select an appropriate VMI for cloning and deploying on cloud nodes. If there is no match found, then a new one is created and configured to match the request. It can be generated by modifying from the closest-fit existing VMI or from scratch. Several concerns would need to be addressed by the cloud providers, such as: (i) How to create an optimal configuration? (ii) Which software packages and their dependencies should be installed? (iii) How to find the best-fit existing VMI and how to obtain a new VMI by modifying this one?

Cloud service providers want to automate this process because the complexity of interdependency between software packages, and the difficulty of maintenance [7] is time-consuming for the creation of standard VMIs. In other words, they want to give users more flexibility when choosing the appropriate VMI to satisfy their requirements, while ensuring benefits for providers in terms of time, operating costs, and resources. In this paper, we present an approach for managing VMI for Cloud Computing environments, providing a way to adapt to the needs of auto-scaling and self-configuring virtual machine images. In this approach, we consider VMIs as a product line and use feature models to represent VMI configurations and model-based techniques to handle automatic VMI deployment and reconfiguration. We claim that this approach makes the management (i.e., creation, configuration and adaption) of virtual image faster, more flexible and easier than the traditional approach. We validate this approach by an example showing that, given a base model representing all available artifacts, one can easily derive a configuration model (a specific use of a subset of artifacts) and generate all needed configuration scripts to generate its corresponding VMI. The paper is organized as follows. Section 2 describes our solution of managing virtual machine image configurations by using feature models and using the model-driven approach for virtual machine image deployment in Cloud Computing environment. Section 3 introduces an example about deploying a Java web application development platform. Section 4 shows the experiment evaluations. Section 5 discusses the related work, and is followed by the conclusion and future work in Section 6.

2   Model-Driven Approach

In this section, we present a model-based approach for image provisioning. This approach uses an image with a minimal configuration, containing the operating system, some monitoring tools, and an *execution model*. The goal of the execution model is to install and configure software packages, after booting the deployed images.

2.1   Feature Modeling for VMI Configuration Management

Our approach uses feature modeling [11] to manage the configuration of virtual-machine images. In terms of configuration derivation, a feature model describes:

- The software packages that are needed to compose a Virtual Machine Image, represented as configuration options.
- The rules dictating the requirements, such as dependent packages and the libraries required by each software component.
- The constraining rules, which specifies how the choice of a given component restricts the choice of other components, in the same Virtual Machine Image.

Feature models have a tree structure, with features forming the nodes of the tree and groups of features representing feature variability. There are four types of feature groups: *Mandatory*; *Optional*; *Alternative*; and *Or*. The model follows some rules when specifying which features should be included in a variant. If a variant contains a feature, then:

- All its *mandatory* child features must also be contained;
- Any number of *optional* child features can be included;
- Exactly one feature must be selected from an *alternative* group;
- At least one feature must be selected from an *or* group.

Feature models support two cross-tree constraints: *Requires*; and *Excludes*. Given two features, f_a and f_b: if f_a requires f_b, then the selection of f_a implies the

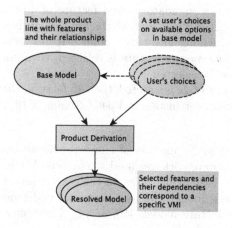

Fig. 1. Feature Modeling Approach

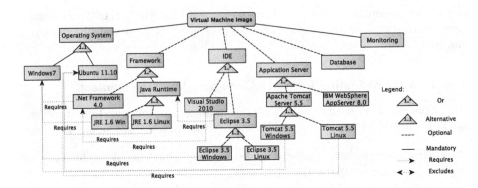

Fig. 2. Feature Diagram Represents a Base Model

selection of f_b; if f_a excludes f_b, then the selection of f_a prevents the selection of f_b.

Our approach deals with two models: base and resolved. The base model represents the whole product line, with all its features, their relationships, and constraints; The resolved model is obtained after the product derivation process, it contains selected features and their dependencies.

Base Model. The base model represents configuration options which would be used for composing a VMI. The elements of the base model are features of the configuration options of a VMI, they represent software packages and their dependencies. These elements become elements of resolved models, according to the resolutions of the corresponding selection models.

Figure 2 depicts a part of based model that represents VMI configuration features. In this model, features and their relationships represent software packages:

- *Operating System* is a mandatory child feature of *Virtual Machine Image*, which must be selected when *Virtual Machine Image* is selected.
- *Operating System* includes alternative child features: *Windows* and *Linux*
- When the *Operating System* feature is selected, then one of *Windows 7* or *Ubuntu 11.10* must be selected.
- If the feature *Ubuntu 11.10* is selected, then all features that require *Windows 7* cannot be selected, for instance: *Visual Studio 2010*, *JRE 1.6 Windows*, etc.

Base models are built by IT experts of cloud providers, who have knowledge about systems and software packages used to compose Virtual Machine Images. The correctness of the base model relies on the correctness of the feature model that represents the base models. Many approaches and tools were proposed to automate analysis of feature models [16, 4, 14]. They offer to validate, check satisfiability, detect the "dead" features and analyze feature models. In our implementation, we use constraints to ensure that the created feature model is valid, and that configurations, which are derived from this feature model, are also consistent with the base model. For example:

- Parent and child features cannot have a mutually exclusive relationship.
- Sibling features cannot be mutually exclusive.
- For two features f_1 and f_2, if f_1 requires f_2, then f_2 cannot require f_1.

Product Derivation. Product Derivation is a process that is responsible for the creation of the final configuration. It supports to derive the VMI configurations from the base model [19]. To create a specific configuration of a VMI, the designer selects some features from the base model and uses a mechanism to produce a suitable configuration. The selection of each feature is checked and validated by the Product Derivation process to ensure the selection is valid. When a feature is selected, the Product Derivation process checks its relationships. Features connected to the selected feature by a mutually exclusive relationship become unavailable on the base model for next selections. All of the features that are required by the selected feature are also selected.

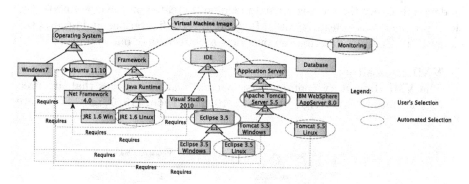

Fig. 3. A Resolved Model Derived by the Product Derivation Process

Resolved Models. A resolved model stores user's feature choices of the base model and their dependencies. It is derived from the Product Derivation process based on user's selection on the base model. A resolved model corresponds to a specific configuration of a Virtual Machine Image. Figure 3 is an example of a resolved model that is derived from the base model presented in Figure 2 with the following user's selections: operating system is Ubuntu 11.10, integrated development environment is Eclipse 3.5, and Apache Tomcat 5.5 for application server. According to the base model, Eclipse 5.5 requires Java Runtime. Both features have two alternative children: Windows and Linux. However, since the selected operating system is Ubuntu 11.10, only the Windows version is available. Addition, since Monitoring is a mandatory feature of Virtual Machine Image it must be selected. By using feature models, cloud providers have flexibility to create Base models representing resources for VMI provisioning. Features represent software packages or hardware options, such as RAM or virtualization technology (e.g., KVM or Xen). These feature could also be used to store other informations: time, cost, memory usage, etc., to support finding optimal configurations. The first time for creating the base models might take time and need experts on software packages and their dependencies. However, once the Base model is created, it helps cloud users during the selection and the creation of VMI configurations, reducing time, complexity, and errors during the manipulation.

2.2 Model-Based Deployment Architecture

Unlike the traditional approach, where software packages are installed and configured when the VMI template is created, the model-driven deployment approach installs and configures software packages at runtime when a VMI template is booted. The approach also supports synchronization of maintenance of the deployed VMIs at runtime. This mechanism allows users to update, remove, and add new components to running VMIs, without image shutdown and redeployment. It is more flexible than the traditional approach.

In our approach, we create models that drive the creation of VMIs instance on demand. Every time a new virtual machine is created on the cloud node, the cloud provider selects features of VMI, generates configurations and applies the model to it. Figure 4 describes an overview architecture of our approach.

– **VMI Repository**
    The VMI Repository contains basic virtual machine images that are used as the initial VMIs: e.g., Ubuntu11.10.img, fedora15.0.img. These are

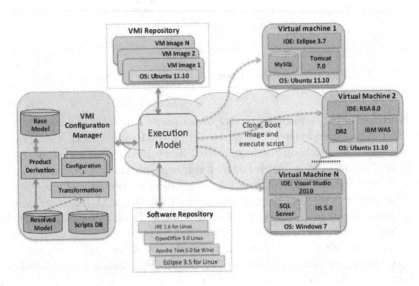

Fig. 4. An Overall Architecture of Model-Driven Approach for VMI Deployment

standard VMIs with minimum configuration, such as operating system and assistance software, like monitoring tools.

- **VMI Configuration Manager**
  The VMI Configuration Manager is responsible for the creation and the management of configurations of virtual machine image to fulfill requested requirements. By using the VMI configuration manager, users can easily select the required software for creating the appropriate virtual machine. It also helps the cloud providers to manage the preparation and provision of resources as per client requirements.
- **Execution Model**
  The Execution Model is responsible for reserving cloud nodes, deploying virtual machines, and executing the corresponding configuration that resulted from the reasoning of VMI Configuration Manager. It is an encapsulation of Ruby and shell script files.
- **Cloud Nodes**
  Cloud Nodes are reserved nodes in the cloud infrastructure for hosting and running virtual machines.
- **Software Repository**
  The Software Repository stores software packages used to compose a VMI. It can be a file server inside the cloud infrastructure or other repositories from the Internet, such as the Debian repository.

2.3 Model-Based Deployment Process

The deployment process deals with the VMI Configuration Manager, the Execution Model, the Software Repositories, and the Cloud Nodes. It includes the following steps:

- **Create a VMI configuration**
  In this step, cloud users interact with the VMI Configuration Manager to select configuration options from the base model. The VMI Configuration

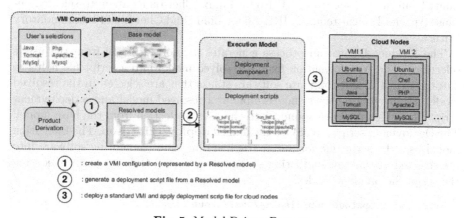

Fig. 5. Model-Driven Process

Manager analyzes the user's choices and generates a resolved model (i.e., a valid configuration of a VMI).

– **Generate a deployment script file**
A resolved model is transformed into a deployment script file for automatic deployment and configuration. In the current implementation, we use Chef[1] to automatic install and configure software on a virtual machine. Chef is an installation software that cloud providers use to deploy, install, and configure software stacks on the cloud nodes at runtime. Chef requires an input file, describing the node configuration: the required software, as well as their role. Actually, the input file is a Ruby or JavaScript Object Notation[2] (JSON) source code.

– **Deploy a standard VMI and apply the deployment script file to the cloud nodes**
The Execution Model, based on the resolved model and deployment script file, selects a standard VMI and launches it on the reserved nodes. After that, it transfers the deployment script to the nodes and executes Chef. Finally, it returns the successful nodes to the cloud user.

3 An Example of the VMI for Java Web Application

To illustrate our approach, we introduce an example of VMI provisioning for the Java Web Application Development platform. The configuration of this VMI includes an operating system, a web application server, a database management system, and a programming language compiler. Cloud users select the required features on the base model by the using VMI Configuration Manager, for example: **Ubuntu, Eclipse, Apache Tomcat**, and **Database**. Figure 6 represents the selection of configuration options from the base model.

A VMI includes only one operating system, so the choice of Ubuntu feature is mutual exclusive with other operating systems and their dependencies. For example, the users can select neither the SQL Server nor the Eclipse for Windows because both features require Windows, which is a mutual exclusive feature of Linux Ubuntu. The features JRE 1.6 for Linux, Chef-Linux are auto-selected because Apache Tomcat requires JRE 1.6 for Linux and Chef-Linux is a mandatory feature.

The Product Derivation process generates a resolved model from the user's selections. The transformation from a resolved model into a script file helps to automatic install and configure software stacks that are selected in the resolved model. Figure 6 also shows the example of a resolved model and a deployment script file, which are corresponding to the user's selection from the base model. The Deployment script is a JSON file, named **deployscript.json**. The Execution model uses the script file for automatic installing and configuring software into the selected virtual image. Listing 1 presents a partial Ruby code for executing the script file on cloud nodes.

---

[1] http://wiki.opscode.com/display/chef/About
[2] http://www.json.org/

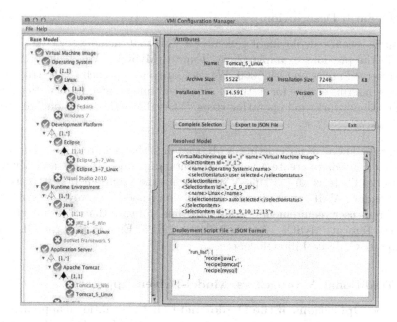

Fig. 6. Example of VMI Configuration Manager

Listing 1. A Partial Code in Ruby of the Execution on the Cloud Nodes

```
Net::SSH::Multi.start do |session|
  # access servers via a gateway
  session.via STRGATEWAY, CONFIG['username']
  deployment["nodes"].each do |node|
    session.use "root@#{node}"
  end
  url = 'http://public.grenoble.grid5000.fr/~tlenhan/TamlnChefScripts/'
  session.exec 'hostname'
  session.loop
  session.exec 'mkdir -p /tmp/chef-solo'
  session.loop
  session.exec 'wget ' url 'deployscript.json'
  session.loop
  session.exec 'chef-solo -j deployscript.json -r ' url 'cookbooks.tgz'
  session.loop
end
```

4 Experiment Evaluation

In this section, we present an experimental evaluation of our approach on the easiness of manipulation and the performance of deployment, in terms of data transfer and deployment duration. The experiment is executed on Grid5000[3], a virtualization infrastructure for research in France. We use Grid5000s tools to reserve nodes and deploy VMIs to the nodes.

---

[3] https://www.grid5000.fr/mediawiki/index.php

4.1 Scenario Description

Our simple scenario deployment generates a VMI that includes selected software stacks in the previous example (Java, Tomcat, MySQL). We deploy this VMI to the reserved nodes on Grid5000. We compare our approach to the traditional approach in terms of time for setting up the environment, amount of data transfer through the network, and operating steps. We evaluate the traditional approach in two cases:

- Case 1: There is no existing VMI that fits the requirements. The cloud provider needs to create a new VMI containing Java, Tomcat and MySQL.
- Case 2: There is an existing VMI that fits the requirements. It is used as a standard VMI for deploying on the cloud nodes. However, for meeting different user requirements, it also contains software that may not be used: Java, Tomcat, MySQL, Apache2, Jetty, PHP5, Emacs, PostgreSQL, DB2-Express C, Jetty, LibreOffice, etc.

4.2 Traditional Approach vs. Model-Driven Approach

Time and Operations of the Deployment. In the traditional approach most decisions are taken by experts, because they require the knowledge of underlying

Table 1. The Operations of Model-Driven Approach and Traditional Approach

Traditional Approach			Model-driven Approach		
Operations	*Handled by*	*Estimated Time*	*Operations*	*Handled by*	*Estimated Time*
1. Find the existing VMI in repository that fit the requirements. • If found: go to operation 3, • If not found: create a new one or modify an existing VMI	Expert (Manually)	1 minute	1. Create a VMI configuration & Generate a deployment script file	Expert & Non-expert (Manually)	2 minutes
2. Create a new VMI • Boot a clean VMI • Install and configure software • Save to an image	Expert (Manually)	11 minutes	2. Reserve 50 nodes & deploy the standard VMI to the nodes	Automatic	8 minutes
3. Reserve 50 cloud nodes & deploy the VMI to the nodes	Expert (Manually)	9 / 12 minutes (*)	3. Copy the deployment file to the running nodes & execute it to install, configure software	Automatic	2 minutes
Total time		21 / 13 minutes (**)	**Total time**		14 minutes

(*) :   9 minutes for case 1, and 12 minutes for case 2
(**):   21 minutes for case 1, and 13 minutes for case 2

systems and software dependencies. Our approach provides a graphical interface, the VMI Configuration Manager, which guides cloud users in the selection of a set of configuration options. After that, the Configuration Manager deploys the new VMI on cloud nodes, making easy to update and to maintain the running VMI. Table 1 shows a comparison between the traditional and the model-driven approaches, in terms of operations and deployment duration. Experiments show that the deployment duration of our approach is slightly better that the traditional approach, if there is an existing VMI that fits the requirements. However, if there is no appropriate VMI and the cloud provider creates a new one, then our approach is faster than the traditional approach.

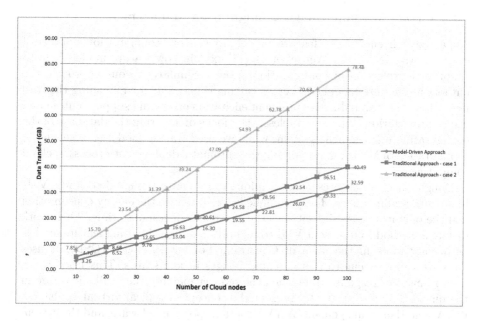

Fig. 7. Data Transfer Through the Network of the VMI Deployment

Data Transfer through the Network. In our experiment, we use a clean image **Squeeze-x64-nsf**[4] (333.587 MB), which is available on the Grid5000's repository. This is also the standard VMI for the case 1 of the traditional approach. In our approach, we use minimal configuration images, only containing an installation software and its dependencies (i.e., Chef). After the installation of the minimal software, the image size is 339.955 MB. In the case 2, unused software is installed for adapting different requirements from users. This makes the size of a standard VMI is much bigger, 803.60 MB. Figure 7 shows that in both cases, the model-driven approach transfers less data than the traditional approach. Especially when the pre-packaged VMI contains more software installed, and deploy to a large number of cloud nodes. In this example, when we

---

[4] https://www.grid5000.fr/mediawiki/index.php/Squeeze-x64-nfs-1.1

deploy 100 cloud nodes, the traditional approach transfers 40.49GB of data for case 1, and 78.48GB of data for case 2, while the model-driven approach only transfers 32.59GB of data. The traditional approach reduces the amount of data in 19.5% and 58.47%, comparing to cases 1 and 2, respectively.

5   Related Work

Our work is related to two areas: Configuration management and the deployment of VMI in cloud environment.

5.1   Virtual Machine Image Configuration Management

Some research efforts use feature models to capture configuration options of complex systems [8, 17]. Wenzel et al. [17] explain how feature models help to simplify the selection of configuration options. Similarly to our approach, the authors use feature models and cross cutting constraints for managing the configuration. This can reduce requirement elicitation errors and support automated choice propagation [10]. Nevertheless, they focus on creating the database of the configuration management system, while we used feature model to manage the configuration of VMIs for supporting the automatic deployment process in cloud computing.

Dougherty et al. [8] present a technique to minimize the number of idle VMs in an auto-scaling queue. The technique helps to reduce the energy consumption and the operating cost and satisfies the constraint of response time. Their work defines a method to represent VMI configuration options by using feature models with constraints in the form of Constraint Solving Problems (CSP). It uses an auto-scaling queue to store created images in idle status. This leads to an improvement of response time when the request matches the available image in the queue. T.Zhang et al. [18] present the concept of typical virtual appliances (TVA) and their management. A TVA contains popular software, and the system can provide a set of frequently used virtual appliances. It helps to minimize the transformation time from an existing virtual appliance to a new one that fits the request. However, in both approaches, the composition of virtual image occurs at design time and at the administrator side, before the system copy and deploys it into cloud nodes. This makes it difficult to synchronize the maintenance and modification of the running images as needed when the amount of running cloud nodes is large. For example, upgrading the software version, or installing a new software package on the running virtual machines. Our approach composes VMI at runtime, when the standard VMI is deployed on cloud nodes. We put the configuration file into the running cloud nodes (they clone the standard VMI), and the installation and configuration occurs inside these nodes. Therefore, it is easy to maintain or modify the running images.

5.2   Virtual Machine Image Deployment

Konstantinou *et al.* [12] describe a model-driven engineering approach for virtual image deployment in virtualized environments. They focus on reusable virtual images and their composition. The authors introduce the concept of virtual solution models. This concept defines the solution as a composition of multiple configurable virtual images. The virtual solution model is an abstract deployment plan and it is platform-independent. According to the specific cloud platform, the model can be transformed into an executable deployment plan[9]. Chieu *et al.* [6, 7] and Arnold *et al.* [3] propose the use of virtual image templates. Their approaches describe a provisioning system that provide pre-installed virtual images according to the deployment scenario. M. Sethi *et al.* [15] present an approach for automated modification of dependency configuration in SOA deployment. In their work, the software stacks are installed and configured at deployment time, transferring smaller VMIs through the cloud network. Sun Microsystems [1] proposes an approach to deploy applications in cloud computing environment. Similarly to our approach, their approach uses shell-script files to execute on running cloud nodes at runtime. However, both approaches need experts on virtual image provisioning. By using feature models to represent the configuration options, our approach can support both experts and non-experts, who lack knowledge about virtual image provisioning and underlying software systems and dependencies. It can reduce errors and improve the consistency of configurations during the composing of VMIs.

6   Conclusion and Future Work

In this paper, we presented a model-driven approach to manage and create configurations, as well as deploy images for virtual machine image provisioning in Cloud Computing. We consider virtual images as product lines, use feature models to capture their configurations, and use model-based techniques for automatic deployment of virtual images. This approach makes the management of virtual image more flexible and easier to use than the traditional approach. On the implementation side, we developed a prototype for validating the approach. It helps cloud users to select configuration options, to create virtual images and to deploy them on cloud nodes. We used Grid5000 as a Cloud Computing environment testbed for deploying virtual images.

The framework includes two major parts: the VMI Configuration Manager and the Execution Model. The VMI Configuration Manager helps cloud users to select configuration options, create a valid configuration of a VMI through a graphical user interface. It also generates deployment script files. The Execution Model uses these files to automatically deploy and configure software into cloud nodes at runtime without any manual intervention.

We compared our approach to the traditional cloud deployment approach in two different scenarios, using an existing compatible VMI and creating a new one. Experiments showed that the model-driven approach helps cloud users to create the configurations and deploy VMIs on demand easily. It minimizes error-prone manual operations. Additionally, our approach reduces the network data transfer, comparing to the traditional approach. Especially, if a pre-packed VMI contains unwanted software. In this case, experiments showed that our approach reduces the data transfer up to 58.47%. It saves network resources during VMIs provisioning in Cloud Computing. Our framework could be extended to support cloud users for estimating the deployment time and operational costs as needed. Therefore, it could improve the performance of virtual machine image provisioning. However, the reasoning engine of our Product Derivation process is still limited with simple constraints of the configuration. It is a challenge to deal with more elaborated configurations that have optimal requirements on the complex constraints of multiple parameters. In the future, we plan to improve the reasoning engine of the Product Derivation process, to deal with more complex configuration options and constraints. We believe that a reasoning engine could enhance the performance of the Product Derivation process in the VMI configuration management. Currently, our prototype only works in the Grid5000 environment. We are improving the prototype to have the ability to work with some open-source cloud platforms, such as OpenNebula, Nimbus, etc.

References

[1] Model-driven application deployment for cloud computing environments. White Paper, Sun Microsystem Inc., 18 pages (January 2010), http://www.techrepublic.com/whitepapers/model-driven-application-deployment-for-cloud-computing-environments/1829151

[2] Armbrust, M., Fox, A., Griffith, R., Joseph, A.D., Katz, R.H., Konwinski, A., Lee, G., Patterson, D.A., Rabkin, A., Stoica, I., Zaharia, M.: Above the clouds: A Berkeley view of cloud computing. Tech. Rep. UCB/EECS-2009-28, EECS Department, University of California, Berkeley (2009)

[3] Arnold, W., Eilam, T., Kalantar, M., Konstantinou, A.V., Totok, A.A.: Automatic Realization of SOA Deployment Patterns in Distributed Environments. In: Bouguettaya, A., Krueger, I., Margaria, T. (eds.) ICSOC 2008. LNCS, vol. 5364, pp. 162–179. Springer, Heidelberg (2008)

[4] Benavides, D., Trinidad, P., Ruiz-Cortés, A.: Automated Reasoning on Feature Models. In: Pastor, Ó., Falcão e Cunha, J. (eds.) CAiSE 2005. LNCS, vol. 3520, pp. 491–503. Springer, Heidelberg (2005)

[5] Buyya, R., Yeo, C.S., Venugopal, S., Broberg, J., Brandic, I.: Cloud computing and emerging it platforms: Vision, hype, and reality for delivering computing as the 5th utility. Future Generation Computer Systems 25(6), 599–616 (2009)

[6] Chieu, T., Mohindra, A., Karve, A., Segal, A.: Solution-based deployment of complex application services on a cloud. In: 2010 IEEE International Conference on Service Operations and Logistics and Informatics (SOLI), pp. 282–287 (July 2010)

[7] Chieu, T., Mohindra, A., Karve, A., Segal, A.: Dynamic scaling of web applications in a virtualized cloud computing environment. In: IEEE International Conference on e-Business Engineering, ICEBE 2009, pp. 281–286 (October 2009)

[8] Dougherty, B., White, J., Schmidt, D.C.: Model-driven auto-scaling of green cloud computing infrastructure. Future Generation Computer Systems 28(2), 371–378 (2012)

[9] Han, R., Guo, L., Guo, Y., He, S.: A deployment platform for dynamically scaling applications in the cloud. In: 2011 IEEE Third International Conference on Cloud Computing Technology and Science (CloudCom), November 29-December 1, pp. 506–510 (2011)

[10] Hubaux, A., Classen, A., Mendonca, M., Heymans, P.: A preliminary review on the application of feature diagrams in practice. In: Proceedings of the 4th International Workshop on Variability Modelling of Software-Intensive Systems - VaMOS (2010)

[11] Kang, K.C., Cohen, S.G., Hess, J.A., Novak, W.E., Peterson, A.S.: Feature-oriented domain analysis (FODA) feasibility study. Tech. rep., Carnegie-Mellon University Software Engineering Institute (November 1990)

[12] Konstantinou, A.V., Eilam, T., Kalantar, M., Totok, A.A., Arnold, W., Snible, E.: An architecture for virtual solution composition and deployment in infrastructure clouds. In: Proceedings of the 3rd International Workshop on Virtualization Technologies in Distributed Computing, VTDC 2009, pp. 9–18. ACM, New York (2009)

[13] Mell, P., Grance, T.: The nist definition of cloud computing. Tech. rep., National Institute of Standard and Technology - NIST (2011)

[14] Mendonça, M., Wasowski, A., Czarnecki, K.: Sat-based analysis of feature models is easy. In: 13th International Conference on Software Product Lines (SPLC 2009), San Francisco, CA, USA (2009)

[15] Sethi, M., Kannan, K., Sachindran, N., Gupta, M.: Rapid deployment of SOA solutions via automated image replication and reconfiguration. In: IEEE International Conference on Services Computing, SCC 2008, vol. 1, pp. 155–162 (July 2008)

[16] Thüm, T., Batory, D.S., Kästner, C.: Reasoning about edits to feature models. In: ICSE, pp. 254–264. IEEE (2009)

[17] Wenzel, S., Berger, T., Riechert, T.: How to configure a configuration management system – an approach based on feature modeling. In: 1st International Workshop on Model-driven Approaches in Software Product Line Engineering (MAPLE 2009) at SPLC 2009, San Francisco, CA (August 2009)

[18] Zhang, T., Du, Z., Chen, Y., Ji, X., Wang, X.: Typical virtual appliances: An optimized mechanism for virtual appliances provisioning and management. Journal of Systems and Software 84(3), 377–387 (2011)

[19] Ziadi, T., Jézéquel, J.M.: Software product line engineering with the UML: Deriving products. In: Käkölä, T., Dueñas, J.C. (eds.) Software Product Lines, pp. 557–588. Springer (2006)

Protocol Conformance Checking of Services with Exceptions

Christian Heike[1], Wolf Zimmermann[2], and Andreas Both[3]

[1] Zuehlke Engineering AG
Wiesenstrasse 10a, CH-8952 Schlieren, Switzerland
christian.heike@zuehlke.com

[2] Universität Halle-Wittenberg, Institut für Informatik, 06099 Halle/Saale, Germany
zimmer@informatik.uni-halle.de

[3] Unister GmbH
Barfußgässchen 11, 04109 Leipzig, Germany
andreas.both@unister-gmbh.de

Abstract. In our previous work we defined a conservative abstraction of the behaviour of service-oriented systems and a contract based on interactions (named service protocol) to be verified. We have achieved modeling unbound concurrency and unbound recursion within this abstraction. However, these works are based only on services that do not raise exceptions. In this paper, we extend our previous work such that service protocols can be verified even if the service interface may raise exceptions.

1 Introduction

Modern software development contains a big share of reusing previously developed software called services. Often these services are developed by third party companies and supplied as Web Service. Our work addresses the topic composability analysis for replaceability, compatibility, and process conformance, which was entitled as a research challenge in [20].

While *stateless* services have no restrictions on the order of the call of operations of the interface, *stateful* services may restrict this order. For example, a file service may expect that a file is first opened for reading, then read operations may follow, and finally the file must be closed. The aim of protocol conformance checking is to statically verify that such protocols are obeyed. Hence, a stateful service should also provide a protocol. In general, this protocol is specified as a finite state machine. However, protocol conformance checking requires to know the behaviour of services. Often, the service providers don't want to provide their code, business process etc., of the service's implementation. In our previous work, we use abstractions [3,5] of the behaviour for that purpose, i.e., each real behaviour corresponds to an abstract behaviour but not vice versa. In our case, the abstract behaviour keeps track of the calls to operations provide by all services in a service-oriented system. Thus, the abstractions must also be

F. De Paoli, E. Pimentel, and G. Zavattaro (Eds.): ESOCC 2012, LNCS 7592, pp. 122–137, 2012.

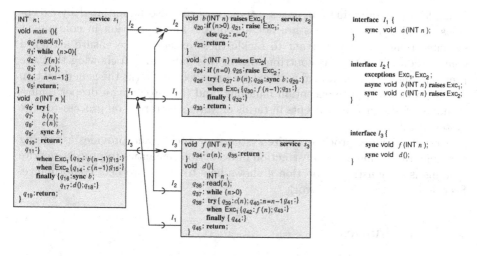

Fig. 1. A Service-Oriented System

published and they can be automatically derived from the source code of the implementation [3,5]. Hence, the implementation of services can still be hidden.

Protocol Conformance Checking can be implemented by verifying the protocol w.r.t. these abstractions. If the protocol conformance is verified, then there is no protocol violation. Abstractions may specify more sequences of operation calls than in the real behaviour. Thus, all real protocol violations are detected but also false alarms are possible. The latter should be avoided as much as possible. Thus, programming language constructs must be abstracted as adequate as possible. In our context, we completely abstract apart from data, but under this restriction the control-flow should be modeled precisely. Currently, abstractions are often specified using Petri-Nets (see e.g. [26,23]), pushdown systems (see e.g. [8,9]), finite state machines (see e.g. [19,25]), or process algebras (see e.g. [7]). Finite state machines and process algebras only allow an adequate modeling of bound concurrency and bound recursion, i.e., the number of parallel threads and the recursion depth are bound by a constant, respectively. [27] shows that with recursion, the language of interactions is not regular but context-free and therefore requires a pushdown-automaton to describe it, i.e., finite state machine or those process algebras not taking into account sequential recursion cannot model it. Furthermore, [27] demonstrates that using finite state machines for abstraction, protocol conformance checking may lead to false positive results if recursive callbacks are present. Unbound recursion can be adequately modeled by pushdown systems, but there is no adequate modeling of unbound concurrency. Petri-Nets may model adequately unbound concurrency but not unbound recursion.

In [3] we have shown that using Mayr's process-rewrite systems [18] both, recursion and parallelism, can be adequately modeled. However, it turned out that the protocol conformance checking problem becomes undecidable. In [3] we have shown an approximation for this model checking problem and how it is possible to deal with it. However, none of these works consider exception handling. As in modern programming languages interactions can also be initiated by exceptions, simplified abstractions are not acceptable for application in component systems. Hence, it is important to tackle these exceptions to ensure a rugged composition of SOAs. The contributions of this paper are (i) showing that the previous concepts cannot deal with exceptions adequately, (ii) the generalization of our previous work to exception handling, and (iii) providing a deeper understanding of abstraction concepts in terms of Mayr's hierarchy on process-rewrite systems [18].

Section 2 defines process-rewrite systems, protocols, and provides a running example. In Section 3, the abstraction of exception semantics to process-rewrite systems is demonstrated. Section 4 shows how to check protocol conformance. Section 5 discusses related work.

2   Preliminaries

In this section, we introduce our model of services and process-rewrite systems according to [18] which are used for describing the abstract behaviour.

A service s *provides* an interface I_s where an interface is a set of type descriptions and procedure signatures with exceptions that may be raised during execution. The implementation of s may call procedures of other services. The *required* interface R_s of s is the set of procedures of other services called by s. A service-oriented system is a directed graph $S \triangleq (WS, C)$ where WS is a set of services such that each $s \in WS$, $p \in R_s$ there is an edge $(s, s') \in C$ with $p \in I_{s'}$. Hence, any call leaving a service $s \in WS$ calls a procedure of another service $s' \in WS$.

There are two kinds of procedures in interfaces, *asynchronous* and *synchronous* procedures. If a synchronous procedure is called, the caller waits until the callee is completed. If an asynchronous procedure is called, the caller and the callee concurrently continue their execution. There might be a synchronize statement **sync** f that is a barrier waiting until the concurrently called procedure f is completed.

Example 1. Fig. 1 shows an example of a service-oriented system consisting of three services s_1, s_2, and s_3 with provided interfaces I_1, I_2, and I_3, respectively. The provided interfaces are shown by filled circles, the required interfaces (partitioned to the called services) are visualized by opened unfilled circles. The service bindings are visualized by arrows. The symbols q_i represent program points indicating each statement. Procedure b of interface I_2 is the only asynchronous procedure. Every other procedure is synchronous. The execution starts with calling *main* of service s_1.

Remark 1. The interface I_s of a service can be specified using WSDL. The exceptions are specified by the **fault**-part in the operations. There are several approaches on Web Service Composition with exception handling, see e.g. [12,16]. In particular, the stub generated from a WSDL interface description of a service s might raise exceptions that can be handled by the client using s.

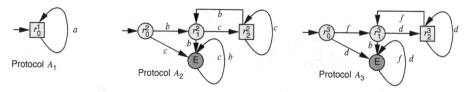

Fig. 2. Protocols of the Services in Fig. 1

Let Q be a finite set. The set $PEX(Q)$ of process-algebraic expressions over Q is the smallest set satisfying:

(i) $Q \subseteq PEX(Q)$

(ii) If $e, e' \in PEX(Q)$ then $e.e' \in PEX(Q)$ and $e \parallel e' \in PEX(Q)$ (*sequential* and *parallel composition*, respectively)

A *process-rewrite system* (short: PRS) is a tuple $\Pi \triangleq (\Sigma, Q, \to, q_0, F)$ where

(i) Q is a finite set (*atomic processes*),

(ii) Σ is finite alphabet disjoint from Q (*actions*),

(iii) $q_0 \in Q$ (the *initial state*)

(iv) $\to \subseteq PEX(Q) \times (\Sigma \uplus \{\lambda\}) \times PEX(Q)$ is a set of *process-rewrite rules* ($\lambda \in \Sigma^*$ is the empty word)

(v) $F \subseteq Q \cup \{\varepsilon\}$ (the set of *final processes*)

The PRS Π defines a derivation relation $\Rightarrow \subseteq PEX(Q) \times \Sigma^* \times PEX(Q)$ (Σ^* is the set of all finite words over Σ) by the following inference rules ($a \in \Sigma \cup \{\lambda\}, x \in \Sigma^*$):

$$\frac{q \xrightarrow{a} q'}{q \xRightarrow{a} q'} \qquad \frac{u \xRightarrow{a} v}{u.w \xRightarrow{a} v.w} \qquad \frac{u \xRightarrow{a} v}{u \parallel w \xRightarrow{a} v \parallel w} \qquad \frac{u \xRightarrow{a} v}{w \parallel u \xRightarrow{a} w \parallel v} \qquad \frac{u \xRightarrow{a} v \quad v \xRightarrow{x} w}{u \xRightarrow{ax} w}$$

$L(\Pi) \triangleq \{w \in \Sigma^* : \exists f \in F \bullet q_0 \xRightarrow{w} f\}$ is the *language accepted by the PRS Π*. Mayr [18] classified the process-rewrite rules according to the class of process-algebraic expressions on the left-hand side and right-hand side, respectively: Class 1 allows only single states, class S only sequential expressions, class P only parallel expressions, and class G allows both, sequential and parallel expressions. An (x, y)-*PRS*, $x, y \in \{1, S, P, G\}$ allows only rules whose left-hand sides belong to class x and whose right-hand sides belong to class y. Note that $(1, 1)$-PRSs correspond to possibly non-deterministic finite state machines (with λ-transitions).

In the context of this paper, we assume that a protocol of a service s is given by a finite state machine $A_s \triangleq (\Sigma_s, R_s, \to_s, r_0^s, F_s)$ where Σ_s denotes the set of operations symbols in the interface of service s, R_s are the states of s, r_0^s is the state when s is started by a client, and F_s is the set of final states. A final state must be reached when the client finishes the use of s. Thus, $L(A_s)$ defines the set of legal sequences of operation calls to s. Fig. 2 shows the state diagrams of protocols of the services in Fig. 1 which are used as an example throughout this paper (final states are indicated by squares and initial states by an arrow without source). If the protocols A_2 and A_3 reach state E, respectively, then a protocol violation occurs. Here, A_2 permits only calls of b followed by a least one call of c; all other sequences lead to an error state.

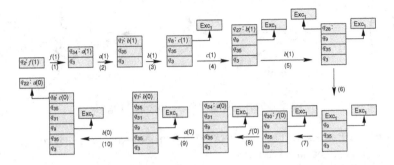

Fig. 3. A Protocol Violation in Fig. 1

Example 2. Fig. 3 shows a possible execution of the service-oriented system in Fig. 1 when the value 1 is read. Steps (1) and (2) are synchronous calls. The program point after the call is pushed onto the runtime stack. Step (3) is an asynchronous call. In this case the stack forks, i.e., it has now two branches: one for the caller and one for the callee. This kind of runtime structure is called a *cactus stack*. [10,14] showed that cactus stack can be used as a runtime system for concurrent processes. The call of $b(1)$ raises exception Exc_1. In a step, all interleavings are possible, i.e. any top element of a stack in the cactus stack can be taken for the next step. In our case, we take the call $c(1)$ (Step 4). Then in (5), $b(1)$ is called, which also raises Exc_1. Since this exception is not handled, the synchronize statement results in Exc_1 (Step (6)). Step (7) shows that now the exception handler in the body of c is being executed and this calls $f(0)$. Then – as above $a(0)$ is called. Note that the branch from q_9 cannot be removed until q_9 is on the top of the (main-) stack.

This execution demonstrates that protocol A_2 is violated because service s_2 receives the calls $b(1)$, $c(1)$, $b(1)$, $b(0)$, i.e., A_2 will be in state E after this sequence. Furthermore, this sequence stems from the execution of an exception handler.

Furthermore, Section 3 defines the use of a service s in service-oriented system S by a PRS $U_s \triangleq (\Sigma_s, Q, \rightarrow, q_0, F)$ where Q is the set of program points in S (i.e., all points before the statements, cf. Fig. 1) and the set of exceptional states, q_0 is the initial program point (the point where the execution starts), and F are the program points of all statements that stop the execution. This set includes in particular the exceptional states. The protocol conformance checking problem checks for each service s of S whether $L(U_s) \subseteq L(A_s)$.

Remark 2. [3,2,5] pointed out that process-rewrite systems provide an adequate modeling technique for unbound recursion and unbound parallelism: Process-algebraic expressions correspond to cactus stacks. For example, the cactus stack in Fig. 3 after step (10) can be represented by the process-algebraic expression $(((q_8\|q_{22}).q_{35}.q_{31}.q_9)\| q_{Exc_1}).q_{35}.q_3$. Thus, process-rewrite systems are an adequate modelling technique for such runtime systems.

Table 1. Abstraction of Control Structures (without Exception Handling) according to [3,2]

Control Structure	Abstraction	Explanation
$q : x := a; q' :$	$q \xrightarrow{\lambda} q'$	Assignments have no interaction. q' is the program point of the statement being executed after $x := a$.
$q : \mathbf{if}(e)\ q' : \cdots$ $\quad \mathbf{else}\ q'' : \cdots$ $\bar{q} : \cdots$	$q \xrightarrow{\lambda} q'$ $q \xrightarrow{\lambda} q''$	No interaction if the conditional is being decided. $\bar{q}$ is the program point of the statement being executed after the last statement of the then- and else-part, respectively.
$q : \quad \mathbf{while}(e)\ q' : \cdots$ $q'' : \cdots$	$q \xrightarrow{\lambda} q'$ $q \xrightarrow{\lambda} q''$	No interaction if the condition is being decided. q is the program point of the statement being executed after the last statement of the loop body.
$q : p(\cdots); q' : \cdots$ $\vdots$ $p(\cdots)\{q'' : \cdots\}$	$q \xrightarrow{\lambda} q''.q'$ (p internal) $q \xrightarrow{p} q''.q'$ (p external)	Call of a synchronous procedure p: The program point q' of the statement to be executed after the call is pushed onto the stack. The execution continues with first program point q'' of p.
$q : p(\cdots); q' : \cdots$ $\vdots$ $p(\cdots)\{q'' : \cdots\}$	$q \xrightarrow{\lambda} q' \parallel q''$ (p internal) $q \xrightarrow{p} q' \parallel q''$ (p external)	Call of an asynchronous procedure p: The execution can be continued concurrently with the statement at program point q' after the call and the statement at the first program point q'' of p
$p(\cdots)\{$ $\cdots q : \mathbf{return}; \cdots$ $\}$	p synchronous: $\quad q.q' \xrightarrow{\lambda} q'$ p asynchronous: $\quad q \parallel q' \xrightarrow{\lambda} q'$ $\quad q' \parallel q \xrightarrow{\lambda} q'$	The current synchronous procedure is left and the execution continues with the statement after the call. The corresponding program point q' was pushed upon call. The last program point of the procedure is erased from the stack. If the procedure is asynchronous, the forked execution is being joined.
$q : \mathbf{sync}\ p; q' : \cdots$ $\vdots$ $p(\cdots)\{\cdots$ $\quad q'' : \mathbf{return}; \cdots\}$	$q \parallel q'' \xrightarrow{\lambda} q'$	The statement after q (at program point q') can only be executed when the previously called asynchronous procedure p returns.

3   Abstraction of Behaviour

We show how the behaviour of services can be abstracted to process-rewrite systems. The states are all program points of the implementations of the services in a service-oriented systems and all exceptional states. Table 1 summarizes the abstraction rules from our previous work. The only difference is that our previous work used $q \xrightarrow{\lambda} \varepsilon$ for a procedure return where ε denotes the empty process. ε is the identity w.r.t. . and $\parallel$. Note that programming language concepts expressing fork-join parallelism (as e.g., in BPEL) can be abstracted analogously to calling asynchronous procedures and synchronize with them, respectively.

A service-oriented system S is abstracted to a process-rewrite system $\Pi_S \triangleq (\Sigma, Q, \rightarrow, q_0, F)$ where $\Sigma = \bigcup_{s \in S} \Sigma_s$ is the set of all procedures in the interface descriptions of the services of S, $Q \triangleq PP \cup Exceptions$, PP is the set of program points, $Exceptions \triangleq \{q_E : E \text{ is an exception}\}$, $\rightarrow$ is defined by Table 1 and Table 2, q_0 is the program point where S starts, $F \triangleq Q_F \cup Exceptions$, and Q_F is the set of program points where the main program returns (i.e., the execution of the program terminates).

Remark 3. In [3], we have shown how Π_S can be constructed in a compositional way. For each $s \in S$, a PRS Π_s is derived and these are glued together to obtain Π_S. For reasons of space, we omit this construction and refer to [3]. In addition to [3] a service-oriented system S might also terminate in an exceptional state. Therefore, these states are also final.

In this paper, we focus on exception handling. Before discussing the abstraction of exception handling, its semantics must be explained. The statement **raise** E raises the exception E. This means the execution is being interrupted, i.e., it is not being continued by the execution of the next statement. If the exception E has been raised outside of **try**-block, then the current procedure stops with the exception E, i.e., the corresponding call raises E. A try statement

> **try** { $\cdots$ }
> **when** E_1 { $\cdots$ }
>
> $\vdots$
>
> **when** E_n { $\cdots$ }
> **finally** { $\cdots$ }

is executed as follows (this is according to *Java, C#, BPEL*): The statements in the try block are being executed as usual. If an exception E is raised, then the block of the first exception handler **when** E_i { $\cdots$ } with $E_i = E$ is executed[1]. If E is different from any exceptions in the exception handlers, the try statement terminates with exception E. The execution of the try statement definitely finishes with the execution of the finally block, no matter what happens inside the try block or the exception handler. This might lead to the fact that a return statement doesn't return from a procedure. For example, the return statement at program point q_{10} in Fig. 1 is not executed because the finally block must be executed. However, this would be different, if there would be no finally block. In this case, the procedure returns as usual.

Table 2 defines the abstraction required for exception handling. Rule (1) is straightforward, it simply rewrites the current state into the raised exceptional state and rule (6) continues with the corresponding exception handler. Rules (2)–(5) are required because the finally block must be executed in any case. For this purpose, the program point q_5 of the first statement of the finally-block is pushed onto the stack. If the execution of the try block doesn't raise an exception, then q_2 is reached, i.e. $q_1 \overset{w}{\Rightarrow} q_2$ for a $w \in \Sigma^*$. Thus, we have $q \overset{\lambda}{\Rightarrow} q_1.q_5 \overset{w}{\Rightarrow} q_2.q_5 \overset{\lambda}{\Rightarrow} q_5$. Thus, the abstraction reaches q_5 as desired. Furthermore, as mentioned above, if a **return**-statement is executed in the try block, then it doesn't return from the procedure. Instead, the finally block is being executed. Suppose that q_1 reaches a program point q' that executes a **return**-statement, i.e. $q_1 \overset{w}{\Rightarrow} q'$ for a $w \in \Sigma^*$. With rule (4) we have $q \overset{\lambda}{\Rightarrow} q_1.q_5 \overset{w}{\Rightarrow} q'.q_5 \overset{\lambda}{\Rightarrow} q_5$ Therefore, the rather complicated semantics of a **return**-statement within a try block is abstracted correctly.

Rules (6) and (7) have a role analogous to rules (2) and (3), respectively, for the corresponding exception handler. However, there is no need to push q_5 onto the stack as it is already there if the handler is being executed, i.e.,

---

[1] This can be easily extended to a subtype hierarchy of exception types.

Table 2. Abstraction of Exception Handling

q : **raise** E;	$q \xrightarrow{\lambda} q_E$	(1)	Raising an exception results in the corresponding exceptional state.

q : **try** $\{q_1 : \cdots$
    $q' :$ **return**; $\cdots$
$q_2 :$ $\}$
    $\cdots$
   when E $\{q_3 : \cdots q_4 :\}$
    $\cdots$
   finally $\{q_5 : \cdots q_6 :\}$
$q_7 : \cdots$
	$q \xrightarrow{\lambda} q_1.q_5$
	$q_2.q_5 \xrightarrow{\lambda} q_5$
	$q'.q_5 \xrightarrow{\lambda} q_5$
	$q_6 \xrightarrow{\lambda} q_7$
		(2)
		(3)
		(4)
		(5)
			q_1 is the program point at the first statement of the try block, q_2 is the program point after the last statement of the try block, q_5 is the program point of the first statement of the finally block, and q_6 is the program point after the last statement of the finally block. A return statement in an exception handler is abstracted to a rule analogous to (4).

	$q_E.q_5 \xrightarrow{\lambda} q_3.q_5$ $q_4.q_5 \xrightarrow{\lambda} q_5$	(6) (7)	q_3 is the program point at the first statement of the exception handling block for exception E and q_4 is the program point after the last statement of the exception handling block for E.
	$q_{E'}.q_5 \xrightarrow{\lambda} q_5.q_{E'}$ $q_6.q_{E'} \xrightarrow{\lambda} q_{E'}$	(8) (9)	E' is an unhandled exception, i.e., the try-block ends with state $q_{E'}$. However, finally must be executed in any case.
sync $p(\cdots)$ **raises** E$\{\cdots\}$ $\cdots q : p(\cdots)$; $q' : \cdots$	$q_E.q' \xrightarrow{\lambda} q_E$	(10)	q' is the program point after the call of p. If E is raised in the body of p and remains unhandled, the call ends with exception E.

async $p(\cdots)$ **raises** E$\{$
    $\cdots q'' :$ **return**; $\cdots\}$
    $\cdots p(\cdots);\cdots$
$q :$ **sync** p; $q' : \cdots$
	$q_E \parallel q \xrightarrow{\lambda} q_E$
	$q \parallel q_E \xrightarrow{\lambda} q_E$
	$q_E \parallel q'' \xrightarrow{\lambda} q_E$
	$q'' \parallel q_E \xrightarrow{\lambda} q_E$
	$q_E \parallel q_{E'} \xrightarrow{\lambda} q_E$
	$q_{E'} \parallel q_E \xrightarrow{\lambda} q_E$
		(11)
		(12)
		(13)
		(14)
		(15)
		(16)
			q' is the program point after synchronization with p. If E is raised in the body of p and remains unhandled, the the call ends with exception E, i.e., the exceptional state is kept after synchronization and return, respectively. If both concurrent executions finish with an exception, there is a non-deterministic choice between one of these exceptions.

it holds $q \xRightarrow{\lambda} q_1.q_5 \xRightarrow{v} q_E.q_5 \xRightarrow{\lambda} q_3.q_5 \xRightarrow{w} q_4.q_5 \xRightarrow{\lambda} q_5$ for a $v, w \in \Sigma^*$. The second last step and the last step use rules (6) and (7), respectively. If a **return**-statement is being executed in the exception handler, the same arguments as for the execution of a **return**-statement in the try-block apply for the correctness of the abstraction. A rule $q_E \to q_3$ would lead to incorrect abstractions in case of nested try blocks where both handle exception E. With the state q_5 in the context it is possible to identify the corresponding exception handler.

Rules (8) and (9) are needed because a try-block or an exception handler might raise unhandled exceptions and the finally-block must alsob be executed under these circumstances. Suppose, it holds $q \xRightarrow{\lambda} q_1.q_5 \xRightarrow{v} q_{E'}.q_5$ for a $v \in \Sigma^*$ and $q_5 \xRightarrow{w} q_6$ for a $w \in \Sigma^*$. Then, a correct abstraction requires $q \xRightarrow{vw} q_{E'}$, i.e., at the end of the try block, the exceptional state is reached. Using the above observations, we obtain $q \xRightarrow{\lambda} q_1.q_5 \xRightarrow{v} q_{E'}.q_5 \xRightarrow{\lambda} q_5.q_{E'} \xRightarrow{w} q_6.q_{E'} \xRightarrow{\lambda} q_{E'}$ using rules (8) and (9). The correctness of rules (10)–(16) is already justified in Table 2.

The use of a service s can be derived from Π_S by replacing all transition rules $e \xrightarrow{f} e'$, $f \notin \Sigma_s \cup \{\lambda\}$, by $e \xrightarrow{\lambda} e'$. Thus, all interactions except calls to service s are ignored.

Example 3. Fig. 4 shows the process-rewrite rules for the abstraction of the service-oriented system in Fig. 1. The initial state is q_0, the set of final states is $F = \{q_9, q_{\mathsf{Exc}_1}, q_{\mathsf{Exc}_2}\}$. With these rules, we can construct a derivation that corresponds to the execution in Fig. 3 (the rule is as a lower index the arrow):

procedure *main*:
(1) $q_0 \xrightarrow{\lambda} q_1$ (2) $q_1 \xrightarrow{\lambda} q_2$ (3) $q_1 \xrightarrow{\lambda} q_5$ (4) $q_2 \xrightarrow{f} q_{34} \cdot q_3$ (5) $q_3 \xrightarrow{c} q_{24} \cdot q_4$ (6) $q_4 \xrightarrow{\lambda} q_5$

procedure *a*:
(7) $q_6 \xrightarrow{\lambda} q_7 \cdot q_{16}$ (14) $q_{Exc_2} \| q_{Exc_1} \xrightarrow{\lambda} q_{Exc_1}$ (20) $q_{Exc_1} \cdot q_{16} \xrightarrow{\lambda} q_{12} \cdot q_{16}$ (26) $q_{16} \| q_{23} \xrightarrow{\lambda} q_{17}$

(8) $q_7 \xrightarrow{c} q_8 \| q_{20}$ (15) $q_{Exc_1} \| q_{Exc_2} \xrightarrow{\lambda} q_{Exc_1}$ (21) $q_{Exc_2} {}_; q_{16} \xrightarrow{\lambda} q_{14} \cdot q_{16}$ (27) $q_{16} \|_, q_{Exc_1} \xrightarrow{\lambda} q_{Exc_1}$

(9) $q_8 \xrightarrow{c} q_{24} \cdot q_9$ (16) $q_{Exc_1} \| q_{Exc_1} \xrightarrow{\lambda} q_{Exc_1}$ (22) $q_{12} \xrightarrow{\lambda} q_{13} \| q_{20}$ (28) $q_{17} \xrightarrow{\lambda} q_{36} \cdot q_{18}$

(10) $q_9 \| q_{23} \xrightarrow{\lambda} q_{10}$ (17) $q_{10} \cdot q_{22} \xrightarrow{\lambda} q_{23}$ (23) $q_{13} \cdot q_{16} \xrightarrow{c} q_{16}$ (29) $q_{18} \xrightarrow{\lambda} q_{19}$

(11) $q_{23} \| q_9 \xrightarrow{\lambda} q_{10}$ (18) $q_{10} \cdot q_{16} \xrightarrow{\lambda} q_{16}$ (24) $q_{14} \xrightarrow{c} q_{24} \cdot q_{15}$ (30) $q_{19} \cdot q_{23} \xrightarrow{\lambda} q_{23}$

(12) $q_{Exc_1} \| q_9 \xrightarrow{\lambda} q_{Exc_1}$ (19) $q_{11} \cdot q_{16} \xrightarrow{\lambda} q_{16}$ (25) $q_{15} \cdot q_{16} \xrightarrow{\lambda} q_{16}$ (31) $q_{19} \cdot q_{35} \xrightarrow{\lambda} q_{35}$

(32) $q_9 \| q_{Exc_1} \xrightarrow{\lambda} q_{Exc_1}$

procedure *b*:
(33) $q_{20} \xrightarrow{\lambda} q_{21}$ (34) $q_{20} \xrightarrow{\lambda} q_{22}$ (35) $q_{21} \xrightarrow{\lambda} q_{Exc_1}$ (36) $q_{22} \xrightarrow{\lambda} q_{23}$

procedure *c*:
(37) $q_{24} \xrightarrow{\lambda} q_{25}$ (42) $q_{28} \| q_{23} \xrightarrow{\lambda} q_{29}$ (47) $q_{Exc_1} {}_; q_{32} \xrightarrow{\lambda} q_{30} \cdot q_{32}$ (52) $q_{32} \xrightarrow{\lambda} q_{33}$

(38) $q_{24} \xrightarrow{\lambda} q_{26}$ (43) $q_{23} \| q_{28} \xrightarrow{\lambda} q_{29}$ (48) $q_{30} \xrightarrow{\lambda} q_{34} \cdot q_{31}$ (53) $q_{33} \cdot q_4 \xrightarrow{\lambda} q_4$

(39) $q_{25} \xrightarrow{\lambda} q_{Exc_2}$ (44) $q_{Exc_1} \| q_{28} \xrightarrow{\lambda} q_{Exc_1}$ (49) $q_{31} \cdot q_{32} \xrightarrow{\lambda} q_{32}$ (54) $q_{33} \cdot q_9 \xrightarrow{\lambda} q_9$

(40) $q_{26} \xrightarrow{b} q_{27} \cdot q_{32}$ (45) $q_{28} \| q_{Exc_1} \xrightarrow{\lambda} q_{Exc_1}$ (50) $q_{Exc_2} \cdot q_{32} \xrightarrow{\lambda} q_{32} \cdot q_{Exc_2}$ (55) $q_{33} \cdot q_{39} \xrightarrow{\lambda} q_{39}$

(41) $q_{27} \xrightarrow{b} q_{28} \| q_{20}$ (46) $q_{29} \cdot q_{32} \xrightarrow{\lambda} q_{32}$ (51) $q_{32} \cdot q_{Exc_2} \xrightarrow{\lambda} q_{Exc_2}$

procedure *f*
(56) $q_{34} \xrightarrow{a} q_6 \cdot q_{35}$ (57) $q_{35} \cdot q_3 \xrightarrow{\lambda} q_3$ (58) $q_{35} \cdot q_{31} \xrightarrow{\lambda} q_{31}$ (59) $q_{35} \cdot q_{43} \xrightarrow{\lambda} q_{43}$

procedure *d*
(60) $q_{36} \xrightarrow{\lambda} q_{37}$ (64) $q_{39} \xrightarrow{c} q_{24} \cdot q_{40}$ (68) $q_{42} \xrightarrow{f} q_{34} \cdot q_{43}$ (72) $q_{44} \xrightarrow{\lambda} q_{45}$

(61) $q_{37} \xrightarrow{\lambda} q_{38}$ (65) $q_{40} \xrightarrow{\lambda} q_{41}$ (69) $q_{43} \cdot q_{44} \xrightarrow{\lambda} q_{44}$ (73) $q_{45} \cdot q_{18} \xrightarrow{\lambda} q_{18}$

(62) $q_{37} \xrightarrow{\lambda} q_{45}$ (66) $q_{41} \cdot q_{44} \xrightarrow{\lambda} q_{44}$ (70) $q_{Exc_2} \cdot q_{44} \xrightarrow{\lambda} q_{44} \cdot q_{Exc_2}$

(63) $q_{38} \xrightarrow{\lambda} q_{39} \cdot q_{44}$ (67) $q_{Exc_1} \cdot q_{44} \xrightarrow{\lambda} q_{42} \cdot q_{44}$ (71) $q_{44} \cdot q_{Exc_2} \xrightarrow{\lambda} q_{Exc_2}$

Fig. 4. Abstraction of the Services in Fig. 1

$q_0 \xrightarrow{\lambda}_{(2)} q_2 \xrightarrow{f}_{(4)} q_{34} \cdot q_3 \xrightarrow{a}_{(56)} q_6 \cdot q_{35} \cdot q_3 \xrightarrow{\lambda}_{(7)} q_7 \cdot q_{16} \cdot q_{35} \cdot q_3 \xrightarrow{b}_{(8)} (q_8 \| q_{20}) \cdot q_{16} \cdot q_{35} \cdot q_3$

$\xrightarrow{\lambda}_{(33)} (q_8 \| q_{21}) \cdot q_{16} \cdot q_{35} \cdot q_3 \xrightarrow{\lambda}_{(35)} (q_8 \| q_{Exc_1}) \cdot q_{16} \cdot q_{35} \cdot q_3 \xrightarrow{\lambda}_{(9)} ((q_{24} \cdot q_9) \| q_{Exc_1}) \cdot q_{16} \cdot q_{35} \cdot q_3$

$\xrightarrow{\lambda}_{(38)} ((q_{26} \cdot q_9) \| q_{Exc_1}) \cdot q_{16} \cdot q_{35} \cdot q_3 \xrightarrow{\lambda}_{(40)} ((q_{27} \cdot q_{32} \cdot q_9) \| q_{Exc_1}) \cdot q_{16} \cdot q_{35} \cdot q_3$

$\xrightarrow{\lambda}_{(41)} (((q_{28} \| q_{20}) \cdot q_{32} \cdot q_9) \| q_{Exc_1}) \cdot q_{16} \cdot q_{35} \cdot q_3 \xrightarrow{\lambda}_{(33)} (((q_{28} \| q_{21}) \cdot q_{32} \cdot q_9) \| q_{Exc_1}) \cdot q_{16} \cdot q_{35} \cdot q_3$

$\xrightarrow{\lambda}_{(35)} (((q_{28} \| q_{Exc_1}) \cdot q_{32} \cdot q_9) \| q_{Exc_1}) \cdot q_{16} \cdot q_{35} \cdot q_3 \xrightarrow{\lambda}_{(45)} ((q_{Exc_1} \cdot q_{32} \cdot q_9) \| q_{Exc_1}) \cdot q_{16} \cdot q_{35} \cdot q_3$

$\xrightarrow{\lambda}_{(47)} ((q_{30} \cdot q_{32} \cdot q_9) \| q_{Exc_1}) \cdot q_{16} \cdot q_{35} \cdot q_3 \xrightarrow{\lambda}_{(48)} ((q_{34} \cdot q_{31} \cdot q_{32} \cdot q_9) \| q_{Exc_1}) \cdot q_{16} \cdot q_{35} \cdot q_3$

$\xrightarrow{a}_{(56)} ((q_6 \cdot q_{35} \cdot q_{31} \cdot q_{32} \cdot q_9) \| q_{Exc_1}) \cdot q_{16} \cdot q_{35} \cdot q_3 \xrightarrow{\lambda}_{(7)} ((q_7 \cdot q_{16} \cdot q_{35} \cdot q_{31} \cdot q_{32} \cdot q_9) \| q_{Exc_1}) \cdot q_{16} \cdot q_{35} \cdot q_3$

$\xrightarrow{b}_{(8)} (((q_8 \| q_{20}) \cdot q_{16} \cdot q_{35} \cdot q_{31} \cdot q_{32} \cdot q_9) \| q_{Exc_1}) \cdot q_{16} \cdot q_{35} \cdot q_3$

$\xrightarrow{\lambda}_{(34)} (((q_8 \| q_{22}) \cdot q_{16} \cdot q_{35} \cdot q_{31} \cdot q_{32} \cdot q_9) \| q_{Exc_1}) \cdot q_{16} \cdot q_{35} \cdot q_3$

At the end of the first line, rules (9) and rules (33) are applicable. It is worth to compare the last expression of the third line with the cactus stack in Fig. 3 after step (3). It has basically the same shape except there are program points q_{32} and q_{16} not present in the cactus stack. These program points are the first program points of the finally blocks and are pushed onto the stack when the corresponding try-statement is executed.

4   Protocol Conformance Checking

For checking the conformance of a protocol of a service s in a service-oriented system S, it must be checked whether $L(U_s) \subseteq L(A_s)$ where the use of s is defined by the PRS $U_s \triangleq (\Sigma_s, Q, \to, q_0, F)$ and $A_s \triangleq (\Sigma_s, R_s, \to_s, r_0^s, F_s)$ is the finite state machine defining the protocol of s. In [3] we have shown that this problem is undecidable for the classes of (x, G) process-rewrite systems, i.e., if sequential compositon and parallel composition occurs in a PRS, the protocol conformance checking becomes undecidable.

We therefore construct in a similar way a PRS K, the *Combined Abstraction*, such $L(K) \supseteq L(U_s) \cap (\Sigma_s^* \setminus L(A_s))$ and check whether $L(K) \neq \emptyset$. The PRS K

$$T_{11} \triangleq \{(r,q) \xrightarrow{\alpha}_K (r',q') : \alpha \in \Sigma_s \cup \{\lambda\} \wedge r, r' \in R_s \wedge q, q' \in Q \wedge (r \xrightarrow{\alpha}_s r') \wedge (q \xrightarrow{\alpha} q')\}$$

$$T_{1S} \triangleq (r,q) \xrightarrow{\alpha}_K (r',q').(r'',q'') : \alpha \in \Sigma_s \cup \{\lambda\} \wedge r, r', r'' \in R_s \wedge$$
$$q, q', q'' \in Q \wedge (r \xrightarrow{\alpha}_s r') \wedge (q \xrightarrow{\alpha} q'.q'')\}$$

$$T_{S1} \triangleq \{(r,q).(r'',q') \xrightarrow{\alpha}_K (r',q'') : \alpha \in \Sigma_s \cup \{\lambda\} \wedge r, r', r'' \in R_s \wedge$$
$$q, q', q'' \in Q \wedge (r \xrightarrow{\alpha}_s r') \wedge (q.q' \xrightarrow{\alpha} q'')\}$$

$$T_{1P} \triangleq (r,q) \xrightarrow{\alpha}_K (r',q') \parallel (r',q'') : \alpha \in \Sigma_s \cup \{\lambda\} \wedge r, r' \in R_s \wedge$$
$$q, q', q'' \in Q \wedge (r \xrightarrow{\alpha}_s r') \wedge (q \xrightarrow{\alpha} q' \parallel q'')\}$$

$$T_{P1} \triangleq \{(r,q) \parallel (r,q') \xrightarrow{\alpha}_K (r',q'') : \alpha \in \Sigma_s \cup \{\lambda\} \wedge r, r' \in R_s \wedge$$
$$q, q', q'' \in Q \wedge (r \xrightarrow{\alpha}_s r') \wedge (q \parallel q' \xrightarrow{\alpha} q'')\}$$

$$T_0 \quad \triangleq \{(r,q) \xrightarrow{\lambda}_K (r',q) : r, r' \in R_s \wedge q \in Q \wedge \exists \alpha \in \Sigma \cup \{\lambda\} \bullet r \xrightarrow{\alpha}_s r'\}$$

Fig. 5. Transition Rules for the Combined Abstraction

belongs to the same class of PRS as U_s and it is $L(K) = L(U_s) \cap (\Sigma_s^* \setminus L(A_s))$ if U_s belongs to one of the classes of (x,y)-PRSs, $y \in \{1, S\}$. Note that $\Sigma_s^* \setminus A_s$ is the language accepted by the finite state machine $\bar{A}_s \triangleq (\Sigma_s, R_s, \rightarrow_s, r_0^s, \bar{F})$ where $\bar{F}_s \triangleq sR_s \setminus F_s$ is the set of all non-final states of A_s.

In [3], we have defined the Combined Abstraction for the class of $(1, G)$-PRS and in [2], we have extended this to the class of (P, G)-PRS. Here, we have to extend it to the class of (G, G)-PRS. It is based on a normalized process-rewrite system that consists only of rules of the forms $q \xrightarrow{\alpha} q'$, $q.q' \xrightarrow{\alpha} q''$, $q \xrightarrow{\alpha} q'.q''$, $q \parallel q' \xrightarrow{\alpha} q''$, and $q \xrightarrow{\alpha} q' \parallel q''$. In [18] it is shown that for any PRS Π there exists a normalized PRS Π' with $L(\Pi) = L(\Pi')$. However, Π' may have more atomic processes.

In order to deal with (G, G)-PRS we slightly change the construction of [3] and base it directly on the construction of a pushdown system in [15] that accepts the intersection of a context-free language and a regular language. The *Combined Abstraction* of $U_s = (\Sigma_s, Q, \rightarrow, q_0, F)$ and $\bar{A}_s = (\Sigma_s, R_s, \rightarrow_s, r_0^s, \bar{F}_s)$ is a PRS $K \triangleq (\Sigma_s, Q_K, \rightarrow_K, q_0^K, F_K)$ where $Q_K \triangleq R_s \times Q$, $q_0^k \triangleq (r_0, q_0)$, $\rightarrow_K \triangleq T_{11} \cup T_{1S} \cup T_{S1} \cup T_{1P} \cup T_{P1} \cup T_0$ as defined in Fig. 5, and $F_K \triangleq F_s \times F$.

The main idea is that for any process-algebraic expression $e \in PEX(Q)$, and any $w \in \Sigma_s^*$ such that $e \xrightarrow{w} f$ for a final process $f \in F$, and any $r \in R_s$ such that $r \xrightarrow{w}_s r_f$ for an $r_f \in F_s$, there is a process-algebraic expression $e' \in PEX(Q_K)$ such that $e' \xrightarrow{w}_K f'$ for a $f' \in F_K$. More precisely, e and e' have the same shape, i.e., e is obtained from e' by removing the first component contained in each atomic process of e'. Formally, there is function $\pi : PEX(Q_K) \mapsto PEX(Q)$ performing this mapping ($\pi((r,q) \triangleq q$ and $\pi(e \circ e') \triangleq \pi(e) \circ \pi(e')$ for $\circ \in \{., \parallel\}$). Furthermore, the top states of e must be in state r. This can be formalized by a partial function $\sigma : PEX(Q_K) \mapsto R_s$ defined by:

$$\sigma((r,q)) \quad \triangleq r \qquad\qquad \sigma(((r,q) \parallel (r,q')) \circ e') \triangleq \sigma((r,q) \circ e')$$
$$\sigma((r,q).e') \triangleq (r,q) \qquad \sigma(((r,q) \parallel (r',q')) \circ e') \triangleq undef$$

for any $e' \in PEX(Q_K)$, $\circ \in \{., \parallel\}$. Note that this means all states on the top of the stacks in a cactus stack have the same protocol state. It is undefined if the protocol state differs. The latter makes no sense because there is only one protocol of service s.

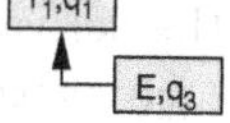

The transition rules T_{11}, T_{1S}, and T_{S1} are a slight generalization of those in [15]. Note that $r \xrightarrow{\lambda}_s r$, and for $a \in \Sigma_s$ it

Fig. 6. Inconsistent Cactus Stack

is $r \xrightarrow{a}_s r'$ iff $r \xrightarrow{a}_s r'$. The transition rules T_{1P} and T_{P1} are straightforward. The ideas stem from [3,2]. The transition rules T_0 are required for maintaining a consistent state of the protocol as demonstrated by Example 4:

Example 4. Consider the finite state machine A_2 in Fig. 2 and suppose that U_s contains the following transition rules $q_0 \xrightarrow{b} q_1 \parallel q_2$, $q_1 \xrightarrow{c} q_3$, $q_2 \xrightarrow{b} q_3$, $q_3 \parallel q_3 \xrightarrow{c} q_4$ where q_4 is the final state. Then $bbcc \in L(U_s) \setminus L(A_2)$, i.e., there is a protocol violation. Without the rules in T_0, we may construct the following derivations:

$$
\begin{aligned}
q_K &\xrightarrow{\lambda} (r_0^2, q_0) && \text{by } T_S \\
&\xrightarrow{b} (r_1^2, q_1) \parallel (r_1^2, q_2) && \text{by } T_{1P} \\
&\xrightarrow{b} (r_1^2, q_1) \parallel (E, q_3) && \text{by } T_{11} \\
&\xrightarrow{c} (r_1^2, q_1) \parallel (E, q_4) && \text{by } T_{11} \\
&\xrightarrow{c} (r_2^2, q_3) \parallel (E, q_4) && \text{by } T_{11}
\end{aligned}
\qquad
\begin{aligned}
q_K &\xrightarrow{\lambda} (r_0^2, q_0) && \text{by } T_S \\
&\xrightarrow{b} (r_1^2, q_1) \parallel (r_1^2, q_2) && \text{by } T_{1P} \\
&\xrightarrow{b} (r_1^2, q_1) \parallel (E, q_3) && \text{by } T_{11} \\
&\xrightarrow{c} (r_2^2, q_3) \parallel (E, q_3) && \text{by } T_{11} \\
&\xrightarrow{c} (r_2^2, q_4) \parallel (E, q_3) && \text{by } T_{11}
\end{aligned}
$$

For none of these two process-algebraic expressions, there are λ-transitions that lead to a final state. Thus, the protocol violation is not detected. The reason is that for both derivations, a change of the protocol state was not taken into account. For both derivations, after the second step, the left operand of $\parallel$ still indicates that A_2 is in state r_1^2 although by the transitions the (final) protocol state E is reached for the right operand. Fig. 6 shows the corresponding cactus stack. Each top element of a cactus stack should have the same protocol state because there is only one protocol and therefore the protocol state must be unique. With the rules of T_0 it is possible to change the protocol state of the left operand to E before applying another transition rule. Thus $(r_1^2, q_1) \parallel (E, q_3) \xrightarrow{\lambda} (E, q_1) \parallel (E, q_3) \xrightarrow{c} (E, q_3) \parallel (E, q_3) \xrightarrow{c} (E, q_4) \in F_K$ for both cases. Hence, the protocol violation is detected.

Lemma 1 ([5]). *Let $U_s \triangleq (\Sigma_s, Q, \to, q_0, F)$ be a PRS , $\bar{A}_s \triangleq (\Sigma_s, R_s, \to_s, r_0^s, \bar{F}_s)$ be a finite state machine, and $K \triangleq (\Sigma_s, Q_K, \to_K, q_0^K, F_K)$ be the Combined Abstraction of U_s and $\bar{A}_s$. Furthermore, let $e \in PEX(Q_K)$ and $w \in \Sigma_s*$ such that $\pi(e) \xrightarrow{w} f \in F$ and $r \in R_s$ such that $r \xrightarrow{w} \bar{r} \in \bar{F}_s$. Then there is a unique $e' \in PEX(Q_K)$ such that $e \xrightarrow{\lambda}_K e'$, $\pi(e') = \pi(e)$, and $\sigma(e') = r$.*

This can be achieved by applying only rules from T_0 (according to Example 4). All protocol states in top elements of the cactus stack of the Combined Abstractions are changed to r.

Theorem 1. *Let $U_s \triangleq (\Sigma_s, Q, \to, q_0, F)$ be a PRS , $\bar{A}_s \triangleq (\Sigma_s, R_s, \to_s, r_0^s, \bar{F}_s)$ be a finite state machine, and $K \triangleq (\Sigma_s, Q_K, \to_K, q_0^K, F_K)$ be the Combined Abstraction of U_s and $\bar{A}_s$. Then $L(U_s) \cap L(\bar{A}_s) \subseteq L(K)$*

Proof. (Sketch) The following stronger claim is proven by induction on the length of the derivation:
For any process-algebraic expression $e \in PEX(Q)$ and any state $r \in R_s$, there is a process-algebraic expression $e' \in PEX(Q)$ with $\pi(e') = e$ and $\sigma(e') = r$ satisfying the following property for each $x \in \Sigma_s^*$: If there is a final state $f \in F$ such that $e \xrightarrow{x} f$ and there is a non-final protocol state $\bar{r} \in \bar{F}_s$ such that $r \xrightarrow{x}_s \bar{r}$ then there is a final state $f_k \in F_K$ such that $e' \xrightarrow{x}_K f_k$ $\hfill (*)$

$$\langle r_0^2, q_0 \rangle \overset{\lambda}{\underset{T_{11}}{\Rightarrow}} \langle r_0^2, q_1 \rangle \overset{\lambda}{\underset{T_{1S}}{\Rightarrow}} \langle r_0^2, q_{34} \rangle \cdot \langle r_0^2, q_3 \rangle \overset{\lambda}{\underset{T_{1S}}{\Rightarrow}} \langle r_0^2, q_6 \rangle \cdot \langle r_0^2, q_{35} \rangle \cdot \langle r_0^2, q_3 \rangle$$

$$\overset{\lambda}{\underset{T_{1S}}{\Rightarrow}} \langle r_0^2, q_7 \rangle \cdot \langle r_0^2, q_{16} \rangle \cdot \langle r_0^2, q_{35} \rangle \cdot \langle r_0^2, q_3 \rangle \overset{b}{\underset{T_{1P}}{\Rightarrow}} ((\langle r_1^2, q_8 \rangle \| \langle r_1^2, q_{20} \rangle) \cdot \langle r_0^2, q_{16} \rangle \cdot \langle r_0^2, q_{35} \rangle \cdot \langle r_0^2, q_3 \rangle$$

$$\overset{\lambda}{\underset{T_{1S}}{\Rightarrow}} ((\langle r_1^2, q_8 \rangle \| \langle r_1^2, q_{21} \rangle) \cdot \langle r_0^2, q_{16} \rangle \cdot \langle r_0^2, q_{35} \rangle \cdot \langle r_0^2, q_3 \rangle \overset{\lambda}{\underset{T_{11}}{\Rightarrow}} ((\langle r_1^2, q_8 \rangle \| \langle r_1^2, q_{\mathsf{Exc}_1} \rangle) \cdot \langle r_0^2, q_{16} \rangle \cdot \langle r_0^2, q_{35} \rangle \cdot \langle r_0^2, q_3 \rangle$$

$$\overset{\lambda}{\underset{T_{1S}}{\Rightarrow}} ((\langle r_2^2, q_{24} \rangle \cdot \langle r_2^2, q_9 \rangle) \| \langle r_1^2, q_{\mathsf{Exc}_1} \rangle) \cdot \langle r_0^2, q_{16} \rangle \cdot \langle r_0^2, q_{35} \rangle \cdot \langle r_0^2, q_3 \rangle$$

$$\overset{\lambda}{\underset{T_0}{\Rightarrow}} (((\langle r_2^2, q_{24} \rangle \cdot \langle r_2^2, q_9 \rangle) \| \langle r_2^2, q_{\mathsf{Exc}_1} \rangle) \cdot \langle r_0^2, q_{16} \rangle \cdot \langle r_0^2, q_{35} \rangle \cdot \langle r_0^2, q_3 \rangle$$

$$\overset{\lambda}{\underset{T_{11}}{\Rightarrow}} (((\langle r_2^2, q_{26} \rangle \cdot \langle r_2^2, q_9 \rangle) \| \langle r_2^2, q_{\mathsf{Exc}_1} \rangle) \cdot \langle r_0^2, q_{16} \rangle \cdot \langle r_0^2, q_{35} \rangle \cdot \langle r_0^2, q_3 \rangle$$

$$\overset{\lambda}{\underset{T_{1S}}{\Rightarrow}} (((\langle r_2^2, q_{27} \rangle \cdot \langle r_2^2, q_{32} \rangle \cdot \langle r_2^2, q_9 \rangle) \| \langle r_2^2, q_{\mathsf{Exc}_1} \rangle) \cdot \langle r_0^2, q_{16} \rangle \cdot \langle r_0^2, q_{35} \rangle \cdot \langle r_0^2, q_3 \rangle$$

$$\overset{b}{\underset{T_{1P}}{\Rightarrow}} ((((\langle r_1^2, q_{28} \rangle \| \langle r_1^2, q_{20} \rangle) \cdot \langle r_2^2, q_{32} \rangle \cdot \langle r_2^2, q_9 \rangle) \| \langle r_2^2, q_{\mathsf{Exc}_1} \rangle) \cdot \langle r_0^2, q_{16} \rangle \cdot \langle r_0^2, q_{35} \rangle \cdot \langle r_0^2, q_3 \rangle$$

$$\overset{\lambda}{\underset{T_0}{\Rightarrow}} ((((\langle r_1^2, q_{28} \rangle \| \langle r_1^2, q_{20} \rangle) \cdot \langle r_2^2, q_{32} \rangle \cdot \langle r_2^2, q_9 \rangle) \| \langle r_1^2, q_{\mathsf{Exc}_1} \rangle) \cdot \langle r_0^2, q_{16} \rangle \cdot \langle r_0^2, q_{35} \rangle \cdot \langle r_0^2, q_3 \rangle$$

$$\overset{\lambda}{\underset{T_{11}}{\Rightarrow}} ((((\langle r_1^2, q_{28} \rangle \| \langle r_1^2, q_{21} \rangle) \cdot \langle r_2^2, q_{32} \rangle \cdot \langle r_2^2, q_9 \rangle) \| \langle r_1^2, q_{\mathsf{Exc}_1} \rangle) \cdot \langle r_0^2, q_{16} \rangle \cdot \langle r_0^2, q_{35} \rangle \cdot \langle r_0^2, q_3 \rangle$$

$$\overset{\lambda}{\underset{T_{11}}{\Rightarrow}} (((((\langle r_1^2, q_{28} \rangle \| \langle r_1^2, q_{\mathsf{Exc}_1} \rangle) \cdot \langle r_2^2, q_{32} \rangle \cdot \langle r_2^2, q_9 \rangle) \| \langle r_1^2, q_{\mathsf{Exc}_1} \rangle) \cdot \langle r_0^2, q_{16} \rangle \cdot \langle r_0^2, q_{35} \rangle \cdot \langle r_0^2, q_3 \rangle$$

$$\overset{\lambda}{\underset{T_{P1}}{\Rightarrow}} (((\langle r_1^2, q_{\mathsf{Exc}_1} \rangle \cdot \langle r_2^2, q_{32} \rangle \cdot \langle r_2^2, q_9 \rangle) \| \langle r_1^2, q_{\mathsf{Exc}_1} \rangle) \cdot \langle r_0^2, q_{16} \rangle \cdot \langle r_0^2, q_{35} \rangle \cdot \langle r_0^2, q_3 \rangle$$

$$\overset{\lambda}{\underset{T_{SS}}{\Rightarrow}} (((\langle r_1^2, q_{30} \rangle \cdot \langle r_2^2, q_{32} \rangle \cdot \langle r_2^2, q_9 \rangle) \| \langle r_1^2, q_{\mathsf{Exc}_1} \rangle) \cdot \langle r_0^2, q_{16} \rangle \cdot \langle r_0^2, q_{35} \rangle \cdot \langle r_0^2, q_3 \rangle$$

$$\overset{\lambda}{\underset{T_{1S}}{\Rightarrow}} (((\langle r_1^2, q_{34} \rangle \cdot \langle r_1^2, q_{31} \rangle \cdot \langle r_2^2, q_{32} \rangle \cdot \langle r_2^2, q_9 \rangle) \| \langle r_1^2, q_{\mathsf{Exc}_1} \rangle) \cdot \langle r_0^2, q_{16} \rangle \cdot \langle r_0^2, q_{35} \rangle \cdot \langle r_0^2, q_3 \rangle$$

$$\overset{\lambda}{\underset{T_{1S}}{\Rightarrow}} (((\langle r_1^2, q_6 \rangle \cdot \langle r_1^2, q_{35} \rangle \cdot \langle r_1^2, q_{31} \rangle \cdot \langle r_2^2, q_{32} \rangle \cdot \langle r_2^2, q_9 \rangle) \| \langle r_1^2, q_{\mathsf{Exc}_1} \rangle) \cdot \langle r_0^2, q_{16} \rangle \cdot \langle r_0^2, q_{35} \rangle \cdot \langle r_0^2, q_3 \rangle$$

$$\overset{\lambda}{\underset{T_{1S}}{\Rightarrow}} (((\langle r_1^2, q_7 \rangle \cdot \langle r_1^2, q_{16} \rangle \cdot \langle r_1^2, q_{35} \rangle \cdot \langle r_1^2, q_{31} \rangle \cdot \langle r_2^2, q_{32} \rangle \cdot \langle r_2^2, q_9 \rangle) \| \langle r_1^2, q_{\mathsf{Exc}_1} \rangle) \cdot \langle r_0^2, q_{16} \rangle \cdot \langle r_0^2, q_{35} \rangle \cdot \langle r_0^2, q_3 \rangle$$

$$\overset{b}{\underset{T_{1P}}{\Rightarrow}} ((((\langle E, q_8 \rangle \| \langle E, q_{20} \rangle) \cdot \langle r_1^2, q_{16} \rangle \cdot \langle r_1^2, q_{35} \rangle \cdot \langle r_1^2, q_{31} \rangle \cdot \langle r_2^2, q_{32} \rangle \cdot \langle r_2^2, q_9 \rangle) \| \langle r_1^2, q_{\mathsf{Exc}_1} \rangle) \cdot \langle r_0^2, q_{16} \rangle \cdot \langle r_0^2, q_{35} \rangle \cdot \langle r_0^2, q_3 \rangle$$

$$\overset{cbcb}{\Longrightarrow} \langle E, q_9 \rangle$$

Fig. 7. A Derivation in a Combined Abstraction (Example 5)

If (*) holds, then the theorem is proven: Let be $x \in L(U_s) \cap L(\bar{A}_s)$. Then, $q_0 \overset{x}{\Rightarrow} f$ for an $f \in F$ and $r_0^s \overset{x}{\Rightarrow}_s \bar{r}$ for a $\bar{r} \in \bar{F}_s$ by the definition of L. Thus, (*) implies that there is a final state $f_k \in F_K$ such that $q_0^K = (r_0, q_0) \overset{x}{\Rightarrow}_K f_K$. Hence, $x \in L(K)$.

The base case is that no transition rule of U_s and A_s is applied, i.e. $f \overset{\lambda}{\Rightarrow} f$ and $\bar{r} \overset{\lambda}{\Rightarrow}_s \bar{r}$. Thus, $(\bar{r}, f) \overset{\lambda}{\Rightarrow}_K (\bar{r}, f) \in F_K$

For the inductive case consider a derivation $e \overset{w}{\Rightarrow} f \in F$ and $r \overset{w}{\Rightarrow}_s \bar{r} \in \bar{F}_s$. CASE: The first step applies rule $q.q' \overset{a}{\to} q''$, $a \in \Sigma_s$: Then $e = q.q' \circ \bar{e}$ for a $\bar{e} \in PEX(Q)$, $\circ \in \{., \|\}$ and $w = ax$ for a $x \in \Sigma_s^*$. Furthermore, $q.q' \circ \bar{e} \overset{a}{\Rightarrow} q'' \circ \bar{e} \overset{x}{\Rightarrow} f$ and $r \overset{a}{\Rightarrow}_s r'' \overset{x}{\Rightarrow}_s \bar{r}$ for a $r'' \in R_s$. By induction hypothesis, there is a $e' \in PEX(Q_K)$ such that $\pi(e') = q' \circ \bar{e}$, $\sigma(e') = r''$, and $e' \overset{x}{\Rightarrow}_K f_K$ for a $f_k \in F_K$. Define $e'' = (r'', q'') \circ \hat{e}$ where $\pi(\hat{e}) = \bar{e}$. By Lemma 1 it holds $e'' \overset{\lambda}{\Rightarrow}_K e'$. Thus, $(r, q).(r', q') \circ \hat{e} \overset{a}{\Rightarrow}_K (r'', q'') \circ \hat{e} \overset{\lambda}{\Rightarrow}_K e' \overset{x}{\Rightarrow}_K f_K$ since $(r, q).(r', q') \overset{a}{\to} (r'', q'') \in T_{S1}$. The proof of this case is completed by observing that $\pi((r, q).(r', q') \circ \hat{e}) = e$ and $\sigma(r, q).(r', q') \circ \hat{e}) = r$.

The case where a rule $q.q' \overset{a}{\to} q''$ is applied at the first step is proven analogously. The only difference is that $r'' = r$ since there is no change in the protocol state. The cases where a rule $q \| q' \overset{a}{\to} q''$ is applied at the first step are proven analogously by using rules from T_{P1}. The other cases can be similarly proven as in [15] and [3].

Example 5 (Combined Abstraction). The Combined Abstraction of the PRS in Fig. 4 and the protocol automaton A_2 in Fig. 2 has 220 atomic processes and 398 transition rules. For reasons of space we therefore only give a derivation demonstrating the protocol violation discussed in Example 2 (the class of the applied transition rule according to Fig. 5 is indicated below the derivation step, T_{SS} is a combination of T_{S1} and T_{1S}), cf. Fig. 7. This derivation should be compared with the derivation in Example 3. Note that all operations different from b and c are replaced by λ since the other operations are not contained in the interface of service s_2.

5   Related Work

Many works on static protocol-checking of components consider local protocol checking on FSMs. The same approach can also be applied to check protocols of objects in object-oriented systems. The idea of static type checking by using FSMs goes back to Nierstrasz [19]. His approach uses regular languages to model the dynamic behaviour of objects, which is less powerful than context-free grammars (CFG). Therefore, the approach cannot handle recursive call-backs. In [17] object-life cycles for the dynamic exchange of implementations of classes and methods using a combination of the bridge/strategy pattern are considered. This approach is also based on FSMs. It comprises dynamic as well as static conformance checking. Tenzer and Stevens [25] investigate approaches for checking object-life cycles. They assume that object-life cycles of UML-classes are described using UML state-charts and that for each method of a client, there is a FSM that describes the calling sequence from that method. In order to deal with recursion, Tenzer and Stevens add a rather complicated recursion mechanism to FSMs. It is not clear whether this recursion mechanism is as powerful as pushdown automata and therefore could accept general context-free languages. All these works are for sequential systems. Schmidt et al. [13] propose an approach for protocol checking of concurrent component-based systems. Their approach is also FSM-based. Thus, it is also unable to deal with recursive call-backs. [3,2] use the restricted class of (P,G) process-rewrite systems and allows thus the adequate modeling of unbound recursion, unbound concurrency, and explicit synchronizations. However, exceptions are not considered in these works.

An alternative approach for an investigation of protocol conformance is the use of process algebras such as CSP (e.g. [1]). These approaches are more powerful than FSMs and context-free grammars. However, mechanized checking requires some restrictions on the specification language. For example, [1] uses a subset of CSP that allows only the specification of finite processes. At the end the conformance checking is reduced to checking FSMs similar to [13]. In [21] behavioural protocol conformance is used to describe a problem similar to ours. In contrast to our approach the developer has to define not only the allowed receivable calls but also the calls of the component. This approach can not handle recursive callbacks, since the verification is reduced to finite state model checking. Many works use process algebras as abstractions for the formal (behavioral) analysis

Table 3. Rule Classes and Programming Language Concepts

Rule	Language Concept	Rule Class
$q \xrightarrow{\alpha} q'$	internal state transition	$(1,1)$
$q \xrightarrow{\alpha} q'.q''$	synchronous procedure call	$(1,S)$
$q \xrightarrow{\alpha} \varepsilon$	regular procedure return	$(1,1)$
$q \xrightarrow{\alpha} q' \parallel q''$	asynchronous procedure call	$(1,P)$
$q \parallel q' \xrightarrow{\alpha} q''$	synchronization	(P,P)
$q.q' \xrightarrow{\alpha} q''.\bar{q}$	exception handling	(S,S)
$q.q' \xrightarrow{\alpha} q''$	exceptional procedure return	(S,S)

α is a function symbol or empty.

of e.g. BPEL applications. [11] uses CSP, while [24] uses CCS-Process-algebras are similar to (P, G)-PRSs. These two works do not verify the behaviour in our sense. To the best of our knowledge, we are not aware of works in protocol conformance checking taking into account unbound recursion, unbound concurrency, and exception handling.

Other works such as [6] use another notion of behavioural conformance as we do. Their notion of conformance basically implies absence of deadlocks and livelocks, i.e. they want to reach a desired state. In contrast, protocols in this work specify sequences of operation calls that must be satisfied, i.e., it is more a safety condition rather than a liveness condition. Furthermore, [6] doesn't abstract the service behaviour from an implementation. The latter is done by [22] who abstract the service implementation to a ZING model. They check also kind of absence of deadlocks as [6] using a simulation relation.

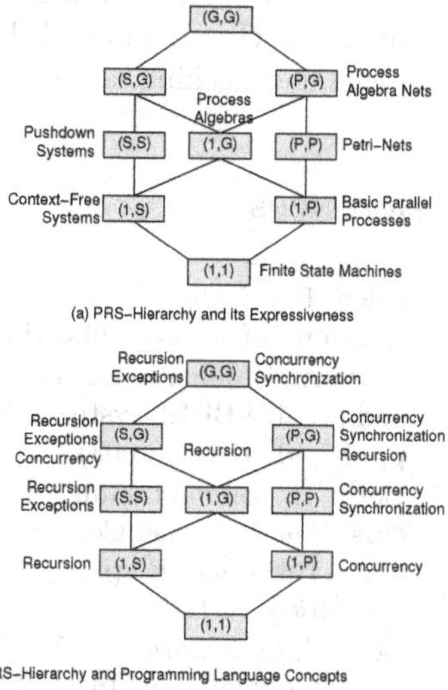

(a) PRS-Hierarchy and its Expressiveness

(b) PRS-Hierarchy and Programming Language Concepts

Fig. 8. PRS-Hierarchy and Expressiveness

6 Conclusions

In this paper we extended our previous work of protocol conformance checking towards exception handling. This approach is capable to represent exception handling even via service interactions. The abstractions are computed using an automatic translation. A more rugged composition of SOAs is now possible. In contrast to our previous work, the most general class of process-rewrite systems is needed for modeling exception handling, unbound recursion, unbound concurrency, and explicit synchronization. Table 3 shows an interesting correspondence between the rule classifications according to Mayr and the adequate modelling of programming language concepts. In particular, it shows what is required for modeling the language concepts if one abstracts completely from data. Thus, we have the correspondence between

Mayr's hierarchy of process-rewrite systems and programming language concepts shown in Fig. 8. In our previous work we had a correspondence to the class Process Algebra Nets. With exception handling we have a correspondence to the general class of process-rewrite systems.

The reachability problem is decidable for each class of PRS while the inclusion problem to regular languages becomes undecidable in any class containing a G, i.e., that includes parallel as well as sequential composition. In a similar way as [3] we have defined a Combined Abstraction that approximates the inclusion problem by a reachability problem such that the approximation is exact iff the process-rewrite system belongs to a decidable class. The reachability problem can be solved by the algorithm in [18].

However, this algorithm requires exponential space (and therefore at least exponential time) in the worst case since the reachability problem for process rewrite systems is EXPSPACE-hard [18]. It is subject to future work to apply some heuristics to get it more efficient. For this, the same ideas as in [2,4,5] may apply. Taking into account data is a challenge: the data types of variables must be abstracted to finite domains. However, this leads to a severe state explosion problem as in classical model checking. Thus, in order to consider data in protocol conformance checking, a more goal-oriented abstraction is required.

References

1. Allen, R., Garlan, D.: A formal basis for architectural connection. ACM Transactions on Software Engineering and Methodology 6(3), 213–249 (1997)
2. Both, A., Zimmermann, W.: Automatic protocol conformance checking of recursive and parallel BPEL systems. In: IEEE Sixth European Conference on Web Services, pp. 81–91. IEEE (2008)
3. Both, A., Zimmermann, W.: Automatic Protocol Conformance Checking of Recursive and Parallel Component-Based Systems. In: Chaudron, M.R.V., Szyperski, C.A., Reussner, R. (eds.) CBSE 2008. LNCS, vol. 5282, pp. 163–179. Springer, Heidelberg (2008)
4. Both, A., Zimmermann, W.: A step towards a more practical protocol conformance checking algorithm. In: 35th Euromicro Conference on Software Engineering and Advanced Applications, pp. 458–465. IEEE (2009)
5. Both, A., Zimmermann, W., Franke, R.: Model checking of component protocol conformance – optimizations by reducing false negatives. Electron. Notes Theor. Comput. Sci. 263, 67–94 (2010)
6. Bravetti, M., Zavattaro, G.: Contract-Based Discovery and Composition of Web Services. In: Bernardo, M., Padovani, L., Zavattaro, G. (eds.) SFM 2009. LNCS, vol. 5569, pp. 261–295. Springer, Heidelberg (2009)
7. Bures, T., Hnetynka, P., Plasil, F.: Sofa 2.0: Balancing advanced features in a hierarchical component model. In: Proc. of the Fourth International Conference on Software Engineering Research, Management and Applications, pp. 40–48. IEEE (2006)
8. Burkart, O., Steffen, B.: Model Checking for Context-free Processes. In: Cleaveland, W.R. (ed.) CONCUR 1992. LNCS, vol. 630, pp. 123–137. Springer, Heidelberg (1992)

9. Burkart, O., Steffen, B.: Pushdown Processes: Parallel Composition and Model Checking. In: Jonsson, B., Parrow, J. (eds.) CONCUR 1994. LNCS, vol. 836, pp. 98–113. Springer, Heidelberg (1994)
10. Dahl, O.-J., Nygaard, K.: Simula: an algol-based simulation language. Communications of the ACM 9(9), 671–678 (1966)
11. Foster, H., Uchitel, S., Magee, J., Kramer, J.: Model-based analysis of Web Services. In: ASE, pp. 152–163. IEEE (2006)
12. Gorbenko, A., Romanovsky, A., Kharchenko, V., Mikhaylichenko, A.: Experimenting with exception propagation mechanisms in service-oriented architecture. In: Proc. of the 4th International Workshop on Exception Handling, pp. 1–7. ACM (2008)
13. Schmidt, H.W., Krämer, B.J., Poernomo, I., Reussner, R.: Predictable Component Architectures Using Dependent Finite State Machines. In: Wirsing, M., Knapp, A., Balsamo, S. (eds.) RISSEF 2002. LNCS, vol. 2941, pp. 310–324. Springer, Heidelberg (2004)
14. Hauck, E.A., Dent, B.A.: Burroughs' b6500/b7500 stack mechanism. In: AFIPS 1968 (Spring): Proc. of the April 30-May 2, 1968, Spring Joint Computer Conference, pp. 245–251. ACM (1968)
15. Hopcroft, J.E., Motwani, R., Ullman, J.D.: Introduction to automata theory, languages, and computation, 2nd edn. Addison-Wesley (2001)
16. Jannach, D., Gut, A.: Exception Handling in Web Service Processes. In: Kaschek, R., Delcambre, L. (eds.) The Evolution of Conceptual Modeling. LNCS, vol. 6520, pp. 225–253. Springer, Heidelberg (2011)
17. Löwe, W., Neumann, R., Trapp, M., Zimmermann, W.: Robust dynamic exchange of implementation aspects. In: TOOLS 29 – Technology of Object-Oriented Languages and Systems, pp. 351–360. IEEE (1999)
18. Mayr, R.: Process rewrite systems. Information and Computation 156(1-2), 264–286 (2000)
19. Nierstrasz, O.: Regular types for active objects. In: Nierstrasz, O., Tsichritzis, D. (eds.) Object-Oriented Software Composition, pp. 99–121. Prentice-Hall (1995)
20. Papazoglou, M.P., Traverso, P., Dustdar, S., Leymann, F.: Service-oriented computing: State of the art and research challenges. Computer, Innovative Technology for Computer Professionals 40(11), 38–45 (2007)
21. Parizek, P., Plasil, F.: Modeling of Component Environment in Presence of Callbacks and Autonomous Activities. In: Paige, R.F., Meyer, B. (eds.) TOOLS EUROPE 2008. LNBIP, vol. 11, pp. 2–21. Springer, Heidelberg (2008)
22. Rajamani, S.K., Rehof, J.: Models for Contract Conformance. In: Margaria, T., Steffen, B. (eds.) ISoLA 2004. LNCS, vol. 4313, pp. 181–196. Springer, Heidelberg (2006)
23. Reisig, W.: Modeling- and Analysis Techniques for Web Services and Business Processes. In: Steffen, M., Zavattaro, G. (eds.) FMOODS 2005. LNCS, vol. 3535, pp. 243–258. Springer, Heidelberg (2005)
24. Salaün, G., Bordeaux, L., Schaerf, M.: Describing and reasoning on web services using process algebra. In: International Conference on Web Services. IEEE (2004)
25. Tenzer, J., Stevens, P.: Modelling Recursive Calls with UML State Diagrams. In: Pezzé, M. (ed.) FASE 2003. LNCS, vol. 2621, pp. 135–149. Springer, Heidelberg (2003)
26. van der Aalst, W.M.P.: Verification of Workflow Nets. In: Azéma, P., Balbo, G. (eds.) ICATPN 1997. LNCS, vol. 1248, pp. 407–426. Springer, Heidelberg (1997)
27. Zimmermann, W., Schaarschmidt, M.: Automatic Checking of Component Protocols in Component-Based Systems. In: Löwe, W., Südholt, M. (eds.) SC 2006. LNCS, vol. 4089, pp. 1–17. Springer, Heidelberg (2006)

Cloud Service Localisation

Claus Pahl

Center for Next Generation Localisation CNGL and CloudCORE Research Centre
School of Computing, Dublin City University
Dublin, Ireland
cpahl@computing.dcu.ie

Abstract. The essence of cloud computing is the provision of software and hardware services to a range of users in different locations. The aim of cloud service localisation is to facilitate the internationalisation and localisation of cloud services by allowing their adaption to different locales. We address the lingual localisation by providing service-level language translation techniques to adopt services to different languages and regulatory localisation by providing standards-based mappings to achieve regulatory compliance with regionally varying laws, standards and regulations. The aim is to support and enforce the explicit modelling of aspects particularly relevant to localisation and runtime support consisting of tools and middleware services to automating the deployment based on models of locales, driven by the two localisation dimensions. We focus here on an ontology-based conceptual information model that integrates locale specification in a coherent way.

Keywords: Cloud services, Service localisation, Service internationalisation, Language and governance localisation.

1 Introduction

Web-enabled software services, particularly in the cloud computing context, can support business and private users on a global scale [2,6]. In regions like Europe, where a multitude of languages are spoken, services are often only developed and deployed to support a single language or region [3]. In particular smaller organisations do often not have the capacity and capability to carry out multi-lingual and multi-regional development. Localisation is the process of adapting digital resources like services and associated data and content to a locale, i.e. the lingual and regulatory environment (restrictions, rules, settings) of a location or region. The emergence of cloud services and the increasing trend towards end-to-end personalisation of service offerings substantiates the need to address this wider understanding of locale and localisation in a dynamic cloud service context.

The wider objectives of cloud service localisation are, firstly, to introduce cloud-centric service localisation techniques, which focus on the localisation of software and interaction at the service interface level, and, secondly, to make the localisation techniques available at runtime for dynamic cloud service localisation and end-to-end personalisation. As there are very few comparable activities, we

F. De Paoli, E. Pimentel, and G. Zavattaro (Eds.): ESOCC 2012, LNCS 7592, pp. 138–153, 2012.

focus in this paper on defining a conceptual information model as the backbone of a wider localisation solution. Based on this, we outline further challenges and possible architectural solutions for this context. A significant part here is devoted to the motivation of cloud service localisation as a new field of investigation.

Often, localisation refers to either languages only or physical locations only. Two different locale dimension are the focus of this investigation that embrace these and widen the concepts of localisation and locale:

- lingual localisation by providing service-level language translation techniques to adopt services (including API, description, models) to different languages,
- regulatory localisation by providing standards-based mappings to achieve regulatory compliance with regionally varying laws and regulations (business rules, standardised name/value mappings, currencies and units, and legal governance/compliance rules in relation to different regions or locations).

Progress beyond the state-of-the-art with respect to the following is aimed at:

- localisation at service interface level - classical forms of software localisation will be expanded to address internationalisation at the interface (API) level. Model mapping and translation form core ingredients to develop a coherent and integrated solution across the locale dimensions here. The challenge is a semantic model integrating heterogeneous translation, mapping and adaptation needs in a single, dynamically processable form.
- adaptation and integration - software adaptation at service-level will be considerably improved by addressing linguistic and regulatory dimensions. This poses a significant challenge, as the current focus of adaptation is only on functional and software quality aspects that are software-technical in nature.
- semantics-enhanced brokering and mediation - matching of services is equally expanded to encompass linguistic and regulatory aspects, here proposed to be included in a locale-centric negotiation process and infrastructure, requiring respective coordination protocols.

We motivate cloud service localisation in the next section. Section 3 defines the conceptual information model and its supporting architecture. In Section 4, we introduce specific localisation techniques. Section 5 discusses some challenges, before we end with a wider discussion of related work and some conclusions.

2   Motivation

Our focus is a platform for service localisation that makes a step from one-size-fits-all services towards end-to-end personalised service offerings based on different locales. Current cloud computing for international settings suffers from localisation and adaptability problems for multiple but different users [18,27], which can be overcome through multi-lingual and multi-regional localisation.

2.1 Application Scenarios and Benefits

Various possible application scenarios can illustrate the benefits of a service localisation solution for the cloud:

- End-user media store&play cloud services. Some cloud media players are currently available in only one language. This form of end-user oriented service interaction would benefit from multilingual access by a mass market. It would involve the localisation (translation) of service description values, interaction text, and other auxiliary text. This can take place statically (prepared localisation) or dynamically (ad-hoc localisation).
- Business-targeted cloud services. A data analysis and storage service as business offerings could be adapted (localised) to be compliant with different standards and regulations for different regional or legal environments - a business-centric service offering requiring a high degree of customisation.
- End-user composed service processes. For instance, public sector applications where governance and regulations are as important as lingual aspects can be composed/configured based on several individual cloud services, adapted by individual users to their specific needs, even dynamically.
- Mediated e-commerce offerings. Telecoms-supported consumer access services are examples, where online shops avail of cloud-based support infrastructure services to allow them to manage their business online.

The second scenario shall be detailed further. A cloud-based data archiving service might need business-oriented service localisation. Sales data from local subsidiaries have to be stored centrally (e.g. in a private cloud) or usage of a low-cost storage provider abroad (in a public cloud) is envisaged. With a focus on regulatory (REG) and lingual (LING) localisation, the following is required:

- LING: translate service data between languages, e.g. from English into German - "Quote" to "Angebot" - based on standards like EANCOM or document-related attributes based on the GS1 standard for documents[1],
- REG: transform data between standards or their variants, e.g. "Quote" translates to "FullQuotation" based on a transformation between different EDIFACT variants and subsets such as EANCOM, EDIKEY, or EDIFICE. Other examples are transformations of currencies or transformation of rules and procedures, e.g. access rights to enable regulatory compliance by enabling legally required recording of activities through service adaptation.

Related data validation and data archiving services might be composed by a broker, which mediates the localisation based on integrated semantically enhanced locale policies. The requestor provides an abstract process that the broker implements - for example to offer locale-specific services abroad for roaming network

---

[1] For illustration, we use the EDIFACT (United Nations rules for Electronic Data Interchange for Administration, Commerce and Transport, http://www.unece.org/trade/untdid/welcome.html) and GS1 standards (supply and demand chains globally and across multiple sectors, http://www.gs1.org/).

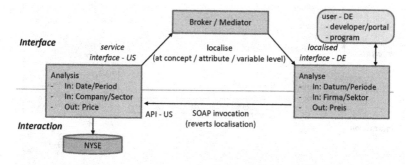

Fig. 1. Localisation of Stock Market Analysis Feature - Focus on Service API

customers (if compatible) using predefined mappings that are deployed dynamically. End-user composition can be applied where the end-user configures a process of different services by different services in different languages. The business searches for best provider internationally for both services, not necessarily as a package. An example is sales records where data is validated for sector categories, e.g. GS1 for sector categorisations, across different languages.

The following illustrates a range of different localisable service artefacts with sample specifications for locales US and DE:

- API: *validate(dataset):result* in US maps to *Validiere(Datensatz):Resultat*
- Semantic Description: *compliant(GS1,dataset)* $\rightarrow$ *validated* is US maps to *einhaltend(GS1,Datensatz)* $\rightarrow$ *validiert* in DE
- Contract: *per_activation = 1 USD (incl. 18% VAT)* and *availability = 98%* in US maps to *pro_Aufruf = 1.35 EUR (incl. 21% MwSt)* and *Verfügbarkeit = 98%* in DE
- Documentation: *service validates dataset for standards compliance* in US maps to *Servce validiert Datensätze aud Einhaltung von Standards* in DE

Note that inter-artefact relationships exist: validate/validated/validates and complaint/compliance as two sets of terms that are internally cross-referenced.

Some progress has been made in the past in the context of Web service internationalisation [24,29]. This has provided a broader framework, particularly addressing data formatting and conversion (e.g. between units) aspects. More complex, rule-based translations are, however, not included.

2.2 Use Case and Requirements

In addition to the demonstration of the need for localisation across a wide spectrum, we chose another use case to elicit more detailed requirements. We use an environment that provides service-level access to stock market information and analyses[2]. A German user might want to access data from the New York

---

[2] This is based on a case study using financial stock market information services from http://xignite.com/ and http://deutsche-boerse.com.

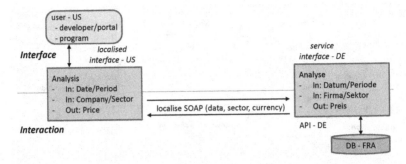

Fig. 2. Localisation of Stock Market Analysis Feature - extends NYSE-specific Analysis Service to include DB-FRA

stock exchange, which is provided in an English format. We present a scenario in which the user can implement a locale-compliant interface, i.e. one that allows technical interaction of service interface and description aspects in German.

At the application-level, two sample calls of a stock market data analysis service for the two locales (US-locale with English as the language and USD as currency and DE-locale with German as the language and EUR as the currency) could be: *Analyse(10/30/2011, logistics)* → *3.82 USD* and *Analysis(30.10.2011, Logistik)* → *4.23 EUR*. Localisable artefacts in this example are

- Date: a format change is needed - which would also apply to time and collation issues,
- Sector: data values describing an industry sector are localised based on a translation between standardised terminologies - which would also apply to product categories,
- Language: operation names (and possibly other interface and model elements) are translated between languages,
- Currency: values are converted - as would be other measurements and units.

This list can be extended: different regulatory environments based on maybe multilingual and standardised glossaries and dictionaries; calculations/conversions based on rules (fixed) or repositories (dynamic); tax rates and customs duties can be added if products are sold; any messages including help and error messages to which text translation would be applied. Typical examples for technical terms that need translation in the banking or stock markets context are (average price - Durchschnittspreis), (main trading phase - Haupthandelsphase), or (volume weighted average - volumengewichteter Durchschnitt) that are based on accepted, often standardised terminologies. Some examples might be defined in terms of classification and categorisation standards: (logistics - Logistik) for a sector or (dairy - Milchprodukte) for product categories.

In the example, the user-DE can discover services based on a German specification and can invoke them based on a German interface. A stock market analysis provider can add a DE-locale to its default US-locale policy. This would result in a correct match in a full negotiation process in which a user searches for services that are provided in a locale-specific way since the provider is able to support

US-to-DE locale mappings if required. In an architecture that implements these localisation translations, service instrumentation would result in a process to be generated and enacted, rather than a single SOAP request as indicated in Fig. 1. This process could comprise service invocation and logging (location) for accountability where the location is a parameter, which indicates where and how records are kept (if ruled by privacy laws). A coordination protocol then governs the exchange of locales and the following SOAP-based application interaction.

The above scenario could be further extended to allow an American user (with locale US) to access a German-language stock market information provider, e.g. for Deutsche Börse, Frankfurt. Localisation can be provided on a SOAP level primarily, see Fig. 2, for automated service activations and interactions.

3   Conceptual Framework

The localisation of possibly brokered and mediated cloud services is the application context in which service localisation takes place - requiring a coherent integrated information model for multi-dimensional localisation and supporting cloud infrastructure to deal with localisation statically and dynamically in an automated form. Our aim is the localisation of the (automated) interaction with software services as dynamic, executable artefacts. What is required to make both software-to-software and user-to-software interaction localisable is interface-level dynamic localisation through translation and adaptation techniques. The conceptual framework we present is comprised of an information architecture, which is essentially an ontology, a systems architecture and an abstract process that would be enacted on the architecture [19,20].

3.1   Information Architecture - Localisable Artefacts

Localisable artefacts are service specifications and models, but also contracts and documentation addressing aspects like interaction in the form of messages and also licensing, usage and access rights, see Fig. 3. Translation between controlled vocabularies is required. If services are not locale-independent, localisation is needed. A locale model is based on locale-affected attributes like time/data format (the localisable artefact is data), language (the localisable artefact is interaction - text and/or dialogues), and collation/ordering (the localisable artefact is data). The user-specific locale models (user locale policies) are applied at the service endpoints after a locale negotiation process with the provider. Services are described in terms of their interfaces (in WSDL): data types, data, operations; more comprehensive models (e.g. the Unified Service Description Language USDL - http://www.w3.org/2005/Incubator/usdl/): functionality, quality, locale (language, currency, units, legal/tax), context (location, device, platform), and documentation (manual, help). Consequently, localisable artefacts are

- service interface: data-level internationalisation and transformation for the different locale dimensions that applies in particular to data (schema and

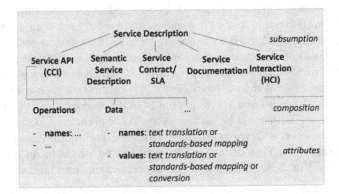

Fig. 3. Localisation Artefact Ontology - Excerpt with Focus on Service API

data-level translation based on EAN Identification, EANCOM/EDIFACT, etc.) and mappings; RESTful HTTP for instance natively supports content-type negotiation for interactions (messages).
– semantic service description and contract: aspects such as licensing, usage and access rights, but also other metadata aspects are subject to translation between controlled vocabularies (data-level translation).

These service descriptions are linked to the generic service description concept through a subsumption relationship. Each of the description types is then decomposed (using an is_part_of relation) into individual description elements, which are subject to localisation. Composition is necessary as a relationship as the subsumption (subtype) idea does not apply between an artefact and its parts. For the service API, operations and data (in the form of input and output parameters or messages) are these individual, localisable elements. Each localisable element has attributes that characterise the localisation technique applied to it. We have indicated their localisation type, which can be text (to be translated using usual MT techniques), standards-based data (where the translation is defined in a predefined glossary) or conversions (e.g. for statically defined measurements or dynamically defined currency conversions). For the given ontology excerpt, the translation type attribute is given. Composition and attributes are intra-artefact properties. There are also inter-artefact properties: is_defined_in and is_explained_in are examples for cross-artefact properties, e.g. a contract refers to a definition of an operation in an API or data is explained in documentation.

The localisation ontology is the foundation, on which later on rules to define localisation policies and actions to be executed for localisation will be introduced.

3.2   Systems Architecture and Process

A service localisation solution consists of guided translations (through ontologies), which may be pre-translated. Static value mappings (cross-language or cross-regulation) and dynamic value mappings need to be combined. A static

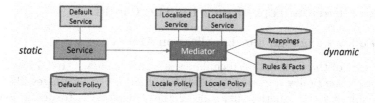

Fig. 4. Localisation Systems Architecture

setting means that localisations are prepared. A system architecture should allow developers to prepare material for multiple locales in advance and check their quality. An intermediary then deploys and executes respective techniques depending on user profile and negotiation, from which SLAs are formed. These are used to govern the invocation of services. In a dynamic setting, an intermediary selects suitable services (involving query translation), carries out negotiation based on best mappings (closest profiles) by using localisation and quality assurance services. Overall, the achievable quality will vary between in-advance and fully-automated scenarios. Corresponding assurance levels will need to be set.

These techniques can be facilitated for service localisation through process adaptation and instrumentation [26]. An intermediary mediates between several clients (at different locations) and several providers (at different locations) by providing this core process with localisation adaptations [23]. Several localisation patterns emerge. In a single-provider setting, one provider supports n (n≥1) locales; in a market-place setting, one client uses a composition of provider services (n>1). Both enact a localisation process based on locale negotiation (brokering) and localisation (mediation) implementing a localisation coordination protocol.

- Dynamic Generation: for regulatory localisation, aspect-oriented instrumentation can be generated on-demand per defined locale, allowing the user control over locale definition
- Configuration Management / Generation: different endpoints (and respective bindings) for different locales are generated for a localised API to which then localisations (translations and mappings) are applied; which of these to use might be dynamically decided
- Negotiation and Coordination: exchange and agreement on locale policies through SOAP headers based on [26] for coordination
- Architecture: data/information integration layer based on ontologies; service localisation layer based on adaptation (user model) and regulatory and lingual localisation; and management through locale negotiation

The process that governs the overall activities is *Negotiation*, followed by *Mediation & Localisation* and *Execution*. Abstract services and locale policies are the negotiation basis, based on which service endpoints give access to application services or instrumented processes, which in turn needs a basis of core services for translation LING, adaptation REG, and necessary instrumentation resulting from these, i.e. is localisation as a service, composed into a process.

4   Localisation Techniques for the Cloud

4.1   Policy Language and Localisation Model

At the core of the localisation techniques is a rule language [16,25,28]: an interoperable locale policy language is needed in addition to languages like WSDL, which captures the functionality side of the service API, to define locale descriptions for both provider and user. The policy language is based on Semantic Web rule principles with underlying ontology support (OWL) for the conceptual aspects. A locale policy defines the individual rules and instrumentations that characterise a locale. In Fig. 5, we define a layered localisation model that connects locales and rule-based locale mappings:

1. An ontology-based base layer captures the different translation types. The ontology defines the localisable artefacts and their relationships (see Fig. 3). Each unit is characterised in terms of a number of attributes:
   - translation unit type: API (data, operation), semantic description, SLAs, or documentation are examples.
   - translation type: standards-based, ad-hoc text translation, conversion based on distinct repositories, called translation memories (TMs) here.
2. Basic rules are provided, like *Locale* or *hasCurr*, on which specific locales can be defined. An example is

$$UKLocale(?l) \leftarrow Locale(?l) \land hasCurr(?l, ?c) \land ?c = GPB$$

Higher level rules allow a locale to be inferred from partial knowledge, e.g. $?c = GBP \rightarrow ?l = UKLocale$ and to detect inconsistencies.

3. Depending on provider and consumer locales, translations might need to be executed. Translations are guided by the locale definitions and use mappings defined in the translations layer (either as pairwise translation units (e.g. text) or as executable conversions (e.g. for measurements or currencies). The overall translation is dynamically assembled from the translation base (memory). The conversion rule for currencies can be dynamically created:

$$UKLocale2DELocale(?l1, ?l2) \leftarrow hasCurr(?l1, ?c1) \land hasCurr(?l2, ?c2) \land$$
$$?c2 = convertCurr(GBP, EUR, ?c1)$$

Mappings appear in a primary form as a translation between locales. However, in some cases, consequential actions need to be added. For instance, dynamic currency conversions need to be added or logging of activities for compliance reasons needs to be added. Actions thus comprise another type of activity than translation. Localisation might entail additional activities such as adding logs for activities.

Locale configuration examples are the metric system of units or a tax system. A locale mapping is compliant if it does not violate any locale configuration. While a coherent conceptual model has been presented in Fig. 5, specific support is needed for the two main localisation dimensions:

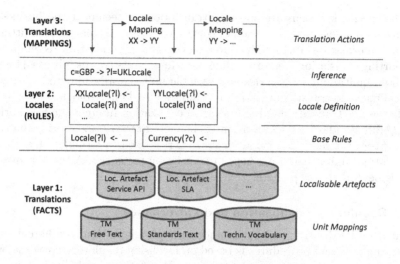

Fig. 5. Conceptual Localisation Model

- Linguistic localisation and machine translation: the challenge is the localisation of service artefacts with little textual context - at design and run-time.
- Regulatory localisation and governance: integrated and coherent adaptation to different regulatory standards and procedures based on semantic, rule-based techniques using multi-locale modelling and discovery using ontologies; and multi-dimensional user and service models and mappings for adaptation.

Consistency is a key motivation behind the rule-based approach. Locale mappings need to be consistent. Inference rules in the rule layer provide the mechanism to detect inconsistencies and enforce correct mappings. An example is that countries use a coherent set of measurements, e.g. the metric system. Also, currencies are linked to fiscal systems defined in a specific language. Since locale mappings are often dynamically assembled from individual translations, their composition needs to be checked for consistency.

4.2 Lingual Localisation and Translation

Localisation of artefacts with little textual context - in prepared and dynamic settings - is the challenge. We propose the translation of technical content based on reduced-context machine translation techniques [12]. We argue that specific techniques are needed to enable reliable translations between formalised, technical content (such as ontologies, service API and service models) [11]. Multi-lingual ontologies form the core of the technique by providing a mapping / glossary (as core translation memory). To enable effective processing, there is a need to consider the merging of prepared translation material with other translations generated on-the-fly. The key concern is the accuracy and quality of the translation, which needs to be trustworthy in automated processing environments.

The specific solutions are ontology translations of technical and business application domains and translation of controlled technical context with little contextual information [12,13]. The outcome consists of translation techniques and supporting translation memories using predefined units (words/phrases) for standardised multilingual glossaries and variable units (words/phrases) - using statistical machine translation (SMT) techniques based on ontological proximity to guide the free translation. XLIFF (XML Localization Interchange File Format), an OASIS standard for localisation exchange - http://www.oasis-open.org/committees/tc_home.php?wg_abbrev=xliff, is used to formulate translations. Translations units (pairs) are kept in translation memories. A further investigation is beyond the scope here.

4.3 Regulatory Localisation and Governance

Regulatory localisation and governance through adaptation to different regulatory standards and procedures is based on localising regulatory concerns, which are often captured in terms and conditions. Regulations apply for instance with respect the identification and description of business entities or the way processes are handled [17,26]. Furthermore, regulatory locale aspects like tax, currencies and units need to be addressed [4,24].

The specific objective here are multi-facetted rules that are modular and composable and that enable interference checking. For data object localisation, we argue here that a multilingual, multiregional schema mapping and integration technique is needed to adapt information to regulations in different regions (in possibly different languages). For SLA translation, we need to enable mappings of a SLA into a different locale that needs to consider the respective standards and procedures. A translation technique needs to ensure quality assurance and accountability of translation. We distinguish physical units like length, size, weight, but also colour and financial aspects like pricing and payment, currency, or tax. The outcome is a set of regulatory rule-based information translation techniques with predefined mappings using standards conversions between lengths and other units and consequential actions (instrumentations) needed when dynamic conversions (e.g. currency) or auxiliary actions (logging) are entailed. Individual definitions are not as much the problems as is keeping consistency.

5   Infrastructures for Cloud Localisation - Directions and Requirements

Two central infrastructure and mediation solutions are needed:

- Coordination: a localisation coordination strategy and protocol to implement the locale negotiation and coordination of localisation for different locales - based on a rule-based solution with a conflict resolution strategy.
- Service Mediation: a brokering and mediation architecture where an intermediary mediates between clients and providers at different locations. Solution components are based on hybrid techniques for guided translation, model mappings (cross-language/regulation) and process adaptation techniques.

We discuss possible directions and techniques here.

The first aspect is semantic technologies for service localisation. Multi-locale modelling and service adaptation using ontologies needs to provide a new approach to semantic service description through locale-specific domain ontologies. Locale-specific domain models are needed. Ontologies provide the formal framework. To define such ontologies, there is a need to consider a data layer and a services layer, each with respective semantic annotations supported. A *multilingual, multi-ontology framework* with corresponding facts, rules and mappings is needed [9]. We suggest to adopt the *linked data* approach followed by other service modelling approaches (like USDL - `http://www.linked-usdl.org/`). The XLIFF translation mapping standard can be converted into RDF.

The second aspect is software brokering - adaptation and mediation of services. Multi-dimensional user and service models and mappings need specific techniques for service adaption and personalisation. A user model developed around a notion of locale is needed to achieve cross-lingual and cross-regional interoperability. To match user models and service profiles, there is a need to formalise and automate mappings between the different models. On the regulatory localisation side, trustworthy conversions between formats and regulations need to be defined, based on guidance from ontologies. On the lingual localisation side, format/meta data translations and translation of values and text need to be facilitated, in both guided and unguided forms.

Brokering and mediation architectures provide a framework for locale mediation based on negotiation and localisation implementation activities [21,22]. We argue here that a *dynamic localisation engine* is needed. This is made up of services providing discovery, locale negotiation (static and dynamic, to generate SLAs and BPEL code, respectively), localisation (lingual and regulatory, prepared and on-the-fly, with quality check). To support this engine, there is a need to define a *localisation process* to govern the individual activities [15]. A repository is proposed to ensure the efficient and effective operation of the engine, which maintains pre-translated content and data/format mappings as translation memories. The outcome is a set of services to negotiate and localise and a repository to keep prepared localisations and schema information.

A locale is a specific type of a context. *Context- or locale-driven service provision* is the aim. From a cloud provider's perspective, this can also be seen as a *multitenancy* problem, where each cloud tenant is defined by its locale. Both aspects are further discussed in Section 6.

6   Related Work

Several areas are related to the subject here, although we provide a different perspective compared to other research publications [10,16,18,28] and work covered by related EU-supported research projects, like SOA4All (www.soa4all.eu), ACSI (www.acsi-project.eu/), 4Caast (4caast.morfeo-project.org/) or mOSAIC (http://www.mosaic-cloud.eu/), which address end-user adaptivity using generic semantic models (SOA4All), software-centric coordination and marketplaces

(ACSI, 4Caast), or multi-cloud provisioning (mOSAIC). Our framework is orthogonal to these efforts towards end-to-end offerings, and unique in its interdisciplinary character focusing on linguistic and regulatory aspects. More general, our proposal relates to the following aspects:

- Software Localisation: localisation of software normally refers to the human consumption, i.e. messages and dialogues produced by the software. We focus on localisation at the service interface level through internationalisation and ontology mapping and translation. The current technology on service internationalisation, which is the closest, is supported by the W3C Service Internationalisation activity [24,29]. The focus there is data level localisation, specifically for dates, currencies and units and common approaches to collation. The necessary solutions are conversions - e.g. statically defined between units or dynamically defined between currencies. Lingual aspects or more complex regulatory or business aspects are not covered, although for instance taxation as a sample concern is mentioned.
- Adaptation and Integration: software adaptation at service-level and data integration are common techniques. An example are schema mappings for data integration, where consistency and semantic preservation are key concerns. We follow ontology-based approaches, using these for semantics preservation, but add a multi-lingual layer using ontology mappings. In a similar context, service/process instrumentation is used to add enhanced processing abilities, but as for data integration and adaption, our focus on lingual and regulatory concerns within a rule-based framework is new.

  Context-awareness of services is a direction that has been covered by a range of contributions [4]. The notion of context is similar to that of locales, reflecting properties of the execution or client environment. However, context usually does not include lingual or regulatory aspects. We propose to adopt and extend respective adaptation and instrumentation techniques [5,14].
  Multi-tenancy is a cloud computing problem [18,27] that requires solutions for different users with different needs to be kept separate.
- Semantic Technologies: matching of services and supporting the negotiation process and infrastructure [7,10,19]. Through ontology mappings, multilingual terminologies and multi-regional regulations can be captured and dynamically processed.

7   Conclusions

Service localisation for cloud computing is a form of service personalisation and adaptation. This focus addresses service engineering principles, methods and tools by allowing service to be adapted to different locales. Services are enabled for seamless integration by providing localisation of services as software in conjunction with related content/data processed and communicated by these services. We have discussed techniques to enable the expansion of service offerings into different markets for cloud solution and application providers, which is a context of significant economic advantage [1,8]. Localisation is a means to bring products and services to markets that are otherwise inaccessible.

Multi-locale services support interoperable clouds contributing to a market of services by allowing services to be internationalised and localised - an aspect of crucial significance for the EU with 27 members, and even higher numbers of local languages and regulatory systems. Service localisation adds to the availability of platforms for easy and controlled development and deployment of value-added services through innovative service front-ends by providing cloud infrastructure services to localise and manage multi-locale services. Localisable services enable lower barriers for service providers and users to develop, select, combine and use value-added services and to allow providers to enter new markets, particularly SMEs without in-house localisation capabilities.

The objectives of this paper were two-fold. Firstly, we presented a conceptual framework to capture the key concerns of multi-lingual, multi-regulatory service localisation as a rule- and ontology-based information model. Secondly, our discussion here aimed to motivate the need for research in service localisation for the cloud to be carried out and analyse the major concerns. In this vein, we tried to identify some directions and concerns to be addressed. The focus of our investigation was, inevitably, limited: program-level localisation, end-to-end cloud personalisation and truly multi-lingual clouds are examples of omissions - which we intend to investigate further. It is also clear that implementation work needs to be done and evaluated - so far, the conceptual solution is only motivated and justified through the discussed case studies.

Acknowledgment. This research is supported by the Science Foundation Ireland (Grant 07/CE/I1142) as part of the Centre for Next Generation Localisation at Dublin City University.

References

1. 451 Group. Report on Cloud Computing 'As-a-service' market sizing - Report II (2010)
2. Armbrust, M., Fox, A., Griffith, R., Joseph, A.D., Katz, R., Konwinski, A., Lee, G., Patterson, D., Rabkin, A., Stoica, I., Zaharia, M.: A view of cloud computing. Comm. ACM 53(4), 50–58 (2009)
3. EU Commission. Report on "The Future of Cloud Computing" - Opportunities for European Cloud Computing Beyond 2010. EU (2010)
4. Bandara, K.Y., Wang, M.X., Pahl, C.: Context modeling and constraints binding in web service business processes. In: Proceedings of the Workshop on Context-Aware Software Technology and Applications, CASTA, pp. 29–32. ACM Press (2009)
5. Baresi, L., Guinea, S.: Towards Dynamic Monitoring of WS-BPEL Processes. In: Benatallah, B., Casati, F., Traverso, P. (eds.) ICSOC 2005. LNCS, vol. 3826, pp. 269–282. Springer, Heidelberg (2005)
6. Buyya, R., Broberg, J., Goscinski, A.: Cloud Computing - Principles and Paradigms. Wiley (2011)
7. Doulkeridis, C., Loutas, N., Vazirgiannis, M.: A system architecture for context aware service discovery. ENTCS, 101–116 (2006)

8. Fingar, P.: Cloud computing and the promise of on-demand business innovation. Intelligent Enterprise (2009)
9. Fu, B., Brennan, R., O'Sullivan, D.: Multilingual Ontology Mapping: Challenges and a Proposed Framework. In: Workshop on Matching and Meaning - Automated Development, Evolution and Interpretation of Ontologies (2009)
10. Fujii, K., Suda, T.: Semantics-based context-aware dynamic service composition. ACM Trans. Auton. Adapt. Syst. 4(2), 1–31 (2009)
11. van Genabith, J.: Metaphors, Logic and Type Theory. Metaphor and Symbol 16(1/2), 43–57 (2001) ISSN 1092-6488
12. van Genabith, J., Crouch, R.: Dynamic and Underspecified Semantics for LFG. In: Dalrymple, M. (ed.) Semantics and Syntax in Lexical Functional Grammar: The Resource Logic Approach, pp. 209–260. MIT Press (1999)
13. Graham, Y., van Genabith, J.: An Open Source Rule Induction Tool for Transfer-Based SMT. The Prague Bulletin of Mathematical Linguistics, Special Issue: Open Source Tools for Machine Translation 91, 37–46 (2009)
14. Kapitsaki, G., Kateros, D., Prezerakos, G., Venierris, I.: Model-driven development of composite context-aware web applications. Information and Software Technology 51, 1244–1260 (2009)
15. Karastoyanova, D., Leymann, F.: BPEL'n'Aspects: Adapting service orchestration logic. In: International Conference on Web Services (2009)
16. Kharbili, M.E., Keil, T.: Bringing agility to business process management: Rules deployment in an SOA. In: 6th IEEE European Conference on Web Services (2008)
17. Leusse, P.D., Dimitrakos, T., Brossard, D.: A governance model for SOA. In: IEEE International Conference on Web Services (2009)
18. Mietzner, R., Unger, T., Titze, R., Leymann, F.: Combining different multi-tenancy patterns in service-oriented applications. In: IEEE International Enterprise Distributed Object Computing Conference (2009)
19. Pahl, C., Zhu, Y.: A Semantical Framework for the Orchestration and Choreography of Web Services. In: International Workshop on Web Languages and Formal Methods, WLFM 2005. ENTCS (2005)
20. Pahl, C.: A Formal Composition and Interaction Model for a Web Component Platform. In: Workshop on Formal Methods and Component Interaction, FMCI 2002 (2002)
21. Pahl, C., Giesecke, S., Hasselbring, W.: An Ontology-Based Approach for Modelling Architectural Styles. In: Oquendo, F. (ed.) ECSA 2007. LNCS, vol. 4758, pp. 60–75. Springer, Heidelberg (2007)
22. Barrett, R., Patcas, L.M., Murphy, J., Pahl, C.: Model Driven Distribution Pattern Design for Dynamic Web Service Compositions. In: International Conference on Web Engineering, ICWE 2006. ACM Press (2006)
23. Pahl, C.: Dynamic Adaptive Service Architecture – Towards Coordinated Service Composition. In: Babar, M.A., Gorton, I. (eds.) ECSA 2010. LNCS, vol. 6285, pp. 472–475. Springer, Heidelberg (2010)
24. Phillips, A.P.: Web Services and Internationalization. Whitepaper (2005), http://www.inter-locale.com/whitepaper/multilingual/ml73-ws-20050524.xml
25. Rosenberg, F., Dustdar, S.: Business rules integration in BPEL - a service-oriented approach. In: 7th IEEE Intl Conference on E-Commerce Technology (2005)
26. Wang, M.X., Bandara, K.Y., Pahl, C.: Integrated constraint violation handling for dynamic service composition. In: IEEE International Conference on Services Computing (2009)

27. Wang, M.X., Bandara, K.Y., Pahl, C.: Process as a Service - Distributed Multi-tenant Policy-based Process Runtime Governance. In: IEEE International Conference on Services Computing, SCC 2010. IEEE Press (2010)
28. Weigand, H., van den Heuvel, W.-J., Hiel, M.: Rule-based service composition and service-oriented business rule management. In: Interdisciplinary Workshop Regulations Modelling and Deployment (2008)
29. W3C. Web Services Internationalization Usage Scenarios (2005), http://www.w3.org/TR/ws-i18n-scenarios/

Quality Architecture for Resource Allocation in Cloud Computing

Kouessi Arafat Romaric Sagbo and Pélagie Houngue

Department of Information Technology
Università Degli Studi Di Milano
26013 Crema, Italy
{kouessi.sagbo,yenukunme.houngue}@unimi.it
http://www.unimi.it

Abstract. Quality features are important to be taken into account while allocating resource in Cloud Computing, since it allows to provide to the users or customers, high Quality of Service (QoS) with best response time as example and respects the Service Level Agreement (SLA) established.

Indeed, it is not easy to handle efficiently resource allocation processes in Cloud, since, the applications deployed on Cloud present non-uniform usage patterns, and the cloud allocation architecture needs to provide different scenarios of resource allocation to satisfy the demands and provide quality. In order to provide the measurement of quality indexes, the Cloud resource allocation architecture needs to be proactive and reactive.

The goal of this paper is to propose a resource allocation' architecture for Cloud Computing that provides the measurement of quality indicators identified between the Key Performance Indicators (KPI) defined by the Cloud Services Measurement Initiative Consortium (CSMIC). Our architecture proposes different resource allocation policies: predictive and reactive. The allocation decisions are taken in this architecture, according to the SLA. Finally, the preliminary experimental results show that our proposed architecture can improve quality in Cloud.

Keywords: Cloud Computing, Resource Allocation, Quality Architecture, Quality of Service.

1 Introduction

Cloud Computing is defined by NIST [1] as: "a model for enabling convenient, on-demand network access to a shared pool of configurable computing resources (e.g. networks, servers, storage, applications and services) that can be rapidly provisioned and released with minimal management effort or service provider interaction".

There are three important services layers in cloud architecture: Software as a Service (SaaS), Platform as a Service (PaaS) and Infrastructure as a Service (IaaS) [3]. Figure 1 shows a basic cloud architecture with the three service layers.

- SaaS allows the consumer to use an application, but it does not control the operating system, hardware or network infrastructure on which the application is running.

F. De Paoli, E. Pimentel, and G. Zavattaro (Eds.): ESOCC 2012, LNCS 7592, pp. 154–168, 2012.

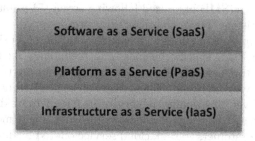

Fig. 1. Cloud basic layers architecture

- PaaS allows the consumer to use a hosting environment for its applications. It controls the applications that run in the environment, but does not control neither the operating system nor the hardware or network infrastructure on which they are running.
- IaaS allows the consumer to use "basic computing resources" such as processing power, storage, networking components, or middleware. The consumer can control the operating system, storage, deployed applications, and probably the networking.

Cloud system provides virtual resources as service through Internet. Then, virtualization is more used in Cloud Computing to provide the resources. Many strategies are used to provide virtual resources and they are grouped under the term "resource allocation".

Resource allocation in Cloud Computing needs to be done automatically and, should have an architecture which contributes to provide quality of service in Cloud. Quality architecture for resource allocation in Cloud Computing means that the architecture will provide performance, scalability, reliability, availability and security.

Our work aims to define an efficient resource allocation' architecture for Cloud Computing which will effectively deliver resources based on the quality metrics defined by [2] and presented in the following sections.

This paper is structured as follows: Section 2 presents the motivations of our work. Section 3 gives an overview of service measurement index following by the related work in section 4. Subsequently, section 5 describes our proposed architecture and section 6 presents the preliminary results obtained from our tests. Finally, section 7 concludes our paper and presents some future works.

2   Motivations

Since the advent of Cloud Computing, there are a lot of cloud providers and services, and it becomes difficult to know which of them actually fulfill the quality requirements.

In order to have good indicators for cloud services, the Cloud Services Measurement Initiative Consortium (CSMIC) [2] has defined some Service

Measurement Indexes (SMI) organized following seven (7) primary service measurement characteristics. These characteristics are designed to become a standard method to help organizations to measure cloud-based business services by taking into account their specific business and technology requirements. Some categories of indicators are defined to allow having good metrics so that to deliver quality of service in Cloud. Then, there is a need to define a standard architecture to deliver this quality of service in Cloud by taking into account these indicators during the resource allocation process. These measurements can help the users and customers to rank cloud service offered by different providers. But, these metrics are not easy to measure, since some are more qualitative and then, difficult to evaluate and the others quantitative, are easy to evaluate. The SLA is often violated during the resource allocation when a good resource allocation procedure is not used and the decision is not taken at time.

With the measurement of these metrics related to the quality delivering in Cloud Computing, it will be easy to know which provider respects the agreement previously established with the users.

Our work is to define a quality architecture for resource allocation and to prove that using this architecture, the cloud provider will fulfill the SLA regarding the Quality of Service level defined in it. Moreover, when the resources are allocated automatically at real-time, these quality indicators can be fulfilled, because in Cloud, all services are based on virtual resources used to provide the services and these resources need to be available over the time without interruption. That gives to cloud the aspect of infinite resources provider.

We aim to show that when cloud architecture has a well-defined and various resource allocation policies and algorithms, it can deliver quality at the end. We do not define in this paper how these metrics are calculated.

3   Overview of Service Measurement Index

The Service Measurement Index (SMI) is a set of business-relevant Key Performance Indicators (KPI's) that provide a standardized method for measuring and comparing a business service regardless whether that service is internally provided or sourced from an outside company [2]. The Service Measurement Index is organized into the following seven (7) characteristics:

- Accountability: this category contains attributes used to measure the properties related to the service provider organization. These properties help the customers to trust in the provider services.
- Agility: this category provides the attributes which indicate how the service can respond quickly and precisely regarding unexpected events or demands with minimal disruption.
- Assurance: this category includes key attributes that indicate how likely it is that the service will be available as specified in the SLA.
- Financial: this category contains the indicators about the cost of the service provided to the customer.

- Performance: this category covers the features and functions of the provided services. It provides the indicators of performance of these services.
- Security and Privacy: this category includes attributes that indicate the effectiveness of the provider's controls on the services access, the protection of data and the physical facilities from which the services are provided.
- Usability: this category contains the indicators which measure the ease of using a service on the Cloud.

Some of these characteristics contribute to have good quality indicators in cloud architecture. The quality features are then more provided by the key performance indicators (attributes) of the following three characteristics: *Agility*, *Assurance* and *Performance*. For simplicity reason, we do not give the definition of the attributes of these characteristics, but they are available in the document provided by the Consortium [2].

The *agility* characteristic has the following attributes:

- Adaptability,
- Capacity,
- Elasticity,
- Extensibility,
- Flexibility,
- Portability,
- Scalability.

The *assurance* characteristic has the following attributes:

- Availability,
- Maintainability,
- Recoverability,
- Reliability,
- Resiliency/Fault Tolerance,
- Service stability,
- Serviceability.

The *performance* characteristic has the following attributes:

- Accuracy,
- Functionality,
- Suitability,
- Interoperability,
- Service Response Time.

The cloud architecture which is able to provide these three categories of metrics ensures the quality requirements for cloud environments.

4   Related Works

The CSMIC [2] has defined the key performance indicators, described in the previous section, that are important to evaluate and rank the cloud providers services based on the SLA.

Our work points out among these indicators, those which contribute to ensure Quality of Service in Cloud when allocating the resources to the services.

The authors of [4] propose a mechanism that evaluates the quality and ranks the cloud provider services based on user requirements. They define some metrics to measure the SMI attributes in order to evaluate the QoS. They provide the way to calculate the metrics for the measurable attributes like the service response time, the sustainability, the suitability, the reliability, the stability and the availability. Moreover, they propose an Analytical Hierachical Process (AHP) based technique to evaluate and rank the cloud services and take into account the user requirements in the SLAs. Their work shows that the attributes defined by CSMIC are useful to compare the Quality of Service provided by the cloud providers. However, their framework proposes to evaluate only the quality quantifiable attributes and does not take into account non-quantifiable indicators.

The authors of [8] propose an architecture and the solutions for resource provisioning oriented-SLA. They show that the resource provisioning can be done in Cloud based on the SLA. They propose to use the SLA to define the quality levels required by the users from the provider. Then, the provider architecture can serve the resources depending on these requirements.

Their evaluation shows that the QoS requirements are met by allocating dynamically the resources and the provisioning is done by optimizing the costs and respecting the QoS level defined in the SLA. However, their works do not ensure the QoS requirements following the attributes defined by the CSMIC in order to minimize the SLAs violation by providing a good level of quality.

The works of Tran et al [9] define the core QoS properties for ranking web services. The attributes that they have defined can be useful to provide quality in Cloud. But, the authors do not evaluate this possibility. Their approach of ranking the web services can be used to classify the service on the Cloud, by adding the specificities of cloud environment.

5   Our Architecture

To provide quality, cloud architecture needs to be designed with a set of requirements which guaranty to this architecture to deliver the service with high level of quality with respect to the Service Measurement Index (SMI) defined by CSMIC in the three categories: *Agility, Assurance* and *Performance.*

Our architecture is organized in unit in such a way as to provide efficient resource allocation in Cloud. This architecture is full-oriented availability of resources by providing multiple scenarios of resource allocation in order to fulfill the SLA agreed with the users and the customers.

Our architecture, depicted in figure 2, is composed by five main units which are the following:

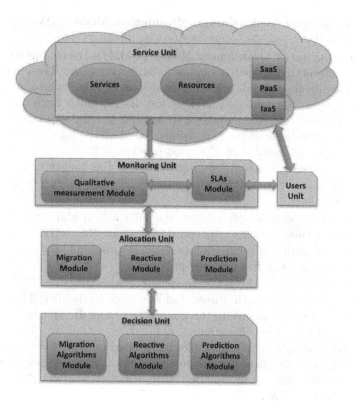

Fig. 2. Resource allocation architecture for quality in Cloud Computing

- Service Unit (SU),
- Monitoring Unit (MU),
- Allocation Unit (AU),
- Decision Unit (DU),
- Users Unit (UU).

1. The Service Unit (SU) presents the cloud services offered by the cloud provider to the users and customers. These services are organized following the cloud three main layers of cloud: SaaS, PaaS and IaaS. This unit manages the virtual resources available to serve each cloud service stack. A resource can be a software like Customer Relationship Management (CRM), a platform such as Google App Engine (GAE) or an infrastructure to deploy and run the virtual resources (Virtual machines and storage). The Service Unit communicates with the Monitoring Unit and the Users Unit by providing the information about the services and their owners.
2. The Monitoring Unit (MU) monitors the cloud service and the resources. It collects information about the services and the resources. It is related to the allocation unit to handle the resource allocation in time to the service. This

unit has two modules: Qualitative Measurement Module (QMM) and SLAs Module (SM).

- The Qualitative Measurement Module (QMM) is the module which manages all metrics to deliver quality in our architecture. These metrics are defined in this module and calculated based on the monitoring information. Since the definition of these metrics can differ from one provider to another, this module takes into account the SLAs specification. This means that these metrics are defined based on the information available in the SLAs provided by the cloud provider.

  The metrics calculated here are related to the quality metrics defined in the three SMI categories mentioned above: *Agility*, *Assurance* and *Performance*.

- The SLAs Module (SM) stores the information about the SLAs and provides these inputs to the QMM to evaluate the metrics. This module is linked with the Users Unit to keep information about each user and the agreement, it has with the provider.

3. The Allocation Unit (AU) is the core of our architecture since all the services in Cloud Computing turn around the resources availability. The service is delivered with high quality to the users, when there are efficient algorithms to handle the resource allocation.

   This unit manages the resource allocation based on the information sent by the MU by offering three possible resource allocation strategies organized in three modules: Migration Module (MM), Reactive Module (RM) and Prediction Module (PM).

   Each module can interact with the others one. The migration can be done following the information provided by the reactive module or the prediction module.

   - The Migration Module (MM) provides well-known algorithms to deliver as a service, the migration of resources from one physical server to another. The migration of resources can be used as allocation of resources technique for the service which does not require high availability (less than 90%) or for server consolidation to prevent future demand of service.

   - The Reactive Module (RM) provides an interface to deliver dynamic resource allocation to the services based on the information sent by the Migration Unit. This module provides some tested algorithms for auto-scaling. The allocation of resources is performed based on the current value of CPU, memory, storage or others load indicators when they reach the predefined threshold. The RM provides common existing strategies for resource allocation in current cloud solutions like RightScale [7] auto-scaling Algorithm.

   - The Prediction Module (PM) delivers resource allocation service using the algorithms based on prediction model. Using the current load information provided by the MU especially the QMM, this module predicts the future load and scales. The prediction algorithms are defined using the common prediction model such as linear regression model, autoregressive of order 1 model and neural network model [5][6].

This module is the most used, since it provides more efficient resource allocation following the results presented by [5][6], and also because in our resource allocation architecture, the main goal is to provide high Quality of Service and the predictive approaches handle better the resource allocation.

The SLAs information are also taken into account in the allocation of resources.

4. The Decision Unit (DU) is the execution unit of the strategy chosen by the AU. This unit has three algorithms modules for each allocation category: Migration Algorithms Module (MAM), Reactive Algorithms Module (RAM) and Prediction Algorithms Module (PAM).

   This unit is designed to use the benefits of modularity, then, the resource allocation algorithms can be defined and tested on this architecture in each module easily without impacting the whole architecture.

   - The Migration Algorithms Module (MAM) runs the migration algorithms.
   - The Reactive Algorithms Module (RAM) runs the reactive algorithms.
   - The Prediction Algorithms Module (PAM) runs the algorithms written following the prediction approach.

5. The Users Unit (UU) manages the users and the customers of cloud services. Each user is in relation with its SLA and services on the Cloud. This unit is then linked to the Service Unit and the Monitoring Unit.

Our architecture takes into account the SLA and users needs in order to perform the resource allocation based on the SLA. This architecture provides quality for the end users, since, it defines the quality metrics identified by us based on the work of CSMIC [2]. Our resource allocation architecture optimizes the quality in Cloud Computing by increasing availability, ensuring scalability and optimizing the response time and others important performance indicators.

In the next section, we provide the first results obtained from the evaluation of our architecture.

6 Performance Evaluation of Our Architecture

To evaluate the performance of our architecture, we have performed a simulation in order to test some behaviours we want to measure. The simulation helps to make repetitive operations and to compare the results. Then, we use CloudSim [10] to evaluate the performance of resource management policies proposed by [11] without energy consideration.

CloudSim is a toolkit to model and simulate Cloud resources and application scheduling. It allows the modeling of virtualized environments, supporting on-demand resource provisioning and their management.

Our resource allocation strategies are inspired by the work of [11]. However, we consider in addition, the cost evaluation of the resource allocation and the impact of migrations process on the SLAs.

A cost is associated to each VM migration. When a migration is completed, there is also a cost for the provider. The customers pay only the VM allocated over the simulation time. Then, we evaluated the profit for the provider as the difference between the total cost of VM allocated and the cost associated to VM migration. The provider uses VMs migration to avoid the saturation on the VMs hosts and then, ensures the infrastructure stability in order to minimize SLAs violation.

This modeling is ongoing and will be available in our future works.

6.1 Testbed

The tests with CloudSim are conducted on one virtual machine running Ubuntu 11.10 64bits, with processor Intel Xeon 4 cores x 2.6 GHz, 50 GB of storage and 8 GB of RAM, hosted by a physical machine Dell PowerEdge 6850 equipped with 4 Intel Xeon Quad core x 2.6 GHz, 16 Gb of RAM and 6 x 146 GB Serial Attached SCSI of storage.

In CloudSim, we have set up the following characteristics:

- A datacenter has 600 homogeneous physical hosts with the following characteristics for each host: Processor Intel Xeon, 2 cores x 2.6 GHz and 4GB of RAM.
- The VMs characteristics are similar to the instance types proposed by the Cloud provider Amazon [12].
- As workload, we use a real system workload trace. These data are provided by CoMon [13] which is a monitoring infrastructure for PlanetLab [14]. The monitoring statistics we used, are about the CPU utilization of more than thousand VMs from servers hosted around the world in more than 500 places. The data collected by CoMon are related to the number of virtual machines that are connected each day.
  In order to perform our simulation, we use the data collected on 22 March 2011 which are available in CloudSim. These data are related to the CPU utilization of 1516 VMs connected that day and the total average of the CPU utilization is less than 10% for 24 hours measurements. The control time is 5 minutes and we have 288 measurements for each VM for one day. We take also the measures for the control time of 15 minutes and 30 minutes.
- As performance metric, the threshold value of the CPU utilization is specified in the SLA and the threshold set up for this simulation varies from 0.6 to 1.0.
- Two techniques are used for the selection of the migrating VM: the Random Selection (RS) and the Minimum Migration Time (MMT) policies proposed by Anton et al in [11]. The MMT policy migrates a VM that requires the minimum time to complete a migration with respect to the other VMs allocated to the same host. The migration time is estimated as the amount

of RAM utilized by the VM divided by the spare network bandwidth available for the host. The Random Selection policy selects a VM to be migrated according to a uniformly distributed discrete random variable.

- The simulation is done also by allowing the migration of VMs and without VMs migration, to see how our architecture can deliver Quality of Service using the appropriate allocation algorithms and migration policies. The VMs migration process does not migrate the storage since, in this case, the storage solution offered by the provider is the network storage (SAN).
- Each migration' cost is arbitrarly fixed at $0.01. The VM allocation' cost is fixed $10 per hour by following the example of Amazon EC2' offers for a dedicated instance with a small configuration.

The Table 1 below, summarizes our Testbed characteristics.

Table 1. Summary of Testbed characteristics

Simulator	CloudSim
Number of Hosts	600
Host features	Intel Xeon - 2 cores x 2.6GHz - 4GB of RAM
VMs features	Amazon EC2 Instance types[12]
Number of VMs	1516
Workload Data	CPU utilization From PlanetLab for one Day
Control Time	Each 5mn - 15mn - 30mn
SLA on CPU utilization	Threshold value from 0.6 to 1.0
VMs selection techniques	Random and Minimum Migration Time policies
Allocation techniques	Without Migration and with migration
VMs Migration cost for the provider	$0.01
VMs allocation cost for one hour	$10

6.2   First Results

We make the measurements for 36 configurations which are summarized in Table 2. We consider the case with migration and without migration for the threshold value of CPU utilization going from 0.6 to 1.0 increasing by 0.2. Then, each line of this table corresponds to 6 simulations. The time control of 5, 15 and 30 minutes are considered.

For each simulation, we measure:

- The number of VMs deallocated before the end of the simulation and we deduct the number of VMs which are running until the end of the simulation.
- The cost of the VMs deallocated before the end.
- The cost of VMs which are running until the end of the simulation.
- The number of Migration.
- The cost of Migration.
- The profit of provider.
- The SLA violation due to migration.

Table 2. Simulations configurations

Time	With Migration		Without Migration	
	Threshold	Policy	Threshold	Policy
5mn	0.6 - 0.8 - 1.0	Random	0.6 - 0.8 - 1.0	Random
5mn	0.6 - 0.8 - 1.0	MMT	0.6 - 0.8 - 1.0	MMT
15mn	0.6 - 0.8 - 1.0	Random	0.6 - 0.8 - 1.0	Random
15mn	0.6 - 0.8 - 1.0	MMT	0.6 - 0.8 - 1.0	MMT
30mn	0.6 - 0.8 - 1.0	Random	0.6 - 0.8 - 1.0	Random
30mn	0.6 - 0.8 - 1.0	MMT	0.6 - 0.8 - 1.0	MMT

The results of the simulations are shown on the pictures below.

Figures 3 (a) and 3 (b) show that the number of migration is proportional to the threshold value of CPU utilization. When, the CPU utilization threshold is increased, the number of migration decreases. These figures show also that the number of migration is less important when the VM is chosen randomly than when the Minimum Migration Time policy is used. Figure 3 (b) demonstrates that when the control time is increased, the number of migration decreases. This happens because the decision to migrate is taken with delay, but the positive result is that the SLAs are taken into account.

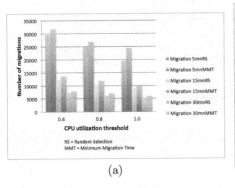
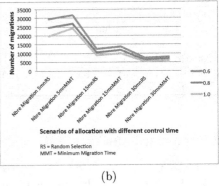

(a)   (b)

Fig. 3. Number of Migration evolution over the control time and the CPU utilization threshold for RS and MMT policies

Figure 4 illustrates the fact that the violation of SLA decreases when the control time increases. The same effects are observed when the VMs migration feature is disabled. In this case, the violation is too important. Our proposal of using resources migration as allocation technique is then justified. The percentage of SLA violation decreases because the migration is done in order to fulfill the agreement with the customers about the CPU utilization threshold.

Figure 5 confirms these observations and we can notice that when the control time increases, there are less violations and when the CPU utilization increases, the violations grow because there are less migrations.

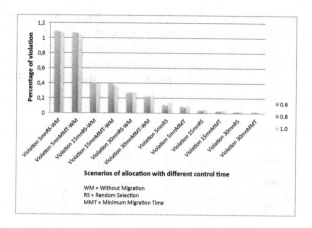

Fig. 4. Percentage of the SLA violation over the control time for RS and MMT policies with and without migration

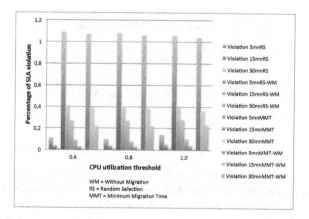

Fig. 5. Percentage of the SLA violation over the CPU utilization threshold for RS and MMT policies with and without migration

The percentage of SLA violation is multiplied by around 10 in each scenario, when the VMs migration is not allowed. This is a positive point for what we are expecting from our architecture. There are a little more violations with RS policy than MMT policy.

Figure 6 illustrates the provider profit. We can notice that this profit increases with the control time, because the decision to deallocate the VMs is taken later and the VMs in some case run one hour more. The number of migrations also decreases with the increase of the control time and the cost associated to the VMs migration has less impact on the profit.

The Random Selection policy increases the profit more than the Minimum Migration Time policy.

These figures also show that without migration, the profit is a little bit higher than the case with migration, but actually, we have to associate a cost to each SLA violation and since the SLA violations are ten times more important than the case with migration, the profit will be reduced considerably. Then, we can still claim that the strategies allowing the use of migration and efficient resource allocation are the best.

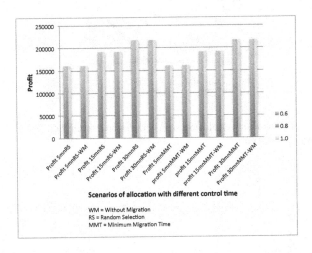

Fig. 6. Provider profit over the control time for RS and MMT policies with and without migration

6.3   Analysis

The results of our simulation show that the resource allocation needs to be done using appropriate and tested algorithms and policies. The provider profit can be important, but the services need to be delivered with high Quality of Service. We need to study which cost' function we can associate to the SLA violation to give a penalty to the provider when the SLA is violated. A tradeoff needs to be found between the profit for the provider and the performance for the customers. By maximizing the profit, the provider has to minimize the SLA violation. For instance, when the control time is increased, the provider has more profit, but this affects the performance of the service delivered.

Moreover, the results show that when the Cloud architecture has various and tested algorithms and policies for resource allocation, the services are delivered with high quality.

7   Conclusion

This work defines the requirements for Cloud architecture to ensure Quality of Service following the metrics defined by CSMIC. We propose an architecture for resource allocation oriented Quality of Service and SLAs fulfilment. The architecture advocates to measure the quantifiable and non-quantifiable metrics and to make the resource allocation based on them and the SLAs pre-established with the customers.

This work shows that by allocating the resources using different allocation techniques, from reactive to predictive, and efficient algorithms and policies for the VMs migration, this architecture can deliver the service to the customers following the SLA and with high quality.

The preliminary experimental results show that, our architecture can improve the Quality of Service when the quality metrics are measured and the allocation of resources are done following these metrics. Moreover, when the resources are allocated following the SLA, the provider's profit is more important.

In the future works, we will evaluate how the security metrics can impact the quality. The next challenge is to define how these qualitative and quantitative metrics can be evaluated and perform our tests in a real world Cloud platform. Finally, we have to model the optimization problem, which will contribute to maximize the provider profit and minimize the SLA violations.

References

1. National Institute of Standards and Technology (NIST), http://www.nist.gov/itl/cloud/index.cfm
2. Cloud Service Measurement Initiative Consortium (CSMIC), Service Measurement Index, http://www.cloudcommons.com/
3. Velte, A.T., Velte, T.J., Elsenpeter, R.: Cloud Computing: A Practical Approach. McGraw-Hill (October 2009)
4. Garg, S.K., Versteeg, S., Buyya, R.: SMICloud: A Framework for Comparing and Ranking Cloud Services. In: 4th IEEE International Conference on Utility and Cloud Computing, pp. 210–218 (2011)
5. Chandra, A., Gong, W., Shenoy, P.: Dynamic resource allocation for shared data centers using online measurements. In: SIGMETRICS 2003: Proceedings of the 2003 ACM SIGMETRICS International Conference on Measurement and Modeling of Computer Systems (2003)
6. Caron, E., Desprez, F., Muresan, A.: Pattern Matching Based Forecast of Non-periodic Repetitive Behavior for Cloud Clients. J. Grid Computing, 49–64 (2011)
7. Rightscale inc., http://support.rightscale.com/
8. Buyya, R., Garg, S.K., Calheiros, R.N.: SLA-Oriented Resource Provisioning for Cloud Computing: Challenges, Architecture, and Solutions. In: Proceedings of the 2011 IEEE International Conference on Cloud and Service Computing (CSC 2011). IEEE Press, USA (2011)
9. Tran, V., Tsuji, H., Masuda, R.: A new qos ontology and its qos-based ranking algorithm for web services. Simulation Modelling Practice and Theory 17(8), 1378–1398 (2009)
10. Calheiros, R.N., Ranjan, R., Beloglazov, A., De Rose, C.A.F., Buyya, R.: CloudSim: A Toolkit for Modeling and Simulation of Cloud Computing Environments and Evaluation of Resource Provisioning Algorithms. Software: Practice and Experience 41(1), 23–50 (2011) ISSN: 0038-0644

K.A.R. Sagbo and P. Houngue

11. Beloglazov, A., Buyya, R.: Optimal Online Deterministic Algorithms and Adaptive Heuristics for Energy and Performance Efficient Dynamic Consolidation of Virtual Machines in Cloud Data Centers. Concurrency and Computation: Practice and Experience (2011), doi:10.1002/cpe.1867, ISSN: 1532-0626
12. Amazon EC2 Instance, http://aws.amazon.com/ec2/instance-types
13. Park, K., Pai, V.S.: CoMon: A mostly-scalable monitoring system for PlanetLab. ACM SIGOPS Operating Systems Review 40(1), 65–74 (2006)
14. PlanetLab, An open platform for developing, deploying and accessing planetary-scale services, http://planet-lab.org

Analysis of Revenue Improvements with Runtime Adaptation of Service Composition Based on Conditional Request Retries

Miroslav Živković[1] and Hans van den Berg[1,2]

[1] TNO, Brassersplein 2,
2612 CT Delft, The Netherlands
miroslav.zivkovic@tno.nl
[2] University of Twente, PO Box 217,
7500 AE Enschede, The Netherlands

Abstract. In this paper we consider the runtime service adaptation mechanism for service compositions that is based on conditional retries. A single retry may be issued while a concrete service within composition is executed. This retry could either invoke the same concrete service or a functionally equivalent service implementing the same task. We determine the optimal moments to terminate the current request and replicate it. The calculation of these moments for each task within the workflow is based on different QoS parameters from Service Level Agreements, like services' response–time distributions and cost–relating parameters. The calculations are performed taking into account the remaining actual time–to–deadline, and the benefit of conditional retry mechanism is illustrated by simulations. We further discuss the impact of costs and response–time distributions' parameters to the solution at hand.

Keywords: Service Oriented Architecture, Optimal Retry Policies, Watchdog Timer, Hazard Rate.

1   Introduction

Composite web services in a service oriented architecture (SOA) aggregate web services that may be deployed and executed within different administrative domains. In the orchestrated scenario composite web service provider acts as an orchestrator that invokes the aggregated services according to a pre–defined workflow. The workflow is based on an unambiguous functionality description of a service ("abstract service"), and several alternatives ("concrete services") may exist that match such a description [1]. With respect to functionality, all concrete services that match the same abstract service are identical.

For commercial success of the composite web service, it is important that the service provider is able to offer the service at attractive price-quality ratios. To this end, the composite service provider (CSP) negotiates Service Level Agreements (SLAs) with the client and third party domains. A service level agreement

F. De Paoli, E. Pimentel, and G. Zavattaro (Eds.): ESOCC 2012, LNCS 7592, pp. 169–183, 2012.

(SLA) is a legal contract that specifies the minimum expectations and obligations that exist between a service provider and a service consumer [2]. Due to the high variability of the service environment, the SLA violations could occur relatively often, leading to providers' losses and customer dissatisfaction.

One of the possible approaches to mitigate the problem of SLA violations is to optimize the running composition instances by adaptation of the composition itself at runtime. In general, the adaptations could be done by means of service rebinding/substitution, or via structural adaptation of the composition [3], [11]. When adaptation is done by service substitution, a service within the composition is exchanged by another one, where, in ideal case both services are functionally equivalent. On the other hand, an interesting possibility that may be applicable in order to satisfy the agreed SLA is to trigger the retry action hoping that the fault was transient [4]. The two basic issues that need to be addressed for any of the mentioned approaches are (1) *when* to perform the adaptation, and (2) how much does it *cost* (time, money, etc.)?

We analyse the runtime adaptation of the orchestrated service composition that is based on *conditional* retry mechanisms. For each task within the service workflow a concrete service has been selected based on some end–to–end optimality criteria, i.e. the service composition has been determined. Services that are not selected are "placed" in the pool of the functionally equivalent services. The concrete services' SLAs contain response–time probability density function, as well as the invocation costs, while the end–to–end SLA contains end–to–end deadline that CSP promises to its clients, as well as reward/penalty (for CSP) when the promised hard deadline is met/missed. We illustrate our scheme in Figure 1. When task i is executed by the concrete service that implements it $(CS_i(1))$, the orchestrator starts the "watchdog timer" with the timeout count value that is set to θ_i for the execution of the selected service. When the counter expires and there is no response generated from the invoked service, the orchestrator terminates the original request, and initiates a new service invocation for the same task (i.e. makes a retry). The new invocation could be submitted, e.g. to the same concrete service as illustrated in Figure 1 for task 2, when timeout counter value θ_2 becomes zero. This may be the case when there is a single implementation of a given workflow task. In case there is more than one implementation of a given task i, the new invocation (retry) could be submitted to another concrete service (e.g. $CS_i(2)$). In the latter case dynamic binding may be required, and once the response from alternative is generated, the execution proceeds with the execution of the next service from the initial composition. When the response from the concrete service is generated before the timeout expires, the orchestrator executes the next task within the workflow. The counter of the timer is set to the new value, e.g. θ_{i+1}, and so on, till all tasks within the workflow have been executed. Based on the fact whether the end–to–end deadline is then met or not, the CSP is rewarded or penalised.

In this paper we analyse the proposed conditional request retry mechanism when a *single* retry is made. This single retry for the executed service is made when, based on service's response–time distribution, it becomes "clear" that

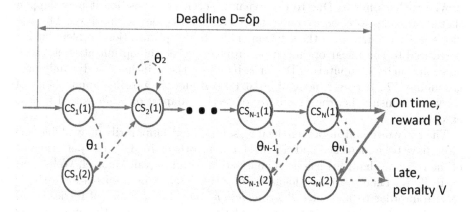

Fig. 1. Runtime service adaptation with conditional retries

the guarantees presented within SLA are jeopardized. In general case, the much faster and more expensive alternative is then executed, which makes it possible for CSP to claim the reward from it's clients. We analyse how the (optimal) values of timeout counter values θ_i could be determined, i.e. the procedure to calculate the time instances when retry should be attempted. We illustrate the impact of response–time distributions and invocation costs specified by services' SLAs to the solution at hand. We indicate which distributions may be considered when retry mechanism is to be applied, and the potential revenue improvements of our scheme. For a given example we determine the optimal position of the retry, i.e. we give an answer to the question whether it would be better to perform the retry the sooner or later during the workflow execution.

The paper is organized as follows: in the next Section we give details of the related work. In Section 3 we describe the system model and the assumptions taken. In Section 4 we explain how to determine the optimal timer values. Based on this analysis, we describe the simulation results for a couple of scenarios in Section 5 and conclude the paper with possible directions for the future work in Section 6.

2   Related Work

QoS–aware service composition within SOA is usually static process, i.e. it deals with determining the "best" available service for the abstract composition during the deployment, e.g. by maximizing some utility function [14] or by combining the local selection and global optimization [15]. The methods an approaches deal with the optimization in a static manner, i.e. the optimal compostion does not change at runtime. More recent work in this area focuses on dynamic, runtime composition solutions and adaptations [9, 10, 12]. For each task invocation, the orchestrator dynamically binds the task of the abstract composition to an actual implementation (i.e., concrete service), selecting it from the pool of service providers that offer it. Due to the dynamic service composition it may happen that every composite service request is served by different composition. The service selection is driven by the solution of a suitable optimization problem, which is reduced to the linear optimization problem [9], or the optimization is based on evolutionary computation [10] or is based on the principles of dynamic programming [12]. However, none of [9,10,12] consider the possible applicability of retry mechanisms, i.e. the possibility of service adaptation *while* actual task is executed.

The retry mechanisms as self–healing solution for temporarily unavailable services, have been identified and classified, among others, in [3,4]. The performance of the retry mechanisms has been analysed in detail by van Moorsel, Wolter, et. al. in [5–7]. Their work has focused on optimal retry mechanisms for a single service in order to *minimize the completion time*. The number of retries could either be finite or infinite, and the completion time when restarting must be less than without restarting. Okamura et. al. in [8] analyse the optimal restart policies when deadline is given. First, they prove that, time–fixed restart time is the best policy even in non–stationary control setting under the assumption of un-bounded restart opportunities. They also analyse the problem of optimal restart when a deadline is given and develop on–line adaptive algorithms for estimating the optimal restart time interval via reinforcement learning. The solutions mentioned focus on minimization of completion time. None of these solutions analyse the problem using the penalty or reward of any kind. The cost of the retries are defined as additional time to re–issue the service request. Besides, the retry mechanism is analysed from the single service point of view.

On the other hand, Yousefi et. al. in [13] describe a strategy for QoS aware service selection which takes advantage of the existing variability in QoS data to provide higher quality services with less cost compared to the conventional QoS aware service selection methods. In their method, *each request* is replicated over multiple independent services to achieve the required QoS. This strategy is clearly sub–optimal as it implies un–necessary request replications (and therefore higher costs) for all those requests that meet the required QoS without request replication. Our approach optimizes request replication from the point of increasing the profit of composite service provider. Therefore, we aim to issue request replication only when it is really meaningful.

3   Considered System Model

In this section we describe the model of the system that we will use for further analysis. We furhtermore adopt some assumptions for the considered system for the model illustrated in Figure 1.

The assumptions and the main features of our model are:

-   We observe the sequential workflow that consists of N tasks to be executed by the orchestrator. How to aggregate some of frequently used workflow patterns and transform the workflow into the sequential one is illustrated, e.g. in [12].

- The selection of candiate services for each task i, $i = 1, \ldots N$ has been performed, and there are at most $M_i = 2$ alternative (concrete) services to be considered, denoted by $CS_i(j)$, $j = 1, 2$. We call the initial service composition the static service composition (SSC).
- We adopt the convention that $CS_i(1)$ is the service selected for static service composition.
- A watchdog timer with timeout value θ_i is associated to workflow task i. Once the timeout expires, and there is no response from the selected service, a retry attempt is made.
- There is only one retry attempt. When request replication is made, the timer is not used till response is obtained.
- When the response is obtained by the orchestrator before θ_i expires, the next task $(i + 1)$ in the workflow is executed, by service $CS_{i+1}(1)$
- In case timer θ_i expires without response generated, the orchestrator invokes the functionally equivalent alternative service $CS_i(2)$ (conditional request replication). In case there is only one service implementing the particular task, the orchestrator attempts a single retry using the same concrete service (i.e. $CS_i(1)$).

In model illustrated at Figure 1 we see the second task is implemented by only one service, and therefore the retry takes place by this service. It is naturally possible this service is temporarily unavailable, or unavailable for a longer period of time. In the latter case multiple retries or some other mechanisms may be applicable, but we do not consider such problem in this paper.

Each concrete service $CS_i(j)$, $i = 1, \ldots, N$, $j = 1, 2$ has a response time represented by the random variable $D_{i,j} \geq 0$. We model the response-time of each concrete service as a black box, which means that $D_{i,j}$ is a random variable for which respective cummulative distribution function (CDF), or equivalent probability density function (PDF) is given. The CDFs and PDFs for concrete services are denoted by $F_{i,j}$ and $f_{i,j}$, respectively. For each concrete service $CS_i(j)$, $i = 1, \ldots, N$, $j = 1, \ldots, M_i$, there is an SLA agreed between the individual service provider (ISP) of that service and the composite service provider (CSP). This SLA contains the following elements:

- The response–time cummulative distribution function, $F_{i,j}$.
- The execution cost $c_{i,j}$ [money unit] per single invocation. From the ISP viewpoint, this value represents reward.

The composite service provider agrees the following SLA with its clients:

- The end-to-end response time penalty threshold δ_p [time unit].
- The fraction of response time realisations p_{e2e} that should be within the deadline δ_p.
- The reward R [money unit] that the CSP gets for executing a single request within penalty deadline δ_p.
- The penalty V [money unit] that the CSP pays to the end customer when the agreed end-to-end deadline is not met.

We therefore adopt a constant penalty function for the composite provider, i.e. a constant payment needs to be made if a given end–to–end response time threshold value is surpassed.

We assume that response times of concrete services are mutually independent, as the services are usually deployed by different service providers. Under this assumption of independence, the end–to–end response time distribution can be determined by taking the convolution of the respective concrete service distributions. Besides, the end–to–end response time distribution of the composite service is therefore calculated as

$$F_{e2e} = F_{1,1} \star F_{2,1} \star \cdots \star F_{N,1},$$

where $\star$ operator represents convolution. *For examples how to calculate the end–to–end response time distribution of some other frequently used workflow design patterns, see* [12].

In case of SSC, the execution costs for the composite service provider are defined as

$$C_{e2e} = c_{1,1} + c_{2,1} + \cdots + c_{N,1},$$

where $c_{i,1}$, $i = 1, \ldots, N$ is the execution cost per individual composite service $CS_i(1)$, $i = 1, \ldots, N$. We take here that $CS_i(1)$ is the service selected during service composition, as already explained.

In case that there is no conditional request replication, the party that owns the orchestrator, i.e. composite service provider has to perform the simple cost analysis for the given end–to–end deadline δ_p, parameters R, V and C_{e2e}. Representing the end–to–end reponse time by random variable D_{e2e}, whose response time distribution is F_{e2e}, the probability for a successful response within δ_p is defined by $p_{e2e} = \mathbb{P}\{D_{e2e} \leq \delta_p\} = F_{e2e}(\delta_p)$. The expected revenue per request for composite service provider in case of SSC could therefore be calculated as

$$\mathbb{E}[R_{e2e}] = -C_{e2e} + p_{e2e} \cdot R - (1 - p_{e2e}) \cdot V =$$
$$= -C_{e2e} - V + p_{e2e} \cdot (R + V).$$

Our goal is to apply the runtime adaptation, i.e. dynamic service composition (DSC) by means of conditional request replication in order to increase the revenue of the composite service provider, CSP. In order to do that, we need to identify *the optimal values* θ_i^*, $i = 1, \ldots, N$ of the timer(s) associated with the execution workflow. The optimality is represented as the profit merit for the composite service provider (CSP).

4   Analysis of the Retry Mechanism

Based on the model description given in Section 3, in this section we will perform analysis of our solution, i.e. the conditional request replication mechanism. We will first illustrate for which response–time distributions the considered mechanism could be considered. Then we perform the analysis of the request replication for the last task in the workflow, and subsequently, we analyse the request replication for other tasks in the workflow. We define the formulae that could be used to find the optimal timeout values.

4.1   Response–Time Distribution

As illustrated in [5–7] when θ_i is restart time, and random variables D and D_θ represent response times without and with retries, the retries could be considered only when expected response time with retry $\mathbb{E}[D_\theta]$ is smaller than response time without retries $\mathbb{E}[D]$, which is defined as

$$\mathbb{E}[D] < \mathbb{E}[D - \theta | D > \theta].$$

Based on this condition, it may be concluded that services with heavy–tailed response–time distributions could be considered for retries. The reason for this is that heavy–tailed distributions have considerable probability mass for relatively high values of response–times. The good indicator of the distributions' suitability for retries is hazard rate. If T is an absolutely continuous non-negative random variable (r.v.), its hazard rate function $h(t)$, $t \geq 0$, is defined by

$$h(t) = \frac{f(t)}{1 - F(t)} = \frac{f(t)}{\bar{F}(t)},$$

where $f(t)$ is probability density function (PDF) of r.v. T, $F(t)$ is cummulative distribution function (CDF) of T, and $\bar{F}(t)$ is the so called survival function of r.v. T. For a *single service, and no costs involved,* under assumptions that

- the restart of a task terminates the previous attempt
- the successive trials are independent

hazard rate is indicative whether retry may be beneficial. The retries are beneficial for services with decreasing hazard rate; it does no harm to retry services with constant hazard rate, and retries should not be done for services with increasing hazard rate.

  Therefore, the recommendations for the services with respect to response–time distributions are:

- Services with heavy–tailed response–time distributions could be used for request replication.
- When task is implemented by a single service that has no decreasing hazard rate, whether the request replication is beneficial should be determined taking into account the costs of execution and expected reward/penalty in such a case.

Another property that we consider for response–time distributions is so called, bimodal, or, in general case, multi–modal distribution. A bimodal distribution is a continuous probability distribution with two different modes, [16]. These appear as distinct peaks (local maxima) in the probability density function, as shown in Figure 2. It appears that number of services deployed today may have multi–modal or bimodal reponse–time distribution, see [17]. The example distribution at given figure indicates that majority of responses are generated within $\delta = 14$ seconds, and the probability this happens is 80%. When choice is to

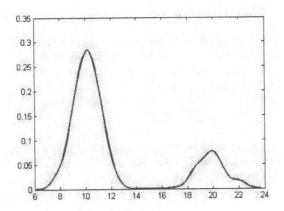

Fig. 2. A typical bimodal response–time distribution, with 80% of the values smaller than 14 seconds

be made between cheap alternative that has bimodal response–time distribution and very expensive service which indicates that response is generated within 5 seconds with, e.g. 95% probability at much higher execution cost, it seems to us reasonable to adopt the following strategy:

1. Use cheaper bimodal (or heavy–tailed) service as the first choice during service composition
2. Set the timeout value to the value that is related to the first maximum (i.e. slightly higher)
3. When the timeout value expires, terminate the current request, and then execute the very expensive alternative.

In case when there is a single implementation of the workflow task, the strategy may be:

1. Calculate the hazard rate of the response–time distribution
2. In case when response–time distribution is with decreasing hazard rate, calulate optimal moments for retries, and set the timeout value to one of the calculated thresholds.
3. In case when response–time distribution is with non–decreasing hazard rate, do not perform the retry mechanism.

In what follows, we will consider the case of expensive services with response–time modelled as lognormal distribution. The support of this distribution are non–negative real values, which overcomes well with the fact that the response–time cannot be negative. Also, the choice of parameters μ and σ of this distribution allow to easily model different response–time distributions.

The PDF $f(t)$ of the lognormal distribution is defined as

$$f(t) = \frac{1}{t\sqrt{2\pi\sigma^2}} \cdot e^{-\frac{\ln t - \mu}{2\sigma^2}}, \ t \geq 0.$$

where μ and σ are so called location parameter and the scale parameter, respectively.

4.2   The Last Task Analysis

Let us suppose that for the example sequential workflow with N tasks, the first $N - 1$ tasks have been executed with the elapsed time τ, which means the time–to–deadline for the last task is $d_n = \delta_p - \tau$. In order to simplify the notation, let us write $c_{N,i} = c_i$, $f_{N,i} = f_i$, $F_{N,i} = F_i$, $i = 1, 2$. Further, let us denote the execution costs of the tasks already executed by C_E (see Figure 3). The expected reward $\mathbb{E}_1$ in case that there is no replication mechanism (SSC) is

$$\mathbb{E}_1 = -c_1 + R \cdot F_1(d_n) - V \cdot (1 - F_1(d_n)) - C_E$$
$$= -C_E - c_1 - V + (R + V) \cdot F_1(d_n).$$

The expected reward consists of costs incurred for the tasks executed (C_E), the cost of the last task execution (c_1), the reward R that is obtained when the task is executed within given deadline d_n with probability F_n, and the penalty V that is paid when deadline d_n is not met, with probability $1 - F_n$. Naturally, when $d_n <= 0$ we have that $F_n = 0$ – in other words, there is "no chance" the deadline would be met. When our approach is applied the expected reward denoted by $\mathbb{E}_{1\to 2}$ is

$$\mathbb{E}_{1\to 2} = -c_1 + R{\cdot}F_1(\theta_n) - C_E + (1 - F_1(\theta_n)){\cdot}$$
$$\cdot\{-c_2 + R{\cdot}F_2(d_n - \theta_n) - V \cdot (1 - F_2(d_n - \theta_n))\}.$$

In this case we see that the reward is obtained either when the first service completes the execution before timeout value θ_n expires, which happens with probability $F_1(\theta_n)$. With probability $1 - F_1(\theta_n)$ we make a conditional retry. When the retry is made, the deadline for the second service is $d_n - \theta_n$ and this deadline is met with probability $F_2(d_n - \theta_n)$, which means that, when timeout expires after θ_n and retry is made, CSP obtains reward R with probability $(1 - F_1(\theta_n)) \cdot F_2(d_n - \theta_n)$. The similar reasoning could be made for the case when penalty is to be paid by CSP.

In order for our method to be applicable, there exists at least one θ such that $\mathbb{E}_1(\theta) \leq \mathbb{E}_{1\to 2}(\theta)$, $0 < \theta < d_n$. The optimal value $\theta_n = \theta_n^*$ is the one for which $\mathbb{E}_{1\to 2}$ reaches maximum at interval $(0, d_n)$. The value $\theta = \theta_n^*$ for which $\mathbb{E}_{1\to 2}$ reaches maximum is determined by solving

$$\frac{\partial \mathbb{E}_{1\to 2}}{\partial \theta}\Big|_{\theta = \theta_n^*} = 0.$$

Elementary transformations give the following expression

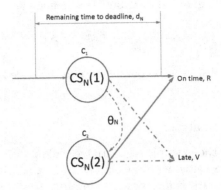

Fig. 3. The execution of the last task with the conditional request replication. Remaining time to deadline is d_n, and the timout value of the timer is θ_n.

$$\frac{f_1(\theta_n^*)}{1 - F_1(\theta_n^*)} + \frac{c_2}{R + V} \cdot \frac{f_1(\theta_n^*)}{1 - F_1(\theta_n^*)} \cdot \frac{1}{1 - F_2(d_n - \theta_n^*)} =$$
$$= \frac{f_2(d_n - \theta_n^*)}{1 - F_2(d_n - \theta_n^*)}.$$

which could also be represented as

$$\frac{f_1(\theta_n^*)}{1 - F_1(\theta_n^*)} \cdot \left\{ 1 + \frac{c_2}{R + V} \cdot \frac{1}{1 - F_2(d_n - \theta_n^*)} \right\} =$$
$$= \frac{f_2(d_n - \theta_n^*)}{1 - F_2(d_n - \theta_n^*)},$$

or, equivalently

$$h_1(\theta_n^*) \cdot \left\{ 1 + \frac{c_2}{R + V} \cdot \frac{1}{1 - F_2(d_n - \theta_n^*)} \right\} = h_2(d_n - \theta_n^*),$$

where h_1 and h_2 are hazard–rate functions, represented by

$$h_1(t) = \frac{f_1(t)}{1 - F_1(t)}$$
$$h_2(t) = \frac{f_2(t)}{1 - F_2(t)}.$$

We see that, other than results from [5–8] cost structure plays important role in determining the optimal timout value θ_n^*. Besides the optimal value does not depend from the costs of the first attempt (c_1 in above example). It is trivial to determine the θ_n^* when the same service ($CS_N(1)$) is considered for the reattempt.

4.3 Analysis of other Tasks in the Workflow

We turn our attention to other tasks in the workflow now. Due to the lack of the space, we would consider the case when there is a single retry within the workflow possible, and would like to determine whether it would be best to apply the given retry scheme either for a) the first task in the workflow, b) the last task N in the workflow or c) the task i in the workflow where $i \neq 1, i \neq N$.

In order to do the fair analysis, we would consider that all services $CS_i(1)$ have the same execution cost c_1. The response–time distributions of the first service in case a), the last service in case b) and service i in case c) are identical and represented by the same bimodal distribution. In all three cases the remaining $N - 1$ response–time distributions are identical (not necessarily bimodal). We want to determine the optimal position (from the revenue point of view) for the alternative service that has execution cost $c_2 > c_1$, and which response–time distribution is lognormal.

Let us analyse the case when retry is considered for the first task in the workflow. Since all response time distributions are known, it is easy to calculate the convolution distribution for the tasks $2 - N$. This means that we have the following cases:

- A: The response from the first service is generated before the retry time-out value θ_1, and end–to–end deadline δ_p is met. The execution costs are
  $$-\sum_{i=1}^{N} c_{i,1} = -N \cdot c_1, \text{ and reward is } R.$$
- B: The response from the first service is generated before the retry timeout value θ_1, and end–to–end deadline δ_p is not met. The execution costs are
  $$-\sum_{i=1}^{N} c_{i,1} = -N \cdot c_1, \text{ and penalty } V \text{ is incurred.}$$
- C: The response from the first service is not generated before the retry timeout value θ_1, so alternative service is invoked. The end–to–end deadline δ_p is met. The execution costs are $-c_2 - \sum_{i=1}^{N} c_{i,1} = -c_2 - N \cdot c_1$, and reward is obtained.
- D: The response from the first service is not generated before the retry timeout value θ_1, , so alternative service is invoked. The end–to–end deadline δ_p is not met. The execution costs are $-c_2 - \sum_{i=1}^{N} c_{i,1} = -c_2 - N \cdot c_1$, and penalty V is paid.

Similar analysis could be performed when the retry is applied at the last workflow task, or when retry is considered for workflow task i, $i \neq 1$, $i \neq N$. The detailed analysis will be omitted here, but, it is no surprise that the biggest benefit is *when retry mechanism is applied for the last workflow task*. This may be explained by the following reasoning: when executing the first task, it is possible to wait a little bit longer before the response is obtained, as the second task, with smaller time–to–deadline is more critical. Therefore it is better to replicate request for the latter task(s) then former. When request is replicated for former task(s) the execution costs increase while the remaining time to deadline decreases significantly. In other words, any longer response times for the first task may be accounted with by the latter task(s). This holds in general for the problem at hand, as any outliers for first task(s) in the workflow may be of limited impact to the final outcome.

5   Experiments

Due to the limited space, we will show here just the very basic experimental results. These apply to the last task in the workflow, and as explained in Section 4 we consider cheap service with bimodal response–time distribution as the one selected during the initial service composition. The alternative is expensive service with *statistically* "superior" lognormal response–time distributions. The bimodal distribution is illustrated in Figure 2 and the two modes have mean values of 10 and 20, respectivelly. The mixture coefficient is 80%, which means that 80% values of response time have the mean of 10, while the remaining 20% values of response time belong to the mode with the mean value of 20. The mean value of lognormal distribution has been set to 0.25, while the variance of this distribution has been set to 4.

For the given deadline δ_p, and the last task in the workflow, the initial selection is cheap service. When timeout θ expires, the retry is made and expensive service is selected. We have varied the timeout value $0 \leq \theta \leq \delta_p$ and determined the expected revenue for given θ. The overview of the simulation parameters and their values used for the experiments are given in Table 1.

Table 1. Overview of model parameters

Parameter	Definition	Value
f_1	Response–time distribution of $CS_i(1)$	Bimodal
f_2	Response–time distribution of $CS_i(2)$	Lognormal
c_1	Cost of invocation of $CS_i(1)$	1
c_2	Cost of invocation of $CS_i(2)$	10
δ_p	End–to–end deadline	
R	Reward per request within deadline δ_p	20
V	Penalty per request not completed within deadline	50
$\mathbb{E}$	Expected revenue without request replication	
$\mathbb{E}_{1\rightarrow 2}$	Expected revenue with request replication	
G	Gain of expected revenue	
θ_i	Timeout value for execution of the task	

The relative gain of expected revenues is calculated as $G = \frac{\mathbb{E}_{1\rightarrow 2}-\mathbb{E}}{\mathbb{E}}$. The value of the deadline δ_p has decreased from 18 down to 3. The simulation results are shown in the graphs presented in Figure 4 and these are also summarized in Table 2. The following observations and conclusions could be made:

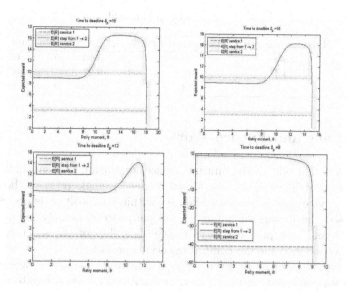

Fig. 4. Overview of the revenue gains for conditional request replication. In clockwise direction, starting from the top left corner, the deadline δ_p is 18, 15, 9 and 12, respectively.

- The scheme has its benefits for certain range of given deadlines, and when applicable, a "window of opportunity" for a retry. This interval becomes smaller as the remaining time to deadline becomes smaller.
- The gain increases as the remaining time to deadline increases. This is the consequence of the fact that it is easier to meet the deadline with the retry when there is more remaining time.
- The gains are possible with retry scheme even when the selected service is not the optimal one. For example, the expected reward for more expensive service (with lognormal response time distribution) is higher for all deadline values ≤ 20. Therefore, one may consider to select this expensive and fast service in such a case. However, we see that, when deadline is, e.g. 18, it is better to *first select* cheap and slow service, and, only when there is no response till e.g. 13 seconds, make a retry. By applying this scheme, much more revenue may be generated for the service provider. This is a consequence to the fact, that a lot of requests would be served by slow service (for given example well over 50%) and the execution costs differ 10 times.
- There is no gain of the proposed scheme when $\delta_p \leq 9$. In such a case the initial service selection should be the fast (and expensive) service. This is noticable from the graph given for δ_p - the expected reward for the whole range of retry moments with initial choice of expensive service is bigger than expected reward of retry scheme, which in turn is bigger than the expected reward when initial choice is cheap (and slow) service.

Table 2. Summary of experimental results

Deadline (δ_p)	Retry moment θ^*	Revenue: with retry	without retry	Revenue gain(%)
18	13.5	16.8	9.94	69.1
15	13.4	16.5	9.91	66.4
12	11.3	14.5	9.88	46.7

6 Summary and Future Work

In this paper we considered the runtime service adaptation mechanism for service compositions that is based on conditional retries. A single retry to the same or alternative service may be issued while task within composition is executed. We have analysed the impact of different QoS parameters, namely response–time distributions and cost parameters to the applicability of the scheme, and the potential revenue gain for the composite service provider.

The analysis has been performed for a relatively simple sequential work-flow, under assumption that response–time distributions are accurate and time–invariant. In practise, however, these distributions change over time, e.g. due temporary overload of the service, and need to be estimated. The estimation is based on response–time measurements over a finite time interval, and therefore may change over time. This needs to be addressed by methods that would recalculate the timeout values, with the main issue of optimal number of recalculations. Next to it, we plan to investigate applicability of the retry mechanism for different workflow patterns and more complex workflows.

Yet another possibility to extend the research is to find the optimal retry mechanisms when penalty function is linearly increasing, with or without the cap. In such a case the minimization of the response time, even when penalty deadline is missed may be the optimal retry scheme.

Acknowledgment. Part of this work has been carried out in the context of the IOP GenCom project Service Optimization and Quality (SeQual), which is supported by the Dutch Ministry of Economic Affairs, Agriculture and Innovation via its agency Agentschap NL.

References

1. Preist, C.: A Conceptual Architecture for Semantic Web Services. In: McIlraith, S.A., Plexousakis, D., van Harmelen, F. (eds.) ISWC 2004. LNCS, vol. 3298, pp. 395–409. Springer, Heidelberg (2004)
2. Ward, C., Buco, M.J., Chang, R.N., Luan, L.Z.: A Generic SLA Semantic Model for the Execution Management of E-business Outsourcing Contracts. In: Bauknecht, K., Tjoa, A.M., Quirchmayr, G. (eds.) EC-Web 2002. LNCS, vol. 2455, pp. 363–376. Springer, Heidelberg (2002)
3. Ardagna, D., Comuzzi, M., Mussi, E., Pernici, B., Plebani, P.: PAWS: A Framework for Executing Adaptive Web-Service Processes. IEEE Software (24), 39–46 (2007)

4. Baresi, L., Ghezzi, C., Guinea, S., Krämer, H.: Towards Self-healing Composition of Services. In: Krämer, B.J., Halang, W.A. (eds.) Contributions to Ubiquitous Computing. SCI, vol. 42, pp. 27–46. Springer, Heidelberg (2007)
5. van Moorsel, A., Wolter, K.: Analysis of Restart Mechanisms in Software Systems. IEEE Trans. on Software Engineering (32), 547–558 (2006)
6. van Moorsel, A., Wolter, K.: Optimal restart times for moments of completion time. IEEE Proc. of Software Engineering 151(5), 219–223 (2004)
7. Wolter, K.: Stochastic Models for Restart, Rejuvenation and Checkpointing. Habilitation thesis, Humboldt-University, Berlin, Germany (2008)
8. Okamura, H., Dohi, T., Trivedi, K.S.: On-Line Adaptive Algorithms in Autonomic Restart Control. In: Xie, B., Branke, J., Sadjadi, S.M., Zhang, D., Zhou, X. (eds.) ATC 2010. LNCS, vol. 6407, pp. 32–46. Springer, Heidelberg (2010)
9. Cardellini, V., Casalicchio, E., Grassi, V., Lo Presti, F.: Adaptive Management of Composite Services under Percentile-Based Service Level Agreements. In: Maglio, P.P., Weske, M., Yang, J., Fantinato, M. (eds.) ICSOC 2010. LNCS, vol. 6470, pp. 381–395. Springer, Heidelberg (2010)
10. Leitner, P., Hummer, W., Dustdar, S.: Cost–Based Optimization of Service Compositions. Journal Trans. on Services Computing (TSC) (to appear)
11. Leitner, P., Hummer, W., Satzger, B., Dustdar, S.: Stepwise and Asynchronous Runtime Optimization of Web Service Compositions. In: Bouguettaya, A., Hauswirth, M., Liu, L. (eds.) WISE 2011. LNCS, vol. 6997, pp. 290–297. Springer, Heidelberg (2011)
12. Živković, M., Bosman, J.W., van den Berg, H., van der Mei, R., Meeuwissen, H.B., Núñez–Queija, R.: Run-time Revenue Maximization for Composite Web Services with Response Time Commitments. In: 26th IEEE Conference on Advanced Information Networking and Applications, AINA (2012)
13. Yousefi, A., Down, D.G.: Request Replication: An Alternative to QoS Aware Service Selection. In: Proceedings of the 2011 IEEE Conference of Service Oriented Computing and Applications (SOCA 2011), pp. 1–4 (2011)
14. Zeng, L., Benatallah, B., Ngu, A.H.H., Dumas, M., Kalagnanam, J., Chang, H.: QoS–aware middleware for web services composition. IEEE Transactions on Software Engineering 30(5), 311–327 (2004)
15. Yang, Y., Tang, S., Xu, Y., Zhang, W., Fang, L.: An Approach to QoS-Aware Service Selection in Dynamic Web Service Composition. In: 3rd IEEE Int. Conf. on Networking and Services (ICNS 2007), pp. 18–23 (2007)
16. Wikipedia: Bimodal distribution,
   http://en.wikipedia.org/wiki/Bimodal_distribution
17. Chen, L., Yang, J., Zhang, L.: Time Based QoS Modeling and Prediction for Web Services. In: Kappel, G., Maamar, Z., Motahari-Nezhad, H.R. (eds.) ICSOC 2011. LNCS, vol. 7084, pp. 532–540. Springer, Heidelberg (2011)

Performance Modeling and Analysis of a Database Server with Write-Heavy Workload

Manfred Dellkrantz[1], Maria Kihl[2], and Anders Robertsson[1]

[1] Department of Automatic Control, Lund University
[2] Department of Electrical and Information Technology, Lund University
Box 118, 221 00 Lund, Sweden
{manfred,maria.kihl}@eit.lth.se,
andersro@control.lth.se
http://www.eit.lth.se/

Abstract. Resource-optimization of the infrastructure for service oriented applications require accurate performance models. In this paper
we investigate the performance dynamics of a MySQL/InnoDB database
server with write-heavy workload. The main objective of our investigation was to understand the system dynamics due to the buffering of disk
operations that occurs in database servers with write-heavy workload. In
the paper, we characterize the traffic and its periodic anomalies caused
by flushing of the buffer. Further, we present a performance model for the
response time of the requests and show how this model can be configured
to fit with actual database measurements.

Keywords: performance modeling, service-oriented analysis, database
server, admission control.

1 Introduction

The processing and control of service-oriented applications, as web applications,
mobile service management systems, media distribution applications, etc., are
usually deployed on an infrastructure of server clusters. The rate at which the
requests arrive can vary heavily both during a single day and during longer
periods, due to user behavior patterns. Scaling for the worst traffic peaks can
be expensive though and will result in most of the capacity being unused most
of the time. Capacity planning and resource optimization is therefore needed,
which require the design of accurate performance models that capture the system
dynamics in high loads.

Previous work on control systems for service-oriented applications and systems has mainly focused on applications with CPU-intensive workload, for example web server systems and databases with read-only requests. For CPU-
intensive workloads previous work has shown that the performance dynamics
are accurately captured by a single server queue model, see for example, [1] and
[4]. However, for applications including large databases (too large to store in
main memory), hard drive dynamics will influence the performance dynamics

F. De Paoli, E. Pimentel, and G. Zavattaro (Eds.): ESOCC 2012, LNCS 7592, pp. 184–191, 2012.

in high loads. Typically the application will need to read data from disk on every database read. Write operations are however often buffered in the server to make them more efficient. For example, in [7] the authors examine different buffering/caching techniques for use with NFS (Network File System).

Writing to persistent media is often a slow process which should be avoided if possible. Further, writing performance is also affected by certain rules of locality. For example, writing sequential data to a hard drive can be many times faster than writing to random sectors. By buffering writes and completing them in sequential order, the writes are executed more efficiently. However, when the buffered writes are actually flushed to disk, the response times of the normal flow of traffic are heavily influenced. The server becomes occupied by work other than that of the normal flow of requests. Therefore, the system dynamics of server systems with write-heavy workload cannot be captured with the single server queueing models proposed for CPU-intensive workload.

In this paper we examine write-heavy workload on a MySQL database server using the engine InnoDB. The database is stored on a magnetic hard drive which results in the database server having to employ heavy buffering to speed up the writes. In the paper, the characteristics of write-heavy workload is examined. We develop a model and configure the model parameters using experiments in our testbed. We show in experiments that the model accurately captures the periodic anomalies that occur when the system needs to empty the buffer.

In Section 2 we present the lab environment used for the database measurements. In Section 3 we characterize the database traffic. In Section 4 we present the model developed for the traffic and discuss how to configure it. We also validate the model with lab measurements.

2   System Description

In this paper, we investigate the dynamics of database servers with write-heavy workload. The models and methods proposed in the paper are based on the results from experiments in our testbed. In this section, we first give an introduction to dirty page caching, which is used in many operative systems and database systems to improve the latencies when writing to disk. Further, we describe our testbed.

2.1   Page Cache

One common way to implement write-buffering is using a page cache. The storage is divided into fixed size pages. When data is written, the page being written to is first read from storage and then changed in memory and marked as dirty. Dirty pages are then kept in memory for some time before it is written back to disk and marked clean.

MySQL has several different storage engines, among them MyISAM and InnoDB. MyISAM has no built in cache for data. Instead it relies on the page caching features of the operating system. In this paper, we have used the storage engine InnoDB, which has its own system of pages which are buffered in the so called *buffer pool*. Pages are written to and read from disk directly using one of several methods for directly accessing the block storage device, bypassing the operating system page cache. The InnoDB engine tries to estimate the speed of the block device and the rate at which new pages are made dirty and from that it calculates how often and how many dirty pages need to be written to disk.

2.2   Testbed

We have used an experimental testbed. The testbed consists of one computer acting as traffic generator, and one database server. The computers were connected with a standard Ethernet switch.

The traffic generator was executed on an AMD Phenom II X6 1055T at 2.8 GHz with 4 GB main memory. The operating system was 64-bit Ubuntu 10.04.4 LTS. The traffic generator was implemented in Java, using the JDBC MySQL connector. The traffic generator used 200 working threads and generated MySQL queries according to a Poisson process with average rate λ queries per second. The behavior of the traffic generator was validated in order to guarantee that it was not a bottleneck in the experiments.

The database server had a 2.0 GHz Celeron processor and 256 MB main memory. The database files are on the system disk which is a standard 3.5" hard drive. It runs the 32-bit version of Ubuntu 10.04.4 LTS (Linux 2.6) and MySQL Server 5.1.41. The InnoDB engine was configured with 16 MB of buffer pool.

The structure of the relations in the database comes from the scalable Wisconsin Benchmark [6] and it has $n = 10^7$ tuples. The structure of the queries used all follow the following pattern:

```
UPDATE <relation> SET unique3=? WHERE unique1=?;
```

The question marks are replaced with uniformly distributed pseudo-random integers in the interval $[0, n[$. This query changes the value of one of the integer attributes of a random tuple.

3   Performance Characterization

In order to investigate the dynamics of a database server with write-heavy workload, we performed a series of experiments in our testbed presented in Section 2. In all the experiments, all requests included a MySQL UPDATE query, causing the system to write one database element to disk. Figure 1 illustrates the system behavior during an experiment where the average arrival rate, λ, was 25 requests per second. The figure shows that the system periodically have to pause the normal work and instead focus on the buffered dirty pages for some time. While the normal response times are below 0.2 seconds, response times of up to one second occur, because of these pauses. The number of requests that have these high response times are affected by the fact that requests are sent and queued up, even when the server is busy with the dirty pages.

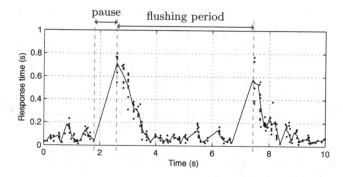

Fig. 1. Response time graph of the InnoDB system, UPDATEs only, with constant Poisson-traffic, $25/s$

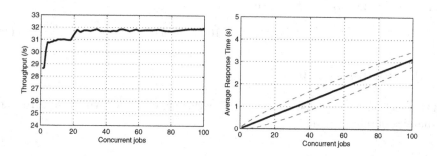

Fig. 2. N/P graph (left) and N/T graph (right) of the InnoDB system, UPDATEs only. Every point was run for 900 seconds.

The average response time as a function of the number of concurrent jobs is from now on referred to as the N/T graph. The throughput as a function of the number of concurrent jobs inside the server at all times is from now on referred to as the N/P graph. The N/T and N/P graphs for our system are shown in Figure 2.

It can be seen in the N/P graph that for a very small number of concurrent requests (up to 10), the throughput is much lower than for a higher number of concurrent requests. This is likely (to some extent, at least) because of network delays and buffering in lower protocol layers.

During high loads, the dirty page cache will be written to disk periodically. The period between two occurrences of disk writing, called the flushing period, depends on the arrival rate. As can be seen in Figure 1, an arrival rate of 25 requests per second results in a flushing period of approximately 5 seconds. Figure 3 shows the response times during an experiment with an average arrival rate of 12.5 requests per second, which results in a flushing period of approximately 10 seconds and an experiment with an average arrival rate of 18.75 requests per

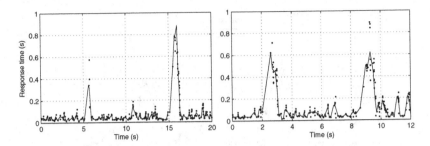

Fig. 3. Response time graph of the InnoDB system, UPDATEs only, with constant Poisson-traffic, $12.5/s$ (left), $18.75/s$ (right)

second, which results in a flushing period of approximately 7 seconds. These experiments show that the period between flushes of the buffer is inversely proportional to the arrival rate, since

$$25 \cdot 5 \approx 12.5 \cdot 10 \approx 18.75 \cdot 7 \qquad (1)$$

4   Performance Model

In this section, we describe our proposed performance model, which captures the dynamics of our system.

4.1   Model Description

We propose a queuing network model shown in Figure 4. The model consists of three parts, a *Network delay (ND)*, a *Job queue (JQ)*, and a *Dirty page buffer (DPB)*. The ND is used to model the reduced throughput at very low numbers of concurrent requests. After passing the ND, requests enter the JQ. As requests are processed by the server, the user is acknowledged and one dirty page equivalent is placed in the DPB. The DPB has a fixed maximum size and when that is reached the server stops processing requests in the JQ and starts to process dirty pages from the DPB instead until the DPB is empty. When the DPB is empty, the server switches back and continues to work on the JQ.

As a request enters the server it is assigned a processing time. Our experiments have shown that the processing time for a request in the JQ and the processing

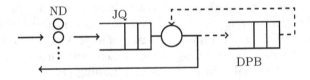

Fig. 4. The Model

time for one dirty page equivalent (T_{proc} and T_{dp}, respectively) can be modeled by an exponential distribution. Further, the time each request spends in the ND (T_{nd}) can be modeled as a sum of a constant and an exponentially distributed random number.

Further, the maximum size of the DPB is denoted DPB_{max} and it is a constant integer number. The maximum length of the DPB and one dirty page equivalent per request determine the inverse proportionality between flush period time and arrival rate shown in Equation (1).

4.2   Parameter Configuration

The model has the following parameters which must be configured:

$$T_{nd} \text{ distribution}, \mathrm{E}\left[T_{proc}\right], \mathrm{E}\left[T_{dp}\right], DPB_{max}$$

The maximum capacity of the DPB can be determined by measuring the period of flushes, p, for some high traffic with throughput P. Since p determines how often the DPB needs to be flushed and P determines how fast new dirty pages are put into the DPB, the max length of the DPB is $DPB_{max} = P \cdot p$.

By examining some experiment with high number of concurrent requests, a lower limit on the duration of the pause in processing ($\min(T_{pause})$) can be determined. By measuring the time between request departures and filtering out those that are $> \min(T_{pause})$, an average on the pause duration (T_{pause}) can be estimated. From these results, the mean of the dirty page processing time is given by $\mathrm{E}\left[T_{dp}\right] = T_{pause} \cdot DPB_{max}^{-1}$.

With the knowledge of T_{dp} and the throughput (P) when keeping high number of concurrent requests, the average processing time T_{proc} can be determined. By assuming that the server is always busy, the throughput can be assumed to be inversely proportional to the total processing time spent on every request. Since the server spends a total of $T_{proc} + T_{dp}$ time on every request, the average for the processing time is given by $\mathrm{E}\left[T_{proc}\right] = P^{-1} - \mathrm{E}\left[T_{dp}\right]$.

The distributions used for the network delay (T_{nd}) are determined by performing an experiment keeping one concurrent request in the system. The response times T are measured. Since the total response time of one single request is the sum of the network delay, the processing time plus that it has a probability of DPB_{max}^{-1} to get $DPB_{max} \cdot T_{dp}$ added, the average network delay is given by $\mathrm{E}\left[T_{nd}\right] = \mathrm{E}\left[T\right] - \mathrm{E}\left[T_{proc}\right] - \mathrm{E}\left[T_{dp}\right]$.

4.3   Model Validation

In order to validate the proposed model, we developed a discrete-event simulation program, written in Java. By using the configuration method described in Section 4.2, we can conclude that the values in Table 1 make a good fit for our database server described in Section 2.

In Figure 5, the cumulative distribution function of the response times from an experiment with arrivals following the Poisson process with an average rate of

Table 1. Fitted model parameters

T_{proc}	Exp(0.0269)
T_{nd}	$0.0025 + $ Exp(0.00049)
DPB_{max}	111
T_{dp}	Exp(0.00433)

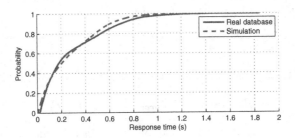

Fig. 5. Cumulative distribution function of response times from InnoDB database system, and the proposed model. Traffic is generated with a Poisson process with average 28 requests per second.

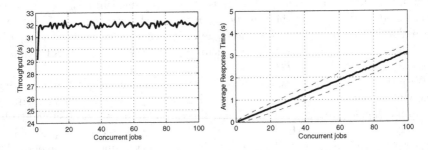

Fig. 6. N/T (top) and N/P (bottom) graph from the simulation of the model. Every number of parallel jobs was run for 900 seconds.

28 requests per second, are shown. One graph shows the results from a testbed experiment and one graph shows the results from the discrete-event simulation of the model. As can be seen in the graphs, the distribution of response times in the model fits accurately with the database experiment.

Further, the N/T and N/P graphs for the simulation is shown in Figure 6. These graphs can be compared with the graphs of the corresponding experiments, shown in Figure 2. The graphs show that the proposed model fits well with the real system.

5   Conclusions

Many service-oriented applications use database servers for storing data. When the applications have a workload that writes to a database stored on hard drives, disk writing optimizations introduce performance dynamics that may be difficult to monitor and control. Traditional queuing system models do not suffice when the response times show these periodic anomalies. In this paper, we have developed a performance model based on queueing systems for database servers with write-heavy workload. We validate our model using experiments in a testbed.

Acknowledgment. This work has been partly funded by the Lund Center for Control of Complex Engineering Systems (LCCC) and the Swedish Research Council grant VR 2010-5864.

References

1. Cao, J., Andersson, M., Nyberg, C., Kihl, M.: Web Server Performance Modeling using an M/G/1/K*PS Queue. In: Proceedings of the 10th IEEE International Conference on Telecommunications (2003)
2. Liu, X., Heo, J., Sha, L., Zhu, X.: Adaptive Control of Multi-Tiered Web Application Using Queueing Predictor. In: Proceedings of: 10th IEEE/IFIP Network Operations and Management Symposium, NOMS 2006 (2006)
3. Kihl, M., Robertsson, A., Andersson, M., Wittenmark, B.: Control-theoretic Analysis of Admission Control Mechanisms for Web Server Systems. World Wide Web Journal 11, 93–116 (2008)
4. Kihl, M., Cedersjö, G., Robertsson, A., Aspernäs, B.: Performance measurements and modeling of database servers. In: Sixth International Workshop on Feedback Control Implementation and Design in Computing Systems and Networks, June 14 (2011)
5. Kamra, A., Misra, V., Nahum, E.M.: Yaksha: A Self-Tuning Controller for Managing the Performance of 3-Tiered Web sites. In: Twelfth IEEE International Workshop on Quality of Service (June 2004)
6. DeWitt, D.J.: The Wisconsin Benchmark: Past, Present, and Future. In: Proceedings of: 9th International Conference on Very Large Data Bases, pp. 8–19. Citeseer (1991)
7. Rago, S., Bohra, A., Ungureanu, C.: Using Eager Strategies to Improve NFS I/O Performance. In: Sixth IEEE International Conference on Networking, Architecture, and Storage (2011)
8. Hsu, W.W., Smith, A.J., Young, H.C.: I/O Reference Behavior of Production Database Workloads and the TPC Benchmarks — An Analysis at the Logical Level. ACM Transactions on Database Systems 26(1), 96–143 (2001)
9. Kleinrock, L.: Queueing Systems: Theory, vol. I. Wiley Interscience, New York (1975)

Mobile Cloud Computing in 3G Cellular Networks Using Pipelined Tasks

Marvin Ferber and Thomas Rauber

Department of Computer Science
University of Bayreuth, Germany
{marvin.ferber,rauber}@uni-bayreuth.de

Abstract. Network latency is often high on mobile devices due to wireless access, e. g., via 3G cellular networks. To better use the ubiquitously available 3G network connections, we propose a pipelining task concept on a single encrypted channel between a mobile device and a cloud resource. This does not only increases wireless bandwidth occupation, it also makes wireless communication more predictable by assuring a high throughput even for small messages. Constantly high throughput allows for a better data transfer time estimation and can thus lead to a more adequate cloud resource selection to assist the mobile application. In an experimental evaluation using streaming image processing, we investigate the performance and applicability of our approach and compare it to the widely used HTTP.

Keywords: mobile cloud computing, image processing, task parallelism, pipelining, 3G cellular network.

1   Introduction

Mobile cloud computing has emerged aiming at assisting mobile devices in processing computationally or data intensive tasks using cloud resources [1, 2]. In this context, mobile image processing tasks often play an important role enabling smart devices to better assist users in every day situations [3–5]. In contrast to mobile computing, network access is a mandatory requirement for cloud computing. The public usage of cloud resources implies a pay-per-use model and, thus, authentication is necessary to use cloud services. As a consequence, all communication between the mobile device and the cloud needs to be encrypted. To make mobile cloud computing even more flexible, dynamic code offloading techniques allow the installation of server code on demand.

Network throughput for publicly available 3G cellular networks depends on the size of the messages transferred, especially for small data transfer. Fig. 1 (left) illustrates the measured throughput over message size for secure SSL-socket connections. This could be adverse for mobile cloud computing, because the number of remote executions in a given period of time, and thus the expected cloud resource load, can often not be predicted adequately. To address these issues, we propose a pipelining task model where remote invocations are represented as

F. De Paoli, E. Pimentel, and G. Zavattaro (Eds.): ESOCC 2012, LNCS 7592, pp. 192–199, 2012.

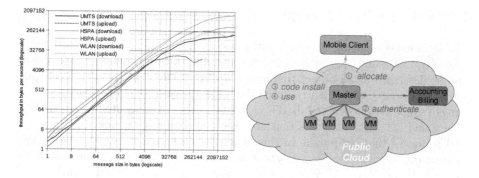

Fig. 1. *Left:* Wireless network characteristics of single SSL socket connections to a VM in the Amazon datacenter in Ireland measured from different places in Bayreuth (Germany) on a Dell Streak 7 Android Tablet. *Right:* Overview of the middleware entities for the mobile cloud computing scenario considered.

tasks. Our contribution is a novel task-based mobile computing approach to execute tasks either on the smart device or remotely. Using pipelining over a single secured socket connection, wireless bandwidth occupation is increased significantly and the throughput even for small tasks is almost constant and, thus, more predictable. This can lead to a better usage of cloud resources and allows for a better on-demand cloud resource selection strategy. Our pipelining task model has been developed for applications that benefit from many (remote) executions using small input/output data, e. g., mobile streaming image processing. Furthermore, we assume the use of public Infrastructure-as-a-Service providers, e. g., Amazon EC2[1], to run the server-side components. As these providers are available for public use and 3G access is available in many places, our approach is applicable to a broad set of applications.

Related approaches for mobile cloud computing do not take into account the cloud resource allocation and the optimization of the bandwidth occupation on the wireless access network. In [6], MARS is presented, a middleware for dynamic remote code execution on mobile devices. MARS is an RPC-based remote execution scheduler that offloads code dynamically based on parameters like the current network connection speed, the expected remote execution time, and the expected energy consumption. MAUI is an advanced middleware for the .NET platform that implements dynamic code offloading for the purpose of energy saving on mobile devices [7]. In contrast to MARS, it performs an online application partitioning in order to select code parts for remote execution.

The rest of the article is structured as follows. In Section 2 we present a model for the mobile cloud computing architecture considered. Section 3 introduces our novel pipelining task approach. In Section 4, a cloud resource selection strategy is presented. In Section 5, our prototypical middleware implementation is evaluated using image processing tasks. Section 6 concludes the article.

---

[1] http://aws.amazon.com/ec2/

2   Mobile Cloud Computing

Mobile cloud computing aims at assisting mobile applications in computationally intensive task using cloud resources. We introduce a task concept, where a task can be described as an object that stores a) input data (byte array), b) output data (byte array), and c) a string that describes the task function. The execution time of single task is denoted as ΔT_{task} for tasks that are executed on the mobile device and ΔT_{remote} for tasks that are executed remotely on cloud resources.

The model that we pursue in this article is illustrated in Fig. 1 (right). We assume that a *cloud resource (virtual machine VM)* is used by a *mobile client* multiple times. The *VM* allocation and remote execution is then performed in the following sequence of steps 1) *VM* resource allocation, 2) authentication, 3) dynamic code offloading and installation, 4) and the actual remote executions. This sequence implies the presence of some kind of proxy entity (*Master*) that performs the *VM* allocation and authentication. After a *VM* has been delivered, the remote execution code is installed directly on the allocated *VM*. A life cycle implementation is necessary, because each *VM* allocation and usage has to be billed. As a result, an explicit destruction of the *VM* needs to be performed by the client in order to stop billing.

According to our middleware model for mobile cloud computing, a sequence of remote task executions is denoted as $\sum_{i=0}^{n} \Delta T_{remote\,i} + \Delta T_{dealloc}$. The composition of different ΔT_{remote} is described in Equations (1) and (2):

$$\Delta T_{remote\,0} = \Delta T_{alloc} + \Delta T_{auth} + \Delta T_{offload} + \Delta T_{comm\,0} + \Delta T_{task\,cloud\,0}, \quad (1)$$

$$\Delta T_{remote\,i} = \Delta T_{comm\,i} + \Delta T_{task\,cloud\,i} \quad , \quad i = 1, \ldots, n. \quad (2)$$

An overhead for allocation and authentication needs to be considered for the first remote execution $\Delta T_{remote\,0}$. Furthermore, the remote execution time for all tasks depends on the cloud resource performance $\Delta T_{task\,cloud}$ and the network communication involved ΔT_{comm}. ΔT_{alloc} describes the time necessary to allocate a *VM* of a given type for the *mobile client*. ΔT_{auth} is necessary to authenticate a *mobile client* in order to implement access restriction to the cloud environment and to bill the *VM* usage accordingly. $\Delta T_{offload}$ describes the time that is consumed by a special first task that is executed on the *VM*. It contains the necessary code as input data and is installed by a common installation task function, e.g., for Java the class files are added to the class path.

The communication time depends on the throughput and the message size. Thereby, we assume that the throughput for single socket connections is a function of the message size (*msg_size*) as it can be recognized in Fig. 1. The communication time can be described as:

$$\Delta T_{comm} = \Delta T_{transfer\,upload} + \Delta T_{transfer\,download}, \quad (3)$$

$$\Delta T_{transfer} = msg\_size \cdot \text{Throughput}(msg\_size), \quad (4)$$

$$msg\_size = \text{encrypt}(\text{marshall}(payload\;data) + protocol). \quad (5)$$

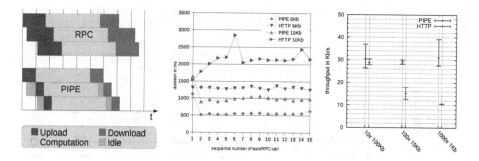

Fig. 2. *Left:* Illustration of three equal tasks with overlapped execution using both approaches. *Middle:* Measured execution times of a sequence of remote executions using UMTS ($\Delta T_{\text{task cloud}}=100$ ms). *Right:* Throughput (min, avg, max) for 1 MB of payload data for different task count using UMTS ($\Delta T_{\text{task cloud}}=0$ s).

3 Pipelining Task Execution

Inspired by work on *HTTP pipelining* such as [8], we apply the pipelining technique to better use the available network bandwidth. A task intended for remote execution is sent to the *VM* using the TCP output channel established. On the server side, incoming tasks are executed according to the number of available CPU cores. Each task is a single processor task. Results of finished tasks are sent back to the *mobile client* using the same TCP connection. Thus, a constant stream between *mobile client* and *VM* is established and bandwidth occupation is maximized. Fig. 2 (left) shows the behavior of the task concept in contrast to an RPC behavior. Therein, RPC calls are overlapped to increase the bandwidth occupation. Because these overlapped calls are not synchronized, communication time for particular calls may increase due to concurring network use.

Results showing the execution time of synthetic benchmarks consisting of a sequence of tasks using the different concepts are shown in Fig. 2 (middle). Only the connection between the *mobile client* and the *VM* is shown. As expected, using the pipelining concept only the first task takes longer for completion in contrast to the subsequent tasks that are sent via the same network stream. For HTTP, the execution time of the different tasks stays the same or may even increase due to concurring invocations. In Fig. 2 (right) the measured throughput for 1 Mb of payload data and different number of tasks is shown. We have conducted 10 measurements for each scenario. It can be seen that the overhead for HTTP with small payload data is much higher. As a result, for the pipelining concept the real network throughput is almost fixed to a value near the maximum for all subsequent remote task executions and thus $\Delta T_{\text{transfer}}$ can be simplified for the pipelining approach to:

$$\Delta T_{\text{transfer PIPE}} = msg\_size \cdot \text{Throughput}_{max}. \qquad (6)$$

This is beneficial, if a computation can be divided into many small tasks, because fine grained progress can be reported on the *mobile client*.

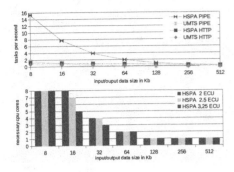

Amazon EC2 instance type characteristics (EU Ireland region)				
	ECUs	Cores	RAM	Cost in USD ECUs/Core
m1.large	4	2	7.5 GB	0.36	2
c1.medium	5	2	1.7 GB	0.186	2.5
m2.xlarge	6.5	2	17.1 GB	0.506	3.25
m1.xlarge	8	4	15.0 GB	0.72	2
m2.2xlarge	13	4	34.2 GB	1.012	3.25
c1.xlarge	20	8	7.0 GB	0.744	2.5
m2.4xlarge	26	8	68.4 GB	2.024	3.25

Fig. 3. *Top:* Task rate$_{max}$ depending on the available network quality. *Bottom:* MIN_{cores} for different EC2 instance groups ($\Delta T_{\text{task cloud}}=1$ s). *Right:* Amazon EC2 instance type characteristics (on-demand instances).

4   Cloud Resource Selection

Although the pipelining approach proposed increases network occupation, the network connection is still the limiting factor. From a sequence of tasks that is transferred between a *mobile client* and a *VM* (each takes ΔT_{comm}) a maximum task rate can be calculated depending on the available network connection:

$$\text{task rate}_{max} = \frac{\text{number of tasks}}{s} = \frac{1}{\Delta T_{\text{comm}}}. \tag{7}$$

Fig. 3 (left) shows the maximum task rate for different network connections using the HTTP and PIPE implementations.

To overlap task execution and data transfer to achieve 100% network occupation, cloud resources with multiple CPU cores may be necessary. In contrast, a second goal is to avoid overprovisioning and thus save money. Cloud resources may differ in single core speed and the number of available CPU cores. Memory is not a relevant factor in this scenario, because each *VM* provides much more main memory than the mobile device itself. As an example for an IaaS provider, we consider the selection of a suitable VM from the portfolio of the Amazon EC2 cloud computing infrastructure. Fig. 3 (right) shows the available instance types. In Amazon EC2, the machine speed is rated in ECUs. As we only have single processor tasks, we calculate the ECU rating per core and classify the available instance types into three groups (2, 2.5, 3 ECUs) by taking into account that a single task execution $\Delta T_{\text{task}}(ECUs)$ scales according to the number of ECUs. When using a different IaaS provider, the rating per core and the creation of groups of similar performance/core ratings can be done accordingly. We do not assume that upload and download can be performed in parallel in a 3G network, because we were not able to measure any significant speedup by doing this. As a result, the number of cores per machine necessary for 100% network occupation for one of the three groups can be calculated as follows:

$$MIN_{\text{cores}} = \frac{\Delta T_{\text{task cloud}}(ECUs)}{\Delta T_{\text{comm}}}. \tag{8}$$

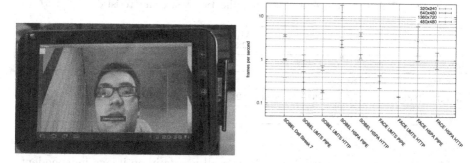

Fig. 4. *Left:* Illustration of the face detecting test application on a Dell Streak 7 Android tablet. *Right:* Frame rates (min, avg, max) for the streaming image processing application using the sobel operator and face detection.

Fig. 3 (bottom) shows MIN_{cores} for $\Delta T_{task\ cloud}(2\,ECU) = 1\,s$ using the HSPA connection. HTTP uses only one core in all cases and thus is not plotted. According to MIN_{cores}, a suitable machine can be selected from Fig. 3 (right). Using the pipelining approach, it is sufficient to know the maximum upload/download speed in order to predict the number of necessary cores adequately.

5   Case Studies

In our prototypical implementation, the task concept is implemented using specific `Task` classes for remote or for local execution. On request, this class is installed on the cloud server using a common install task. The install task adds the transferred precompiled class file to the Java class path of the server. An object of the desired `Task` class in Java is instantiated using `Class.forName()`. Note that remote and local `Task` classes can have completely different implementations, which is necessary to support potentially different system libraries (Standard Java API and Android API). On the Android platform, only the type of network can be identified, such as EDGE, UMTS, or HSPA, but not the exact network link speed. However, the current link speed can be determined by the user using tools like Speedtest[2].

To show the practical applicability of the proposed pipelining approach, we have included image processing algorithms from *Face Detection in Color Images*[3] and *ImageProx*[4] into an Android application. The application is implemented as a streaming camera picture processing application that takes camera images, processes them and displays the modified results in a loop. Thus, a frame rate per second can be measured. We have used a Dell Streak 7 for the investigations. It uses Android 3.2 and owns an Nvidia Tegra 2 Dual-core ARMv7 CPU (1 GHz) and 512 Mb RAM.

---

[2] http://www.speedtest.net/

[3] http://sourceforge.net/projects/facedetectionin/

[4] http://www.3programmers.com/mwells/research.html

Table 1. Image processing application test characteristics

	Upload	Download	ΔT_{task}	$\Delta T_{task\ cloud}$ (2.5 ECUs)	task rate$_{max}$ (UMTS/HSPA)	MIN_{cores} (2.5 ECUs) (UMTS/HSPA)
320x240 (Sobel)	ca. 7 Kb	ca. 12 Kb	280 ms	25 ms	ca. 1,5/ca. 17,8	1/1
640x480 (Sobel)	ca. 22 Kb	ca. 29 Kb	990 ms	80 ms	ca. 0,5/ca. 6,3	1/1
1360x720 (Sobel)	ca. 54 Kb	ca. 85 Kb	2500 ms	250 ms	ca. 0,2/ca. 2,4	1/1
480x480 (Face)	ca. 20 Kb	ca. 21 Kb	–	ca. 1000 ms	ca. 0,6/ca. 7,5	ca. 1/ca. 7

The sobel operator [9] can be applied to all points in an image independent from the other pixels. So, a task-based version of this algorithm works on small buckets of the image. In contrast, the face detection algorithm can hardly be decomposed, because it consists of a workflow of dependent operations and intermediate data must be kept in main memory. We were not able to execute this kind of algorithm on the Dell Streak 7, unless image size is smaller than 64x48.

We have measured the frame rates for the different 3G configurations and have compared them to the pure device performance using different image resolutions. Fig. 4 shows the minimum, maximum and average values for a 100 s measurement of the sobel operator task. The frame rates do not include the allocation and code installing phase. For the sobel operator task, a `c1.medium` instance at the Amazon EC2 datacenter in the EU region has been used. Image size in transfer data and processing times of the tasks are given in Table 1. The results show that the pipelining approach is much faster than the RPC approach via HTTP. For HTTP, we have allowed up to eight parallel connections to achieve a better bandwidth occupation. In comparison to the device speed of the Dell Streak 7, we have been able to achieve reasonable speedups only for the HSPA scenario. However, for another device, the results could be different.

Using the face detection algorithm based on skin color [10], we only used a resolution of 480x480 for our investigations, because each task takes around 1 s to process on a 2.5 ECU/core machine, which is recognized as a delay in the image stream on the device. When decreasing the picture size the chance of detecting faces also decreases because of the bad picture quality. Using this configuration, we chose a `c1.medium` instance for UMTS and a `c1.xlarge` instance for HSPA. The frame rates of the face detection application are shown in Fig. 4. We have measured a CPU utilization of 38% on the `c1.medium` instance and 61% on the `c1.xlarge` instance using Amazon EC2 CloudWatch. The results show that the cloud resource selection strategy proposed is sufficient for the application considered. A demonstration of the face detection application on the Dell Streak 7 is given in Fig. 4.

Furthermore, it could be observed that the link quality of the tested 3G connections is varying over time. This can be recognized in Fig. 2 (right) and in Fig. 4 by the difference between minimum and maximum values. Moreover, when a cell change is performed in the 3G network, the connection can be stalled for several seconds. Thus, it is preferable not to move around, e. g. in a car, when using a cloud-assisted mobile application.

6   Conclusion

We have presented a pipelining approach that achieves a better network occupation in 3G cellular networks than an RPC-like HTTP implementation. Based on the communication improvements, we have also presented a strategy to select a suitable cloud resource from Amazon EC2 based on data size and network link speed. Tests have shown that the selected machines achieved the expected load while the cost can be kept as low as possible. As a result, ubiquitously available 3G connections are better applicable to realize cloud-assisted mobile image processing applications for smart devices. However, dynamic code offloading using a public IaaS provider still needs to be initiated by the user, because cloud resource allocation time is paying off only if the subsequent usage period is much longer, which can hardly be known in advance. Finally, the performance in 3G cellular networks can often not be assessed adequately, but it has significant influence on the remote execution time and needs to be verified by the user.

References

1. Guan, L., Ke, X., Song, M., Song, J.: A Survey of Research on Mobile Cloud Computing. In: Proc. of the 10th Int. Conf. on Computer and Information Science (ICIS), pp. 387–392. IEEE (2011)
2. Dinh, H.T., Lee, C., Niyato, D., Wang, P.: A Survey of Mobile Cloud Computing: Architecture, Applications, and Approaches. Wireless Communications and Mobile Computing (2011)
3. Chen, D., Tsai, S., Hsu, C., Singh, J., Girod, B.: Mobile Augmented Reality for Books on a Shelf. In: Proc. of the Int. Conf. on Multimedia and Expo. (ICME), pp. 1–6. IEEE (2011)
4. Girod, B., Chandrasekhar, V., Chen, D., Cheung, N., Grzeszczuk, R., Reznik, Y., Takacs, G., Tsai, S., Vedantham, R.: Mobile Visual Search. IEEE Signal Processing Magazine 28(4), 61–76 (2011)
5. Chen, D., Tsai, S., Vedantham, R., Grzeszczuk, R., Girod, B.: Streaming Mobile Augmented Reality on Mobile Phones. In: Proc. of the Int. Symp. on Mixed and Augmented Reality (ISMAR), pp. 181–182. IEEE (2009)
6. Cidon, A., London, T., Katti, S., Kozyrakis, C., Rosenblum, M.: MARS: Adaptive Remote Execution for Multi-Threaded Mobile Devices. In: Proc. of the Workshop on Networking, Systems, and Applications on Mobile Handhelds, pp. 1–6. ACM (2011)
7. Cuervo, E., Balasubramanian, A., Cho, D., Wolman, A., Saroiu, S., Chandra, R., Bahl, P.: Maui: Making Smartphones Last Longer with Code Offload. In: Proc. of the Int. Conf. on Mobile Systems, Applications, and Services, pp. 49–62. ACM (2010)
8. Kaspar, D., Evensen, K., Engelstad, P., Hansen, A.: Using HTTP Pipelining to Improve Progressive Download over Multiple Heterogeneous Interfaces. In: Proc. of the Int. Conf. on Communications, pp. 1–5. IEEE (2010)
9. Nixon, M., Aguado, A.: Feature Extraction & Image Processing. Academic Press. Academic (2008)
10. Hsu, R.L., Abdel-Mottaleb, M., Jain, A.K.: Face Detection in Color Images. IEEE Transactions on Pattern Analysis and Machine Intelligence 24(5), 696–706 (2002)

Cloud User-Centric Enhancements of the Simulator CloudSim to Improve Cloud Deployment Option Analysis

Florian Fittkau, Sören Frey, and Wilhelm Hasselbring

Software Engineering Group, Christian Albrechts University of Kiel, Germany

Abstract. Cloud environments can be simulated using the toolkit Cloud-Sim. By employing concepts such as physical servers in datacenters, virtual machine allocation policies, or coarse-grained models of deployed software, it focuses on a cloud provider perspective. In contrast, a cloud user who wants to migrate complex systems to the cloud typically strives to find a cloud deployment option that is best suited for its sophisticated system architecture, is interested in determining the best trade-off between costs and performance, or wants to compare runtime reconfiguration plans, for instance. We present significant enhancements of CloudSim that allow to follow this cloud user perspective and enable the frictionless integration of fine-grained application models that, to a great extent, can be derived automatically from software systems. Our quantitative evaluation demonstrates the applicability and accuracy of our approach by comparing its simulation results with actual deployments that utilize the cloud environment Amazon EC2.

1 Introduction

The toolkit CloudSim [2] can simulate cloud environments. It focuses on concepts like CPU scheduling strategies, detailed physical host models, and virtual machine (VM) allocation policies. Hence, it takes the cloud provider perspective. However, for migrating an application into the cloud, a cloud user typically wants to find a cloud deployment option (CDO) that delivers the best trade-off between costs and performance, whereas many details of the underlying platform remain unknown. In the context of deploying software on a cloud platform, a CDO can be seen as a combination of decisions concerning the selection of a cloud provider, the deployment of components to a number of virtual machine instances, the virtual machine instances' configuration, and specific runtime adaptation strategies. The set of combinations of the given choices forms a huge design space that is infeasible to test manually [5]. Thus, simulating CDOs can significantly simplify reasoning about appropriate solutions for cloud users.

We developed the simulation tool CDOSim [3] that can simulate the costs, response times, and SLA violations of a CDO. For these purposes, we utilized and substantially extended the cloud simulator CloudSim by means of elasticity,

F. De Paoli, E. Pimentel, and G. Zavattaro (Eds.): ESOCC 2012, LNCS 7592, pp. 200–207, 2012.

price models, and remote calls between virtual machine instances. In this paper, we present our enhancements to CloudSim that facilitate a dedicated cloud user view. Our separation of these perspectives follows the definition of the cloud role model by Armbrust et al. [1]: A *cloud provider* offers the *cloud users* the resources in terms of the utility computing paradigm. We report on a case study that uses the public cloud environment Amazon EC2 and demonstrates the accuracy of our CloudSim enhancements.

The remainder of the paper is structured as follows. Section 2 overviews CDOSim. Our CloudSim enhancements are presented in Section 3. Afterwards, Section 4 evaluates the enhancements with the help of a case study, before the related work is described in Section 5. The final Section 6 draws the conclusions and outlines the future work.

2   The Cloud Deployment Option Simulator CDOSim

CDOSim builds on CloudSim [2]. It is a toolkit for the modeling and simulation of cloud environments. With CloudSim, the simulation of distributed environments and corresponding model entities, e.g., virtual machines, scheduling strategies, and data centers, can be conducted using a single computer. Network connections between data centers and data center brokers can also be simulated.

In contrast, our tool CDOSim enables the simulation of different cloud deployment options for software systems that have—often automatically—been reverse-engineered to Knowledge Discovery Metamodel (KDM)[1] code models. KDM is used for representing the architecture of the application under study. CDOSim integrates in our cloud migration framework CloudMIG [4] and is available online as a plug-in for the corresponding tool CloudMIG Xpress.[2] CloudMIG utilizes so called cloud profiles to model, for example, the provided resources, services, and pricing of a cloud environment. In the context of those cloud profiles, CDOSim can simulate the occurring costs, response times, and SLA violations of a CDO. Different VM scheduling strategies of the cloud providers are implicitly measured by our benchmark (for details see Fittkau [3]). CDOSim utilizes Structured Metrics Meta-Model (SMM)[3] models for describing workload profiles. In SMM, the measurement, the measure, and the observation timestamps of each call to the service are described. Furthermore, CDOSim can start or shutdown virtual machine instances based on the average CPU utilization of allocated virtual machine instances resulting from arbitrary workload patterns. Furthermore, the initial VM instance type and the number of instances that shall be run at the beginning of the simulation can be configured. To dynamically start and stop VM instances and to utilize other VM instance types according to varying workload intensities, CloudMIG Xpress provides so called runtime adaptation rules. These rules can be simulated by CDOSim too.

---

[1] http://www.omg.org/spec/KDM/, last accessed 2012-06-29.

[2] http://www.cloudmig.org/, last accessed 2012-06-29.

[3] http://www.omg.org/spec/SMM/, last accessed 2012-06-29.

3   Cloud User-Centric Enhancements of CloudSim

The next Sections 3.1 to 3.7 describe our enhancements of CloudSim in detail.

3.1   CPU Utilization Model Per Core

CloudSim provides a pure random-based CPU utilization model because the CPU utilization is often rather random from a cloud provider perspective. However, from the cloud user perspective we can approximate the CPU utilization because of additional knowledge concerning an application's structure in combination with a recorded workload profile. The CPU utilization is a major predictor indicator for the performance of a VM instance. For this purpose, we implemented a CPU utilization model that follows the conducted work for an application call.

3.2   Starting and Stopping Virtual Machine Instances on Demand

In CloudSim, the virtual machine instances cannot be comfortably started on demand at runtime. They have to be created before the simulation begins or when the simulation is stopped. Hence, there exists no convenient way to simulate automatic elasticity in CloudSim. The CloudSim authors provide a way to stop the simulation and then change the configuration. However, using this approach to enable elasticity would result in stopping the simulation, for example, each minute and testing if the configuration would have to be altered. This activity should be an internal function and as cloud users we should only need to define adaptation rules. We implemented this feature into CloudSim.

Adaptation rules are required for starting and terminating instances on the basis of occurring events or the exceeding of thresholds. An example for an adaptation rule is "start a new VM instance when for 60 seconds the average CPU utilization of allocated nodes stays above 70 %."

CloudSim effectively limits this amount because only a restricted quantity of hosts can be added upfront and each host has a limited capacity as well. We extended CloudSim such that with every virtual machine instance a new host, that fits the needs of the virtual machine instance, is added dynamically at runtime.

3.3   Delayed Cloudlet Creation

CloudSim requires all Cloudlets, which model an application calculation, to be started at the beginning, if we ignore the unapt method of stopping the simulation at a defined timestamp. With this behavior web applications cannot be modeled in a realistic way because all requests would start at the beginning of the simulation and in parallel. Hence, we enhanced CloudSim such that Cloudlets are extended by an attribute *delay*, which corresponds to the time when the Cloudlet should be sent for processing. Hence, we can now handle flexible and realistic usage profiles.

3.4   Delayed Start of Virtual Machines

In CloudSim, a creation of a virtual machine results in instant availability of the VM instance. Our conducted tests showed that there is an average delay of, for example, one minute on our private Eucalyptus cloud which is typically not negligible. Therefore, we implemented an event for the delayed creation of VMs. The former creation method is triggered by this new event handler.

3.5   Configurable Timeout for Cloudlets

In web applications, there is typically a configurable response timeout. After this timeout, an answer is useless because the client or server closed the connection. Most web servers would recognize when a user closes the connection by timeout and would terminate the corresponding task that calculates the answer. This results in savings of CPU time. Hence, we also implemented a timeout for calls to application logic. Every Cloudlet that is executing, paused, or waiting, can get canceled after a configurable timeout.

3.6   Enhanced Debt Model

The debt model in CloudSim is kept coarse-grained and in particular, it's implementation uses just a basic calculation mechanism. Modeling the current debt model of Amazon EC2, for instance, is not possible with this debt model. Hence, we implemented a debt model that follows the pricing model of CloudMIG Xpress and takes a time span for which the debts are calculated. For instance, for modeling the on demand VM instance debt model of Amazon EC2, every begun hour the price for the running VM is added to the debts. Furthermore, the debt model for bandwidth usage is modeled as a step function like done by Amazon EC2. For example, the first gigabyte of traffic is free of charge, above one gigabyte to 10,000 gigabytes, every gigabyte costs 0.12$ at the time of this writing.

3.7   Method Calls and Network Traffic between Virtual Machine Instances

In CloudSim, each Cloudlet runs on one virtual machine instance. It can be moved to other virtual machine instances but a Cloudlet, e.g., representing an object-oriented method, cannot "call" other Cloudlets.

We wanted to simulate the explicit calling of methods between different virtual machine instances and on the same instance. For example, a use case for this is the calling of web services on other virtual machine instances. For this purpose, we had to implement a new Cloudlet scheduler. For example, assume *method1* which should execute on *VM1* and should synchronously call *method2* on *VM2*. *Method1* is represented by *Cloudlet1*. Before *Cloudlet1* is executed, the scheduler searches in the source code of *method1* for methods that are called by *method1*. A call to *method2* is found and the *Index Service* is queried for the location where *method2* is running. The *Index Service* returns *VM2* and for *method2* the new *Cloudlet2* is created on *VM2*. Then, *Cloudlet1* pauses itself, meaning other Cloudlets can process on *VM1*. Assume *method2* conducts no method calls. Therefore, *Cloudlet2* processes and then wakes up *Cloudlet1* on finish. *Cloudlet1* can now process or call other methods.

4   Case Study

We conducted a case study to show that our CloudSim enhancements perform in a valid, realistic way. We utilized our developed tool CDOSim, which includes our CloudSim enhancements, to reproduce a real run we conducted on Amazon EC2. Further evaluations of CDOSim, which also show its scalability, can be found in Fittkau [3]. We utilize iBatis JPetStore 5.0[4] in the case study.

4.1   Methodology

We compare the measured values with simulated values per minute. The values we compare are CPU utilization, instance count, costs, and response times. As a metric, we utilize the relative error for each of those aspects in percent values. For calculating the relative error at timestamp t, the simulated value is subtracted from the measured value and then divided by the measured value. The relative error (RE) for the whole run is calculated by summing up the relative error for each timestamp and then dividing the value by the number of timestamps. For details we refer to Fittkau [3]. All percent values will be truncated after the second decimal place. We feature four different REs. RE_{CPU} stands for the relative error of the CPU utilization. RE_{IC} is the relative error of the VM instance count. RE_{Costs} is the relative error of the costs output. RE_{RT} marks the relative error of the response times. Due to space limitations, we only provide the plots for the CPU utilization. For comparing whole runs, we introduce the overall relative error ($OverallRE$) which is the arithmetical mean of the four former described relative errors. The $OverallRE$ should remain below 30 % to have results that are sufficiently accurate [8].

4.2   C1: Case Study Using Single Core Instances

Goal. Our goal for this case study is to show that our CloudSim enhancements are valid by simulating a conducted run, that used single core instances.

Experimental Setting. The workload intensity function that is used in the case study origins from a service provider for digital photos. It represents a day-night-cycle workload that's pattern can be considered typical for regional websites. It starts with a few requests at night and increases in the morning. Then, it peaks at about 3,500 requests per minute in hour 10 and slowly decreases to about 3,000 requests per minute at noon. Afterwards, there is a second peak in hour 20 with about 5,800 requests per minute which decreases until midnight.

---

[4] http://sf.net/projects/ibatisjpetstore/, last accessed 2012-06-29.

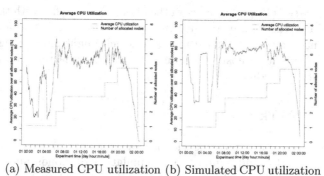

(a) Measured CPU utilization (b) Simulated CPU utilization

Fig. 1. Average CPU utilization of allocated nodes

The simulation takes place on the basis of a workload from a run that was conducted on Amazon EC2 incorporating *m1.small* instances. The adaptation strategy is 90 % CPU utilization for starting a new instance and 10 % CPU utilization for terminating a running instance. The run starts with one instance, which will not be terminated.

Results. Fig. 1 shows the average CPU utilization of the allocated nodes. In Fig. 1(a), the measured CPU utilization on Amazon EC2 and in Fig. 1(b) the simulated CPU utilization by CDOSim are presented. Over time, the instance count in the simulation and the conducted run is approximately equal. The CPU utilization is also roughly equal except from the beginning to hour 6. In this time period, the simulated CPU utilization differs by an offset of about 10 %.

The relative error for the CPU utilization is $RE_{CPU} = 30.64$ %. The average difference per minute is 12.04 % CPU utilization. The relative error of the instance count is $RE_{IC} = 1.32$ %. The overall difference of the instance minutes amounts to 28 instance minutes. The incurred costs account for 6.745\$ for the Amazon EC2 run. The simulation costs result in 7.125\$, which is $RE_{Costs} = 5.63$ %. The relative error for the response times is $RE_{RT} = 37.57$ %. The average difference per minute is 120.29 milliseconds. The overall relative error for this scenario amounts to $OverallRE = 18.79$ %.

Discussion of the Results. The relative error for the CPU utilization is 30.64 % which we attribute mainly to the differences from hour 1 to hour 6 which most probably resulted from the performance variations of *m1.small* instances on Amazon EC2 [3]. The relative error of 1.32 % for the instance count shows that the number of instances that were utilized in the conducted run can be sufficiently well reproduced. The relative error of 5.63 % for the costs is also low and shows that the corresponding reproduction is sufficiently accurate. The relative error for the response times is 37.57 %. We attribute this rather high value to the high response times that were simulated in hour 20 [3]. The overall relative error of 18.79 % is below our 30 % threshold and thus, we conclude that the simulation sufficiently well reproduces the conducted run in total.

Threats to Validity. The performance of the instances can differ with the location where the VM instances are spawned in a public cloud. The performance can also be influenced by the workload intensity which might have changed during the run on the executing host. We cannot control these factors and thus, they stay as a threat to validity.

5   Related Work

GroudSim is a tool for simulating clouds environments. It was developed by Ostermann et al. [10] and supports the simulation of clouds and grids. The equivalent to Cloudlets in CloudSim are GroudJobs in GroudSim. Failures of different components can be defined in GroudSim. They are then generated in a defined interval for a specific registered resource. In contrast to CloudSim, GroudSim is not under active development.

Another cloud simulator is MDCSim [7]. It is especially designed for in-depth analysis of multi-tier data centers and can estimate the throughput, response times, and power consumption. In contrast to CloudSim, its simulation is configured into three layers, namely a communication layer, kernel layer, and user-level layer for modeling the different aspects of a cloud.

GreenCloud [6], which is an extension to the network simulator Ns2, enables the simulation of energy-aware cloud computing data centers. It is designed for the simulation of detailed energy consumption of data center components like servers, switches, and links, and packet-level communication patterns. On the contrary, CDOSim focuses on the cloud user perspective which often has no knowledge about the internal components of a data center.

Nuñez et al. [9] developed the simulation platform iCanCloud for modeling and simulating cloud computing architectures. It bases on the SIMCAN simulation framework and can predict the trade-off between costs and performance of a particular application in a specific cloud environment and configuration. Existing software systems can only be modeled manually with iCanCloud, whereas CDOSim utilizes KDM models that can often be extracted automatically.

6   Conclusion and Future Work

A wide range of different cloud deployment options (CDOs) has to be assessed by a cloud user during a cloud migration. Basic CDOs are the selection of a cloud provider, suitable VM instance types, and runtime adaptation strategies, for instance. Due to the infeasibility of manually testing all CDOs, the best ratio between high performance and low costs can be found by utilizing simulators like CloudSim. CloudSim is a very useful toolkit for simulating cloud environments. It follows the cloud provider perspective but it lacks support for the cloud user view, which restrains the possibilities to simulate CDOs.

Therefore, this paper presented our enhancements to CloudSim that establish a cloud user perspective for simulating CDOs with our developed tool named CDOSim. We presented a case study that utilizes the public cloud provider

Amazon EC2. It showed that the simulation results that were produced by incorporating our CloudSim enhancements are reasonably near to the conducted run concerning accruing costs and performance on Amazon EC2.

Most future work lies in further adaptations to CloudSim. For enabling efficient automatic CDO optimization support that requires plenty of simulations, CloudSim should be extended to support parallel simulations.

References

[1] Armbrust, M., Fox, A., Griffith, R., Joseph, A.D., Katz, R.H., Konwinski, A., Lee, G., Patterson, D.A., Rabkin, A., Stoica, I., Zaharia, M.: Above the Clouds: A Berkeley View of Cloud Computing. Tech. Rep. UCB/EECS-2009-28, EECS Department, University of California, Berkeley (February 2009)

[2] Calheiros, R.N., Ranjan, R., Beloglazov, A., De Rose, C.A.F., Buyya, R.: CloudSim: a toolkit for modeling and simulation of cloud computing environments and evaluation of resource provisioning algorithms. Software: Practice and Experience 41, 23–50 (2011)

[3] Fittkau, F.: Simulating Cloud Deployment Options for Software Migration Support. Master's thesis, Software Engineering Group, University of Kiel, Kiel, Germany (March 2012)

[4] Frey, S., Hasselbring, W., Schnoor, B.: Automatic Conformance Checking for Migrating Software Systems to Cloud Infrastructures and Platforms. Journal of Software Maintenance and Evolution: Research and Practice (2012), doi:10.1002/smr.582

[5] Grundy, J., Kaefer, G., Keong, J., Liu, A.: Guest Editors' Introduction: Software Engineering for the Cloud. IEEE Software 29, 26–29 (2012)

[6] Kliazovich, D., Bouvry, P., Khan, S.: GreenCloud: a packet-level simulator of energy-aware cloud computing data centers. The Journal of Supercomputing, 1–21 (2010), doi:10.1007/s11227-010-0504-1

[7] Lim, S.H., Sharma, B., Nam, G., Kim, E.K., Das, C.: MDCSim: A multi-tier data center simulation, platform. In: IEEE International Conference on Cluster Computing and Workshops 2009, pp. 1–9 (August 2009)

[8] Menasce, D.A., Almeida, V.A.F.: Capacity Planning for Web Services: Metrics, Models, and Methods. Prentice Hall International (September 2001)

[9] Nuñez, A., Vázquez-Poletti, J.L., Caminero, A.C., Carretero, J., Llorente, I.M.: Design of a New Cloud Computing Simulation Platform. In: Murgante, B., Gervasi, O., Iglesias, A., Taniar, D., Apduhan, B.O. (eds.) ICCSA 2011, Part III. LNCS, vol. 6784, pp. 582–593. Springer, Heidelberg (2011)

[10] Ostermann, S., Plankensteiner, K., Prodan, R., Fahringer, T.: GroudSim: An Event-Based Simulation Framework for Computational Grids and Clouds. In: Guarracino, M.R., Vivien, F., Träff, J.L., Cannataro, M., Danelutto, M., Hast, A., Perla, F., Knüpfer, A., Di Martino, B., Alexander, M. (eds.) Euro-Par- 2010 Workshop. LNCS, vol. 6586, pp. 305–313. Springer, Heidelberg (2011)

PaaSSOA: An Open PaaS Architecture for Service Oriented Applications

Claudio Guidi[1], Paolo Anedda[2], and Tullio Vardanega[1]

[1] Department of Mathematics, University of Padova, Italy
{cguidi,tullio.vardanega}@math.unipd.it
[2] CRS4, Technology Park, Pula (CA), Italy
paolo.anedda@crs4.it

Abstract. In this paper we present PaaSSOA, our vision for a next-generation PaaS layer intended for openness and federation for the support of service oriented applications in the Cloud. PaaSSOA provides for the design of service oriented applications into the Cloud. Its architecture follows a service oriented design style and facilitates interoperation between the PaaS and possibly heterogeneous IaaS layers. We describe the architecture of PaaSSOA and present the early results we have obtained from a first prototype implementation.

1 Introduction

In the context of the Cloud Computing paradigm, the Platform-as-a-Service (PaaS) layer operates as the connection tier between the Infrastructure-as-a-Service (IaaS) layer, where the computing, the storage and the networking infrastructures are multiplexed among the users through the use of virtualization technologies, and the Software-as-a-Service (SaaS) layer, where applications become available to the user. The PaaS provides all the functionalities required for the development, the deployment and the monitoring of services as seen from the standpoint of the SaaS. The PaaS also governs the resource requests that must be made to the underlying IaaS to meet the service level agreements separately defined at both the SaaS and the IaaS levels: the former between the user and the application provider; the latter between the application provider and the infrastructure owner.

The concept we present here is named PaaSSOA and it follows from work we started in [1]. PaaSSOA aims at establishing a proof-of-concept initial model, equipped with a prototype, for facilitating the development and the standardization of PaaS frameworks by capturing the main functions which characterize the Cloud from the PaaS perspective and the interactions the PaaS has to have with the two adjacent levels in the Cloud SPI stack. The use of a Service Oriented Architecture for designing a reference model for the PaaS has two main advantages: on the one hand, it allows for a standard and well-defined separation between PaaS and IaaS and between PaaS and SaaS; on the other hand it also guarantees high flexibility, adaptability and modularity within the PaaS itself, which

F. De Paoli, E. Pimentel, and G. Zavattaro (Eds.): ESOCC 2012, LNCS 7592, pp. 208–209, 2012.

are very desirable qualities. The architecture of PaaSSOA is built upon some basic blocks that supply the basic services the PaaS level should provide. Tools offer the web production tools classically available for SaaS development; Functions provide the core resource management functionalities, such as for example monitoring and Service Level Agreement (SLA) negotiation; SaaS Gateway is in charge of publishing the deployed service for exploitation in the end-user space; and PaaS Gateway deals with PaaS federation. Finally, the Service Container block is in charge of hosting all the services deployed within PaaSSOA. The hosting task is achieved by means of a service called *SOABoot* which is executed in each Virtual Machine provided by the IaaS and it is able to receive service description and execute them.

2 PaaSSOA

Figure 1 depicts a representation of the layers needed for integrating PaaSSOA with the IaaS. Such an architecture is a fundamental facilitator to providing, at the level of the PaaS, the needed abstraction for managing services as basic resources without having to negotiate with the bare machines on which they will be run. Such an abstraction is obtained by means of two layers: *the virtual machines* and the *SOABoot*. As usual, the former is provided by the IaaS, whereas the latter is a specialized service, unique to PaaSSOA, which starts at the boot of every individual virtual machine and it is able to receive services to be deployed and executed.

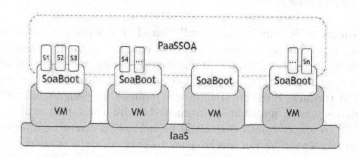

Fig. 1. PaaSSOA resources. Virtual machines (VM) are supplied by the IaaS layers, whereas SOABoots are PaaSSOA components executing services S_1, S_2, S_3, ..., S_n.

Reference

1. Guidi, C., Anedda, P., Vardanega, T.: Towards a new paas architecture generation. In: CLOSER 2012 - Proceedings of the 2nd International Conference on Cloud Computing and Services Science, Porto, Portugal, April 18-21, pp. 279–282. ScitePress (2012)

Context Mediation as a Linked Service

Pierre De Vettor[1], Michael Mrissa[1], and Carlos Pedrinaci[2]

[1] CNRS, Université de Lyon
LIRIS UMR5205, Université Lyon 1,
69622 Villeurbanne
pierre.de-vettor@etu.univ-lyon1.fr
[2] Knowledge Media Institute, The Open University,
Milton Keynes, MK7 6AA, UK

Background and Motivation. The past few years have seen important advances in the domain of Semantic Web Services (SWS), especially in data mediation. Most work in the area has focused on the semantic alignement of input/output concepts at design time, and on schema-level integration [1]. Correct communication is not guaranteed even when two services are connected to each other with compatible input/output concepts. Indeed, conceptually compatible data may not be usable when data representation and scaling conflicts occur. To address this problem, which we refered to as the *contextual heterogeneity* problem, we rely on the Minimal Service Model [2] and operate with Linked Services as SWS that offer explicit semantics. In this paper, we present our Mediation as a Service (MaaS) architecture and demonstrate its applicability with a running scenario and a prototype.

Mediation as a Service. The overall idea of this paper is to provide an architecture, accessible as a service and that enables on-the-fly mediation over compatible services based on the automated discovery and injection of mediation services at runtime, i.e. services able to convert data from one context to an other, at runtime. Such an architecture requires, at design time, (1) to provide enough semantic information to make data interpretation explicit, and at runtime, (2) to identify data that could be subject to diverging interpretations and (3) to trigger mediation mechanisms to perform data transformation. We rely on semantic descriptions of services, expressed with the MSM model associated with the Quantities, Units, Dimensions and Data Types ontologies[1]. These semantic annotations bring us means to formally describe exchanged data and their contextual sensitivity, but also to add information concerning any additional restrictions about the data to be exchanged. We attach input and output data (Message Parts) of our services to concepts of our domain ontology (e.g. Price) and to sets of meta-attributes that represent their contextual sensitivity (e.g. currency unit, VAT rate, etc.).

Fig. 1 illustrates the operational steps of our architecture with a purchase order scenario. We consider a user, who wants to buy products from Moon via the

---

[1] http://www.qudt.org/

F. De Paoli, E. Pimentel, and G. Zavattaro (Eds.): ESOCC 2012, LNCS 7592, pp. 210–211, 2012.
© Springer-Verlag Berlin Heidelberg 2012

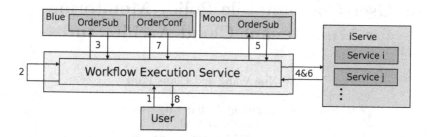

Fig. 1. Our MaaS architecture

Blue seller service. Our MaaS architecture builds around a service called Workflow Execution Service (WES), which takes as input a workflow representation and the input data required for the composition (step 1). The WES handles runtime analysis of the data exchanged and their contextual sensitivity in order to detect context heterogeneity issues (step 2). For each data flow of the composition, it extracts contextual information from the descriptions of involved services. Between each service execution (steps 3, 5 and 7), if the contextual information presents an incompatibility, the WES generates discovery queries at runtime to find services that can alleviate these incompatibilities. These queries are send to the iServe[2] platform, a Linked Service warehouse, which returns the most relevant service to perform the mediation task, e.g. unit conversion service (steps 4 & 6). This service is transparently injected within the workflow.

Discussion. In this paper, we define an architecture for Mediation as a Service (MaaS). Our system provides a way to automatically interconnect services that are compatible and to perform context-based data mediation at runtime. Our approach benefits from the respect of the service-oriented paradigm (promoting loose coupling, service reuse and composition), through the design of a Mediation as a Service architecture available as a generic Linked Service interface, the independence from workflow languages and the use of standard service description for semantic annotation. In our architecture, the WES automatically generates discovery queries when detecting contextual heterogeneity. This could serve as a basis for a truly generic and extensible infrastructure for solving runtime mediation problems.

References

1. Nagarajan, M., Verma, K., Sheth, A.P., Miller, J., Lathem, J.: Semantic interoperability of web services - challenges and experiences. In: ICWS, pp. 373–382. IEEE Computer Society (2006)
2. Pedrinaci, C., Domingue, J.: Toward the Next Wave of Services: Linked Services for the Web of Data. Journal of Universal Computer Science 16(13), 1694–1719 (2010)

---

[2] http://iserve.kmi.open.ac.uk/

User-Customisable Policy Monitoring for Multi-tenant Cloud Architectures

Ming-Xue Wang and Claus Pahl

School of Computing, Dublin City University
Dublin, Ireland
{mwang,cpahl}@computing.dcu.ie

Abstract. Cloud computing needs end-user customisation and personalisation of multi-tenant cloud service offerings. Particularly, QoS and governance policy management and monitoring is needed. We propose a user-customisable policy definition solution that can be enforced in multi-tenant cloud offerings through automated instrumentation and monitoring. Service processes run by cloud and SaaS providers can be made policy-aware in a transparent way.

Keywords: Cloud architecture, Policy customisation, Monitoring.

1 Introduction

Cloud customers should to be allowed to better control and customise cloud offerings through specific management interfaces. This is a multi-tenancy environment where users have varying requirements [1]. Governance and QoS issues are concerns usually split between provider and user. This requires a monitoring and enforcement platform, where these policies can be configured. Two key objectives of our policy definition, instrumentation and monitoring solution can be singled out. Firstly, user-configured policy management for multi-tenancy allows end-user customisable cloud computing. Secondly, our process-level policy management works not only for service-level offerings, but also for process-level architectures, where the provider implements an offered service as a process (cloud prosumers that provide service mashups).

2 Overview of the Framework

Our framework for user-controlled management of policies in multi-tenancy cloud provisionings facilitates the (self-)management (specification and monitoring) of cloud resources in order to optimise usage (the provider perspective) based on monitoring compliancy and to ensure SLA compliance (the user perspective) based on monitoring policies [2]. Our assumption for the service-level solution is that services processes (rather than individual services) are enacted by SaaS providers or users. These are customer policy-enhanced provider processes or customer processes which are customer policy-enhanced.

A management scalability problem for multi-tenancy applications arises if different users have different requirements [1,3]. A configurable policy monitoring

F. De Paoli, E. Pimentel, and G. Zavattaro (Eds.): ESOCC 2012, LNCS 7592, pp. 212–213, 2012.

technique is the proposed solution [2,4]. Customisation of policy management requires a fine-granular multi-tenancy model, where end users can configure and enact (remotely) their specific requirements. Two types of interfaces in cloud applications exist that are internally enacted through service proceses: the upload and management of resources, which can be executed by a provider BPEL process, and functionality that the application uses as a process (the cloud acts as middleware). Policy monitoring is a customer service.

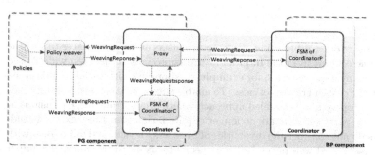

- A policy model allow users to specify dynamic quality and governance requirements. We use rule-based context modelling for policies to capture user-specific requirements and settings [5]. We have implemented user-side components for policy customisation, instrumentation, monitoring and validation.
- A policy coordination and instrumentation software tool that instruments cloud services at process level with the user policies for governance and QoS monitoring [6,7]. For the process view, mashups (composition) need to address composition of functionality as well as composition of quality aspects and their respective policy specifications. Monitoring provides feedback for policy customisation - implemented as a listener service for the process.

References

1. Mietzner, R., Unger, T., Titze, R., Leymann, F.: Combining different multi-tenancy patterns in service-oriented applications. In: Intl. Enterprise Distributed Object Computing Conf. (2009)
2. Wang, M.X., Bandara, K.Y., Pahl, C.: Integrated constraint violation handling for dynamic service composition. In: Intl. Conf. on Services Computing (2009)
3. Erradi, A., Maheshwari, P., Tosic, V.: Policy-Driven Middleware for Self-adaptation of Web Services Compositions. In: van Steen, M., Henning, M. (eds.) Middleware 2006. LNCS, vol. 4290, pp. 62–80. Springer, Heidelberg (2006)
4. Zeng, L., Lei, H., Jeng, J.J., Chung, J.Y., Benatallah, B.: Policy-driven exception-management for composite web services. In: Intl. Conf. E-Comm Tech. (2005)
5. Pahl, C., Zhu, Y.: A Semantical Framework for the Orchestration and Choreography of Web Services. In: International Workshop on Web Languages and Formal Methods, WLFM 2005. ENTCS (2005)
6. Wu, Y., Doshi, P.: Making bpel flexible and adapting in the context of coordination constraints using ws-bpel. In: Intl. Conf. on Services Computing (2008)
7. Pahl, C.: A Formal Composition and Interaction Model for a Web Component Platform. In: Workshop on Formal Methods and Component Interaction, FMCI 2002 (2002)

Enabling Co-browsing Service across Different Browsers and Devices

Bin Cheng, Sachin Agarwal, and Daniele Abbadessa

NEC Laboratories Europe, Heidelberg, Germany

Abstract. Co-browsing allows several users at different places to surf the same content from the Internet at the same time. It has been widely used in many user scenarios, for example, co-shopping with social friends or assisted customer care services. To enable such a service, some recent studies propose a web-enabled approach where browser plugins/extensions or third-party software are no longer required. However, those existing studies do not consider the diversities of browsers/devices and fail to deal with personalized web pages. With a special focus on these issues, this paper presents the detailed design and implementation of our web-enabled co-browsing system, namely *CoSurfen*. Some important strategies for web-based co-browsing are first discussed, for instance, *cookie mapping*, *event-loop detection*, *event reduction*, and *page transition*. Using these strategies, CoSurfen is able to provide an efficient web-based co-browsing service across different browsers and devices. Our initial evalutation results demonstrate its scalability, efficiency, and usability. Based on the current design, CoSurfen can be also extended to provide a cloud-based co-browsing service.

1 Introduction

Co-browsing enables two or more users at different locations to browse the same web page at the same time. It allows any user to see what the other participants are doing on the same web page in nearly real-time. With these features, co-browsing service can be used in many scenarios. For instance, Internet service providers can use it for effective customer support. Also, Internet users can use it for online shopping with their friends so that they can easily get some opinions and recommendations from their friends about which product to buy. Co-browsing facilitates great collaboration and communication for many Internet applications.

Early co-browsing systems were software-enabled, usually requiring all users to install some client software or browser plugin/extensions before the users can start to cobrowse a web page with others. For example, MSN Messenger and GoToMyPC [2] support co-browsing, but they require the users to first install a client software. In reality, there are lots of barriers for users to use such a software-enabled co-browsing. First, it requires the installation of some software, either an native application or a browser extension. The new software installation takes some time and might cause some software installation issues. Second, the

F. De Paoli, E. Pimentel, and G. Zavattaro (Eds.): ESOCC 2012, LNCS 7592, pp. 214–229, 2012.

users might have security concerns about the installed software, because of its possibility to perform malicious actions to the user's local machine after the installation.

With recent technology, we are able to provide co-browsing as a pure web-enabled service. That means, in order to use the co-browsing service, users do not need to install any software except a normal browser, which is usually pre-installed. This way to use co-browsing is also quite straightforward and secure. Whenever the users want to establish a co-browsing session for a web page, they just need to copy the URL of the page and click some buttons. By integrating with existing online social networks like Facebook, the co-browsing service allows the users to invite their trusted online friends to join the established session. As a web service, co-browsing is executed in an isolated environment provided by the browser. Under the security policy constraints of the browser, no damage to the user's local computer is possible by the co-browsing service. With all of these features, our web-enabled co-browsing can be a convenient cloud service for the users to use across different browsers and devices.

Web-enabled co-browsing is desirable to the users, but it is quite challenging to implement due to the following facts.

- First, existing devices are *highly diversified* in terms of performance capacity and properties. For instance, PCs, tablet, and smartphones are different types of devices and they have completely different screen sizes and computation power. The same web page could have different loading times and content layout on these devices. This affects synchronization during co-browsing. Also, major browsers are not standardized and they may have *different interfaces* for the same functionality. We have to deal with this compatibility issue of browsers, because co-browsing is supposed to work on all these environments in real-time and in a synchronized manner. Dealing with the diversity across browsers and devices is the big challenge for web-enabled co-browsing.
- Second, the content of some web pages can be highly *personalized and dynamic*, especially for online shopping web sites. Currently, browser cookies are commonly used to identify individual users for showing them personalized content accordingly. However, co-browsing is supposed to show the same content to several different users in the same session. To deal with the personalized and dynamic web pages without any change to the user browser and the original web site is another challenge.

Our experience shows that these issues are important for designing and deploying a practical web-enabled co-browsing system. Although previous studies propose some approaches to web-enabled co-browsing, none of them focus on the issues mentioned above. To solve these issues is challenging; it requires a deep understanding on how the browsers work and a broad knowledge background of contemporary web technologies, like HTML5 [3], CSS, jQuery, and JavaScript. In this paper, we present methods to tackle these challenging issues and share our experience of designing and implementing an efficient web-enabled co-browsing service across different browsers and devices.

2 Design

2.1 Architecture

As shown in Fig. 1, the whole co-browsing system consists of three components: *web proxy*, *cobrowser modules*, and *event coordinator*.

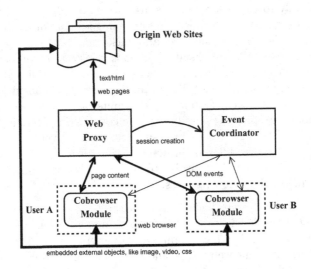

Fig. 1. Architecture of our co-browsing system

Web proxy works as a web server to provide a HTTP-based interface for the user to create a co-browsing session for any given web page. Once the session is established, web proxy will return a new URL with the generated session ID to the user and also notify the event coordinator to be ready to receive and propagate user events for this co-browsing session. By requesting the URL with the session ID, users can join the session and fetch the web page that they want to cobrowse with others. On receiving the requests from the users, the web proxy starts to fetch the web pages from the original web site, injects the code of the cobrowser module into the pages, and then forwards these pages to the users.

A cobrowser module is a JavaScript library running within the user browsers. Whenever a user performs any operation on the web page and triggers events such as mouse move, click, or page scroll, the embedded cobrowser modules capture the events, propagate them to the other users' cobrowser modules through the event coordinator, and also replay any events received from the event coordinator.

The event coordinator is responsible for managing all the co-browsing sessions and the associated users, ordering the received events and propagating them to the users in the same session. In addition, in order to facilitate user communication, text-based chatting is also supported in our co-browsing service. Therefore, the event coordinator also provides instant messaging functionality.

In our co-browsing service, all participants in the same session are the controllers being allowed to make some changes to the current web page, either by moving the mouse or by highlighting some lines of text on the page. We are trying to synchronize the activities from all participants in nearly real time so that we can ensure that *everybody in the same session can see the same thing* when they are using different devices and different browsers. In the following sections, we discuss the detailed challenges and explain our solutions toward achieving an efficient and scalable co-browsing service.

2.2   Web Proxy

In order to inject some code into the web page that the users are about to cobrowse with others, we have to let the users send their HTTP requests to our web proxy first. To do so, we cannot expect the users to change their browsers' proxy configurations, because in that case all HTTP requests from the user's browser will be forwarded to our web proxy, no matter whether they wish to use the co-browsing service or not. Also, this violates our design goal that no changes are required from the users. Therefore, we design the following mechanism for users to fetch the content of the cobrowsed web pages.

Fig. 2 gives a concrete example to illustrate the HTTP request timeline when the first user establishes the co-browsing session and starts to cobrowse *www.abc.com*. First, the first user sends the web proxy a HTTP request A, which contains a '*create*' command and the specified page URL. Then the web proxy returns a unique session ID (*SID*) to the user. Using this SID, the user generates a '*join*' request B and sends it to the web proxy to join the session. After that, the web proxy will reply the user's browser with a new cookie, which contains the SID and a unique peer ID (*PID*), and then redirect it to another HTTP request C. The unique PID is assigned by the web proxy to identify each participant in the same session. After the cookie is set up, all of the requests from the user

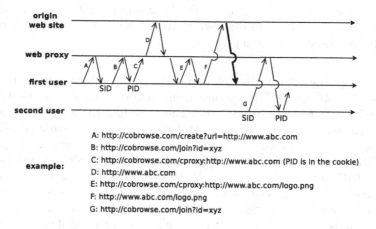

A: http://cobrowse.com/create?url=http://www.abc.com
B: http://cobrowse.com/join?id=xyz
C: http://cobrowse.com/cproxy:http://www.abc.com (PID is in the cookie)

example:

D: http://www.abc.com
E: http://cobrowse.com/cproxy:http://www.abc.com/logo.png
F: http://www.abc.com/logo.png
G: http://cobrowse.com/join?id=xyz

Fig. 2. Workflow to establish a session and join the session

side will automatically attach this cookie so that the web proxy and the event coordinator can identify which session and which user the requests are coming from. On receiving the request C with a separator keyword '*cproxy*', the web proxy will extract the real URL D of the cobrowsed web page and start to fetch its content from the origin web site. After the content returns, the web proxy will inject the code of the cobrowser module into it and then send the modified content to the user. Therefore, what the user receives is the slightly modified web page embedded with our cobrowser module.

As we see in Fig. 2, the first user automatically joins the co-browsing session right after he/she creates the session. To join the established session, a user just needs to open the session URL, which contains the corresponding session ID like the request B. After that, the underlying process of joining the session is the same for every participant. To be convenient for sharing the session URL to other participants, our system integrates with the existing social network Facebook. Therefore, the first user can send out the session URL to any online friends through Facebook. For the users on mobile devices, they can also join the session by scanning a QR-code associated with the session URL.

Request Bypassing. Notice that, for the user's browser, the HTML document of the requested page comes from the web proxy at the domain of 'cobrowse.com'. So the absolute location of any embedded objects with a relative path will be referred to this domain name. However, to get the right location of these embedded objects, we should refer to the real URL of the web page, which points to the origin web site. The solution to this problem is to add a '<*base*>' tag into the header part of the web page, as the web proxy injects some code into this web page. The added '<*base*>' tag can specify the right base URL for all relative URLs in this web page so that the web proxy can reconstruct the real URL and fetch the page content from the original web site. In addition, the embedded objects could be images, videos, CSS files, JS files, XMLHTTPRequest, or iframes. For static image or video objects we do not need to modify them. As the requests E and F in Fig. 2 illustrate, the web proxy will detect this kind of requests and redirect them to the original web site so that we can largely offload the traffic overhead of the web proxy.

Cookie Mapping. When the web proxy fetches the web page from the origin web site, the returned HTTP response might contain some cookies used by the origin web site for identifying the user and recording the context of user behaviors. To cobrowse the web sites with personalized and dynamic web pages, e.g. amazon.com, this returned cookie needs to be shared among the participants. Otherwise, the participants might not see the same content even through the page URL is the same for them. If the web proxy just passes the response over to the user browser, the browser will not accept those cookies, because the cookies are bound to the original web site, instead of the web proxy's domain. Our solution is to let the web proxy create a table to remember the mapping between the cookies and the origin web sites. Whenever the web proxy receives a request from the user, it can ascertain the right cookie from the table to communicate with the original web site. In addition, the following two observations are important to make this solution work correctly. First, the web proxy needs to send the received cookies to the user browser. That is because in some cases the JavaScript code within the cobrowsed web page refers to the cookies for generating the subsequent HTTP requests or URL links. Second, the web proxy needs to send the entire cookie table to the newly-joined users so that they can catch up with the current status of the co-browsing session.

Page Caching. Whenever one of the users in the same session triggers a new HTTP request, the event will be propagated to all others. They are all going to request the same web page simultaneously. In this case, caching the received page on the web proxy can avoid repeatedly fetching the same web page from the original web site in a short period time. This way we can not only guarantee that the users in the same session can see the same content from the same click, but also reduce the overhead of the web proxy.

To maintain this page cache, an important question is how to determine the lifetime of each page. In the page cache, each page is identified by its original page URL plus the related co-browsing session ID. In the same session, the requests to the same original page URL might lead to different contents from the original web site when the requests are generated at different time or in different contexts. Therefore, we cannot simply keep the received page until the co-browsing session ends. For the received page from the original web site, the 'Cache-Control' header in its HTTP response specifies whether the web page is cacheable and how long we can cache it. If 'Cache-Control' is 'private', that means this page is not supported to be cached. But in our case, to cache it for a short period time is still meaningful in order to serve simultaneous requests from all participants. In our implementation, the lifetime of a non-cacheable object is 5s. For theose cacheable objects, we remove them from the page cache after the session ends.

2.3 Cobrowser Module

A cobrowser module is a pure JavaScript code file, injected into the requested page by the web proxy and loaded by the user browser. When the page document is ready, the whole page might be not fully loaded because the browser is still requesting the external objects, such as images and iframe documents. However, as soon as the page document is ready and its elements are displayed, the user will be able to do some operations, like click a URL or move the mouse. Those operations should be synchronized. Therefore we should start our co-browse module before the page is presented to the user. Currently the cobrowser module is bound with the 'ready' event of the document, which guarantees that the cobrowser module can start to work once the document is ready.

To synchronize the user operations associated with any element in the web page, we need a way for anybody in the same session to uniquely identify the element. There are two methods to do this. The first method is to assign a unique ID to each element in the document. The second method is to use the route path of each element in the document. The route path is an array to record which child node we will choose to reach the destination element, starting from the root element of the document. The first method is more efficient than the second one because because it is faster and causes less network traffic. In our design we use both methods, but the second method is used only when the targeted element has no assigned ID, for example text elements or the newly-created dynamic elements.

URL Modification. When a user clicks some elements in the current page, like URLs or buttons, a HTTP request could be triggered to open a new page. To continue to synchronize user behaviors, we should inject our co-browser module into the new page as well. Therefore, to ensure that the HTTP request goes to our web proxy, we need modify some properties of those elements before the request is triggered. For example, we change the '*href*' or 'action' properties of <*a*>, <*button*>, <*area*>, and <*form*> to make them refer to the domain of the web proxy. Opening more than one documents for users at the same time can cause some confusion to the users. That is because, if two users stay on two different current web pages, they can not see the interactions from each other. To avoid this, we also change the '*target*' property of each elements.

Event Capture and Reply. According to the framework behind modern web browsers, user operations associated the web page are first captured by the browser UI interface and then generate the UI events. These events are given to the JavaScript Engine to update the DOM tree and further affect what we see on the page. By synchronizing the events, we should be able to synchronize what users can see in the same co-browsing session. There are a set of events which can affect the content shown to the user on his device screen. To be able to replay these events within the other user browsers, we need to capture the required information for each event in the first place.

To be more efficient, we divide the events into two types: *synchronous events* and *asynchronous events*. For synchronous events, we have to hijack them first and then send them to the event coordinator for a centralized ordering, and finally the event coordinator broadcasts them to anyone in the same session, including the user who triggers this event. Thereafter, the synchronous events can be replayed by all users in the same order without inconsistency. For example, the click event to open a new page or typing event belongs to synchronous events. For asynchronous events, we capture them and propagate them to others through the event coordinator. But unlike synchronous events, we will immediately give the captured asynchronous events to the local browser right after we send them out to the event coordinator. Therefore, the propagation of asynchronous events causes nearly no delay to the current user. For example, mousemove, the most frequent event, is an asynchronous event. This design choice leads to much better user experience.

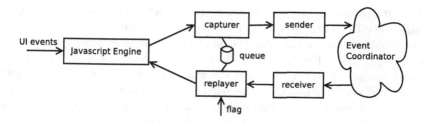

Fig. 3. Method to avoid event-looping

Event-Looping Detection. There is an *event-looping* issue when we distribute the synchronous events. As Fig. 3 shows, when the event replayer receives a synchronous event message from the event coordinator through the event receiver, it will simulate the related event and give it to the JavaScript Engine. Then the JavaScript Engine will trigger the event capturer to propagate the same event again, therefore forming a loop. We propose two methods to avoid this event-looping for different type of events. For some synchronous event like clicks or keyboard typing, we are able to call the browser's APIs to create a new event object to simulate it. This new event object goes to the event capturer through the JavaScript Engine. When we create the new event object, we will attach a *flag* property to it. By checking whether the captured event object has this flag property, the event capture can determine whether the event object is from the event replayer. If the event has this flag property, the event capturer will discard it. Unfortunately, for some event like page scrolling, modern browsers do not provide an interface for us to directly create the related event object. But we are able to call some function to generate the same effect. In this case, we come up with the second method to solve this problem. We set up a queue between the event replayer and the event capturer. The queue saves the received synchronous event messages. By comparing the captured event to the recorded event messages in the queue, the event capturer can judge whether it needs to discard this event to avoid event-looping.

Relative Positioning. The users might join the co-browsing session from different devices with different screen sizes or different resolutions. Given the same HTML document from the web proxy, the page layout might be much different on different devices, because some of the elements with relative positioning property in the web page change their position according to the window size and the screen resolution. In this case, using the direct position property to synchronize the mousemove events can result in a completely wrong position on the other users' screens. To solve the problem above, we use a *relative positioning* strategy to calculate the position of the mouse. Here is how it works. A mouse event has two properties, *clientX* and *clientY*, which are relative to the upper-left corner of the window. Its target element has the OffsetParent property, which represents the offset position of the current element relative to its parent element.

These three properties are widely supported by all major browsers. By going through the offsetParent property from the target element of a mouse event to the root element, we can calculate the offset of the target element relative to the current page, denoted as (oX, oY). Then we can further calculate the offset of the mouse event relative to its target element, denoted as $(RX, RY) = (clientX - oX, clientY - oY)$. When the other participants receive RX and RY, they can derive the position of the mouse on their own screens based on the offset of the local target element associated with this mouse event.

2.4   Event Coordinator

The event coordinator manages all of the co-browsing sessions. As Fig. 4 shows, within each session, we use three major objects, *page*, *connection*, and *user*, to manage its web pages, data connections, and participants respectively. As the users continue to cobrowse, a number of web pages are opened in the same session. In some case, the opened main page might contain an embedded sub-page, e.g. the inline *iframe* showing some advertisement. This means two pages could be active at the same time in the same session. To establish the data communication between the cobrowse module and the event coordinator, a bidirectional connection is created for each opened page, including the main page and the embedded sub-page. Currently, this bidirectional connection can be implemented based on the existing technologies, like XHR or websocket. According to our previous measurement study, XHR is more widely supported by modern browsers but less efficient as compared to websocket. In our implementation, we prefer to use websocket if the user's browser can support it. As the users open web pages from one to another, a new connection is created and the old connection is disclosed, which further trigger the related page objects to be created or discarded. Also, the event coordinator maintains a user list for each session to adapt to the joining of the new users and the leaving of the existing ones. Several timers are also set up to check the health of these objects. In addition, the event coordinator handles synchronous events and asynchronous events differently. For synchronous events, it will send them to every user on the same page, including the one that generates the event. For asynchronous events, it will just send them to all the other users on the same page.

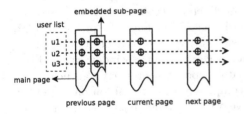

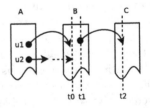

Fig. 4. Session management on the event coordinator

Fig. 5. An example to illustrate page transition

Page Transition. As the users cobrowse, the current web page is changed from one to another. Each change is called a *page transition*. Several events can fire a page transition, for example, clicking some URL, submitting a form, or clicking the forward or backward button of the browser. The cobrowse module can capture most of these events and further synchronize them, but it has no way to capture the forward or backward event of the browser. When the users click the forward, backward, or refresh button of the browse, a new HTTP request will be directly issued by the browser and the data connection between the cobrowse module and the event coordinator must be reestablished. This poses two challenges. *First*, how can we synchronize this type of event? Because of the security concerns, modern browsers do not provide any interface for the JavaScript code in the web page to hook forward or backward. However, we can detect them by checking the page transition on the event coordinator side. This gives us the chance to further synchronize them among the participants. *Second*, the bidirectional communication between the cobrowse module and the event coordinator are based on a series of temporary connections, rather than a persistent connection. Because whenever the user clicks the refresh, forward, or backward button, the existing connection will be closed and a new connection will be needed for event synchronization.

As an example, Fig. 5 shows how we deal with the synchronization of page transition based on non-persistent connections. Suppose that two users *u1* and *u2* are browsing the current page *A* in the same session. In the following co-browsing procedure, several different cases might happen. Both of these two users can trigger a page transition, either by opening a link or by clicking the forward/backward button. A page transition is detected by the event coordinator when a new connection is established to create a new page object. Then the new page object becomes the current page. To notify the other users to catch up in the same session, a *NAVIGATE* command will be sent to them through their existing connection with the previous page.

Event Reduction. The reason why we need to reduce some mouse move events comes from the following facts: 1) we target different devices, including laptop, desktop computers and tablets and the performance of these devices is very different. Some of them might be not powerful enough to replay all received mouse movement events from the co-browsing server in a synchronized manner; 2) mousemove is the most frequent and intensive event, accounting for 99% of all propagated events. For a mobile device with less computation capacity, replaying all mousemove events in a real time and synchronized way is nearly impossible. A naive solution to address this problem is to simply discard some mousemove events before the events are propagated to others. The event coordinator still receives all mousemove events from the original user who generate these events and then decides how much of these mousemove events will be sent out to other users, according to the capability of their devices. If the user comes with a browser on PC, he/she will receive all mousemove events without any precision loss. If the user comes with a browser on a slow smartphone, the selective event reduction will be turned on for him/her.

3   Implementation

Based the above design, we implemented a proof-of-concept co-browsing system, called *CoSurfen*. *CoSurfen* is a pure web-enabled solution and does not require users to install anything except a standard web browser. No configuration change to the user's browser is needed. Currently, our co-browsing service is working with all major modern browsers, including Chrome, Firefox, Safari, and Internet Explorer, across all major mobile devices like iOS/android based smartphone and tablet.

CoSurfen is mainly implemented in JavaScript. The cobrowse module is written in JavaScript, using the jQuery library. Based on the *nodejs* [4] platform, we implemented our cobrowse server, which consists of the web proxy and the event coordinator. Nodejs is a platform built on Chrome's JavaScript runtime for easily building fast, scalable network applications. With an event-driven, non-blocking I/O model, nodejs is lightweight and efficient, perfect for data-intensive real-time applications. Currently, lots of third parties libraries are available on the nodejs platform for developers. Using nodejs, we are able to use JavaScript to implement both the cobrowse module and the cobrowse server. To establish the bi-directional data communication between the browse module and the co-browse server, we used the socket.io library, which is also based on the nodejs platform and can automatically choose a suitable way to transfer the underlying data package according to the capability of the user's browser.

4   Performance Evaluation

4.1   Setup

We have internally deployed *CoSurfen* in our lab network. The whole deployment environment consists of one Linux server and three clients with different operating systems and hardware configurations. The Linux server is running the cobrowse server. The clients connect to the lab network through different networks, running different browsers on PC, iPad, and iPhone respectively. Table 1 lists the details of the entire setup environment. Based on this setup, we evaluated the performance of our system. The initial evaluation results are reported as follows, in terms of latency, scalability and usability.

4.2   Performance

Event Messages. We monitor the size of all event messages on the cobrowse server side. Here each event message contain the required information for replaying the event on the other browsers. For example, a typing event message contains both the properities of the typing event and the associated letter typed by the user. Totally, the cobrowse server handles 14 types of event messages. Fig. 6 shows the average message size for each type of event. Note that the message size across all events is 325 bytes on average, ranging from 83 bytes to 330 bytes. In addition, Fig. 7 shows the percentage of each event message. This

Table 1. The setup environment

	Type	OS	Browser	Hardware
Co-browse Server	1U blade server	Ubuntu 10.04 LTS	-	2 Intel Xeon CPU 3.6GHz, 8GB memory, Ethernet
Client	PC	Windows 7	Chrome, Safari, IE, Firefox	4 Intel i7 CPU 2.7GHz, 4GB memory, Ethernet
	iPad	iOS 4.2	Mobile Safari	1GHz Apple A4, 256 MB memory, WiFi
	iPhone	iOS 4.0	Mobile Safari	1GHz Apple A4, 512MB memory, WiFi
Network	PC, blade server, and WiFi AP are connected to the same Ethernet with the 100Mbps capacity iPad and iPhone are connected to the same network through WiFi			

result shows that mousemove, mouseover, mouseout, and touchmove are the top 4 ranked events in terms of event frequency. As we can see, the touch and mouse events are dominated, accounting for 95% of all the generated events. Reducing these events properly without losing too much precision can dramatically improve system efficiency. This is the motivation for the event reduction algorithm in our system.

Propagation Latency. We also measure the latency of event propagation. In our implementation, socket.io is used to propagate the captured events. We did a very simple PING-PONG test to calculate how much latency can be caused in the event propagation [6]. Fig 8 shows the results when the given message size is 325 bytes and 93 bytes respectively. Notice that the socket.io performs differently on different browsers and networks. We have the following observations. First, Internet Explorer (IE) on the PC performs very badly because it uses XHR-polling, instead of WebSocket. In the experiment, we use IE9, which does not support WebSocket. Second, in terms of the performance of WebSocket on Chrome, Safari, and Firefox, Chrome and Safari are doing much better than

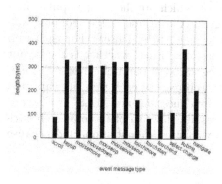

Fig. 6. Size of each event message

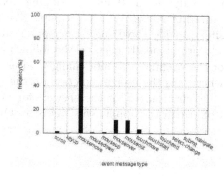

Fig. 7. Frequency of each event message

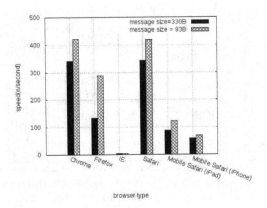

Fig. 8. Speed of event propagation across different browsers

Firefox. The difference comes from either the implementation of the socket.io library or the WebSocket implementation in the browsers. Third, the performance of WebSocket on Mobile devices is much worse than that on PCs due to the wireless network and the processing capacity. According to these three observations, we can clearly see the gap of event propagation latency across different devices and browsers. This diversity indicates that dealing with the diversities caused by different browsers and different devices in web-based co-browsing is important and necessary. This is exactly why we propose a special design to achieve page-level consistency in our co-browsing system. Finally, when the size of event message goes down, the performance of WebSocket goes up, especially for Firefox. Therefore, it helps to only put the required properties or data into the event messages.

4.3   Usability

To measure how well CoSurfen can support the existing dynamic web sites, we manually tested 50 online shopping web sites, which are the most popular ones ranked by Alexa [1] in its "shopping" category. All of these online shopping web sites provide cookie-based personalized web pages to end users. For each web site, we manually checked the following questions. First, whether is the layout of the original web site changed after going through our web proxy? Second, whether is the user interaction on the first web page of each web site captured and synchronized? If the answers for both two questions are "YES", we regard CoSurfen can support this web site. Our results show 45 of these 50 web sites can be supported by CoSurfen. The rest 5 web sites are not supported because they are HTTPs based.

5   Limitations

Based on our experience with CoSurfen, we also identify the following limitations of web-enabled co-browsing systems.

First, the current design does not support the HTTPs-based web sites. For HTTPs-based web sites, their web pages are encrypted by the original web server and only the authenticated user is allowed to see the decrypted content. With our current architecture, the intermediate web proxy is not able to inject the code of the cobrowse module into the HTTPs-based web page.

Second, with the current system architecture and design, we have to assume that the co-browsing service provider is fully trusted. This assumption makes sense only when the privacy associated with the co-browsed content and user interactions is not a concern for the users. However, in some cases, like online banking, the user would not like any other participants to see his/her private information on the web page, like the account number or the balance. Also, the users do not want the co-browsing server to watch what they are doing within the co-browsing sessions. To meet these requirements is out of the scope of this paper. We leave it as the future work.

6   Related Work

The concept of co-browsing has occurred for more than a decade. Many studies have been done to solve the problems related to co-browsing. Roughly, they can be categorized into two types: *Software-enabled Co-browsing* and *Web-enabled Co-browsing*.

For software-enabled co-browsing, users have to install something before co-browsing, either a software client or software-enabled co-browsing browser extension/plugin. This affects its ease of use and raises some security concerns to users. On the other hand, since the implementation of software-enabled co-browsing is not limited by the browsers' standard APIs, it has more capabilities to do something advanced. For example, the co-browsing client from GoToMyPC [2] propagates the cobrowsed web page as an image. This method to synchronize user behaviors on the cobrowsed web page is more generic but much more heavy than just sending the fired DOM UI events or the update of the DOM tree, because it causes lots of network traffic. CoFox [8] can record the user behaviors on the cobrowsed web page and propagate them as a live video stream. Using a Firefox browser plugin, RCB [15] can implement co-browsing without using any intermediate server. Similar to RCB, LiCob [13] proposed a lightweight distributed architecture for native-application based co-browsing. Also, as a software-enabled solution, CoLab [10] explored the topology organization issue of a distributed co-browsing system.

For web-enabled co-browsing, its implementation is limited by browsers. As the web technologies evolve, however, we are able to build more efficient web-enabled applications in the browser. For example, some measurement studies [9] [6] already points out that HTML5 Websocket [5] gives us lots of opportunities to build real-time web applications. Several previous [12] [8] [11] studies have discussed how to provide web-enabled co-browsing service with different focuses. For example, Esenther [8] first presented a web-enabled co-browsing system, which implemented an instant co-browsing for relatively simple web pages in the master-slaver mode. Lowet [11] proposed some general approaches to the co-browsing of dynamic web pages. Our work is similar to them, but we stay more focused on providing web-enabled co-browsing across different devices and browsers. For example, we target to the situation where users in the same co-browsing session are using different devices with different network connections, computation capacities, browsers, screen sizes and display resolutions. To handle those diversities is the new challenge that we mainly solved in our work. Although several previous studies [14] [7] already discussed co-browsing among mobile devices, they all focused on the page level synchronization and did not synchronize the detailed user interactions within the cobrowsed web page.

7   Conclusion and Future Work

In this paper we present the detailed design and implementation of our web-enabled co-browsing system and explore the strategies to make it working across browsers and devices in an efficient way. More specifically, we make the following contributions.

- To make our co-browsing system adapt to different devices, we propose a relative positioning approach to the synchronization of mousemove events, which can more precisely show users' mousemove positions on the screens with different resolutions and different window sizes.
- We present several strategies to make our service more efficient. For example, we improve the page caching mechanism to deal with cacheable and non-cacheable pages; we use a request bypassing strategy to largely offload our server's overhead; we separate events into asynchronous events and synchronous events and handle them differently to achieve better user experience; we implement an event reduction strategy to speed up the event rendering on mobile devices.
- We propose a page transition detection solution to support forward and backward operations for better user behavior synchronization and also present a cookie mapping strategy to synchronize personalized web pages.

Currently, our co-browsing service can support most HTTP-based web sites, including highly dynamic online shopping web sites. Based on the current design and implementation, we can deploy the CoSurfen system in the cloud to have a more scalable solution, by adding a session-based front-end scheduler. For the future work, we are interested in investigating the way of providing web-enabled co-browsing for HTTPS-based web sites and the related privacy-preserving issue.

Acknowledgement.   We would like to thank Sabah Al-Sabea and Joao da Silva for their initial contributions to this work.

References

1. alexa (2012), http://www.alexa.com/topsites/category/Top/Shopping
2. Gotomypc (2012), http://www.gotomypc.com
3. Html5 (2012), http://www.html5rocks.com
4. nodejs (2012), http://nodejs.org
5. websocket (2012), http://dev.w3.org/html5/websockets
6. Agarwal, S.: Real-time web application roadblock: Performance penalty of html web sockets. In: Proceedings of IEEE International Conference on Communications (June 2012)
7. Coles, A., Deliot, E., Melamed, T., Lansard, K.: A framework for coordinated multi-modal browsing with multiple clients. In: Proceedings of the 12th International Conference on World Wide Web, WWW 2003, pp. 718–726. ACM, New York (2003)
8. Esenther, A.W.: Instant co-browsing: Lightweight real-time collaborative web browsing. In: Proceedings of the 18th International Conference on World Wide Web (WWW 2002) (May 2002)
9. Gutwin, C.A., Lippold, M., Graham, T.C.N.: Real-time groupware in the browser: testing the performance of web-based networking. In: Proceedings of the ACM 2011 Conference on Computer Supported Cooperative Work, CSCW 2011, pp. 167–176. ACM, New York (2011)
10. Hoyos-Rivera, G., Gomes, R., Willrich, R., Courtiat, J.-P.: Colab: A new paradigm and tool for collaboratively browsing the web. IEEE Transactions on Systems, Man and Cybernetics, Part A: Systems and Humans 36(6), 1074–1085 (2006)
11. Lowet, D., Goergen, D.: Co-browsing dynamic web pages. In: Proceedings of the 18th International Conference on World Wide Web (WWW 2009) (March 2009)
12. Maly, K., Zubair, M., Li, L.: CoBrowser: Surfing the web using a standard browser. In: Proceedings of World Conference on Educational Multimedia, Hypermedia and Telecommunications, pp. 1220–1225 (June 2001)
13. Santos, R.O., Oliveira, F.F., Antunes, J.C.P., Martinello, M., Guizzardi, R.S.S., Gomes, R.L.: Licob: Lightweight collaborative browsing. In: IEEE/WIC/ACM International Joint Conferences on Web Intelligence and Intelligent Agent Technologies, vol. 3, pp. 571–574 (September 2009)
14. Wiltse, H., Nichols, J.: Playbyplay: collaborative web browsing for desktop and mobile devices. In: Proceedings of the 27th International Conference on Human Factors in Computing Systems, CHI 2009, pp. 1781–1790. ACM, New York (2009)
15. Yue, C., Chu, Z., Wang, H.: RCB: A simple and practical framework for real-time collaborative browsing. In: Proceedings of the USENIX Annual Technical Conference (June 2009)

Device Token Protocol for Persistent Authentication Shared across Applications

John Trammel, Ümit Yalçınalp, Andrei Kalfas, James Boag, and Dan Brotsky

Adobe Systems Incorporated, 345 Park Avenue, San Jose, USA
{jtrammel,lyalcina,akalfas,jboag,dbrotsky}adobe.com

Abstract. This paper describes a protocol for enabling shared persistent authentication for desktop applications that comprise a common suite by extending the OAuth2.0 protocol. OAuth2.0 is the de facto standard for developing and deploying federated Identity. Our extension enables the users to authenticate and authorize on devices that host a suite of applications that are connected to backend services and systems at Adobe. It is the backbone of our subscription and licensing infrastructure for the Adobe Creative Suite® 6 and Adobe Creative Cloud™. The extended protocol works without storing users credentials on a per application basis but rather uses device identities that are managed on a centralized server to enable increased security and management capabilities for a set of applications on the device. We describe the protocol is in detail, its inherent characteristics, how it extends OAuth2.0, and how it is used in practice.

Keywords: Authentication, Identity Management, OAuth2.0, Authorization.

1   Introduction

1.1   Problem

Today, software clients and applications are available on heterogeneous devices, including tablets, smart phones, and desktops. In addition, in a world where companies are beginning to develop and deploy multiple applications, user access should be accomplished in a manner that is both user-friendly and secure, and also recognizes that specific context; the user should not be required to enter separate user authentications for each application from the same vendor on a particular device. We faced this issue when we needed to deploy subscription services to multiple applications that were offered on the desktop that comprised Adobe Creative Suite and Adobe Creative Cloud membership.

In today's mobile applications, each application manages access control for the user and it is configured separately. As new applications are added, access for the user is configured anew for each application. Furthermore, a user's credentials are typically stored on the device via encryption rather than by identifying the device and the authorizations of the specific user for the device.

There are many applications in the industry that are currently use stored user credentials for authentication and authorization. Examples include email access from

F. De Paoli, E. Pimentel, and G. Zavattaro (Eds.): ESOCC 2012, LNCS, 7592, pp. 230–243, 2012.

different vendors on the iPhone, twitter account settings on iOS or Android devices, etc. These approaches require user credentials to be stored on a per application basis.

When there are multiple applications from the same vendor on the same device, this approach becomes cumbersome and error prone. Although the user may be governed by a centralized identity service that may also support Federated Identity, security on the device can only achieved by replicating user credentials on the device on a per application basis. This is clearly not desirable.

Without a centralized mechanism on the client, a management problem occurs when the user, in a heterogeneous landscape, needs access to more devices and applications. This is a problem space that other vendors have begun to recognize: Google Application Manager on the Android platform [4] has centralized account management in a single source in the client machine. However, that implementation still stores user credentials on the client.

This leaves related areas open for further improvement: security and remote management. Mobile devices may be broken, stolen, or lost. Therefore, the ability to remotely manage and revoke authorizations on mobile devices is highly desirable to reduce data security risks. In addition, companies need to be able to terminate access for users, perhaps due to personnel changes, from a central server and have that change take affect on all associated remote devices.

Note that several web and mobile applications keep track of user authentication from the specific device. For example, Facebook and Bank of America Online Banking [5] keep track of the specific devices that the user authenticates from in their applications. Thus, device tracking is important to utilize for the added security and management, but it has not been fully utilized in conjunction with decoupling user credentials from the authentication and authorization process.

The OAuth2.0 Protocol [1] has become widely used for granting access to clients of services and applications. However, a persistent token that decouples users credentials, and that can cater to multiple client applications, rather than a single one, has not been targeted by this protocol in the state of the art, literature or standardization.

1.2   Solution

We developed a novel mechanism, a **persistent device token**, for securely persisting authentication for a user that can be used *by a set of authorized applications on a device* (laptop, desktop, mobile phone, tablet, etc.).

The device token is unique to a specific device and user and can be used by one or many applications. It can be persisted, but it is non-transferable, meaning that it cannot be transferred to another device or to another user. This mechanism

- is secure (because a device token is usable only on the device and by the user for which it was issued.)
- does not require the persistence of user credentials on the device.
- enables revocation of authorizations remotely – outside of the presence of the device on a centralized service that is dedicated to identity management.

- is configurable because it allows for server side control over which client applications can make use of the mechanism.

An implementation of this concept has been developed and delivered as an extension to the OAuth2 [1] + OpenID-Connect protocol [2], specifically as a new **grant type.** We assume that the reader is familiar with the OAuth2.0 [1] protocol reading this paper. This extension to OAuth2 and OpenID-Connect is currently in use within the Adobe Creative Suite product line and Adobe Creative Cloud.

The extension presented does not currently exist in OAuth2 or OpenID-Connect protocols, as most applications ARE NOT configured like a suite or a group of applications on a device basis. However, this need is rapidly emerging as companies like Adobe begin developing and deploying multiple applications for its constituent user bases on devices.

Today, almost all Adobe software that connects to Adobe web services use a backend service called IMS (Identity Management Service). IMS centralizes the workflows for all clients that require authentication and authorization to various Adobe hosted services and it provides federated identity support. IMS supports OAuth2.0 [1] and OpenID- Connect Protocol [2]. IMS also provides centralized common UI workflows that are targeted to clients on specific device types, such as desktop, browser, mobile device, etc.

The protocol presented in this paper is currently being deployed worldwide as part of the Adobe Creative Suite 6.0 and Adobe Creative Cloud [6] offerings on the desktop. It is integrated with the Adobe Application Manager that manages single sign on, device tokens and user authorization with IMS on the desktop for all client applications and extensions that reside on the desktop.

2   Detailed Protocol

2.1   Overview

This protocol has the following characteristics and behaviors:

1. A new grant type, named Device Token is introduced. This grant type is similar to the authorization grant type, with a key difference: while the authorization code is bound to a specific client-id, the device token is bound to a specific device and a user and may be used to create access tokens for authorized clients applications on the same device. Note that there are many applications on the same device where each has a different client_id.
2. This grant type is most appropriate for client applications that reside locally on the device (native, AIR, etc.), and not appropriate for server back-ends or web-apps that are intended to run in a system-browser.

The client-application must adhere to specific requirements in the system:

a. Client applications must be specifically authorized to use the device token grant type and be configured in advance of deployment.

   b. Client applications must share secure access to and generation algorithms for the device-identifier.

   c. Client applications must generate the device-identifier via an algorithm, shared by the coordinating applications, each time the application launches or intends to use the device token.

   d. Client applications must not persist the device-identifier in its final form.

3. The following recommendations apply to the generation of device-identifiers for use on various platforms/environments. These recommendations do not represent the actual implementation details of Adobe's applications, but rather are illustrative descriptions, appropriate for publication:

Part	Description
platform	A code specific for the platform (ios, android, win, mac, linux)
user identifier	A user id that uniquely identifies a user on the specific platform. Needed for devices that allow multiple users, where there is a need to limit device token portability between users on the same device.
profile identifier	A unique identifier for a profile. Users may have multiple profiles where there is need to distinguish different patterns and entitlements of use, such as home vs. work. Needed for devices that allow multiple users when there is a need to limit device token portability between groups/profiles on the same device.
System device identifier	The device identifier of the specific platform. OS or system appropriate value.

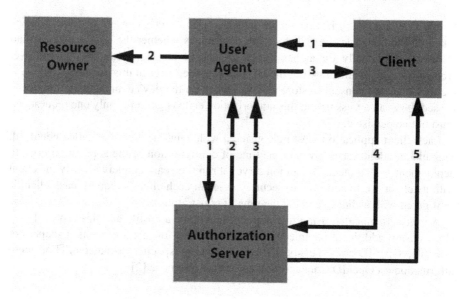

Fig. 1. Device Token Flow Diagram with OAuth2.0

An excerpt from early documentation for the device token protocol follows and refers to the accompanying flow diagram. It has been edited to remove some details deemed confidential or not relevant. Terminology from OAuth2.0 is used in the flow diagram in Figure 1 and the descriptions of the steps involved. In the detailed API documentation that follows, the protocol described builds on top of the specific calls of OAuth2.0 [1].

1. The client initiates the flow by directing the resource owner's user-agent to the device authorization endpoint (at the Authorization Server). The client includes its device identifier, client identifier, requested scope, local state, and a redirection URI to which the authorization server will send the user-agent back once access is granted.
2. The authorization server authenticates the resource owner (via the user-agent). The user has the option to persist data on the device. If the user agrees to save data on the device, the authorization server releases a device token, otherwise it returns an authorization code.
3. Assuming the authentication is successful, the authorization server redirects the user-agent back to the client using the redirection URI provided earlier. Depending on the user's consent, the redirection URI includes either a device token or an authorization code and any local state provided earlier by the client.
4. The client, providing either a device token or an authorization code, requests an access token from the authorization server. This transaction requires the client to authenticate.
5. The authorization server validates the client credentials and the device token or authorization code. If valid, it responds back with an access token.

In this flow, the authorization server depends on the user's consent to store a device token on the client device. This consent determines whether the device token would be used subsequently for authentication instead of an authorization code and user credentials. This is illustrated in the UI flow provided later in this document below. If the user does not consent to store a device token on the device, an authorization code is used to get an access token; this authorization code is good for only one request and must not be persisted.

Each client application must be registered with a unique identifier called **client_id**. This unique identifier is given at the time of configuration of the application prior to deployment so that the authorization server at run time can uniquely identify the client with its client_id. In addition, to securely transmit each client's request, each client is configured with a client_secret at the time of registration.

A user authenticated using this protocol may have a profile and this protocol may also transmit additional parameters that are specified for this user using a scope. For example, OpenID may be specified to get these specific parameters. For more information on OpenID Connect profiles, see the reference [2].

2.2   Detailed Protocol

Device Token Request: The client constructs the request URI by adding the following parameters to the query component of the authorization endpoint URI using the `"application/x-www-form-urlencoded"`.

Parameter	Mandatory	Description
response_type	true	Must be "device"
device_id	true	It is up to clients to generate and provide the device ID. Refer to SHA256 [3].
device_name	false	If specified, can be used to present to the user a user-friendly name of the device.
redirect_uri	false	If missing, the server will use the default redirect URI that is provisioned when the client was registered during the configuration.
client_id	true	The client identifier that is provided for the application during the registration phase.
scope	true	The scope of the access request expressed as a list of comma-delimited, case sensitive strings. *Details of scope parameter values not presented.*
locale	false	The locale to be used in the user interface, supplied in the format *language_country*. Default is en_US.
state	false	*Details around usage of state parameter not presented.*
dc	false	*Details around usage of dc parameter not presented*

Device Token Response: If the user agrees to persist data on the device, the server issues a device token and delivers it to the client by adding the following parameters to the query component of the redirection URI using the `"application/x-www-form-urlencoded"` format:

Parameter	Mandatory	Description
device_token	true	The device token bound to the device.
state	false	If present in the device token request

If the user did not agree to persisting data on the device, IMS will fallback to releasing an authorization code. The query component of the redirection URI using the `"application/x-www-form-urlencoded"` will contain:

Parameter	Mandatory	Description
code	true	The authorization code.
state	false	If present in the device token request

Error Response: If the client identifier provided is invalid, the server informs the resource owner of the error and does not redirect the user-agent anywhere. If the request fails for another reason, the server informs the client by adding the following parameters to the query component of the redirection URI using the "application/x-www-form-urlencoded" format:

Parameter	Mandatory	Description
error	true	A single error code with the values from bellow.
error_description	false	Additional information about the error.

error_code	Description
access_denied	If user did not authorize the client application. For instance this can happen when the user clicks on the Cancel button in the login screen.
access_denied_no_cookies	If the server detects that cookies are disabled.

Example: In the examples below, the tokens are abbreviated for clarity and designated by mnemonics, such as <DEV_TOKEN>.

Device Token Request

```
GET
/ims/authorize/v1?client_id=AXX_YYY&response_type=device&
&device_id=MA4Y2KfwV1av8soWHoOnmubOiFWhXOg-
nwePp9dExqU&device_name=Mac&redirect_uri=http%3A%2F%2Fsto
phere.adobe.com&scope=openid HTTP/1.1
Host: ims-host.adobelogin.com
```

Device Token Response with device token

```
HTTP/1.1 302 Moved Temporarily
Server: Apache-Coyote/1.1
Set-Cookie: relay=0526317f-3e77-46c1-8b19-957a06a9b2e8;
Path=/
Cache-Control: no-store
P3P: CP="IDC DSP COR CURa ADMa OUR IND PHY ONL COM STA"
X-RHH: B8E1750B964EE62AB7C147F0EDF12803
Location:
http://stophere.adobe.com?device_token=<DEV_TOKEN>
Content-Type: text/html;charset=UTF-8
Content-Language: en-US
Transfer-Encoding: chunked
Content-Encoding: gzip
Vary: Accept-Encoding
Date: Mon, 14 Nov 2011 12:50:01 GMT
```

Device Token Response with authorization code

```
HTTP/1.1 302 Moved Temporarily
Server: Apache-Coyote/1.1
Set-Cookie: relay=08da1a84-9179-4720-95c5-c871fdc69063;
Path=/
Cache-Control: no-store
P3P: CP="IDC DSP COR CURa ADMa OUR IND PHY ONL COM STA"
X-RHH: B8E1750B964EE62AB7C147F0EDF12803
Location: http://stophere.adobe.com?code=<AUTHR_CODE>
Content-Type: text/html;charset=UTF-8
Content-Language: en-US
Transfer-Encoding: chunked
Content-Encoding: gzip
Vary: Accept-Encoding
Date: Mon, 14 Nov 2011 12:50:14 GMT
```

Access Token Request with a Device Token: The client makes a request to the token endpoint by adding the following parameter using the "application/x-www-form-urlencoded" format in the HTTP request entity-body:

Parameter	Mandatory	Description
grant_type	true	Must be "device"
device_id	true	It is up to clients to generate and provide the device ID. Refer to SHA256 [3].
device_token	true	The device token received at the previous step.
client_id	true	The client_id credential received during the registration phase.
client_secret	true	The client_secret credential received during the registration phase.

Access Token Response: The server issues an access token and a refresh token, and constructs the response by adding the following parameters to the entity body of the HTTP response with a 200 (OK) status code.

Parameter	Mandatory	Description
access_token	true	The access token
refresh_token	true	The refresh token
expires_in	true	The lifetime in milliseconds of the access token. For example, the value "360000" denotes that the access token will expire in one hour from the time the response was generated.

In addition to the above parameters, the server will include in its response attributes from the user's profile based on the requested scope as specified in the Device Token Request. The parameters may be included in the entity body of the HTTP response using the appropriate media type. For example "application/json" media type will serialize the parameters into a JSON structure.

Error Response: The server responds with an HTTP 400 (Bad Request) status code and includes the following parameters with the response:

Parameter	Mandatory	Description
error	true	A single error code with the values from below

error code	Description
invalid request	If creating an access token fails due to internal errors.
invalid_client	If the client credentials are not correct.
unsupported_grant_type	If the client_id does not have the appropriate grant_type set.
access_denied	If the device token is invalid or if it was released for a different device id.

Example: *Access Token Request with a device token*

Access Token Request with Device Token

```
POST /ims/token/v1 HTTP/1.1
User-Agent: curl/7.21.4 (universal-apple-darwin11.0)
libcurl/7.21.4 OpenSSL/0.9.8r zlib/1.2.5
Host: ims-host.adobelogin.com
Accept: */*
Content-Length: 740
Content-Type: application/x-www-form-urlencoded
grant_type=device&device_id=MA4Y2KfwV1av8soWHoOnmubOiFWhX
Og-
nwePp9dExqU&device_token=<DEV_TOKEN>&client_id=<YOUR_CLIE
NT_ID>&client_secret=<CLIENT_SECRET>
```

Access Token Response

```
HTTP/1.1 200 OK
Server: Apache-Coyote/1.1
Set-Cookie: relay=0c122e22-58be-4c5d-b215-d362b9142c71;
Path=/
Cache-Control: no-store
P3P: CP="IDC DSP COR CURa ADMa OUR IND PHY ONL COM STA"
X-RHH: B8E1750B964EE62AB7C147F0EDF12803
Content-Type: application/json;charset=UTF-8
```

```
Transfer-Encoding: chunked
Date: Mon, 14 Nov 2011 13:17:56 GMT
{"token_type":"bearer","expires_in":86399952,"refresh_tok
en":"REFRESH_TOKEN","access_token":"ACCESS_TOKEN"}
```

Access Token Request with an Authorization Code: The client makes a request to the token endpoint by adding the following parameter using the "application/x-www-form-urlencoded" format in the HTTP request entity-body:

Parameter	Mandatory	Description
grant_type	true	Must be "authorization_code".
code	true	The authorization code previously received.
client_id	true	The client_id credential received during the registration phase.
client_secret	true	The client_secret credential received during the registration phase.

The server validates the client credentials and ensures that the authorization code was issued to that client. Note that an authorization code may be used only once but the device token can be stored and reused to grant access.

Example: With an authorization code a client can request an access token as follows:

```
POST /ims/token/v1 HTTP/1.1
Host: ims-na1-dev1.adobelogin.com
Content-Type: application/x-www-form-urlencoded
grant_type=authorization_code&client_id=THE_CLIENT_ID&cli
ent_secret=THE_CLIENT_SECRET&code=AUTHR_CODE
```

Access Token Response: IMS issues an access token and a refresh token, and constructs the response by adding the following parameters to the entity body of the HTTP response with a 200 (OK) status code.

Parameter	Mandatory	Description
access_token	true	The access token.
refresh_token	true	The refresh token.
expires_in	true	The lifetime in milliseconds of the access token. For example, the value "360000" denotes that it will expire in one hour from the time the response was generated.

In addition to the above parameters, the server may include in its response attributes from the user's profile based on the requested scope specified within the

Device Token Request. Again, the parameters are included in the entity body of the HTTP response using the specific media-type, such as `"application/json"` which will serialize the parameters into a JSON structure.

IMS will check the client credentials and the authorization code and if they are OK it will send back a response.

Access Token Error Response: IMS responds with an HTTP 400 (Bad Request) status code and includes the following parameters with the response:

Parameter	Mandatory	Description
error	true	A single error code with the values from below.
error_description	false	Additional information about the error.

error_code	Description
invalid_request	If creating an access token fails due to internal errors
invalid_client	If the client_id was not provisioned or the client_secret does not match.
unauthorized_client	If the client_id does not have the appropriate grant_type set.
access_denied	If the authorization code / refresh token is not valid or the authorization code was released to a different client_id.

2.3   Persistence of Device Tokens

There are two different approaches in persisting device tokens on a device:

1) A client application may store the device token in the client application or user specific storage, akin to how many applications store user credentials today (e.g., Mac OS X Keychain). Since this approach requires each application to implement the protocol itself, it would require duplicative, coordinated implementations if used by multiple applications.

2) Another alternate is to develop a separate account management library that manages device tokens and related authentication tokens for a series of applications. This library is responsible for storing the device token on behalf of the user as well as generating authentication tokens for specific applications that need authentication and authorization. Basically, the client and the user-agent in the workflow are coupled and encapsulated in a library that allows multiple applications to use the same mechanism on the device. This approach decouples the applications from security and persistence concerns, while bringing the benefits of security and manageability.

There are use cases when is it desirable to disallow the storage of a local device token. The ability to enable local storage of a device token is configurable. If the user is allowed to store a device token locally, that option can be presented in the following manner shown in Figure 2.

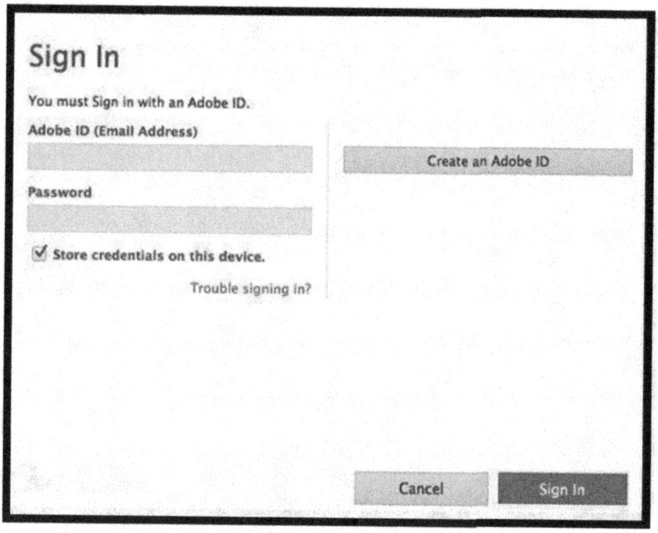

Fig. 2. Signing In when Local Device Token Storage Enabled

In use cases where the device tokens will always be stored locally, the user can be informed of this via a user experience as exemplified in Fig. 3.

In the case when third party identity providers (such as Google, Yahoo or Facebook) handle authentication, the login UI is fixed and cannot be modified to prompt for device token storage. In these cases the server will show an *interstitial* page asking for consent to store the tokens locally. This is exemplified in Figure 4.

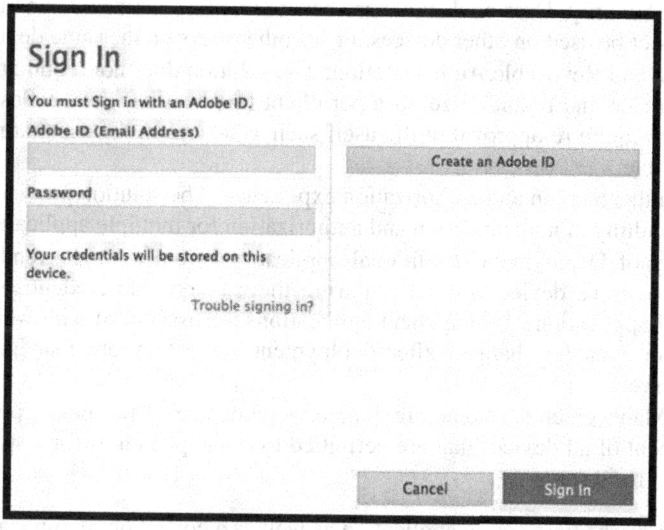

Fig. 3. Mandatory persistence on device

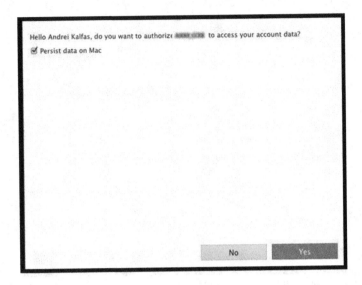

Hello Andrei Kalfas, do you want to authorize ▓▓▓ to access your account data?

☑ Persist data on Mac

No   Yes

Fig. 4. Interstitial with third party providers

3   Conclusion

We presented a novel extension to the OAuth2.0 protocol using device tokens and a new grant type to authenticate and authorize a user for multiple applications on a single device. A device token is not transferable but is persistable.

Our approach has the following advantages:

- Enhanced Security. User credentials are never stored on the device and the device token cannot be used on other devices, or for other users on the same device.
- Permanent and Revocable Authentication: The solution does not require the user to re-authenticate and re-authorize on a per client (application) basis unless changes occur that require re-approval of the user, such as new terms of use that need to be agreed to, etc.
- Unified authentication and authorization experience: The solution provides a single way of handling of authentication and authorization for multiple applications.
- Scalability of Deployment: Additional applications from a single vendor can be added to a user's device without requiring them to provide credentials for each additional application. Which client applications are associated with which device tokens can even be changed after deployment since they are managed from a central server.
- Remote Management: Tokens are remotely revocable. This makes possible the management of all devices that are permitted to run applications for a specific user on a centralized server.

The solution works for a single application as well as a collection of applications. The security (not storing credentials on the client and non-transferable device tokens) and manageability benefits apply to both configurations.

The protocol discussed in this paper is being deployed along with the Adobe Creative Suite 6.0 and Adobe Creative Cloud.

Acknowledgements. The Adobe Creative Suite, Adobe Create Cloud and IMS are corporate efforts. We thank the members of the IMSLib, OOBE and CEP teams in their endless efforts in developing, debugging and testing the client library that enables all applications that are managed by Adobe Application Manager on the desktop; the IMS team for supporting this protocol addition with IMS. We also thank the Business Architecture team in reviewing and making comments to the drafts of this paper, in particular Lois Gerber, Bob Murata, Shyama Padhi and Chris Tuller.

References

1. OAuth Working Group, Hammer, E. (ed): IETF, The OAuth2.0 Authorization Protocol draft 28 (2012), http://tools.ietf.org/html/draft-ietf-oauth-v2-28
2. OpenId Foundation, Open ID Connect Protocol Suite (2012), http://openid.net/connect/
3. IPSec Working Group, Frankel, S., Kelly, S.: The HMAC-SHA-256-128 Algorithm and Its Use With IPsec (2002), http://w3.antd.nist.gov/iip_pubs/draft-ietf-ipsec-ciph-sha-256-01.txt
4. Google, Android Account Manager API (2012), http://developer.android.com/reference/android/accounts/AccountManager.html
5. Bank of America, Online Banking FAQ (2012), http://www.bankofamerica.com/onlinebanking/index.cfm?template=site_key-accesslb
6. Adobe Creative Cloud^{TM} (2012), http://creative.adobe.com
7. Adobe Creative Suite® (2012), http://www.adobe.com/products/creativesuite.html

Simplified Authentication and Authorization for RESTful Services in Trusted Environments

Eric Brachmann[1,*], Gero Dittmann[2], and Klaus-Dieter Schubert[2]

[1] Dresden University of Technology, 01062 Dresden, Germany
`eric.brachmann@tu-dresden.de`
[2] IBM Systems & Technology Group, 71032 Boeblingen, Germany
`gero@ieee.org, kdschube@de.ibm.com`

Abstract. In some trusted environments, such as an organization's intranet, local web services may be assumed to be trustworthy. This property can be exploited to simplify authentication and authorization protocols between resource providers and consumers, lowering the threshold for developing services and clients. Existing security solutions for RESTful services, in contrast, support *untrusted* services, a complexity-increasing capability that is not needed on an intranet with only *trusted* services.

We propose a central security service with a lean API that handles both authentication and authorization for trusted RESTful services. A user trades credentials for a token that facilitates access to services. The services may query the security service for token authenticity and roles granted to a user. The system provides fine-grained access control at the level of resources, following the role-based access control (RBAC) model. Resources are identified by their URLs, making the authorization system generic. The mapping of roles to users resides with the central security service and depends on the resource to be accessed. The mapping of permissions to roles is implemented individually by the services. We rely on secure channels and the trusted intermediaries characteristic for intranets to simplify the protocols involved and to make the security features easy to use, cutting the number of required API calls in half.

Keywords: Authentication, Authorization, Intranet, Representational state transfer (REST), Role-based access control (RBAC), Security, Web services.

1 Introduction

Organizations usually deploy protected intranets with restricted access. This paper presents an approach to simplify security protocols within these trusted environments for a gain in agility.

Consider, for instance, engineers who commonly share large amounts of data, such as test or analysis results, across a development department. To be more

---

* Brachmann was with IBM Germany R&D at the time of this work.

F. De Paoli, E. Pimentel, and G. Zavattaro (Eds.): ESOCC 2012, LNCS 7592, pp. 244–258, 2012.

productive, they often write scripts and tools for this data. Sharing these tools can increase the productivity of an entire organization. In spite of this positive impact, providing such resources is often not part of the engineers' job descriptions. A framework to facilitate and encourage resource sharing must hence provide easy access and an instant payoff for engineers in order for the system to be used and extended. Furthermore, access has to be possible using a wide variety of programming languages because developers often have strong and diverse preferences and limited flexibility in this regard.

Web services meet these requirements, as they facilitate the sharing of both data and functionality, thus supporting heterogeneity and distributed ownership. RESTful services implemented with HTTP and XML are particularly suitable because they leverage well-known technologies for which libraries are available in many programming languages. The fixed API of HTTP provides a uniform way to access all resources. Frameworks like *Ruby on Rails* render the generation of RESTful services even easier. In our context, these technologies enable developers to rapidly implement their own services and to write scripts that employ services made available by their peers.

However, access to design data must be controlled and restricted, requiring authentication and authorization of users. Although our target are services that reside within the trusted internal network of an organization, certain users may not be allowed to see, use or edit certain resources. Hence, authorization is necessary to manage access rights, and authentication is needed to reliably identify users in the first place. Incorporating such security features should not require much initial training or knowledge of complicated protocols so that it remains easy for developers to implement libraries for their preferred programming languages themselves.

From our aim to build our service system in an intranet environment we derive some assumptions that help us achieve the desired simplicity of the security framework. First, all channels are encrypted and authenticated by using the TLS/SSL protocol. Thereby we largely eliminate the possibility of eavesdropping and man-in-the-middle attacks. Second, we trust all services in the system: We suppose that services perform only legitimate actions on behalf of the user. An intranet for which these assumptions hold we call *trusted*.

However, we want to avoid storing user passwords on clients and sending them to custom-built services. Furthermore, users should only have to provide their credentials once or once every few days. After that, access to services has to be possible without entering credentials again. Therefore, the system has to offer single sign-on.

We propose a central security service with an API comprised of three methods. The first method is called by users and trades the user credentials for a security token that facilitates single sign-on to the complete service system. The token is stored on the client and sent along with every service request. The second method is called by services to validate a token and with it the authenticity of the requesting user. The third method is called by services to check whether the user is allowed to act in a certain role on a certain resource. This final call determines whether a user has sufficient rights for a request. We use roles to bundle permissions of groups of users and associate them with individual resources for fine-grained access control. The security service provides the necessary mapping of users to roles and resources, and offers functionality for their administration.

The remainder of this paper is organized as follows: Section 2 surveys existing web service security solutions. Section 3.1 provides an overview of the architecture of our framework with a brief description of all components. Sections 3.2 and 3.3 describe how we handle centralized authentication and authorization, respectively. In Sect. 4 we elaborate on how we implemented the central security service, and Sect. 5 concludes the paper.

2 Related Work

Security extensions for web services have been defined in the WS-Security, WS-Trust, and WS-Federation standards. The first two specify how to secure SOAP messages and how identification tokens can be attached and exchanged. WS-Federation deals with the issue of propagating identity proof between disparate security realms. These protocols add up to complex frameworks for authentication and authorization for SOAP-based web services. Similar developments for REST, in contrast, have not yet gained momentum.

Typical RESTful services exploit the HTTP protocol. The basic means of authentication in this context are HTTP Basic and HTTP Digest. They specify how to send user credentials to a service. However, to resend them with every access requires them to be stored at the client, posing a potential security risk. In fact, we want to avoid sending such sensitive information to application services altogether.

Web authentication protocols inspired by Kerberos[1], such as WebAuth[2] or the Central Authentication Service (CAS)[3], achieve this by trading credentials for tokens and transmitting them instead, providing centralized authentication and single sign-on. Construction and exchange of their tokens follow sophisticated patterns to support untrusted services. As our target services reside in a protected intranet environment, the complexity of those protocols is an unnecessary burden for service developers. Existing client libraries are designed for protecting web sites, for example, by forwarding users to login forms that cannot be used by headless clients such as automated data-processing scripts.

Web-based systems on a trusted intranet may use simpler cookie-based SSO solutions, such as the one presented in [4]. These propositions rely on a web browser for storing cookies and offer no centralized authorization management.

The Security Assertion Markup Language (SAML) [5] and the eXtensible Access Control Markup Language (XACML) [6] are often used in SOAP-based systems for authentication and authorization requests and to exchange policy information. There is, however, no established binding of these protocols for HTTP-based RESTful services. Moreover, we only need a fraction of the SAML features and, therefore, have opted for a less complex and natively RESTful protocol. Nevertheless, our architecture would also work with SAML. Our authorization approach follows the SAML philosophy with separate identity provider

(IdP) and service provider (SP). Our authorization system follows the XACML architecture with a central policy decision point (PDP) and distributed policy enforcement points (PEPs). Exchanging policy information is outside the scope of this paper.

A RESTful interface for XACML Policy Decision Points to handle authorization is proposed in [7]. RESTful messages are translated to SOAP and forwarded to the central authorization component. This approach is useful for an intranet that is already equipped with a running XACML infrastructure or for exploiting the rich expressiveness of XACML for access control. Otherwise, there is little gain to justify the translation overhead introduced.

In [8], a cookie scheme is combined with role-based authorization. Session cookies stored by the client contain information about the user. These cookies are cryptographically protected by a message authentication code so that the user cannot change the information they contain. Authorization is implemented by introducing user and role object classes in LDAP. Organizations already deploying LDAP user directories need to change their existing LDAP schema accordingly, which might not be feasible.

Hecate [9] is a framework that provides centralized authorization for RESTful resources. The authors propose an XML dialect to define access rules for all available resources of the system, including the possibility of resource-aware filtering for fine-grained access control. However, service developers need to learn a new XML dialect for protecting their resources. Moreover, Hecate does not deal with authentication.

OpenID [10] is a protocol offering decentralized authentication, which has limited benefit in intranet solutions where services typically belong to the domain of a single identity provider.

Thanks to its widespread deployment, oAuth [11] has received much attention in the area of authentication and authorization. However, it covers the specific use case of granting third parties access to private user resources and hence does not fit our scenario.

Our framework offers centralized authentication with single sign-on capabilities and centralized authorization, both accessed through a RESTful services API. It exploits the properties of a trusted intranet to provide a lean protocol API and easy access to its security features.

3   Framework

3.1   Overview

Figure 1 shows the architecture of our framework. The central components are the services themselves. They offer resources that users access for their everyday work. Access should be simple, and the creation of new services should be feasible for development engineers in addition to their core responsibilities. Therefore, our services follow a RESTful design. Simple services may just provide access to data records from a database and support handy, data-specific queries. Composite services combine or extend the functionality of one or more other services. Users access either type of service via a client. A client may be a web application or some other kind of graphical user interface. A client may also be a command-line tool or a custom-built script that interacts with services on behalf of the user to carry out a specific task. Authentication and authorization are managed in a centralized manner by the security service. Users interact with the security service to prove their identity. The security service is connected to the organization's user directory to check credentials. Services interact with the security service to validate the identity of a requesting user and possibly to check the user's access rights for an access-restricted resource.

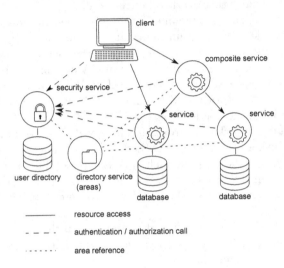

Fig. 1. Architecture of the security framework. Line styles represent the different types of interaction.

In our framework authorization rules are associated with special resources called *areas*. An area may be a department, a project, or a data-specific unit. Areas serve as reference points for groups of resources in the service system. An area directory service holds these area resources and thereby provides common references for services and the security service to map role-area pairs to groups of users. The notion of areas is borrowed from the Jazz platform [12].

3.2   Authentication

Authentication is the process of proving the user's identity to the service she attempts to interact with. It ensures that only legitimate members of the organization use the service and is the foundation for authorization. For a reliable identification, a user and a service share a secret that only they know, i.e., the user's credentials. In this way, when receiving the credentials a service can be sure that the associated user is at the sending end. To relieve the services from managing user credentials and authentication logic themselves, we introduce a central authority that handles authentication for all services.

Tokens. In our proposed solution, this central authority is implemented by the security service (see Fig. 1). A user sends his credentials only to the security service, and only once. The security service verifies the credentials against the user directory of the organization, which stores the credentials of all employees, for example as part of LDAP user profiles. If the credentials are valid, the security service creates a token for the user. A token identifies a user for a certain period of time, e.g., several days. During this time, a user does not need to present the credentials again but presents this token instead. A security token in our framework is an opaque string that does not carry any information itself. Instead, the security service keeps a table that maps tokens to users and that also contains the expiration dates of tokens. A token contains 20 random letters and digits to prevent a brute-force attack from guessing it. Our system would also work with cryptographic tokens, e.g., to detect manipulation attempts.

In contrast to other systems like CAS, our tokens are not bound to individual services. The CAS protocol [3] describes several types of tokens (called *tickets* there). Most important are ticket-granting tickets and service tickets. Ticket-granting tickets are stored in a cookie on the client. The client sends them to the CAS server to obtain service tickets. The client then attaches the service ticket to a service request. The service checks the user's authenticity by validating the service ticket with the CAS server. Service tickets can only be validated once and are bound to one service. Tickets that were eavesdropped by attackers are therefore useless and pose no security risk.

We, however, prevent eavesdropping by using secure channels. In our case, the restrictions that CAS places on service tickets are an unnecessary burden. If security tokens expire after the first validation, users have to request new tokens for every service access. Our users should have to request their security token only once. If tokens are bound to services, composite services cannot forward them to other services without additional communication with the security service. As we trust our services to be uncorrupted, we want to allow them to reuse tokens on behalf of the user for simplicity of the protocol. In this way, a composite service can access other services on behalf of the user without requesting new tokens. The receiving service will process the request as if it had come directly from the user.

Accessing a Service. All services in our framework require that requests be augmented with a security token identifying the requesting user. Access without a token is not permitted and returns an error (see Fig. 2). Therefore, a user without a valid token who wishes to use a service first performs an authentication call to the security service, providing her credentials. She receives a token in return that may be reused for several days until it expires. Now, to access a service, she passes this token along with the HTTPS call, for example as an additional GET parameter or as an HTTPS header.

Upon receiving a request, a service checks whether a token is provided. It extracts the token and sends it to the security service for validation. A token is valid if there is a corresponding entry in the token table and its expiration date has not passed. The security service responds with the user name associated with

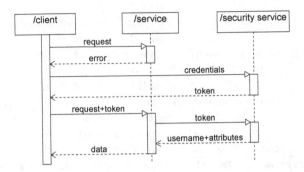

Fig. 2. Authentication protocol. A service denies an unauthenticated request. The user performs authentication by trading his credentials for a security token. The authenticated request is granted.

the token, possibly together with additional user attributes that might be of use in the domain of the service system. The security service responds with an error code if the token cannot be found in the token table or if it has expired. Upon receiving a positive answer, the original service processes the user request after checking the user's authorization if necessary (see Sect. 3.3). Once the service has verified the identity of the user, it may establish a session with this user to prevent unnecessary authentication calls during further communication.

3.3 Authorization

Although the identity of a user has already been verified in the preceding authentication steps, a service might still have to decline a request if the resource to be accessed is sensitive and the user lacks sufficient clearance. We manage the required authorization at the resource level and integrate it with our central security service to relieve services of the burden of managing user groups and associating them with authorization rules. This central authorization corresponds to the concept of a policy decision point as defined by the XACML standard [6]. Based on the decision of the security service, the services controlling a resource grant or deny access, acting as policy enforcement points.

User Groups, Roles and Areas. The security service manages user groups and roles. According to the role-based access control (RBAC) model [13], a role represents a responsibility in the context of an organization. User groups, on the other hand, often reflect the structure of an organization. We exploit existing user groups by assigning roles to entire groups rather than individual users, leaving user management with the group owners rather than duplicating it for roles. Our role definitions are generic and can hence be reused by multiple services for multiple resources. We make the mapping of roles to user groups dependent on the resources to ensure that the same generic role can be associated with different users for different resources. For instance, the role "admin" might require membership in the group "management" for resource "A", but membership in the group "engineers" for resource "B".

In contrast to this centralized portion of the RBAC model, the mapping of roles to permissions stays with each individual service. Permissions denote rights to perform particular actions[1] that often depend on the service and the particular resource. It is hence insufficient to grant or block access to a service or a function as a whole. A user might be entitled to use a service to manipulate resource "A" but not to do the same with resource "B". However, when services provide access to large amounts of data it is inconvenient to manage authorization rules for every single resource.

We therefore have a directory service that provides a representation of the logical structure of our organization in the form of areas (see Fig. 1). Areas are resources that serve as authorization reference anchors. Our services associate each resource they provide with an area, and authorization rules also refer to areas. In this way, the area directory serves as a common dictionary for services and the security service to map resources to authorization rules. It does not have to implement any further functionality, but may store meta-information with the areas.

In fact, any REST service and even multiple services might be used as area directory as long as reference resources, i.e., areas, are provided. The difference between arbitrary resources and areas is of a semantic nature. Any resource that is being referenced by authorization rules becomes an area, and any service that holds such resources becomes an area directory. The security service reflects this flexibility by representing areas with URLs that can point to any REST resource. Thereby, regarding authorization, we support heterogeneous organizational structures.

Each service in our system knows to which areas its resources belong. The security service, in turn, maintains area-specific mappings of roles to user groups. To perform a given action, a user must be assigned particular roles. For example, instructing a service to delete data records might require the role "admin", whereas merely reading those same records requires the role "consumer". The security service implements the authorization mapping by managing lists of roles, user groups and areas (see Fig. 3). Areas are represented by their URL, pointing to the area directory that holds the area in question. Roles are represented only by name; they do not carry any further information. The security service is only responsible for answering the question whether a user has a certain role in an area; it does not specify what a user in a certain role is allowed to do as these permissions are service-specific. The services requiring authorization are themselves responsible to determine the level of access a role grants. This arrangement has the advantage that service owners don't require the assistance of a security-service administrator to define or change the mapping of role-area pairs to permissions.

---

[1] Although we deal with RESTful services, permissions are not necessarily limited to CRUD operations.

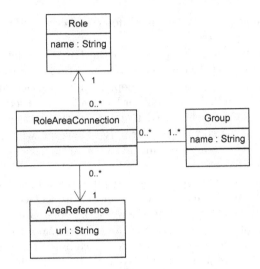

Fig. 3. Authorization classes. Group objects hold authorized users for unique role-area pairs.

For each level of access we want to distinguish for an area, we define an appropriate role and establish a relationship to the area reference via a role-area connection (see Fig. 3). This connection contains the information which groups of users may act on the area in that role. By holding the user group information in the role-area connection objects, we facilitate the definition of generic, reusable roles.

Without loss of generality we restrict our discussion to *core RBAC* while our approach may be extended to also support hierarchical roles and separation-of-duty constraints.

Accessing a Resource. When receiving a request, a service determines the roles required to perform the requested action. It also determines the area the accessed resource belongs to. The service then sends the security token of the user, the URL of the area, and the role that matches the requested access to the security service. The security service checks whether the user is a member of all the groups that have been specified for that particular area-role combination. If the user is lacking a group membership or the role or the area cannot be found in the first place, the security service will respond with an error code. In this case, the original service will deny access. If the user is a member of all the necessary groups, the security service will signal success and access will be granted.

Figure 4 gives an example of the complete authorization process. Fig. 4a shows the three services involved and some of the data they hold. The area directory reflects the structure of an organization with two departments. "Department X" runs two projects named "project foo" and "project bar". A service offers a "unit test report" resource that belongs to "project foo" and an "integration test report" resource that belongs to "project bar". For each of the four standard REST operations, the service contains a mapping to the role that is necessary to perform that operation on the report. The security service knows for every area, e.g., "project foo", which groups a user has to be member of to act in a certain role on that area.

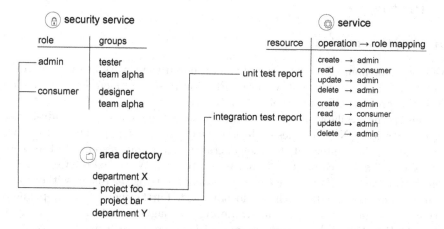

(a) Example data held by the services involved. Arrows between the services and the directory represent references.

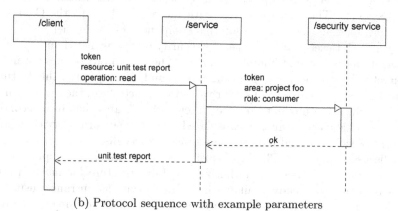

(b) Protocol sequence with example parameters

Fig. 4. Authorization example

Figure 4b shows how a user request is processed. The user wants to read the "unit test report". The client sends this request and the user's token to the service. The service determines that the "unit test report" belongs to the area "project foo" and that the role "consumer" is necessary to read that report. It sends a query to the security service whether the user is a "consumer" of resources associated with "project foo". The security service knows that a user has to be a member of the groups "designer" and "team alpha" to act in the role "consumer" on "project foo". If the user is a member of both groups, the security service will approve the query, and the service will send the "unit test report" to the client.

4   Prototype

4.1   Implementation

We have implemented a prototype of the proposed framework in Ruby on Rails 3.0.3. For service deployment, we use a Phusion Passenger module with enabled TLS/SSL protection on an Apache web server.

Some of the available single sign-on (SSO) solutions come with ready-to-use implementations. None of these solutions meet all of our requirements, but we deploy one of them internally for the generation and the management of security tokens as well as the connection to our user directory. We picked the Central Authentication Service (CAS) because it uses opaque strings as tokens without any cryptographic overhead, which we do not need. Furthermore, CAS implementations are available for many programming languages including Ruby, namely rubyCAS [14]. RubyCAS directly supports LDAP user directories. However, any CAS implementation should work.

Note that no service except the security service communicates directly with the CAS server. The security service with its lean API wraps the CAS server completely, making the latter an internal component of the former.

We use CAS ticket-granting tickets as security tokens as they do not expire after validations and are not bound to services. The CAS protocol does not include the direct validation of ticket-granting tickets and, consequently, this feature is missing in CAS implementations. Our validation process uses the ticket-granting ticket to request an auxiliary service ticket and validates that in a second internal call. This mechanism is encapsulated within the security service, whereas CAS service tickets would require users to issue two calls.

As discussed in Sect. 3.3, the security service contains a mapping of user groups to roles and areas for authorization. Infrastructure for managing user groups is typically already available in an organizations' intranet, usually as part of a user directory. It would therefore be redundant to implement groups as lists of users in the security service. It is more convenient to reuse the group infrastructure or even preexisting groups of the user directory. Our RoleArea-Connection object (see Fig. 3) is associated with a list of LDAP groups from our organization's user directory. When an authorization request for a particular user reaches the security service, the latter connects to the user directory and retrieves all groups this user is member of. The security service then compares these user directory groups with the list of group names associated with the requested role and area. If the user is a member of all necessary groups, access is granted. We decided to require the user to be member of *all* listed groups to facilitate the formation of intersections of groups. Thereby, we are able to bind access rights to user sets below the granularity of groups. This is not possible if membership in only *one* of the listed groups would suffice. For additional flexibility both schemes could be combined.

4.2 API

Our overall approach results in the following API for the security service:

issue_token. This method is called by a client POSTing the credentials of a user to the security service. Credentials consist of user name and password and are sent as POST data. If the user is found in the user directory and the password matches, the security service responds with the HTTP status 200 OK with the security token contained in the HTTP body. If the credentials are invalid, the security service responds with the HTTP code 401 Unauthorized.

check_token. This method is called by services checking the identity of a user who provided a security token along with her request. The method is called by an HTTP GET, with the security token passed as a parameter within the query string. If the token is found in the token table and has not expired, the security service responds with the HTTP code 200 OK. The response body contains an XML document with the corresponding user name and the associated list of group memberships found in the user directory. If the token is invalid, the security service responds with the HTTP code 401 Unauthorized.

check_authorization. This method is called by a service if a user requests access-controlled resources that may only be seen by users in a certain role. The method has three parameters: the security token of the requesting user, the area the requested resource belongs to, and the role matching the access. The method is called by an HTTP GET along with all three parameters. If the security token is invalid, the security service responds with the HTTP code 401 Unauthorized. If role or area cannot be found, the security service responds with the HTTP code 404 Not Found. This indicates that administrative action is necessary to create a authorization mapping for the service. If the mapping is found but the user is not a member of all required groups, the security service responds with the HTTP code 403 Forbidden. If the user has all required memberships, the security service responds with 200 OK.

The security service also provides an API for creating all necessary authorization mapping objects (see Fig. 3). This API follows a RESTful design, i.e., the individual objects are created, read, updated or deleted by using HTTP POST, GET, PUT or DELETE, in some cases with an XML representation of the resource in the HTTP body. Note that this API is not used by services or clients, but is accessed only by administrators. Writing one central, convenient interface should suffice. We have implemented a web interface for this purpose, using Ruby on Rails.

Table 1 compares the protocol API complexity of CAS and of our proposed framework in terms of HTTP calls to the central security service. It lists three

Table 1. Protocol comparison of CAS and our framework. For an explanation of the CAS tickets, see [3].

Step	CAS	Our Framework
Login	2 calls (get login ticket, get ticket-granting ticket)	1 call (get token)
Service Access	2 calls (get service ticket, access with service ticket)	1 call (access with token)
Proxy Access	2 calls + 1 passive call (get proxy ticket, access with proxy ticket + receive proxy-granting ticket)	1 call (access with token)

use cases: A user gains access to the service system in the *Login* case. She sends a request to a service in the *Service Access* case, and a service sends a requests to another service in the *Proxy Access* case. Note that this comparison does not consider the authorization aspect, which is not supported by CAS. In our framework, a service can verify user authorization with one call (see *check_authorization*).

Compared with existing systems like CAS, our framework does not require complex request-response interactions. A user can perform any security-related action with one simple HTTP call. This makes it very easy to access our framework from any programming language with support for HTTP and XML.

4.3   Deployment

We used our framework to implement a set of services for an internationally distributed engineering department developing high-performance processor chips. The services are accessed via a web front-end or by command-line scripts written in Python. The web server redirects an unauthenticated web client to a log-in page. For shell scripts, we wrote a tool that asks the user for credentials, trades them for a token with the security service, and stores the token in a shell environment variable from where service clients can pick it up. This mechanism provides single sign-on from a shell and enables automatically scheduled scripts that cannot ask any user for credentials: They can run with a token a user fetched beforehand.

We also made available a Ruby library for service developers who build upon the Ruby on Rails framework. This library implements the communication with the security service and supports queries to other services within the framework. It can also help in the creation of Ruby client scripts. A separate Python library facilitates the creation of Python client scripts.

5 Conclusion

In this paper we have proposed a security framework for RESTful services deployed in the protected domain of an intranet. A central security service handles authentication and authorization for the services in the system, relieving services of the burden of managing users, groups and authorization rules. Because the services are trusted and run within the confines of a secure environment, we have been able to simplify the API for authentication and authorization.

Users authenticate by trading their credentials for a security token which identifies a user until it expires. The token is attached to each service call. Upon receiving a token, a service validates it with the security service. It can also check whether the user has been granted a particular role for the requested resource. The security service contains a mapping of user groups to roles, and dedicated resources called *areas*. Services grant access if the user has been granted the necessary role for the requested area. As all services are trusted, the framework enables them to use the user token to access other services on behalf of the user, greatly simplifying service composition.

We have presented an implementation of our security service using available software libraries. The prototype enables engineers to consume and create access-controlled services for improved collaboration in support of their work. As the framework is composed of simple HTTP-based RESTful services and the presented protocols cut the number of required API calls in half, we have lowered the barrier for engineers to include security features into their custom-built scripts and services, requiring only little training.

Acknowledgements. The authors wish to thank Chris Giblin, Olaf Zimmermann and Charlotte Bolliger of IBM Research for their considerable help in improving the original manuscript. We also thank Michael Schäfer of IBM Germany R&D for his invaluable support with implementing the system described.

References

1. MIT: Kerberos: The network authentication protocol,
   http://web.mit.edu/kerberos/
2. Schemers, R., Allbery, R.: WebAuth technical specification,
   http://webauth.stanford.edu/protocol.html
3. Mazurek, D.: CAS protocol (May 2005), http://www.jasig.org/cas/protocol
4. Samar, V.: Single sign-on using cookies for web applications. In: Proceedings of the 8th Intl. Workshops on Enabling Technologies: Infrastructure for Collaborative Enterprises (WETICE 1999), Stanford, CA, USA, pp. 158–163. IEEE (1999)
5. OASIS: SAML specifications, http://saml.xml.org/saml-specifications
6. OASIS: OASIS eXtensible Access Control Markup Language (XACML) TC, http://www.oasis-open.org/committees/xacml/
7. Mirza, Q.K.A.: Restful implementation of authorization mechanisms. In: Proceedings of the International Conference on Technology and Business Management (ICTBM 2011), Dubai, UAE, pp. 1001–1010. INFOMS (March 2011)

8. Gutzmann, K.: Access control and session management in the HTTP environment. IEEE Internet Computing 5, 26–35 (2001)

9. Graf, S., Zholudev, V., Lewandowski, L., Waldvogel, M.: Hecate, managing authorization with RESTful XML. In: Proceedings of the 2nd International Workshop on RESTful Design (WS-REST 2011), Hyderabad, India, pp. 51–58. ACM (March 2011)

10. Recordon, D., Reed, D.: OpenID 2.0: A platform for user-centric identity management. In: Proceedings of the 2nd Workshop on Digital Identity Management (DIM 2006), Fairfax, Virginia, USA, pp. 11–16. ACM (November 2006)

11. Hammer-Lahav, E.: The OAuth 1.0 protocol. RFC 5849, IETF (April 2010)

12. Jazz Community: Jazz, https://jazz.net/

13. ANSI: American national standard for information technology – Role based access control. ANSI INCITS 359-2004, ANSI (February 2004)

14. Zukowski, M.: RubyCAS-Server, http://code.google.com/p/rubycas-server/

How to Federate VISION Clouds
through SAML/Shibboleth Authentication

Massimo Villari, Francesco Tusa, Antonio Celesti, and Antonio Puliafito

Dept. of Mathematics, Faculty of Engineering, University of Messina,
Viale F. D'Alcontres 31, 98166, Messina, Italy
{mvillari,ftusa,acelesti,apuliafito}@unime.it
http://mdslab.unime.it

Abstract. Federation is currently finding a wide argumentation in Cloud Computing. The federation among cloud operators should allow new opportunities and businesses even making the role of SMEs crucial in these new scenarios. In this work, we provide a solution on how to federate Storage Cloud providers, enabling the transparent and dynamic federation among storage suppliers adding new functionalities for end-users. VISION Cloud represents the reference architecture dealing with Storage Clouds, and our work attempts to design a solution applied on VISION, but suitable for any similar architecture.

Keywords: Cloud Computing, VISION Cloud, Federation, Security, Authentication, SAML, Shibboleth.

1 Introduction

Nowadays, most cloud providers can be considered as "islands in the ocean of the cloud computing" and do not present any form of cooperation. Recently, world wide SDOs are trying to overcome the current limitations. In particular, all standardization boards are looking at how enforcing concepts as: *interoperability*, *portability*, *data and services mobility*, *system openess*, and *federation*. Currently, we are assisting to a new trend in which cloud computing is dominated by the idea to federate clouds involving computation, storage and networking. Nevertheless, even though Federation is becoming a "buzzword" there is still a long way to go toward the establishment of a worldwide Cloud ecosystem including thousands of cooperating clouds.

Recently, many academic and industry organizations have tried to add federation features to their existing cloud architectures, but the process for making these architectures federation-enabled is not so trivial at all. In fact, often clouds are not natively conceived for cooperating with other clouds and the addition of federation features might deeply impact their architectures. Moreover, federation can have many different meanings, and its impact on a cloud architecture also depends on the target that cloud designers would like to achieve.

VISION Cloud [1] is a European FP7 Project, funded by EC in 2010. The high-level goal of VISION Cloud is to increase the global competitiveness of

F. De Paoli, E. Pimentel, and G. Zavattaro (Eds.): ESOCC 2012, LNCS 7592, pp. 259–274, 2012.

the European ICT industry by introducing a virtualized infrastructure for cost-effective delivery of data-intensive and media-rich services, providing comprehensive data interoperability and mobility, QoS and security guarantees.

The main contribution of this paper is firstly to discuss how federation can affect a cloud architecture analyzing the VISION Cloud architecture, and secondly to propose a possible technical solution for the achievement of a secure federation between different VISION Clouds leveraging the IdP/SP model and adopting the Security Assertion Markup Language (SAML) [5] and the Shibboleth [7] technologies.

The paper is organized as follows. In Section 2, we provide an overview regarding the general cloud federation concept. Section 3 discusses related works. In Section 4, we introduce the VISION Cloud architecture and in Section 5, we motivate the impact of the federation. In Section 6, we propose a solution-enabling authentication to access federated resources deployed in different VISION Clouds. In Section 7, we provide several implementation highlights using the Shibboleth technology. Section 8 concludes the paper.

2   The Perspective of Cloud Federation

Doing a parallelism with the Internet, which is considered a *network of networks*, "Cloud federation" cannot be simply considered as *Cloud of Clouds*. As the networks composing the Internet are governed by the policies, which define access control rules, also the Clouds composing a federation need to be regulated by policies defining their relationships. But the definition of such relationships is not simple because the cloud federation can theoretically consider many possible scenarios, depending on the business model, which the involved Clouds want to accomplish.

A "Cloud Federation" can be defined as a relationship between two or more independent homogeneous/heterogeneous Cloud platforms which establish a trusted federation agreement in order to benefit of a particular form of business advantage. This latter definition is quite generic and does not specify which type of relationship may be established between Clouds.

The concept of cloud federation implies several more evolved and complex scenarios than the current ones where Clouds are independent and isolated from each other, or where they merely use the services provided by other Clouds. In fact, federated cloud scenario involves more than the simple provisioning of services from a Cloud to another, and therefore it needs to rely on closer relationships between Clouds. But in order to establish such "closer relationships" achieving a "high cooperation federation", several issues concerning both the compatibility among heterogeneous Cloud platforms need to be addressed.

An indispensable requirement is that the federation agreements do not have to affect all the assets of the Clouds having relationships with other Clouds. In fact, the federation has to respect the local management and policies, but at the same time it has to enable the involved Clouds to control and use part or the whole range of resources lent by other Clouds. Typically these resources are storage and computational capabilities which Clouds use for the allocation of *aaS. The access to the federated resources is regulated by a priori federation agreements which define how each federated Cloud can "borrow" the resources of other Clouds and how each federated Cloud can "lend" the resources to other federated Clouds. Examples of federation scenarios include: "Capability Enlargement and Resource Optimization", "Provisioning of Distributed *aaS", "Service Consolidation and Power Saving".

3 Related Works

Hereby, we describe the current state-of-the-art in cloud computing, emphasizing federation aspects. A few works are available in literature related to cloud federation. The main reason is that several pending issues concerning security and privacy still have to be addressed, and a fortiori, is not clear what cloud federation actually means and what the involved issues are [3]. Nowadays, the latest trend to federate applications over the Internet is represented by the Identity Provider/Service Provider (IdP/SP) model [4]. Examples are SAML, Shibboleth, and OpenID [6]. Such solutions, considered alone, do not solve the cloud federation issues. In fact, the federation problem in cloud computing is greater than the one in traditional systems. The main limit of the existing federation solutions is that they are designed for static environments requiring a priori policy agreements, whereas clouds are high-dynamic and heterogeneous environments, which require particular security and policy arrangements. Keeping in mind the cloud federation perspective, several security issues are already picked out. Interoperability in federated heterogeneous cloud environments is faced in [8], in which the authors propose a trust model where the trust is delegated between trustworthy parties which satisfy certain constrains. Instead, the data location problem is treated in [9] where it is proposed a privacy manager to solve the problems of the data compliance to the laws of different jurisdictions.

An interesting work is presented in [10]. The authors made up an identity federation broker for service cloud. They looked at federation but considering SaaS services in which SAML is used as the basic protocol. They introduced a trusted third party as a trust broker to simplify the management of identity federation in a user centric way. In our view the proposed architecture shows good motivations but the solution is rather complex because many components, gateways, software modules (plug-in) are introduced.

In [11], the authors provide a model for Cloud Storage RESTFul based, following the SNIA directives. They introduced a *trust estimation system (TES)*, for evaluating the level of trustiness among Cloud Service Providers (CSPs), but it is not clear how they estimate this quality of relationship among servers. However the work is interesting because they modified Shibboleth for supporting their model and allowing transparent web redirections (RESTFul based) among the parties. Ranjan and Buyya [12] describe a decentralized and distributed cloud federation based on the Aneka middleware that combines PaaS enterprise clouds, overlay networking, and structured peer-to-peer techniques to create scalable wide-area networking of compute nodes for high-throughput computing. It is interesting the work done in [18], that tries to find a SSO solution suitable for Cloud environments. Rochwerger et al [13] address the federation between several IaaS RESERVOIR-based clouds. An even more decentralized vision is offered in Cloud@Home [14], a PRIN Project founded by the Italian Ministry of Education facing the cloud federation problem from the point of view of the volunteer computing paradigm. Another FP7 European Project is CONTRAIL [15], which aims to develop a system with an integrated approach to virtualization, offering services for IaaS Cloud Federation. Other initiatives aiming to develop virtual infrastructure management systems with features supporting the IaaS cloud federation are CLEVER [16] and OpenNebula [17].

4   The VISION Cloud Architecture

In this section we describe VISION Cloud, the reference architecture adopted in the rest of the paper. The VISION Cloud (VC) architecture is aimed to the accomplishment of an abstraction of raw massive data. The VC abstraction allows to enrich storage service, taking into account a semantic classification and cataloguing of data, using XML tags, systems hints, user profiles and behaviors. In particular VC deals with the opportunity to provide new innovations:

- *Raise the Abstraction Level of Storage.* A new data model enabling the encapsulation of storage into objects with user-defined and system-defined attributes.
- *Computational Storage.* Computational agents (storlets) released into the cloud and activated by events on data.
- *Content-Centric Storage Access.* Access to data objects through information about their content and its relationships, rather than details of underlying storage containers
- *Advanced Capabilities for Cloud-based Storage.* Support multi-tenancy, guarantee secure and authorized access to the data and services, check compliance with standards and regulations, optimize service provision with regard to cost, monitor, analyze and manage SLA considering content-related terms.
- *Data Mobility and Federation.* A layer enabling unified access to data across storage clouds and federation of data objects maintained by users across different administrative domains.

As depicted in Figure 1 VC deploys its software stack inside each node compounding the basic element of a cluster. As it is possible to notice in Figure 1, at cluster level VC has servers equipped with basic software GPFS-SNC and CASSANDRA (as intra-cluster distributed configuration) and Linux, Apache and Tomcat (as intra-server stand-alone configuration).

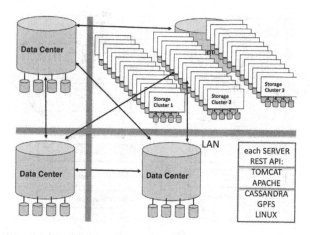

Fig. 1. VISION Cloud Physical Model. At bottom on Right Side, the basic existing software stack of a server composition is depicted.

5 The Federation between VISION Clouds

In the VISION Cloud model different actors exist. In the following, we will pay more attention on *Tenants*, *Users*, and *Containers* that are deeply involved in our scenario. A *Tenant* is an organization that subscribes for and receives storage cloud services. A *Tenant* may represent a commercial firm, a governmental organization, or any other organization, including any group of one or more individual persons. A user is the entity that actually uses (consumes) VISION Cloud's storage services. The term user may refer to a person or to an application/program. A user belongs to one and only one *Tenant*. We note that a person might own a user account in more than one *Tenant*, but this is opaque to VISION Cloud. A *Tenant* administrator creates *Users* and manages them. A user has an identifier (unique within his *Tenant*) and may have credentials allowing him to authenticate himself to VISION Cloud. Data objects are stored in containers. Each data object resides within the context of a single container. Each *Tenant* has its own set of users and its own name space for its containers.

Commonly, an independent VISION Cloud stores data objects in its own containers. Federation allows to VISION Cloud providers to leverage new business benefits. In fact, a VISION Cloud provider might decide to federate itself with other VISION Cloud providers for different reasons including:

- **Storage capability enlargement.** If a VISION Cloud runs out of storage capabilities, it can request external storage capabilities to external providers.
- **Geographical data placement.** Providers can require to store data objects closer to his/her geographical location.
- **Resource consolidation.** In order to reduce the energy consumption, according to target conditions, a VISION Cloud might decide to migrate data object into another VISION Cloud.

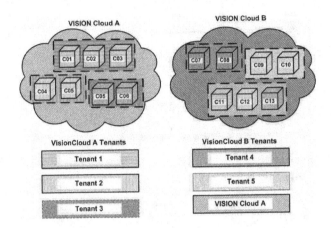

Fig. 2. Federation between two VISION Clouds in a storage capability enlargement scenario

In the rest of the paper, in order to analyze the VISION Cloud federation, we will focus on a storage capability enlargement scenario. Figure 2 depicts an environment including two VISION Clouds each one acts on a different administrative domain. VISION Cloud A holds *Tenants* 1, 2, 3. *Tenant 1* holds *Containers* C01, C02,and C03. *Tenant 2* holds *Containers* C04 and C05. *Tenant 3* holds *Containers* C06 and C07. As VISION Cloud A receives instantiation requests for further containers, it decides to establish a federation with VISION Cloud B. As consequence, VISION Cloud B creates in its data center a *Tenant* "VISION Cloud A" holding *Containers* C11, C12, and C13. VISION Cloud B simply sees the three *Containers* as data of VISION Cloud A and it is not able to determine to which particular *Tenants* of VISION Cloud A they belong. On the other hand, VISION Cloud A associates *Container* C11 to *Tenant 1*, *Container* C12 to *Tenant 2*, and *Container* C13 to *Tenant 3*.

Despite the obvious advantages, the aforementioned scenario raises several security issues:

- A VISION Cloud performs an authentication in another one in order to establish a federation hence deploying containers.
- VISION Cloud B has not to be aware who is the effective holder of each *Container* of the *Tenant* "VISION Cloud A". This information hiding is very important because it allows to avoid possible unfair competition between different federated VISION Clouds.

Regarding *Users* interactions:

- The *User* needs to be authenticated by the corresponding *Tenant* gaining access to all his own *Containers* hosted in both the local and external VISION Clouds.
- The *User* needs to perform a Single Sign-On authentication on the *Tenant*, gaining access to all its *Containers* without further log-in.

Issues related to Cloud interactions are out of the scope of this paper and will not analyzed in the following.

6 VISION Cloud Security Infrastructure

6.1 Current Authentication in VISION Cloud

According to the VISION Cloud architectural document, *Tenants*, in order to authenticate their *Users*, may select one of the following authentication options:

1. Authentication with an internal identity manager provided by the VISION Cloud as part of the *User Services* in the *Global View* (GV, which provides a set of distributed cloud-wide services that are logically global).
2. Authentication with his existing identity management server (e.g. Identity Provider), which is located at the customer premises.

In the current VISION Cloud architecture, the only supported authentication option is the one based on the internal identity management service, operating on LDAP service. Figure 3 points out the process by means of a client request is handled in VISION Cloud: upon receiving a client request, the *Request Processor* will call the *Access Manager* to authenticate the request. The *Access Manager* will call the *Identity and Access Policy Services* to do the actual authentication with the relevant identity management server (lying in the User Services). In particular, the *Authentication Service* is called within the *Identity and Access Policy Services* for checking all data access requests and management operations that require *User* identity verification. This latter is validated interacting with the *Identity and Policy Repository*. The *Identity and Access Policy Services* also includes a *Federation Manager* that will provide (in future implementations) the interface for SAML assertions. Since the current VISION Cloud implementation does not provide any Federation feature, this component is not used yet. In the following Section, starting from the *Identity and Access Policy Services* component, with particular attention on the Federation Manager, we will introduce our decentralized security solution.

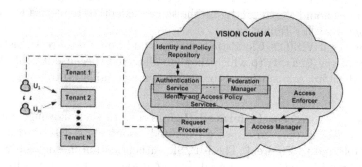

Fig. 3. Authentication based on the internal identity management service

6.2   Authentication through Tenant IdP for Federation

According to the SAML terminology, the basic authentication system includes three main entities: Subject, Service Provider (SP) or Relaying Party (RP), and Identity Provider (IdP) or Asserting Party. The subject is the entity, which wants to perform the authentication. It can be a person using a Desktop/Web/Mobile application or a software system. The SP is the system authenticating a subject. The IdP is a system asserting authentication claims to the SP regarding a subject. When an authentication request coming from a subject arrives to the SP, it redirects the request to the IdP. If the subject has not been authenticated yet, the subject needs to perform an authentication on the IdP, gaining access to one or more SPs relaying on the IdP without further authentications (hence achieving SSO).

Figure 4 points out a scenario involving VISION Cloud A, VISION Cloud B, N *Tenants* and M *Users*. More specifically, services made available from Vision Cloud A are exploited by its *Tenants* $T_1, T_2, \cdots, T_N$ and T_2 in turn offers services to Users $U_1, U_2, \cdots, U_M$. Differently from the centralized approach, here we assume that the *User* authentication is managed from each *Tenant* independently through an IdP (one for each Tenant): $IdP_{T_1}, IdP_{T_2}, \cdots, IdP_{T_N}$. Now, let us consider a particular situation where VISION Cloud A run out its own resources and, for matching anyway the service allocation requests coming from its Tenants, asks further resources to an external provider VISION Cloud B. This might be considered as a resource federation example among VISION Cloud A and VISION Cloud B. The latter, in order to allocate resources for the former, will create a new *Tenant* named VC_A that logically stores all the *Containers* associated to the *Tenants* of VISION Cloud A (VC_A) that have been deployed on VISION Cloud B (VC_B). In general, *Containers* in VISION Cloud are identified and accessed using a mapping with the DNS as follows: $C_1.T_2.VC_A.eu$ represents the *Container* C_1 belonging to the tenant T_2 on VISION Cloud A; $C_1.T_{VC_A}.VC_B.eu$ identifies the *Container* C_1 belonging to *Tenant* T_{VC_A} on VISION Cloud B. When building up resources federation among different VISION Clouds, we retain the two following requirements have to be satisfied:

- a User should be allowed to access a remote federated resources transparently: he should conveniently use the same credentials exploited for authenticating with his Tenant;
- the external VISION Cloud that provides additional resources must not be aware of the *Tenants* to which they are allocated (because it could be considered *unfair competition* according to commercial laws).

How the User Access Federated Resources. In the following, the logical steps needed by a *User* to access a federated resource are described using the example referred to Figure 4. The IdP/SP authentication mechanism we introduce can be still used when internal *Tenant* resources are accessed by a User. Even though both scenarios can be managed with our approach, in the following we will discuss only the one regarding resource Federation. The system behavior

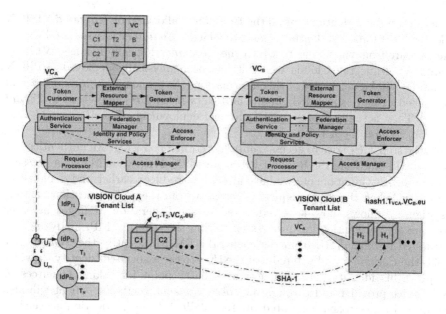

Fig. 4. Authentication in a Federated VISION Cloud scenario

is described through logical steps that are not explicitly reported in Figure for granting its readability. In step 1, VISION Cloud A runs out its resources (e.g., storage space) and, for satisfying the requests of *Tenant* T_2, asks and receives the rights to deploy *Containers* on VISION Cloud B. As consequence of this resource federation, a new *Tenant* named VC_A is created on VISION Cloud B: it will gather *Containers* logically belonging to *Tenants* of VISION Cloud A that are actually deployed on VISION Cloud B. In this particular example, we are assuming these external *Containers* are associated to *Tenant* T_2. As the Figure shows, on VC_A, *Tenant* T_2 includes logical *Containers* C_1 and C_2, physically allocated on VC_B, owned by *Tenant* T_{VC_A}.

In order to track the allocation of *Containers* on external VISION Clouds, the Federation Manager of VC_A, in particular its sub-component *External Resource Mapper*, will maintain a resource mapping table (as represented in Table 1) where each row consists of the following information: *Container* name, tenant and VC (i.e., the external provider where the resource is deployed). For each couple of fields [container, tenant] it is possible to compute a hash representing a unique identifier through the SHA-1 (160 bits). Using this hash, it will be possible to

Table 1. Example of a Resource Mapping table

Container	Tenant	VC
C_1	T_2	B
C_2	T_2	B

generate a unique identifier for all the *Containers* allocated on federated VISION Clouds. Most importantly, the *Tenant* to which a *Container* is associated will be known only from the Cloud to which the *Container* logically belongs (VISION Cloud A), while the Clouds where it has been physically deployed (VISION Cloud B) will be not aware of this information (the economic *unfair competition* is avoided). Figure shows federated *Containers* H_1 and H_2 associated to *Tenant* T_{VC_A}. They actually represent the physical deployment of *Containers* C_1 and C_2 from *Tenant* T_2 of VC_A.

In the step 2, U_1 tries to access *Container* C_1 of T_2 on VC_A. An authentication request will flow from the Request Processor to the Federation Manager crossing all the security components we have already introduced earlier and depicted in Figure 3. When the client request is received from the Authentication Service, as Figure 4 shows, now it is redirected to the Federation Manager in order to start the authentication process exploiting the external IdP: analyzing the requested resource URL from the client, the FM will identify the *Tenant* that holds the *Container* and will redirect the User to the associated Identity Provider to prove his identity. The FM acts as a entry point for asking resources to the service provider and through its *Token Consumer* sub-component will also consume Users's token generated by Tenants'IdP. If authentication succeeded, U_1 receives a token that can be used to access all the *Containers* of T_2 for which he is authorized (i.e., for which the User holds access right in the ACL). The *Token Consumer* on the FM will check if the token has been issued by one of the VC_A *Tenants* and if the *Tenant* asserts the User identity. In this example, User U_1 is a valid User of *Tenant* T_2 of VISION Cloud A and the token will lead to a successful authentication process.

After the authentication is accomplished, in step 3 the authorization process starts: since U_1 asked for *Container* C_1, the authorization components of VC_A will control the related access rights. Querying the *Identity and Policy Repository*, the *Access Enforcer* verifies the access rights of U_1 on the container The FM will be notified by the Access Enforcer about the authorization response that will be saved in a local cache. If authorization is successful, the resource access continues. As represented in Table 1, *Container* C_1 just represents a logical map to the physical *Container* $hash1.T_{VC_A}.VC_B.eu$ deployed on VISION Cloud B. This means that, once the token is consumed by the *Token Consumer* in the FM, the resource will not be really accessed on VC_A. U_1. In order to retrieve the physical container, VISION Cloud B has to be involved and an authentication/authorization process may be performed there. U_1 will need to be authenticated from *Tenant* T_{VC_A} on VISION Cloud B that holds the *Container* H_1 associated to C_1.

Before the User can be redirected on the remote VISION Cloud for accessing the physical container, the FM has to verify how the requested *Container* has been mapped on the remote federated VISION Cloud: in order to carry out this operation, in step 4, through the *External Resource Mapper* component, it will look up the Federation Resource Mapping table for retrieving the remote

VISION Cloud where the *Container* associated to the key value [Container, Tenant] = $[C_1, T_2]$ is deployed.

Right now, User U_1 has been authenticated on VC_A, his access rights to Container C_1 have been verified and the FM of VC_A knows the remote path where the associated physical container. Furthermore, U_1 holds a token issued by *Tenant* T_2. Unfortunately, this token cannot be directly used to perform authentication on the logical *Tenant* T_{VC_A} on VISION Cloud B, because it has been issued by *Tenant* T_2 of VC_A. In addition, one of the requirements we want to satisfy refers into avoid the possibility that VC_B may known which *Tenants* are exploiting its resources through Federation. In order to solve the authentication problem across organizational boundaries and introducing SSO authentication for Users, we should need a mechanism by means of Cloud A delegates its identity for accessing Federated Resources on external Providers.

If a User holds a token issued by his *Tenant* IdP, the FM in VC_A will generate a new token for him: in the example, after that the U_1 identity and his rights have been verified, a new token that will be used for accessing the remote federated resource is generated by the *Token Generator* asserting that:

- U_1 identity is verified by one of the *Tenant* of VISION Cloud A but the information about the specific *Tenant* identity is omitted for avoiding unfair competition issues with the Federated Cloud.
- User U_1 is authorized to access *Container* $hash1.T_{VC_A}.VC_B.eu$ on the Federated VISION Cloud B.

In the example pointed out in Figure 4, since the token is associated to a valid User of *Tenant* T_2 that, in turn represents a valid *Tenant* for VISION Cloud A, the new token generation will be correctly accomplished. The new token will state that User U_1 is recognized by VISION Cloud A. The new token does not contain any explicit reference to the *Tenant* to which U_1 belongs but just a reference to it that is known only from VC_A . The new token will be signed using the private key of the Federation Manager (e.g., X.509) for preventing data tampering.

Once the token has been generated, *User* U_1 receives it from the FM of VC_A and it is redirected to VISION Cloud B to the URL identifying the resource that has to be accessed. In this example, the URL will be the location of the *Container* hash1: $hash1.T_{VC_A}.VC_B.eu$. User U_1 forwards his *Container* request to VISION Cloud B: *Container* $hash1.T_{VC_A}.VC_B.eu$ belongs to *Tenant* T_{VC_A}.

In order to access the resources, an authentication request is generated and will be managed according to the flow we have already described above. From the Request Processor, the request is propagated across the authentication components and is caught from the FM of VC_B. The token provided by U_1 will be consumed from the *Token Consumer* of the FM that will check its issuer (verifying the token digital signature). If the issuer is equal to the name of the logical tenant where federated resource are allocated (in this example VB_A) the asserted identity of U_1 will allow the User to be recognized. Furthermore, also the authorization assertion within the token will be checked and, in this case will allow U_1 to access the *Container* $hash1.T_{VC_A}.VC_B.eu$.

In the example of Figure 4 if U_1 needs to access the *Container* C_2 of *Tenant* T_2 will present his token to the *Token Consumer* of the FM. The token will certify that U_2 is a valid *User* of *Tenant* T_2 and since the authentication has been already performed, if U_1 is enabled to access C_2, an authorization assertion is generated and is added to the content of the U_1 The new token is digitally signed again because its content has been modified. From now on, U_1 will be able to access both *Containers* C_1 and C_2 on the remote VISION Cloud B.

7   Secure Federation through Shibboleth Authentication

In the previous Section, we discussed how to integrate federation features within the VISION Cloud architecture, especially focusing on authentication system adopting the IdP/SP model. Here, we will discuss several Shibboleth [7] implementation highlights for the authentication of the *Users* of *Tenants* accessing to *Containers* deployed in different federated VISION Clouds. Shibboleth is one of the major solutions implementing the SAML protocol and the IdP/SP model.

In order to establish a federation between different VISION Cloud providers, it is needed to perform two phases of authentication.

- Cloud Authentication. A VISION Cloud performs an authentication in another VISION Cloud in order to establish a federation hence deploying containers.
- User Authentication. A *User* of a *Tenant* performs an authentication in the *Tenant's* IdP accessing all its *Containers* placed in both the local and external VISION Clouds. The data object location is transparent for the *User* that only interact with his/her reference local VISION Cloud.

In this Section, considering the architectural solution already discussed in the previous Section, we specifically focus on how to achieve the "User Authentication", discussing several implementation highlights using Shibboleth. According to the SAML. According to our infrastructure, the Shibboleth subject is the *Tenant's User*, and the Shibboleth SP is the *token consumer* of the *Federation Manager* component. Moreover, assertions sent by the *Tenant's* IdP are caught by the FM, rearranged by the *External Resource Mapper* and forwarded by the *Token Generator* to the *Token Consumer* of the federated VISION Cloud hosting the containers.

7.1   The Shibboleth SP

The Shibboleth SP, in a Linux system is represented by the *shibd* demon integrated in the Apache Web Server by means of the *mod_shib* module. In the following, we report the main parameters adopted to configure the SP:

- **SP - entityID**: https://sp.shib.org/shibboleth
- **SP - metadata**: sp-metadata.xml
- **SP - credentials**: sp-key.pem sp-cert.pem

Commonly, the settings of the *shibd* daemon are defined by the *shibboleth2.xml*. In the following several highlights of this configuration file are depicted. *SP - shibboleth2.xml*

```
<SPConfig xmlns="urn:mace:shibboleth:2.0:native:sp:config"
    xmlns:conf="urn:mace:shibboleth:2.0:native:sp:config"
    xmlns:saml="urn:oasis:names:tc:SAML:2.0:assertion"
    xmlns:samlp="urn:oasis:names:tc:SAML:2.0:protocol"
    xmlns:md="urn:oasis:names:tc:SAML:2.0:metadata"
    logger="syslog.logger" clockSkew="180">
<!-- ... -->
  <RequestMapper type="Native">
        <RequestMap applicationId="default">
            <Host name="sp.shib.org">
                <Path name="authenticationagent/home" authType="shibboleth"
                requireSession="true" requireSessionWith="Intranet"/>
            </Host>
        </RequestMap>
    </RequestMapper>
<!-- ... -->
<ApplicationDefaults id="default" policyId="default"
        entityID="https://sp.shib.org/shibboleth"
      homeURL="https://sp.shib.org/authenticationagent/home"
      REMOTE_USER="eppn persistent-id targeted-id"
      signing="true" encryption="true">
<!-- ... -->
<Sessions lifetime="28800" timeout="3600" checkAddress="false"
        handlerURL="/Shibboleth.sso" handlerSSL="true"
        exportLocation="https://sp.shib.org/Shibboleth.sso/
        GetAssertion" exportACL="127.0.0.1"
        idpHistory="false" idpHistoryDays="7">
        <SessionInitiator type="Chaining" Location="/Login"
        isDefault="true" id="Intranet" relayState="cookie"
        entityID="https://idp.shib.org:8443/idp/shibboleth">
              <SessionInitiator type="SAML2" acsIndex="1"
              template="bindingTemplate.html"/>
                  <SessionInitiator type="Shib1" acsIndex="5"/>
            </SessionInitiator>
<!-- ... -->
  <MetadataProvider type="Chaining">
    <MetadataProvider type="XML" file="idp-metadata.xml"/>
    <MetadataProvider type="XML" file="sp-metadata.xml"/>
    </MetadataProvider>
  <CredentialResolver type="File" key="sp-key.pem" certificate="sp-cert.pem"/>
</ApplicationDefaults>
```

More specifically, we can distinguish:

- **SPConfig:** It contains the name spaces of the SP configuration
- **RequestMapper:** It maps the quest with the associated applications.
  - *Host name*: SP hostname.
  - *Path*

   * *name*:redirect path.

   * *requireSessionWith*: Associated Session Initiator id.

– **ApplicationDefaults:** settings for a default *Session Initiator*.
- *entityID*: SAML entityID used in the SP.
- *homeURL*: URL where the SP redirect the client.
- *signing*: if *true* the SAML messages will be signed.
- *encryption*: if *true* the SAML messages will be crypted.

– **SessionInitiator:** It checks the handlers starting the authentication process with the SP.
- *entityID*: SAML entityID of the used IdP.

– **MetadataProvider:** It sets the sources of metadata used by the SP.
- *file*: path of the metadata file.

– **CredentialResolver:** It allows to the SP to access its credential as public and private keys.
- *key*: Path of the file containing the private key in PEM format.
- *certificate*: path of the file containing the certificate in PEM format.

7.2   The Shibboleth IdP

The Shibboleth IdP receives authentication request from *Users* through SPs. It provides information regarding the identity of *Users* issuing attributes (or authentication token), interacting with a LDAP server. So that, it represents a point of certification. In the following, we report the main parameters adopted to configure the IdP:

– **IDP - entityID**: https://idp.shib.org:8443/idp/
– **IDP - metadata**: idp-metadata.xml
– **IDP - credenziali**: idp.key idp.crt
– **LDAP - hostname**: ldap://localhost:389
– **LDAP - base dn**: ou=Users,dc=shibidp,dc=home
– **LDAP - user dn**: cn=Manager,dc=shibidp,dc=home
– **LDAP - password**: shibidp

The Shibboleth IdP is released as web application that can be deployed in a *servlet container*. In our testbed, we specifically used Tomcat. As already pointed out, the Shibboleth IdP perform authentication by means of an LDAP server containing *User* accounts. In our testbed, we choice to use *OpenLDAP*.

 In the following, we report the main IdP configuration. For the deployment of the IdP it was necessary to modify the *server.xml* file placed in the Tomcat configuration directory, adding an appropriate *Connector https* on port 8443. *IDP - server.xml*

```
<Connector port="8443"
protocol="org.apache.coyote.http11.Http11Protocol"
SSLImplementation="edu.internet2.middleware.security.
tomcat6.DelegateToApplicationJSSEImplementation"
```

```
scheme="https"
SSLEnabled="true"
clientAuth="false"
secure="true"
keystoreFile="/opt/shibboleth-idp/credentials/idp.jks"
keystorePass="administrator" />
```

Regarding the metadata structure, it is needed to add the *IDPSSODescriptor* tag inside the *EntityDescriptor* tag indicating the parser which is starting the IdP. Regarding the configuration file, it was required to enable the user authentication by means of username and password. This is possible modifying the *conf/handler.xml* file as follows: *IDP - handler.xml*

```
<!-- Login Handlers -->
<!--<ph:LoginHandler xsi:type="ph:RemoteUser">
<ph:AuthenticationMethod>
    urn:oasis:names:tc:SAML:2.0:ac:classes:unspecified
  </ph:AuthenticationMethod>
  </ph:LoginHandler>-->
<!-- Username/password login handler -->
<ph:LoginHandler xsi:type="ph:UsernamePassword"
    jaasConfigurationLocation="file:///opt/shibboleth-idp/conf/login.config">
<ph:AuthenticationMethod>
    urn:oasis:names:tc:SAML:2.0:ac:classes:PasswordProtectedTransport
</ph:AuthenticationMethod>
</ph:LoginHandler>
```

8   Conclusions and Remarks

Nowadays both industry and academic initiatives are trying to add federation features in cloud architecture, but this task is not trivial at all. In this paper, starting from the VISION Cloud architecture, we studied a methodology for the integration of federation features. More specifically, we analyze the impact of our solution in the original architecture, also proposing a possible implementation based on SAML/Shibboleth. Currently the VISION Cloud project is at the second year, and one of the major objectives is the addition of federation capabilities. Nevertheless, further issues need to be faced yet.

Acknowledgments. The research leading to the results presented in this paper has received funding from the European Union's Seventh Framework Programme (FP7 2007-2013) Project VISION-Cloud under grant agreement number 217019.

References

1. Vision-Cloud Project (March 2012), http://www.visioncloud.eu/
2. Storage Networking Industry Association (SNIA): Cloud Data Management Interface (CDMI) (September 2011), http://www.snia.org/tech_activities/ publicreview/CDMI_SNIA_Architecture_v1.0.1.pdf

3. Leavitt, N.: Is cloud computing really ready for prime time? Computer, 15–20 (January 2009)
4. Liberty Alleance Project, http://projectliberty.org
5. SAML V2.0 Technical Overview, OASIS (January 2012), http://www.oasis-open.org/specs/index.php#saml
6. OpenID Authentication 2.0, OpenID Foundation (2007), http://openid.net/specs/openid-attribute-exchange-2_0.html
7. The Shibboleth system standards (January 2012), http://shibboleth.internet2.edu/
8. Li, W., Ping, L.: Trust Model to Enhance Security and Interoperability of Cloud Environment. In: Jaatun, M.G., Zhao, G., Rong, C. (eds.) CloudCom 2009. LNCS, vol. 5931, pp. 69–79. Springer, Heidelberg (2009)
9. Pearson, S., Shen, Y., Mowbray, M.: A Privacy Manager for Cloud Computing. In: Jaatun, M.G., Zhao, G., Rong, C. (eds.) CloudCom 2009. LNCS, vol. 5931, pp. 90–106. Springer, Heidelberg (2009)
10. Huang, H.Y., Wang, B., Liu, X.X., Xu, J.M.: Identity federation broker for service cloud. In: 2010 International Conference on Service Sciences (ICSS), pp. 115–120 (May 2010)
11. Srinivas, M., Srinivas, B., Marx, R.: Article: A unique approach to element management and secure cloud storage backup for sensitive data. IJCA Special Issue on Communication and Networks comnetcn, 1–5 (2011)
12. Ranjan, R., Buyya, R.: Decentralized overlay for federation of enterprise clouds. In: Handbook of Research on Scalable Computing Technologies (2009)
13. Rochwerger, B., Breitgand, D., Epstein, A., Hadas, D., Loy, I., Nagin, K., Tordsson, J., Ragusa, C., Villari, M., Clayman, S., Levy, E., Maraschini, A., Massonet, P., Munoz, H., Toffetti, G.: Reservoir - when one cloud is not enough. Computer 44, 44–51 (2011)
14. Cunsolo, V., Distefano, S., Puliafito, A., Scarpa, M.: Applying software engineering principles for designing cloud@home. In: CCGRID, pp. 618–624 (2010)
15. Contrail, Open Computing Infrastructures for Elastic Services, http://contrail-project.eu/
16. Tusa, F., Celesti, A., Paone, M., Villari, M., Puliafito, A.: How clever-based clouds conceive horizontal and vertical federations. In: ISCC, pp. 167–172 (2011)
17. Milojicic, D.S., Llorente, I.M., Montero, R.S.: Opennebula: A cloud management tool. IEEE Internet Computing 15(2), 11–14 (2011)
18. Reich, C., Rubsamen, T.: Shibboleth Web-proxy for Single Sign-on of Cloud Services. In: CLOSER, Proceedings of the 2nd International Conference on Cloud Computing and Services Science, Porto, Portugal, pp. 89–95 (2012)

The Secure Enterprise Desktop:
Changing Today's Computing Infrastructure

Thomas Gschwind, Michael Baentsch, Andreas Schade, and Paolo Scotton

IBM Research, Zurich, Switzerland

Abstract. An end-user computing environment is characterized by an image which is the ensemble comprising operating system, applications and data) and by the hardware where the image is running. One can essentially distinguish two fundamental approaches: either the image is installed on a given end-user owned computer or the image is run on a server and is remotely accessed by the user through a remote desktop. Both approaches, however, have a disadvantage. In the former case, no network connectivity is required as the image is stored on the local computer, this data is lost when the computer such as a notebook is lost or stolen. Moreover, in an enterprise environment, it is very difficult to control that image and apply patches, check for viruses etc. While the latter approach waives these shortcommings, a continuous network connection is required to work with that virtual machine which may not be always available. With the Secure Enterprise Desktop, we bridge this gap and allow users to use their computer image locally or remotely and ensure that their computer image is continuously synchronized.

1 Introduction

With the prevalence of cloud services, users expect more and more that their data is accessible from all over the world and on all types of devices. This desire is addressed with services such as Microsoft's SkyDrive, Apple's iCloud, or the Google Drive but they cover only the user's data and not the entire computing desktop (application, preferences, printers, firewall settings, etc.), an essential part of the protection mechanism for securing enterprise data access.

The Secure Enterprise Desktop goes one step further, it does not only store the user's data in the cloud (public or private) but it stores the entire desktop image in the cloud and synchronizes that image as necessary with locally available storage. This approach ensures that the entire desktop is replicated to any other computer and the user does not have to worry about the availability of the applications needed or even different computer configurations.

Maintaining the entire computer image in the cloud is also appealing to corporations. Today, many employees do their work on dedicated corporate computers. Many corporations do not want private computers to be used because typically they are less secure. Using our approach private computers can be used with the corporate image stored in the cloud (Bring Your Own Device) while ensuring the company's security standards. This is beneficial when employees are abroad and want to access their private and corporate data.

F. De Paoli, E. Pimentel, and G. Zavattaro (Eds.): ESOCC 2012, LNCS 7592, pp. 275–276, 2012.

2   The Secure Enterprise Desktop

Several challenges need to be solved for maintaining the entire computer image in the cloud.

Computer Images are Large. Copying the entire computing image onto the client computer and starting the OS would take too long. Our approach allows users to start working in their environment while the image is being downloaded from or synchronized with the server. We use a device driver that accesses the image from the cloud via iSCSI running within a securely bootstrapped and encrypted connection, that caches any block that has been download over the network on the local hard drive, and that downloads all remaining blocks in the background [1].

Continuous Backup. All blocks that are modified by the user can be written back directly into the cloud provided that there is network connectivity. When there is no network connectivity, our device driver marks blocks written back to the local cache as dirty and writes them back to the server when the connection to the corporate network is reestablished. Only blocks that have been modified by the local OS have to be written back.

Security. When a computer is started with the Secure Enterprise Desktop, for security reasons, we cannot rely on any locally installed software as it may be infected with viruses or not even available. The Secure Enterprise Desktop therefore must be booted from a boot device that cannot be tampered with and serves as authentication key, the IBM ZTIC [2]. This boot device then starts a virtualization layer into which the actual users desktop is booted. All data including caches are encrypted and only decrypted with the ZTIC.

Bring Your Own Device. When the system is to be used with a private computer we may not overwrite the data already stored on the local computer. This limitation is addressed by requiring a part of the computers hard disk to be unpartitioned, or by storing the encrypted cache within the normal users file system. Both approaches have their respective advantages and disadvantages.

3   Conclusions

The migration of entire computer images into the cloud allows users to take their desktop to wherever they go. In addition when the computer is lost, they can buy a new computer (with or without OS), boot the computer from their mobile trust anchor (performing secure boot and authentication) and continue where they have left off.

References

1. Clerc, D., Garcés-Erice, L., Rooney, S.: Os streaming deployment. In: IPCCC. IEEE (2010)
2. Weigold, T., Kramp, T., Hermann, R., Höring, F., Buhler, P., Baentsch, M.: The Zurich Trusted Information Channel – An Efficient Defence Against Man-in-the-Middle and Malicious Software Attacks. In: Lipp, P., Sadeghi, A.-R., Koch, K.-M. (eds.) TRUST 2008. LNCS, vol. 4968, pp. 75–91. Springer, Heidelberg (2008)

Cloud Computing:
U.S. and E.U. Government/Military Approach

Antonio Mauro

University of Northwest, USA
University of Modena and Reggio Emilia, Italy

Abstract. At the moment Cloud Computing is an important model to transfer applications, data and services. Companies, Government and private people are using the cloud for a lot of services such as backup or data storage. The Government uses a particular approach to move their applications into the cloud. For this reason the United State (US), has published more documents that describe these procedures. The European Union (EU) uses another approach but the topic is in continuous evolution. To understand the Federal Cloud Computing strategy in the US and in the EU, it is important to know some Federal documents published by NIST, ENISA, CIO Council, etc.

1 Introduction

For government work that is related to the cloud, it is important to understand the reference documents for Cloud Computing Standard and architecture, what is the Cloud Computing Strategy and why and how the US and EU use the cloud for their applications. It is likely that the same procedures and approaches can be used for private use or Enterprice use and to get more confidence in this technology. The US has more interesting use cases in the Government scope and tactical while the EU has a few use cases in the healthcare, research and academic scopes.

2 The European Approach

The Cloud Computing Strategy is an important project for the European Commission [1,2,3]. In particular the focus is "The Digital Agenda" [4]. The procedure is divided in three steps: legal, technical and marker. Each step has strong implications on how to implement the technology, for instance, in the context of privacy and data protection, forensics, security, etc. At the moment, the EU has some important use cases in academic, research, scientific and government environment.

3 The US Approach

The US launched the "The Cloud First Program" in 2009 and "The Cloud Computing Strategy" in 2011 [5,6,7]. These programs are very different from the EU

F. De Paoli, E. Pimentel, and G. Zavattaro (Eds.): ESOCC 2012, LNCS 7592, pp. 277–278, 2012.
© Springer-Verlag Berlin Heidelberg 2012

because the US is a federation of States and hence, it is somewhat easier to implement new guidelines. A particular working group is called "FedRAMP" (Federal Risk and Authorization Management Program) [8]. The role of this working group is to reduce redundant processes across government by providing security authorizations and continuous monitoring of cloud systems, established to provide a standard approach to assessing and authorizing cloud computing services and products. The first strategy is divided in pillars: Simplifying Acquisition of Cloud Computing Solution, Budgeting, Cloud Computing Pilot Projects, Guidance to Agencies and Policy Planning & Architecture. A new Cloud Computing Strategy was published in July 2012.

4   Conclusions

Comparing the different approaches used by the EU and the US helps us to better understand the methodology and procedures to move applications and data into the cloud, especially in a governmental context. Some topics are still open such as the Forensics procedures or the use of the cloud for crime but the regulations mentioned so far are an important starting point to stimulate discussion.

References

1. European Commission: Towards a European Cloud Computing Strategy, http://ec.europa.eu/information_society/activities/cloudcomputing/index_en.html
2. ENISA: Cloud Computing Risk Assessment, http://www.enisa.europa.eu/activities/risk-management/files/deliverables/cloud-computing-risk-assessment/
3. ENISA: Cloud Computing: Benefits, Risks and Recommendations for Information security
4. European Commission: The European Digital Agenda, http://ec.europa.eu/information_society/digital-agenda/index_en.html
5. Kundra, V.: Federal Cloud Computing Strategy (February 2011), http://www.cio.gov/documents/federal-cloud-computing-strategy.pdf
6. Department of Defense: Cloud Computing Strategy (July 2012), http://www.defense.gov/news/DoDCloudComputingStrategy.pdf
7. NIST: Cloud Computing Collaboration Website, http://collaborate.nist.gov/twiki-cloud-computing/bin/view/CloudComputing/
8. US General Services Administration: FedRAMP, http://www.gsa.gov/portal/category/102371

Smart Work Industry Best Practices for Business and IT

Hans-Peter Hoidn[1] and Peter Utzinger[2]

[1] IBM, Zurich, Switzerland
[2] IBM, Lugano, Switzerland

Abstract. Enterprises must respond faster to changing customer expectations and business demands. The major observation is today that we cannot just work harder, and that we cannot just dedicate more resources; thus we must work smarter. Therefore the major question to be answered is: How do businesses evolve to adapt and respond dynamically? We will explain by industry examples how today's technology approaches enable smarter solutions. These solutions are better adapted to business needs, and they are faster implemented.

1 Inhabiting the Smarter Planet

Global trends and economic conditions are affecting businesses around the world, and the pace of change is accelerating. Businesses must work smarter to survive and to succeed. Dynamic Enterprises are the heart of this smart work. They enable faster response to changing customer expectations and business demands. We outline how a roadmap for implementing a Smart Cloud solution can be based on best practices for a Business Process Management life cycle, Service Oriented Architecture practice, methodology, and governance. The solution roadmap will focus business and IT value.

2 About the Speakers

Hans-Peter Hoidn is Executive Architect with a very strong architectural background doing architecture more than 15 years with a strong focus on Service-Oriented Architecture (SOA) and Enterprise Architecture (EA). Peter Utzinger is a Business Architect at IBM with focus on cloud solution architectures.

F. De Paoli, E. Pimentel, and G. Zavattaro (Eds.): ESOCC 2012, LNCS 7592, p. 279, 2012.
© Springer-Verlag Berlin Heidelberg 2012

Author Index